Interconnecting Data Centers Using VPLS

Nash Darukhanawalla, CCIE No. 10332

Patrice Bellagamba

Cisco Press

800 East 96th Street

Indianapolis, IN 46240

Interconnecting Data Centers Using VPLS

Nash Darukhanawalla, Patrice Bellagamba

Copyright© 2009 Cisco Systems, Inc.

Published by:
Cisco Press
800 East 96th Street
Indianapolis, IN 46240 USA

Printed in the United States of America

First Printing   June 2009

Library of Congress Cataloging-in-Publication Data:

Darukhanawalla, Nash, 1963-

Interconnecting data centers using VPLS / Nash Darukhanawalla and Patrice Bellagamba.

   p. cm.

ISBN-13: 978-1-58705-992-6 (pbk.)

ISBN-10: 1-58705-992-4 (pbk.)

1. Extranets (Computer networks)   2. Internetworking (Telecommunication)   3. Electronic data processing departments.   4. Cisco IOS.   I. Bellagamba, Patrice, 1959-   II. Title.

TK5105.875.E87D37 2010

004.6—dc22

2009020207

ISBN-13: 978-1-58705-992-6

ISBN-10: 1-58705-992-4

Warning and Disclaimer

This book is designed to provide information about interconnecting data centers using Virtual Private LAN Service (VPLS). Every effort has been made to make this book as complete and as accurate as possible, but no warranty or fitness is implied.

The information is provided on an "as is" basis. The authors, Cisco Press, and Cisco Systems, Inc., shall have neither liability nor responsibility to any person or entity with respect to any loss or damages arising from the information contained in this book or from the use of the discs or programs that may accompany it.

The opinions expressed in this book belong to the author and are not necessarily those of Cisco Systems, Inc.

Trademark Acknowledgments

All terms mentioned in this book that are known to be trademarks or service marks have been appropriately capitalized. Cisco Press or Cisco Systems, Inc., cannot attest to the accuracy of this information. Use of a term in this book should not be regarded as affecting the validity of any trademark or service mark.

Corporate and Government Sales

The publisher offers excellent discounts on this book when ordered in quantity for bulk purchases or special sales, which may include electronic versions and/or custom covers and content particular to your business, training goals, marketing focus, and branding interests. For more information, please contact: **U.S. Corporate and Government Sales**   1-800-382-3419   corpsales@pearsontechgroup.com

For sales outside the United States please contact: **International Sales**   international@pearsoned.com

Feedback Information

At Cisco Press, our goal is to create in-depth technical books of the highest quality and value. Each book is crafted with care and precision, undergoing rigorous development that involves the unique expertise of members from the professional technical community.

Readers' feedback is a natural continuation of this process. If you have any comments regarding how we could improve the quality of this book, or otherwise alter it to better suit your needs, you can contact us through email at feedback@ciscopress.com. Please make sure to include the book title and ISBN in your message.

We greatly appreciate your assistance.

Publisher: Paul Boger

Associate Publisher: Dave Dusthimer

Executive Editor: Mary Beth Ray

Managing Editor: Patrick Kanouse

Senior Development Editor: Christopher Cleveland

Project Editor: Jennifer Gallant

Editorial Assistant: Vanessa Evans

Book Designer: Louisa Adair

Composition: Mark Shirar

Cisco Representative: Eric Ullanderson

Cisco Press Program Manager: Anand Sundaram

Copy Editor: Keith Cline

Technical Editors: Cesar Carballes and Yves Louis

Indexer: Brad Herriman

Proofreader: Apostrophe Editing Services

Americas Headquarters
Cisco Systems, Inc.
San Jose, CA

Asia Pacific Headquarters
Cisco Systems (USA) Pte. Ltd.
Singapore

Europe Headquarters
Cisco Systems International BV
Amsterdam, The Netherlands

Cisco has more than 200 offices worldwide. Addresses, phone numbers, and fax numbers are listed on the Cisco Website at **www.cisco.com/go/offices.**

CCDE, CCENT, Cisco Eos, Cisco HealthPresence, the Cisco logo, Cisco Lumin, Cisco Nexus, Cisco StadiumVision, Cisco TelePresence, Cisco WebEx, DCE, and Welcome to the Human Network are trademarks; Changing the Way We Work, Live, Play, and Learn and Cisco Store are service marks; and Access Registrar, Aironet, AsyncOS, Bringing the Meeting To You, Catalyst, CCDA, CCDP, CCIE, CCIP, CCNA, CCNP, CCSP, CCVP, Cisco, the Cisco Certified Internetwork Expert logo, Cisco IOS, Cisco Press, Cisco Systems, Cisco Systems Capital, the Cisco Systems logo, Cisco Unity, Collaboration Without Limitation, EtherFast, EtherSwitch, Event Center, Fast Step, Follow Me Browsing, FormShare, GigaDrive, HomeLink, Internet Quotient, IOS, iPhone, iQuick Study, IronPort, the IronPort logo, LightStream, Linksys, MediaTone, MeetingPlace, MeetingPlace Chime Sound, MGX, Networkers, Networking Academy, Network Registrar, PCNow, PIX, PowerPanels, ProConnect, ScriptShare, SenderBase, SMARTnet, Spectrum Expert, StackWise, The Fastest Way to Increase Your Internet Quotient, TransPath, WebEx, and the WebEx logo are registered trademarks of Cisco Systems, Inc. and/or its affiliates in the United States and certain other countries.

All other trademarks mentioned in this document or website are the property of their respective owners. The use of the word partner does not imply a partnership relationship between Cisco and any other company. (0812R)

About the Authors

Nash Darukhanawalla, CCIE No. 10332, has more than 25 years of internetworking experience. He has held a wide variety of consulting, technical, product development, customer support, and management positions. Nash's technical expertise includes extensive experience in designing and supporting complex networks with a strong background in configuring, troubleshooting, and analyzing network systems.

Nash has been with Cisco for more than 10 years and is currently an engineering manager in the Enhanced Customer Aligned Testing Services (ECATS) group in the Advanced Services organization.

Nash graduated with a bachelor of science degree in physics and computer science from the University of Bombay, India, and is a CCIE in routing and switching. He has written several white papers on various technologies and recently wrote the *System Assurance Guide on High Availability Campus Network Design — Routed Access Using EIGRP or OSPF.*

Patrice Bellagamba has been in the networking industry for more than 25 years and has spent more than 10 years in engineering development. He is a consulting engineer and a recognized expert in IP and MPLS technologies. He is one of the influencers in the development of MPLS and has led MPLS techtorials at Networkers in Europe since its inception.

He is also the inventor of the Embedded Event Manager (EEM) semaphore concept and is the designer of the VPLS-based solutions that this book describes.

Patrice holds an engineering degree from the École Supérieure d'Electricité, one of France's prestigious Grandes Écoles and a top institution in the field of electrical and computer engineering. He has written several Cisco white papers on the use of MPLS technology.

About the Technical Reviewers

Cesar Carballes, double CCIE No. 2152-R&S and Dial, is a solutions architect with the Cisco Advanced Services Architecture and Design Team. Cesar has more than 27 years of internetworking experience. At Cisco, he has been working on large and complex networking projects for multinational enterprise and ISP customers, primarily in Europe. Cesar is recognized as a subject matter expert in data center interconnectivity technologies and has deployed or supervised the deployment of some of the solutions that this book describes. Cesar holds a bachelor's degree in physics from the Universidad Complutense de Madrid. In 1981, he was awarded the Philips Young Scientific Award for his work in energy exchanges and electrical motors. He has been an active member of the IEEE Communications Society since 1989. Cesar has resided in Belgium since 1995.

Cesar has been with Cisco for more than 13 years, and previously held positions at Motorola, Eurocomercial, and Nixdorf Computers.

Yves Louis has been in the computing and networking industries for more than 25 years. He has been with Cisco for more than 9 years and was one of the key members in the central European team working on next-generation IP network infrastructure.

As a consulting engineer, Yves supports large enterprise projects for strategic customers and recently has been working on the new generation of switching technologies, developing IP network support for routing and switching, network services for application optimization and security, and network virtualization for data centers.

He was one of the first to understand issues customers were facing in the area of data center virtualization and has provided guidance and ideas about bringing this book's architectural solutions to the global data center infrastructure.

Yves holds a degree in computer engineering from the Control Data Institute. He has written several white papers on network solution architectures and recently wrote a blueprint to provide recommendations enabling broadcasters to deploy their enterprise network architecture to support the Media Workflow Platform (MWP).

Dedications

From Nash:

This book is dedicated to my wife, Anahita, to my children, Jennifer and Malcolm, to my dad, Sorab, and to Firuza and Farzin, who have always been there for me and have never doubted my dreams. Thank you for your support, understanding, and encouragement. I also dedicate this book to my beloved brother Khushroo, who is no longer with us but would have been very proud to see this book published.

From Patrice:

The book is dedicated to those who gave me strength and support throughout my life, to my wife, Danielle, who gives me so much, and to my mentor, Christian, who left us so early. It is also dedicated to those I love so much, my children, Gauthier and Manon. And a special dedication to Yves, who inspired this book and was instrumental in its review.

Acknowledgments

The authors would like to acknowledge and thank the following individuals for their contributions, support, advice, and encouragement.

Khalil Jabr has been a key driver in bringing awareness of the solutions in this book to the U.S. market. He is a recognized expert in many of the technologies that this book discusses, which has allowed him to drive improvements in products and protocols within Cisco.

Mukhtiar Shaikh offered assistance on various technology implementations. Credit goes to him for working with us to formulate a proposal for validating the designs in this book under the Cisco Validated Design program.

David Jansen has been actively promoting data center interconnect solutions to customers throughout the United States and is a leader in educating customers in large technology forums.

Pooja Aniker, Harisha Badhya, Wei Gao, Anowarul Huq, Gopi Itagi, David Liang, Stephanie Lu, Charlene Luo, Ambrish Mehta, Kevin Hoan Tran, Priyanka Vora, and Xiaojie Zhang deserve special mention. Validation of the designs presented in this book would not have been completed without their expertise, dedication, and perseverance.

Special recognition goes to Ambrish, whose leadership and expertise were instrumental to the overall success of the project. Xiaojie provided a significant contribution by proposing and providing the proof of concept for the all pseudowire up/up solution that this book describes.

Paul Riskin deserves special mention, because without him, completion of this book would not have been possible within our aggressive timeline. He was invaluable in bringing what began as a concept to what became this book. We thank him for his advice and assistance with transforming the structure, prose, and format of this book.

This project started as a proposal from a small group of experts in the field, and with the support of the management it has now evolved into a set of solutions that can be used by a large segment of the enterprise, service provider, and application service provider markets. Special thanks go to the ECATS management, Nigel Townley and Mo Amirkalali, for providing their unwavering guidance and support during every phase of this rather long initiative.

We also want to express our sincere thanks to Mary Beth Ray, Christopher Cleveland, and the entire production team who graciously accommodated our deadline slip and yet met the publishing date.

Contents at a Glance

Contents

Icons Used in This Book

Router Multilayer Switch Route/Switch Processor Switch

Data Center Switch Optical Services Router Blade Chassis with Pass thru Modules

Aggregation Layer Switch with Integrated Service Modules

Server Network Cloud Ethernet Connection

Command Syntax Conventions

The conventions used to present command syntax in this book are the same conventions used in the IOS Command Reference. The Command Reference describes these conventions as follows:

- **Boldface** indicates commands and keywords that are entered literally as shown. In actual configuration examples and output (not general command syntax), boldface indicates commands that are manually input by the user (such as a **show** command).

- *Italic* indicates arguments for which you supply actual values.

- Vertical bars (|) separate alternative, mutually exclusive elements.

- Square brackets ([ ]) indicate an optional element.

- Braces ({ }) indicate a required choice.

- Braces within brackets ([{ }]) indicate a required choice within an optional element.

Introduction

This book presents Virtual Private LAN Service (VPLS)-based solutions that provide a high-speed, low-latency network and Spanning Tree Protocol (STP) isolation between data centers. The book also includes detailed information about issues that relate to large Layer 2 bridging domains and offers guidance for extending VLANs over Layer 3 networks using VPLS technology.

The solutions presented in this book have been validated under the Cisco Validated Design System Assurance program. All solutions were validated with a wide range of system tests, including system integration, fault and error handling, and redundancy. Testing also verified the end-to-end flow of both unicast and multicast unidirectional traffic. Voice, using components of the Cisco Unified Communications solution, was also implemented and verified.

The solutions in this book were developed because globalization, security, and disaster recovery considerations are driving divergence of business locations across multiple regions. In addition, organizations are looking to distribute workload between computers, share network resources effectively, and increase the availability of applications. With the ultimate goal of eliminating all downtime and sharing data across regions, enterprises are deploying geographically dispersed data centers to minimize planned or unplanned downtime, whether it is caused by a device failure, security breach, or natural disaster.

As data centers grow in size and complexity, enterprises are adopting server virtualization technologies to achieve increased efficiency and use of resources. In addition to providing resource optimization, virtualization strategies offer data protection, which enables enterprises to build disaster recovery solutions and provide high availability, scalability, flexibility, and business continuity.

Server virtualization technologies include the following:

- **VMotion:** Allows an individual virtual machine (such as Windows Server) to be dynamically moved to another VMware server. A dedicated VLAN is required for VMotion traffic so that virtual machines can be moved without affecting users. In addition, the group of servers that VMs are balanced between must be in the same Layer 2 domain, because attributes such as an IP address cannot change when a virtual machine moves. Therefore, all VMware servers, including the source VMware server, must have connections to the same VLAN.

- **NIC teaming:** Servers that include only one network interface card (NIC) are susceptible to many single points of failure, such as a failure of the NIC, its network cable, or the access switch to which it connects. A solution developed by NIC vendors, NIC teaming eliminates this single point of failure. In this solution, special drivers allow two NICs to be connected to separate access switches or to separate line cards on the same access switch. If one NIC fails, the other NIC assumes the IP address of the server and takes over operation without disruption. Types of NIC teaming solutions include active/standby and active/active. All solutions require Layer 2 adjacency for the teamed NICs.

- **Server clusters:** High-availability (HA) server clusters have become key components of IT strategies as organizations need to increase processing power, distribute workloads between computers, share network resources effectively, and increase the availability of applications. HA clusters typically are built with two separate networks: a public network to access the active node of the cluster from outside the data center, and a private network to interconnect the nodes of the cluster for private communications. The private network connection is also used to monitor the health and status of each node in the HA cluster using the heartbeat system. This solution requires that the network is capable of handling any kind of failure without causing a split-brain condition that could lead to duplicate instances of services and even the corruption of data on shared storage devices. The private network is a nonrouted network that shares the same Layer 2 VLAN between the nodes of the cluster even when extended between multiple sites.

These virtualization technologies have resulted in an expansion of Layer 2 domains, which in turn has increased the spanning-tree domain at the network level. STP was developed to handle a network with a small diameter, so an enterprise network with geographically dispersed data centers needs an effective solution for Layer 2 connectivity between multiple sites.

Also, during the process of migrating physical servers from one location to another, it is much easier to extend the Layer 2 VLAN and maintain the original configuration of the systems, thus avoiding IP address renumbering. Even during a phased migration period, when just part of the server farm is being relocated, the Layer 2 adjacency is often required across the entire server farm to ensure business continuity.

As data center resources and security requirements continue to grow, organizations must connect multiple data centers over larger distances. As a result, organizations are facing additional challenges such as maintaining the high availability of applications and dealing with complex multisite interconnections.

Objective of This Book

This book provides design guidance, configuration examples, and best practices for deploying a single IP/MPLS-based network to interconnect data centers ensuring high availability Layer 2 connectivity with STP isolation in the core. Customers who have already deployed a separate optical network for Layer 2 extension can also take advantage of these solutions to reduce infrastructure and maintenance costs.

This book addresses issues that are related to large Layer 2 bridging domains and provides guidance for extending VLANs using VPLS technology.

This book also examines in detail the technologies that offer such solutions, explains the benefits and trade-offs of various solutions, and describes a variety of deployment options. The deployment model that an organization chooses depends on the complexity of the requirements, the protocols currently deployed in the data centers, the scalability required, and many other factors.

Who Should Read This Book

This book is intended for systems professionals and system engineers who are designing solutions for interconnecting data centers that ensure high availability Layer 2 connectivity and STP isolation. Service providers that offer metro Ethernet leased-line aggregation and Layer 2 transport services can also benefit from these solutions that provide large-scale Layer 2 extension.

Cisco Validated Design Program

The Cisco Validated Design (CVD) program designs, tests, and documents systems and solutions to facilitate faster, more reliable, and more predictable customer deployments. The program includes Cisco Validated Design and CVD System Assurance.

Cisco Validated Design

Cisco Validated Designs are systems or solutions that have been validated through architectural review and proof-of-concept testing in a Cisco lab. Cisco Validated Design provides guidance for deploying new technologies or for applying enhancements to existing infrastructure.

CVD System Assurance

The Cisco Validated Design System Assurance is a program that identifies systems that have undergone architectural- and customer-relevant testing.

A CVD certified design is a highly validated and customized solution that meets the following criteria:

■ Reviewed and updated for general deployment

■ Achieves the highest levels of consistency and coverage within the Cisco Validated Design program

■ Solution requirements successfully tested and documented with evidence to function as detailed within a specific design in a scaled, customer representative environment

■ Zero observable operation impacting defects within the given test parameters; that is, no defects that have not been resolved either outright or through software change, redesign, or workaround

For more information about Cisco CVD program, refer to http://tinyurl.com/6gxuk2.

How This Book Is Organized

The material in this book is presented in a building-block fashion that takes you from the legacy deployement models for data center interconnect (DCI) and problems associated with extending Layer 2 networks, through VPN technologies, to various Multiple Spanning Tree (MST)-, Embedded Event Manager (EEM)- and generic routing encapsulation (GRE)-based deployment models, and beyond. Although this book is intended to be read cover to cover, it is designed to be flexible and allow you to easily find information that applies to your needs.

The chapters cover the following topics:

- **Chapter 1, "Data Center Layer 2 Interconnect"**: This chapter provides an overview of high availability clusters. It also explains DCI legacy deployment models and problems associated with extending Layer 2 networks.

- **Chapter 2, "Appraising Virtual Private LAN Service"**: This chapter discusses Layer 2 and Layer 3 VPN technologies and provides introductions to VPLS, pseudowires, EEM, and MPLS.

- **Chapter 3, "High Availability for Extended Layer 2 Networks"**: This chapter focuses on design components such as maximum transmission unit (MTU), core routing protocols, and convergence optimization techniques to achieve high availability.

- **Chapter 4, "MPLS Traffic Engineering"**: This chapter explains the implemetation of MPLS-TE for load repartition of Layer 2 VPN traffic over parallel links. It also introduces Fast Reroute (FRR) for faster convergence.

- **Chapter 5, "Data Center Interconnect: Architecture Alternatives"**: This chapter highlights several options for implementing DCI. In addition, this chapter provides guidance for selecting an appropriate solution based on your requirements (such as scalability and ease of implementation).

- **Chapter 6, "Case Studies for Data Center Interconnect"**: This chapter provides case studies that relate to the DCI solutions that this book describes.

- **Chapter 7, "Data Center Multilayer Infrastructure Design"**: This chapter highlights the Cisco data center multitier model and provides information about network topology, hardware, software, and traffic profiles used for validating the designs in this book.

- **Chapter 8, "MST-Based Deployment Models"**: This chapter covers "MST in pseudowire" and "isolated MST in N-PE" solutions and provides configuration details for implementing these solutions.

- **Chapter 9, "EEM-Based Deployment Models"**: This chapter explains "EEM sema-phore protocol," which was developed to achieve N-PE redundancy in the absence of ICCP. In addition, this chapter describes various EEM-based VPLS and Hierarchical VPLS (H-VPLS) solutions, provides in-depth theory about the operation of each solution, and provides configuration details.

- **Chapter 10, "GRE-Based Deployment Models"**: This chapter provides VPLS and H-VPLS solutions over an IP network using VPLSoGRE (VPLS over GRE).

- **Chapter 11, "Additional Data Center Interconnect Design Considerations"**: This chapter introduces other technologies or issues that should be considered when designing DCI solutions.

- **Chapter 12, "VPLS PE Redundancy Using Inter-Chassis Communication Protocol"**: This chapter introduces ICCP protocols and provides various redundancy mechanisms and sample configurations.

- **Chapter 13, "Evolution of Data Center Interconnect"**: This chapter provides a brief overview of the emerging technologies and the future of DCI.

- **Glossary**: This element provides definitions for some commonly used terms associated with DCI and the various deployment models discussed in the book.

The authors have also written several documents, including *Interconnecting Geographically Dispersed Data Centers, High Availability Clusters, Layer 2 Extension Between Remote Data Centers*. These documents cover a few key concepts from this book and are freely available on Cisco.com.

Chapter 1

Data Center Layer 2 Interconnect

Many enterprises are making fundamental changes to their business processes by using advanced IT applications to achieve enhanced productivity and operational efficiencies. As a result, the underlying network architecture to support these applications is evolving to better accommodate this new model.

As data availability becomes a critical requirement, many businesses are devoting more resources to ensure continuous operation. Enterprises are provisioning dedicated networks to guarantee performance metrics for applications without compromising security.

Although maintaining uninterruptible access to all data center applications is desirable, the economics of business-continuance require network operators to prioritize applications according to their importance to the business. As a result, data centers need a range of business-continuance solutions to accommodate this goal, from simple tape backup and remote replication to synchronous mirroring and mirrored distributed data centers.

Enterprises can enhance application resilience in several ways, including the following:

- Removing single points of server failure by deploying high-availability clusters or load-balancing technology across web and application servers

- Extending the deployment of these clusters in different data centers to protect against major disruptions

User access is as important as downtime protection and data recovery. Following a disruption, how long can the business afford for users to be without access to applications? Companies are employing technologies such as Global Site Selector that enable users to manually or automatically connect to an alternative site running the application they need.

Businesses run tens and often hundreds of applications, each of which might have differing continuance requirements, measured in a time-to-recovery and data-loss perspective. IT groups need to match the associated characteristics and cost of a business-continuance solution to the potential business and consider which technologies to deploy where problems impact data, applications, and user access.

Cisco delivers scalable, secure, and cost-effective technology that helps enterprises build end-to-end backup and recovery solutions and disaster recovery solutions. These solutions include the following:

- High-availability data center networking and storage-area networks for nonstop access to applications and data

- Synchronized distributed data centers for continuous service over WANs in the event of site disruptions

- Synchronous disk mirroring and replication over WANs for fast recovery and zero data loss

- Asynchronous data replication over IP networks for remote data protection

- Consolidated backup to tape or near-line disk and remote electronic vaulting over enterprise-wide storage networks for consistent protection of distributed data

Each of these solutions requires the appropriate network infrastructure to help ensure that user-specific availability, performance, distance, and latency requirements are met. In addition, enterprises require a resilient, integrated business-continuance network infrastructure to protect three key areas in the event of a disruption:

- Data

- Applications

- User access

Overview of High-Availability Clusters

High-availability (HA) clusters operate by using redundant computers or nodes that provide services when system components fail. Normally, if a server with a particular application crashes, the application is unavailable until the problem is resolved. HA clustering remedies this situation by detecting hardware/software faults, and immediately providing access to the application on another system without requiring administrative intervention. This process is known as *failover*.

HA clusters are often used for key databases, file sharing on a network, business applications, and customer services such as e-commerce websites. HA cluster implementations attempt to build redundancy into a cluster to eliminate single points of failure. These implementations include multiple network connections and data storage that connects via storage-area networks (SAN).

HA clusters usually are built with two separate networks:

- **The public network:** Used to access the active node of the cluster from outside the data center

■   **The private network:** Used to interconnect the nodes of the cluster for private communications within the data center and to monitor the health and status of each node in the cluster

Public Network Attachment

For the public network (facing the nodes cluster), the server often is enabled by a dual-homing mechanism with one network interface card (NIC) configured in active state and one NIC configured in standby state. If a link to the active NIC fails, or the NIC loses connectivity with its default gateway, the operating system performs a failover. A NIC failover for a public network has no affect on cluster availability because the heartbeat mechanism and NICs in active/standby mode for public access are two separate hand-check mechanisms.

The network design must provide the highest availability for the LAN infrastructure. To achieve this goal, the teaming service or dual-homing should be distributed between different access switches, which in turn should be connected to different aggregation switches, as illustrated in Figure 1-1.

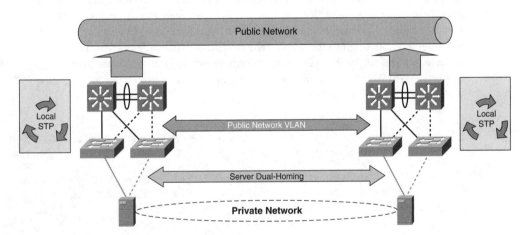

Figure 1-1   *Extending the public network.*

Private Network Attachment

The private network primarily carries cluster heartbeat, or keepalive, messages. Other server-to-server communications that occur on this private network include the following:

■   Cluster data

■   Cluster file system data

■   Application data (back-end)

The private network is a nonrouted network that shares the same Layer 2 VLAN between the nodes of the cluster even when extended across multiple sites. In a campus cluster environment, heartbeats are sent via the private network from node to node of the HA cluster using a proprietary Layer 2 (nonroutable) protocol. The servers manage the I/O by sending traffic over all interfaces and by preventing traffic from being sent over a failing path. This approach provides resiliency in the event of a NIC failure on a server.

The heartbeat is the most important component of the cluster that uses the private network interconnection. However, if all paths go down for more than 10 seconds (applicable for most HA clusters), a *split-brain* situation can occur, which prompts the cluster framework to check the number of votes and decide which server or servers will continue as the members in the cluster. Nodes that lose cluster membership assume that they are isolated, and any applications that run on those nodes terminate. Surviving nodes know that the nonsurviving nodes have stopped, and the cluster will then restart the applications.

Although some HA cluster vendors recommend disabling Spanning Tree Protocol (STP) for the private interconnect infrastructure, such a drastic measure is neither necessary nor recommended when using Cisco Catalyst switches. In fact, Cisco has since provided the *PortFast* feature, which puts an access port into forwarding mode immediately after link up without losing loop-detection capabilities. To avoid connectivity delays, PortFast must be enabled on all access interfaces connecting cluster nodes. This rule also applies to any servers connected to the switch. The IEEE also defines the PortFast concept within the Rapid STP 802.1w standard under the *edge port* designation. In addition, Cisco supports Per-VLAN Spanning Tree, which maintains a spanning-tree instance for each VLAN configured in the network.

Note   For detailed information about HA clusters, refer to the Windows HPC Server 2008 site at http://www.microsoft.com/HPC/.

For detailed information about STP PortFast configuration to resolve server/workstation startup connectivity delay, refer to the Cisco document Using PortFast and Other Commands to Fix Workstation Startup Connectivity Delays, available at http://tinyurl.com/2e29bw.

For detailed information about designing a network for extended HA clusters, refer to the following Cisco white paper A: "Technology and Networking Guide for High Availability Clusters Extended Across Multiple Data Centers," at http://tinyurl.com/cb4f3k.

Data Center Interconnect: Legacy Deployment Models

Several transport technologies are available for interconnecting the data centers, each of which provides various features and allows different distances, depending on factors such as the power budget of the optics, the lambda used for transmission, the type of fiber, and so forth.

Consider the features of the LAN and SAN switches that provide higher availability for the data center interconnect (DCI) before considering some of the available technologies. The convergence time required for the application also is important and should be evaluated.

The list that follows describes common transport options:

- **Dark fiber:** Dark fiber is a viable method for extending VLANs over data center or campus distances. The maximum attainable distance is a function of the optical characteristics (transmit power and receive sensitivity) of the LED or laser that resides in a small form-factor pluggable (SFP) or Gigabit Interface Converter (GBIC) transponder, combined with the number of fiber joins, and the attenuation of the fiber.

- **Coarse wavelength-division multiplexing (CWDM):** CWDM offers a simple solution to carry up to eight channels (1 Gbps or 2 Gbps) on the same fiber. These channels can carry Ethernet or Fiber Channel. CWDM does not offer protected lambdas, but client protection allows rerouting of the traffic on the functioning links when a failure occurs. CWDM lambdas can be added and dropped, allowing the creation of hub-and-spoke, ring, and meshed topologies. The maximum achievable distance is approximately 60 miles (100 km) with a point-to-point physical topology and approximately 25 miles (40 km) with a physical ring topology.

- **Dense wavelength-division multiplexing (DWDM):** DWDM enables up to 32 channels (lambdas), each of which can operate at up to 10 Gbps. DWDM networks can be designed either as multiplexing networks that are similar to CWDM or with a variety of protection schemes to guard against failures in the fiber plant. DWDM also offers more protection mechanisms (splitter protection and Y-cable protection), and the possibility to amplify the channels to reach greater distances.

Note   For details about data center transport technologies, refer to Chapter 2 of *Data Center High Availability Clusters Design Guide*, available at http://tinyurl.com/ct4cw8.

In nearly all of these deployment models, costs associated with deploying and maintaining a dedicated optical network is one of the biggest concerns. Also, there is no STP isolation. Depending on the nature of the problem, issues in one data center will affect other data centers. Another disadvantage is the lack of load balancing across redundant paths due to blocked links in the core network.

Problems Associated with Extended Layer 2 Networks

A common practice is to add redundancy when interconnecting data centers to avoid split-subnet scenarios and interruption of the communication between servers, as illustrated in Figure 1-2. The split-subnet is not necessarily a problem if the routing metric makes one site preferred over the other. Also, if the servers at each site are part of a cluster and the communication is lost, mechanisms such as the quorum disk avoid a split-brain condition.

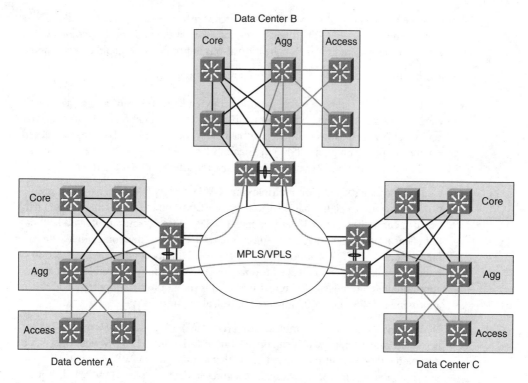

Figure 1-2 *Layout of multiple data center interconnect with redundant N-PEs in each data center.*

Adding redundancy to an extended Ethernet network typically means relying on STP to keep the topology loop free. STP domains should be reduced as much as possible and limited within the data center. Cisco does not recommend deploying the legacy 802.1d because of its old timer-based mechanisms that make the recovery time too slow for most applications, including typical clustering software.

An extended Layer 2 network does introduce some problems to contend with, however.

STP operates at Layer 2 of the Open Systems Interconnection (OSI) model, and the primary function STP is to prevent loops that redundant links create in bridge networks. By exchanging bridge protocol data units (BPDU) between bridges, STP elects the ports that eventually forward or block traffic.

The conservative default values for the STP timers impose a maximum network diameter of seven. Therefore, two bridges cannot be more than seven hops away from each other.

When a BPDU propagates from the root bridge toward the leaves of the tree, the age field increments each time the BPDU goes through a bridge. Eventually, the bridge discards the BPDU when the age field goes beyond maximum age. Therefore, convergence of the spanning tree is affected if the root bridge is too far away from some bridges in the network.

An aggressive value for the max-age parameter and the forward delay can lead to an unstable STP topology. In such cases, the loss of some BPDUs can cause a loop to appear. Take special care if you plan to change STP timers from the default value to achieve faster STP convergence.

Unlike legacy STP, Rapid STP (RSTP) converges faster because it does not depend on the timers to make a rapid transition. However, STP does not provide the required robustness for large-scale Layer 2 deployments:

■ Network stability is compromised as a result of slow response to network failures (slow convergence). Even new spanning-tree developments such as RSTP and Multiple Spanning Tree (MST) assume good-quality physical connections such as dark fiber or WDM connections. These STP protocols are not built to accommodate frequent link-flapping conditions, high error rates, unidirectional failures, or nonreport of loss of signal. These typical and frequent behaviors of long- and medium-distance links could lead to STP slow convergence or even instability.

■ The primary reason for multisite data centers is disaster recovery. However, because data centers typically require Layer 2 connectivity, failure in one data center can affect other data centers, which could lead to a blackout of all data centers at the same time.

■ A broadcast storm propagates to every data center, which, if uncontrolled, could result in network-wide outage.

■ STP blocks links, which prevents load balancing of traffic across redundant paths in the core network.

Note   For understanding and tuning STP timers and the rules to tune them when absolutely necessary, refer to the Cisco document, "Understanding and Tuning Spanning Tree Protocol Timers," available at http://tinyurl.com/7ppqq.

Summary

This chapter provided an overview of HA clusters, legacy deployment models for interconnecting data centers, and problems related to extending Layer 2 networks. The solutions that this book presents address these issues in more detail and provide guidance for designing and deploying DCI.

## Chapter 2

Appraising Virtual Private LAN Service

High-availability requirements of virtualization technologies, the costs associated with deploying and maintaining a dedicated fiber network, and technology limitations have led to the development of Virtual Private LAN Service (VPLS)-based solutions. These solutions provide multipoint Layer 2 (L2) connectivity services across geographically dispersed data centers over a Layer 3 (L3) network infrastructure.

Key objectives for using L3 routing rather than L2 switching to interconnect data centers include the following:

- Resolve core link-quality problems using L3 routing technology

- Remove data center interdependence using spanning-tree isolation techniques

- Provide storm-propagation control

- Allow safe sharing of infrastructure links for both L2 core and L3 core traffic

- Adapt to any data center design such as Rapid Spanning Tree Protocol (RSTP)/Rapid Per-VLAN Spanning Tree Plus (RPVST+), Multiple Spanning Tree (MST), Virtual Switching System (VSS), Nexus, and blade switches

- Allow VLAN overlapping and therefore virtualization in multitenant or service provider designs

The following sections discuss virtual private network (VPN) technologies and some associated challenges in detail.

VPN Technology Considerations

Ethernet switching technology has a long and successful record for delivering high bandwidth at affordable prices in enterprise LANs. With the introduction of 10-Gbps

Ethernet switching, the outstanding price/performance of Ethernet provides even greater price/performance advantages for both enterprise and service provider networks.

In attempting to deliver Ethernet-based multipoint services, service providers are evaluating and deploying two types of multipoint architectures: L3 VPNs and L2 VPNs.

Layer 3 Virtual Private Networks

The most common L3 VPN technology is Multiprotocol Label Switching (MPLS), which delivers multipoint services over a L3 network architecture. MPLS L3 VPNs offer many attractive characteristics for delivery of multipoint services, including the following:

- The use of a variety of user network interfaces (UNI), including Frame Relay, Asynchronous Transfer Mode (ATM), and Ethernet

- The scalability of MPLS for wide-area service deployments

- The capability to access multiple L3 VPNs from the same UNI

- The ability for an end user to add new customer edge (CE) nodes without having to reconfigure the existing CE nodes

- Robust quality of service (QoS) implementation, allowing differentiated packet forwarding according to application characteristics

- The capability to support stringent service level agreements (SLA) for high availability

However, MPLS L3 VPNs do impose certain provisioning requirements on both service providers and enterprises that sometimes are unacceptable to one or the other party. Some enterprises are reluctant to relinquish control of their network to their service provider. Similarly, some service providers are uncomfortable with provisioning and managing services based on L3 network parameters as is required with MPLS L3 VPNs.

Layer 2 Virtual Private Networks

For multipoint L2 VPN services, service providers have frequently deployed Ethernet switching technology using techniques such as 802.1Q tunneling (also referred to as tag stacking or QinQ) as the foundation for their metro Ethernet network architecture.

Switched Ethernet service provider networks support multipoint services, also referred to as *transparent LAN services* (TLS), which provide a good example of L2 VPN service supported over L2 network architecture.

Switched Ethernet network architectures have proven to be successful in delivering high-performance, low-cost L2 VPN multipoint services by service providers in many countries. However, as the size of these switched Ethernet networks has grown, the limitations of the scalability of this architecture has become increasingly apparent:

- Limited VLAN address space per switched Ethernet domain

- Scalability of spanning-tree protocols (IEEE 802.1d) for network redundancy and traffic engineering

- Ethernet MAC address learning rate, which is important to minimize broadcast traffic resulting from unknown MAC addresses

These limitations, which are inherent in Ethernet switching protocols, preclude the use of Ethernet switching architectures to build L2 VPN services that scale beyond a metropolitan-area network (MAN) domain.

To address the limitations of both MPLS L3 VPNs and Ethernet switching, and because classical L2 switching was not built for extended, large-scale networks, innovations in network technology have led to the development of VPLS.

VPLS Overview

Virtual Private LAN Service (VPLS) is an architecture that provides multipoint Ethernet LAN services, often referred to as transparent LAN services (TLS), across geographically dispersed locations, using MPLS as transport.

Service providers often use VPLS to provide Ethernet multipoint services (EMS). VPLS is being adopted by enterprises on a self-managed MPLS-based MAN to provide high-speed any-to-any forwarding at L2 without the need to rely on spanning tree to keep the physical topology loop free. The MPLS core uses a full mesh of pseudowires (PWs; described in the next section) and split horizon to avoid loops.

To provide multipoint Ethernet capability, Internet Engineering Task Force (IETF) VPLS drafts describe the concept of linking virtual Ethernet bridges by using MPLS PWs. At a basic level, VPLS is a group of virtual switch instances (VSI) that are interconnected by using Ethernet over MPLS (EoMPLS) circuits in a full-mesh topology to form a single, logical bridge.

A VLAN can be extended across multiple segments by using a bridge or a switch, so it is not constrained to a single wire. A bridge or a switch monitors each incoming Ethernet frame to determine its source and destination MAC addresses. A bridge or switch uses the source MAC address to build a table of device addresses that are attached to its ports. The bridge or switch uses a destination address to make a forwarding decision. If the frame is a broadcast or multicast frame or its destination address is unknown to the bridge or switch, the frame is forwarded (flooded) to all ports except the receiving port. This flooding process is called a *learning bridge mechanism*.

In concept, a VSI is similar to this bridging function. In both technologies, a frame is switched based on the destination MAC address and membership in an L2 VPN (a VLAN). VPLS forwards Ethernet frames at L2, dynamically learns source MAC address-to-port associations, and forwards frames based on the destination MAC address. If the destination address is unknown, or is a broadcast or multicast address, the frame is flooded to all ports associated with the virtual bridge. Therefore, in operation, VPLS offers the same connectivity experienced as if a device were attached to an Ethernet switch by linking VSIs using MPLS PWs to form an "emulated" Ethernet switch.

Because of the flooding behavior, loops in bridged networks are disastrous. There is no counter such as the Time-To-Live (TTL) field in an IP header at the frame level to indicate how many times a frame has circulated a network. Frames continue to loop until an entire network is saturated and the bridges can no longer forward packets. To prevent loops in a network, bridges or switches use Spanning Tree Protocol (STP) to block any ports that might cause a loop. VPLS offers an alternative to the STP control plane and limits STP to local sites.

Compared to traditional LAN switching technologies, VPLS is more flexible in its geographic scaling. Therefore, CE sites might be within the same metropolitan domain, or might be geographically dispersed on a regional or national basis. The increasing availability of Ethernet-based multipoint service architectures from service providers for both L2 VPN and L3 VPN services is resulting in a growing number of enterprises transitioning their WANs to these multipoint services. VPLS is playing an increasingly important role in this transition.

The VFI identifies a group of PWs that are associated with a VSI.

Figure 2-1 shows the use of VFIs using MPLS PWs to form an "emulated" Ethernet switch.

VPLS is an emerging technology intended to provide an emulated LAN service across the MPLS core network. The service is a multipoint architecture to connect remote sites at Layer 2.

VPLS consists of three primary components:

- **Attachment circuits:** Connection to CE or aggregation switches, usually Ethernet but can be ATM or Frame Relay

- **Virtual circuits (VCs or PWs):** Connections between Network-facing Provider Edges (N-PEs) across MPLS network based on draft-martini-l2circuit-trans-mpls-11

- **VSI:** A virtual L2 bridge instance that connects attachment circuits to VCs

The VPLS specification outlines five components specific to its operation:

- **VPLS architecture (VPLS and Hierarchical VPLS [H-VPLS]):** The Cisco 7600 series routers support flat VPLS architectures and Ethernet edge H-VPLS topologies.

- **Autodiscovery of PEs associated with a particular VPLS instance:** The Cisco 7600 series routers support manual neighbor configuration and Border Gateway Protocol (BGP) autodiscovery.

- **Signaling of PWs to interconnect VPLS VSIs:** The Cisco 7600 series routers use Label Distribution Protocol (LDP) to signal draft-martini PWs (VC).

- **Forwarding of frames:** The Cisco 7600 series routers forward frames based on destination MAC address.

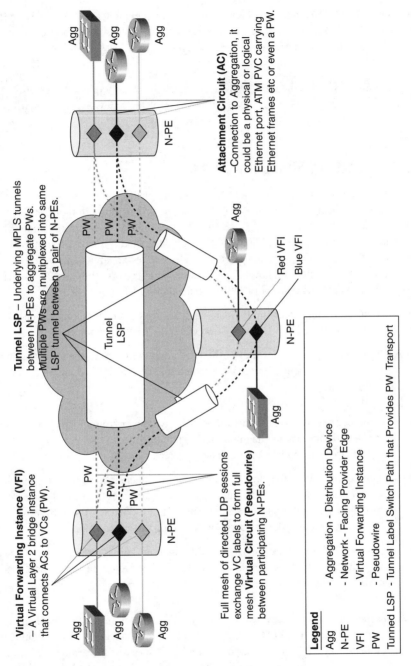

Figure 2-1 *Schematic representation of VPLS components.*

■ **Flushing of MAC addresses upon topology change:** In Cisco IOS Software Release 12.2(33)SRC1 and later, Cisco 7600 series routers support MAC address flushing and allow configuration of a MAC address aging timer.

Note   For more information about VPLS, refer to the Cisco document "*Cisco IOS MPLS Virtual Private LAN Service: Application Note*," available at www. http://tinyurl.com/c6k6ot.

Understanding Pseudowires

A PW is a point-to-point connection between pairs of PE routers. It is bidirectional and consists of a pair of unidirectional MPLS VCs. The primary function of a PW is to emulate services such as Ethernet, ATM, Frame Rely, or time-division multiplexing (TDM) over an underlying core MPLS network through encapsulation into a common MPLS format. The PW is a mechanism that carries the elements of an emulated service from one PE router to one or more PEs over a packet-switched network (PSN). A PW is a virtual connection that, in the context of VPLS, connects two VFIs.

In Ethernet switching extension, PWs are used to cross-connect (xconnect) either physical ports, subinterfaces, or VLANs (SVI or VFI) over MPLS transport.

When used as a point-to-point (P2P) Ethernet circuit connection, the PW is known as EoMPLS, where the PW is created using targeted LDP. This P2P connection can be used in the following modes:

■ **Xconnect ports (EoMPLS port mode) with whatever frame format on the port (that is, with or without the dot1q header):** In this mode, the xconnected port does not participate in any local switching or routing.

■ **Xconnect port VLAN (also known as subinterfaces):** Allows selective extraction of a VLAN based on its dot1q tag and P2P xconnect packets. Local VLAN significance is usually required in this mode and is supported today only on an Ethernet Service (ES) module's facing edge, also known as facing the aggregation.

■ **Xconnect SVI (interface VLAN) in a P2P fashion:** This approach requires a shared port adapter interface processor (SIP) or ES module facing the core (also called facing the MPLS network).

PWs are the connection mechanisms between switching interfaces (VFIs) when used in a multipoint environment (VPLS). This approach allows xconnecting SVI in a multipoint mode by using one PW per destination VFI with MAC address learning over these PWs.

PWs are dynamically created using targeted LDP based on either a neighbor statement configured in the VFI or automatically discovered based on Multiprotocol BGP (MP-BGP) announcements. This feature is beyond the scope of this book because it requires BGP to be enabled in the network.

In Cisco IOS Software Releases 12.2(33)SRB1 and 12.2(33)SXI, the targeted LDP IP address for the PW, can be independent from the LDP router ID, which is required for scalability and load balancing.

PWs can be associated to PW classes that would specify creation options such as transport of the PWs via MPLS Traffic Engineering (TE) tunnels. This approach allows full control of load repartition on the core links and permits Fast Reroute (FRR) protection to accelerate convergence on link or node failures. This protection against core link failure is achieved by locally repairing the label switch paths (LSP) at the point of failure, allowing data to continue to flow while a new end-to-end LSP is being established to replace the failure. FRR locally repairs the protected LSPs by rerouting them over backup tunnels that bypass failed links or nodes.

VPLS to Scale STP Domain for Layer 2 Interconnection

EoMPLS requires that STP be enabled from site to site to provide a redundant path, so it is not a viable option for large-scale L2 extensions of bridge domains.

VPLS is a bridging technique that relies on PWs to interconnect point-to-multipoint virtual bridges. Because VPLS is natively built with an internal mechanism known as split horizon, the core network does not require STP to prevent L2 loops.

Figure 2-2 shows three remote sites connected via a multipath VPLS core network.

Redundancy with VPLS, as shown in Figure 2-3, is difficult. In a single N-PE, split horizon prevents traffic from looping from one PW to another. However, with dual N-PEs per site, traffic can traverse the link between the dual N-PEs or via the aggregation switches, creating a loop.

The design goal is to maintain the link between aggregation switches in forwarding mode. At the same time, a goal is to block VPLS-associated traffic from traversing the inter-N-PE link within a data center, allowing only one N-PE to carry traffic to and from the VPLS cloud.

Even though a VPLS bridge is inherently protected against L2 loops, a loop-prevention protocol must still be used against local L2 loops in the access layer of the data centers where cluster nodes are connected. Therefore, for each solution described in this book, VPLS is deployed in conjunction with Embedded Event Manager (EEM) to ensure loop prevention in the core based on the full mesh of PWs and redundant N-PEs in each location. Edge node or edge link failure is protected against by using VPLS and EEM to customize the solution behavior based on network events as they occur.

An active/standby path-diversity protection mechanism is provided per VLAN using VPLS to ensure one L2 connection to VPLS at a time. This mechanism is known as *VPLS with EEM in N-PE.*

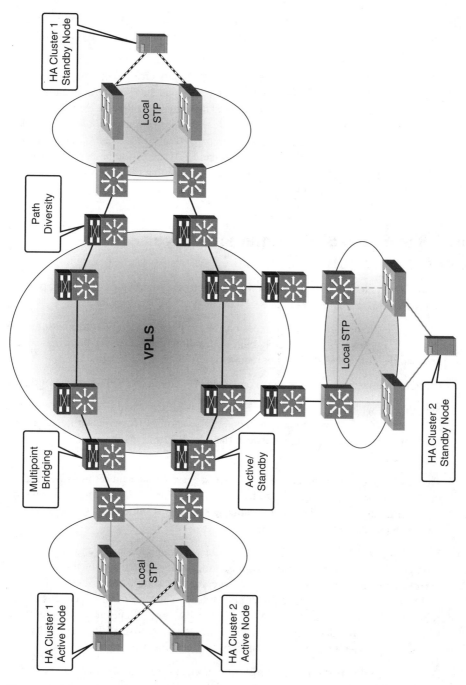

Figure 2-2   *Multipath VPLS with STP isolation.*

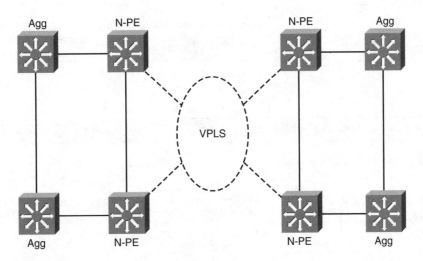

Figure 2-3 *Redundant N-PEs within the data center.*

H-VPLS Considerations

VPLS requires the creation of one VFI for each bridge domain that is to be extended across an L3 core network. Some organizations might require many VLANs to be extended between geographically dispersed data centers. However, creating the hundreds of VFIs that would be required in this case is not practical.

One of the options for scaling VLAN transport via VPLS is to use additional 802.1Q encapsulation, which is known as *QinQ*. QinQ is the Cisco implementation of the IEEE 802.1ad standard and specifies how to double-tag a frame with an additional VLAN. A frame that enters an interface configured for QinQ encapsulation receives a core VLAN number. In QinQ encapsulation, the edge VLAN number is hidden, and frames are switched based on this core VLAN.

Figure 2-4 illustrates H-VPLS encapsulation. In the original Ethernet frame, the payload is tagged with the 802.1Q edge VLAN number and with the destination (DA) and source (SA) MAC addressees. To aggregate and hide the edge VLANs, QinQ inserts an additional 802.1Q core VLAN number, as shown in the QinQ frame. However, the DA of the incoming Ethernet frame is used for forwarding. In addition, VPLS adds the two labels that LDP provides. One label points toward the destination N-PE (core label), the other label identifies the PW, so it points to the correct VFI.

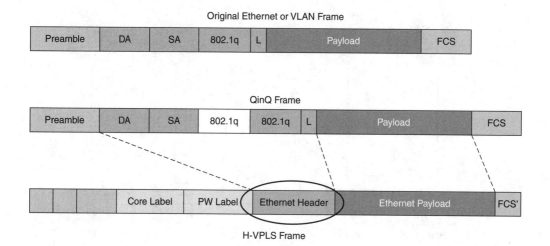

Figure 2-4   *H-VPLS encapsulation.*

EEM

The Cisco IOS Embedded Event Manager (EEM) is a unique subsystem within Cisco IOS Software. EEM is a powerful and flexible tool to automate tasks and customize the behavior of Cisco IOS and the operation of the device. EEM consists of Event Detectors, the Event Manager, and an Event Manager Policy Engine.

You can use EEM to create and run programs or scripts directly on a router or switch. The scripts are called *EEM policies* and can be programmed with a simple command-line interface (CLI) or by using a scripting language called Tool Command Language (Tcl). Policies can be defined to take specific actions when the Cisco IOS Software recognizes certain events through the Event Detectors. The result is an extremely powerful set of tools to automate many network management tasks and direct the operation of Cisco IOS to increase availability, collect information, and notify external systems or personnel about critical events.

EEM helps businesses harness the network intelligence intrinsic to Cisco IOS Software and gives them the capability to customize behavior based on network events as they happen, respond to real-time events, automate tasks, create customer commands, and take local automated action based on conditions detected by Cisco IOS Software.

EEM is a low-priority process within IOS. Therefore, it is important to consider this fact when using EEM on systems that are exposed to environments in which higher-priority processes might monopolize routers' CPU resources. Care should be taken to protect the routers' CPU from being hogged by higher-priority tasks such as broadcast storms. Recommended practice dictates allocating more time for low-priority processes using the IOS command **process-max-time 50**. In addition, control-plane policing (CoPP), storm control, and event dampening should also be deployed to prevent CPU hog.

Note   The Cisco document *"Cisco IOS Embedded Event Manager Data Sheet"* provides detailed information about EEM, and is available at www. http://tinyurl.com/3hrdm7.

MPLS

Multiprotocol Label Switching (MPLS) combines the performance and capabilities of L2 (data link layer) switching with the proven scalability of L3 (network layer) routing. MPLS enables enterprises and service providers to build next-generation intelligent networks that deliver a wide variety of advanced, value-added services over a single infrastructure. MPLS also makes it possible for enterprises and services providers to meet the challenges of explosive growth in network utilization while providing the opportunity to differentiate services, without sacrificing the existing network infrastructure. The MPLS architecture is flexible and can be employed in any combination of L2 technologies. This economical solution can be integrated seamlessly over any existing infrastructure, such as IP, Frame Relay, ATM, or Ethernet. Subscribers with differing access links can be aggregated on an MPLS edge without changing their current environments because MPLS is independent of access technologies.

Integration of MPLS application components, including L3 VPNs, L2 VPNs, TE, QoS, Generalized MPLS (GMPLS), and IPv6 enable the development of highly efficient, scalable, and secure networks that guarantee SLAs.

MPLS delivers highly scalable, differentiated, end-to-end IP services with simple configuration, management, and provisioning for providers and subscribers. By incorporating MPLS into their network architectures, service providers can save money, increase revenue and productivity, provide differentiated services, and gain competitive advantages.

Label Switching Functions

In conventional L3 forwarding mechanisms, as a packet traverses the network, each router extracts all the information relevant to forwarding the packet from the L3 header. This information is then used as an index for a routing table lookup to determine the next hop for the packet.

In the most common case, the only relevant field in the header is the destination address field, but in some cases, other header fields might also be relevant. As a result, the header analysis must be performed independently at each router through which the packet passes. In addition, a complicated table lookup must also be performed at each router.

In label switching, the analysis of the L3 header is done only once. The L3 header is then mapped into a fixed-length, unstructured value called a *label*.

Many headers can map to the same label, as long as those headers always result in the same choice of next hop. In effect, a label represents a *forwarding equivalence class* (that is, a set of packets that, however different they might be, are indistinguishable by the forwarding function).

The initial choice of a label need not be based exclusively on the contents of the L3 packet header. For example, forwarding decisions at subsequent hops can also be based on routing policy.

After a label is assigned, a short label header is added in front of the L3 packet. This header is carried across the network as part of the packet. At subsequent hops through each MPLS router in the network, labels are swapped, and forwarding decisions are made by means of MPLS forwarding table lookup for the label carried in the packet header. Therefore, the packet header does not need to be reevaluated during packet transit through the network. Because the label is a fixed length and unstructured, the MPLS forwarding table lookup process is both straightforward and fast.

MPLS LDP

MPLS Label Distribution Protocol (LDP) allows the construction of highly scalable and flexible IP VPNs that support multiple levels of services.

LDP provides a standard methodology for hop-by-hop, or dynamic label, distribution in an MPLS network by assigning labels to routes that have been chosen by the underlying Interior Gateway Protocol (IGP) routing protocols. The resulting labeled paths, called label switch paths (LSP), forward label traffic across an MPLS backbone to particular destinations.

LDP provides the means for label switch routers (LSR) to request, distribute, and release label prefix binding information to peer routers in a network. LDP enables LSRs to discover potential peers and to establish LDP sessions with those peers for the purpose of exchanging label binding information.

MPLS LDP Targeted Session

The **mpls ldp neighbor targeted** command is implemented to improve the label convergence time for directly connected LSRs. When the links between the neighbor LSRs are up, both the link and targeted hellos maintain the LDP session. When the link between neighboring LSRs goes down, the targeted hellos maintain the session, allowing the LSR to retain labels learned from each other. When the failed link comes back up, the LSRs can immediately reinstall labels for forwarding use without having to reestablish their LDP session and exchange labels again.

Cisco recommends the use of the **mpls ldp neighbor targeted** command to set up a targeted session between directly connected MPLS LSRs when MPLS label forwarding convergence time is an issue.

The following commands set up a targeted LDP session with neighbors using the default label protocol:

```
lon-n-pe1# config t
Enter configuration commands, one per line.  End with CNTL/Z.
lon-n-pe1(config)# mpls ldp neighbor 10.76.70.12 targeted ldp
lon-n-pe1(config)# mpls ldp neighbor 10.76.70.21 targeted ldp
```

```
lon-n-pe1(config)# mpls ldp neighbor 10.76.70.22 targeted ldp
lon-n-pe1(config)# mpls ldp neighbor 10.76.70.31 targeted ldp
lon-n-pe1(config)# mpls ldp neighbor 10.76.70.32 targeted ldp
```

Limit LDP Label Allocation

Normally, LDP advertises labels for IP prefixes present in the routing table to all LDP peers. Because the core network is a mix of IP and MPLS architecture, you must ensure that the advertisements of label bindings is limited to only a set of LDP peers so that not all traffic is label switched. All other traffic should be routed using IP.

The **no mpls ldp advertise-labels** command prevents the distribution of any locally assigned labels to all LDP neighbors.

In the following example, a standard access control list (ACL) used on N-PE routers limits the advertisement of LDP bindings to a set of LDP peers that match access list 76. Therefore, it is a best practice to use a separate IP block for N-PE loopback interfaces for L2 VPN services:

```
lon-n-pe1# config t
Enter configuration commands, one per line.  End with CNTL/Z.
lon-n-pe1(config)# mpls ldp advertise-labels for 76
lon-n-pe1(config)# access-list 76 permit 10.76.0.0 0.0.255.255
```

MPLS LDP-IGP Synchronization

The LDP-IGP synchronization feature specifically refers to synchronization of IP path and MPLS labels to prevent traffic from being black-holed. The algorithm used to build the MPLS forwarding table depends on the IP routing protocol in use. It is important to ensure that LDP is fully converged and established before the IGP path is used for switching traffic. The IP path is not inserted in the routing table until LDP has converged.

The command syntax necessary to configure the LDP-IGP synchronization feature is as follows:

```
lon-n-pe1(config)# router ospf 1
lon-n-pe1(config-router)# mpls ldp sync
```

Note For detailed information about MPLS LDP-IGP synchronization, refer to the Cisco document "*MPLS LDP-IGP Synchronization*," available at www. http://tinyurl.com/d5cux5.

MPLS LDP TCP "Pak Priority"

MPLS LDP uses TCP to establish adjacency before exchanging network information. During heavy network traffic, LDP session keepalive messages can be dropped from the outgoing interface output queue. As a result, keepalives can time out, causing LDP sessions to go down. Use the **mpls ldp tcp pak-priority** command to set high priority for LDP messages sent by a router using TCP connections.

> **Note**   Configuring the **mpls ldp tcp pak-priority** command does not affect previously established LDP sessions.

MPLS LDP Session Protection

MPLS LDP session protection maintains LDP bindings when a link fails. MPLS LDP sessions are protected through the use of LDP hello messages. When you enable MPLS LDP, the LSRs send messages to locate other LSRs with which they can create LDP sessions.

If the LSR is one hop from its neighbor, it directly connects to that neighbor. The LSR sends LDP hello messages as User Datagram Protocol (UDP) packets to all the routers on the subnet. The hello message is called an *LDP link hello*. A neighboring LSR responds to the hello message, and the two routers begin to establish an LDP session.

If the LSR is more than one hop from its neighbor, it does not directly connect to the neighbor. The LSR sends out a directed hello message as a UDP packet, but as a unicast message specifically addressed to that LSR. The hello message is called an *LDP targeted hello*. The nondirectly connected LSR responds to the hello message, and the two routers establish an LDP session.

MPLS LDP session protection uses LDP targeted hellos to protect LDP sessions (for example, two directly connected routers that have LDP enabled and can reach each other through alternate IP routes in the network). An LDP session that exists between two routers is called an *LDP link hello adjacency*. When MPLS LDP session protection is enabled, an LDP targeted hello adjacency is also established for the LDP session. If the link between the two routers fails, the LDP link adjacency also fails. However, if the LDP peer can still be reached through IP, the LDP session remains up, because the LDP targeted hello adjacency still exists between the routers. When the directly connected link recovers, the session does not need to be reestablished, and LDP bindings for prefixes do not need to be relearned. Thus, MPLS LDP session protection improves LDP convergence following an outage by using LDP targeted discovery to retain previously learned label bindings. To configure MPLS LDP session protection, enter the following commands:

```
1on-n-pe1# config t
Enter configuration commands, one per line. End with CNTL/Z.
1on-n-pe1(config)# mpls ldp session protection
```

> **Note**   For more information about MPLS LDP session protection, refer to the Cisco document "*MPLS LDP Session Protection*," available at www. http://tinyurl.com/cfmvrm.

Summary

As explained in this chapter, VPLS is an important part of a solution for extending L2 connectivity across geographically dispersed data centers. The MST-based, EEM-based, and generic routing encapsulation (GRE)-based solutions that this book describes incorporate this technology.

## Chapter 3

High Availability for Extended Layer 2 Networks

The following design components must be considered to achieve high availability when extending Layer 2 networks:

- Maximum transmission unit (MTU) evaluation for intersite core transport

- Core routing

- Convergence optimization

This chapter focuses on the components listed to achieve high availability.

MTU Evaluation for Intersite Transport

As in any Ethernet encapsulation technology, MTU is an important aspect to consider. The packet-switched network (PSN) must be configured with an MTU that is large enough to transport a maximum-size Ethernet frame that is encapsulated with a control word, a pseudowire (PW) demultiplexer, and a tunnel encapsulation. If the tunneling protocol is Multiprotocol Label Switching (MPLS), the largest frame increases by at least 8 bytes. Other tunneling protocols might have longer headers and therefore require larger MTU values.

Figure 3-1 illustrates the fields in the Ethernet frame with MPLS encapsulation.

An MTU calculation summary is as follows:

    Core header = 14 bytes

    VPLS encapsulation = 12 bytes

    Customer L2 Frame = 18 bytes (includes 4 bytes FCS)

    Customer VLAN = 4 bytes (QinQ option)

    Customer PDU = 1500 bytes

    Ethernet MTU = 1548 bytes

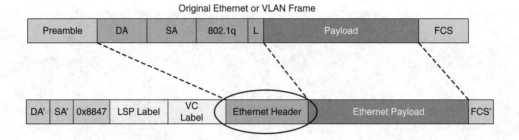

Figure 3-1   *Ethernet frame with MPLS encapsulation.*

The MTU of links between N-PE and P routers must be the same at each end of the link and across all the PWs in the mesh. If the Fast Reroute (FRR) option is configured in the core to achieve sub-50-ms backup time, the MTU value must be increased by 8 bytes to allow two additional labels, one for the primary tunnel and second label for the backup tunnel.

Note   Fragmentation within an MPLS network is not allowed. It is important to configure the MTU appropriately so that traffic is not dropped in the core or the service provider network.

The preceding MTU calculation assumes that only a plain Ethernet or dot1q frame has to be transported. If larger Ethernet frames, such as giant or jumbo frames, require transport, the IP MTU or MPLS MTU must be increased to accommodate these frames.

To configure an MTU of 1548, enter the following:

```
lon-n-pe1# config t
Enter configuration commands, one per line.  End with CNTL/Z.
lon-n-pe1(config)# interface ten 3/8
lon-n-pe1(config-if)# mtu 1548
```

Table 3-1 describes the fields in an Ethernet frame with MPLS encapsulation.

Table 3-1   *Fields in Ethernet Frame with MPLS Encapsulation*

Field	Size in Bytes	Purpose
Core destination MAC address	6	Destination MAC address of the next-hop router
Core source MAC address	6	MAC address of the egress interface of the Network-facing Provider Edge (N-PE) router
EtherType MPLS	2	—
Label switch path (LSP) label	4	Core switching label (null label when the N-PE routers between data centers are directly connected)
VC (PW) label	4	Identification of remote virtual forwarding instance (VFI), pointing to PW label of remote VFI
Control word	4	Always 00.00.00.00 because control word is not used in VPLS
End-device destination MAC address	6	Known to the N-PE, but hidden to the core due to VPLS encapsulation
End-device source MAC address	6	Known to the N-PE, but hidden to the core due to VPLS encapsulation
EtherType = 802.1Q	2	H-VPLS with QinQ at edge of N-PE
802.1Q field	2	Customer VLANs
Length/type	2	Pointing to IP packet or other frame
Packet data unit (PDU)	1500	Up to 1500 bytes
FCS	4	
Ethernet MTU Total	**1548 bytes**	

Note   Chapter 2, "Appraising Virtual Private LAN Service," discusses PWs in greater detail. Chapter 4, "MPLS Traffic Engineering," discusses FRR in greater detail.

Core Routing

Virtual Private LAN Services (VPLS) is a virtual private network (VPN) class that supports the connection of multiple sites in a single bridged domain over an MPLS or IP network.

The principle architectures for building a Layer 3 core network to enable integration of Layer 2 traffic are as follows:

■   Mixed MPLS/IP core

■   Pure MPLS core

■   Pure IP core

Mixed MPLS/IP Core

Figure 3-2 shows the most common architecture, in which Layer 3 is pure IP, independent of MPLS, and Layer 2 is pure MPLS. In this architecture, N-PE is the MPLS node and functions both as a plain IP router for Layer 3 connectivity and as an N-PE for Layer 2 traffic.

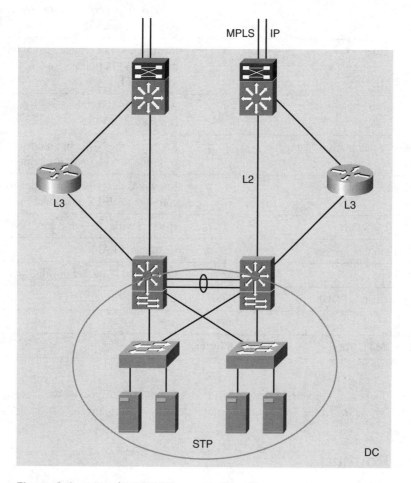

Figure 3-2   *Mixed MPLS/IP core model.*

MPLS is a layered technology in which the control plane relies on the IP routing protocol. The IP routing topology information is used to build and maintain the MPLS forwarding table. So, the first step to create an MPLS network is to determine an Interior Gateway Protocol (IGP). The following sections describe the two approaches that you can use to make this determination.

Different IGP for IP Core and MPLS

One approach to creating an MPLS network is to select an IGP other than the one used in the IP core. The advantages of this approach include smooth integration of MPLS without affecting existing routing, isolation of the MPLS service from the edge, and protecting key services from noncore failures.

IGP optimization can be performed without affecting user traffic when different IGPs are used in the MPLS-enabled core network and within the data centers.

In addition, this approach simplifies control of the semaphore because it is restricted only to the core. Depending on the routing protocol in the IP core network, the IGP for MPLS core could be Open Shortest Path First (OSPF) or Intermediate System-to-Intermediate System (IS-IS).

Same IGP for IP Core and MPLS

Another approach to creating an MPLS network is to use the same IP routing protocol that the IP core network uses. This approach is the simplest option. However, take care to control semaphore loopback advertisement to avoid reinjecting these semaphore loopback routes of other data centers from the data center edge.

Embedded Event Manager (EEM)-based solutions achieve the detection of node failures through the advertisement of peer loopback interfaces through the core IGP. You must configure a distribute list on all Layer 3 links between core and N-PE routers to avoid learning of these routes in the event of dual WAN link failure (link between N-PE to P routers and inter-N-PE link). Otherwise, EEM will be unable to detect this failure, thus black-holing all traffic that was originally being forwarded by the failed N-PE. Figure 3-3 illustrates this situation.

Example 3-1 shows the configuration of a distribute list on an N-PE router.

Example 3-1   *Configuring a Distribute List on an N-PE Router*

```
Router (config)# router ospf process
Router (config-router)# distribute-list 1 in N-PE to data center core router
interface
Router (config-router)# access-list 1 deny host route of semaphore loopbacks of
remote data centers
Router (config-router)# access-list 1 permit any
```

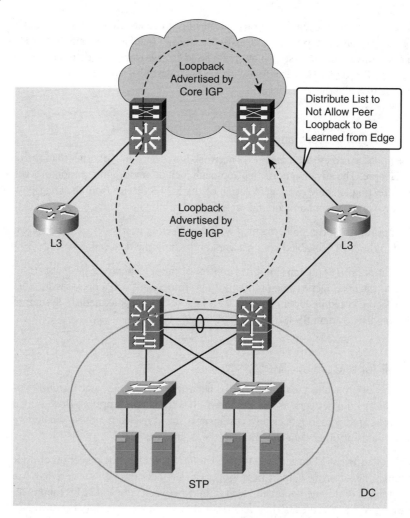

Figure 3-3   *Application of a distribute list that blocks the N-PE from learning peer loopback addresses via the data center edge.*

Pure MPLS Core

Data centers often operate in dynamic multitenant environments such as multitenant office buildings. These deployments are designed to accommodate subsidiaries' data center consolidation or to offer service to multiple independent entities. Security is a paramount requirement when the core network is shared in a multiservice transport solution and is a primary reason for deploying MPLS in the enterprise core networks. The deployment of Virtual Routing and Forwarding (VRF) for Layer 3 and virtual forwarding instance (VFI) for Layer 2 traffic also provides flexibility and ease of integration of Layer 2 data center interconnect (DCI) because the core is already enabled to transport MPLS labels.

In this pure MPLS core model, illustrated in Figure 3-4, all traffic is transported via MPLS labels.

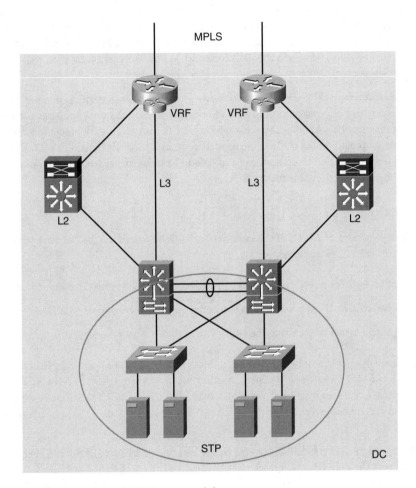

Figure 3-4 *Pure MPLS core model.*

In the pure MPLS core model, Layer 2 and Layer 3 traffic benefit from MPLS technology in the following ways:

- **Virtualization:** MPLS VRF provides the capability to configure and maintain two or more routing domains. Each routing domain has its own set of interfaces and its own set of routing and forwarding tables within the same router. MPLS VRF also enables support for two or more VPNs where IP addresses can overlap between different VPNs.

- **Traffic engineering:** MPLS Traffic Engineering (MPLS-TE) optimizes the routing of IP traffic within the constraints imposed by the capacity of the core network, sometimes also referred to as the *backbone*. Traffic flows have bandwidth and media requirements, prioritization of flows, and so on. Hence, these flows can be routed across a network based on the resources that the traffic flow requires and the resources available in the network. This capability allows network operators to provision links by partitioning loads and avoid link oversubscription, thus guaranteeing end-to-end quality of service (QoS) through the core. MPLS-TE employs *constraint-based routing* in which the path for a traffic flow is the shortest path that meets the resource requirements (constraints) of the traffic flow.

- **Fast Reroute (FRR):** Because core networks carry a large amount of critical traffic, protection and restoration of link and node failures in the core becomes the key component of the overall architecture. FRR provides protection by preestablishing a backup path that is ready to be used as soon as a failure is detected. FRR also provides restoration by dynamically calculating a new path as soon as the failure has been detected and propagated.

Pure IP Core

The deployment of MPLS in the core network might not always be the best option, particularly in the following cases:

- Intersite links leased from service providers that provide only IP connectivity.

- The existing IP core network is too complex for integration of MPLS.

- Data center traffic exiting the enterprise network must be encrypted.

In these situations, a better solution is a direct encapsulation of VPLS or Ethernet over MPLS (EoMPLS) traffic into generic routing encapsulation (GRE), or MPLS encapsulated at the data center egress point via MPLS over GRE (MPLSoGRE). Also, any crypto engine can be deployed if the IP traffic (L3 VPN or L2 VPN over GRE) needs to be encrypted.

In the pure IP core model, all Layer 2 traffic is tunneled using MPLSoGRE. Figure 3-5 illustrates the pure IP core model.

Some of the possible solutions mentioned earlier have the following characteristics:

- **EoMPLSoGRE approach:** When using a Cisco 7600 series router as the N-PE, EoMPLSoGRE is supported only in port mode or subinterface mode, which allows the point-to-point cross-connect of interconnect edge devices.

  When using a Cisco Catalyst 6500 series switch as the N-PE, EoMPLSoGRE can interconnect switched virtual interfaces (SVI) and can provide support for port and subinterface mode. When interconnecting SVIs, the N-PE can participate in local Spanning Tree Protocol (STP) or execute 802.1Q in 802.1Q (QinQ) and tunnel all incoming VLANs to a QinQ VLAN.

- **VPLSoGRE approach:** As of this writing, VPLSoGRE is supported only on Cisco Catalyst 6500 switches with the SIP-400 module. One GRE tunnel is configured on

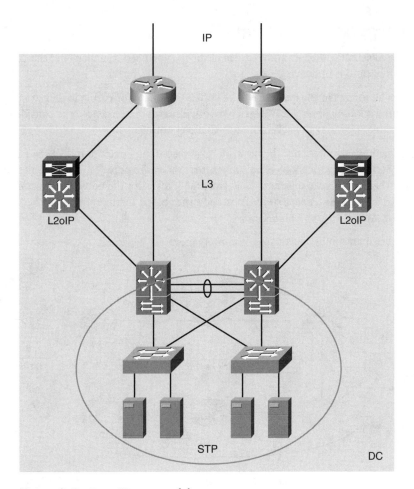

Figure 3-5 *Pure IP core model.*

the N-PE for each N-PE in remote data centers for encapsulation of VPLS traffic.
MPLS must be enabled on the tunnel endpoints.

■ **MPLSoGRE approach:** When all the Layer 2 and Layer 3 traffic must be encapsulated into IP, a solution is to use a dedicated router to perform encapsulation and
another router as the N-PE for standard L2 VPN implementation.

These successive encapsulations will increase packet MTU. The GRE header is 24
bytes, while the L2 VPN header can be up to 30 bytes, leading to 1554-byte MTU;
however, this total byte count does not include the additional core link header.

These approaches, in which MPLS traffic is encapsulated in GRE, are less efficient than
plain MPLS imposition. In addition, if the IP traffic, L3 VPN, or L2 VPN over GRE must
be encrypted, deployment of an IP crypto engine should be evaluated.

Convergence Optimization

Before discussing the key convergence elements, you need to understand the definition and implications of convergence.

When all routers in a network have the correct routing information in their routing tables, the network has converged. When a network achieves convergence, it is considered to be in a stable state, and all packets are routed along optimal paths.

When a link or router fails, the network must reconfigure itself to reflect the new topology by updating routing tables, possibly across the entire network. Until the network reconverges, it is in an unstable state. The time it takes for the network to reconverge is known as the *convergence time.* This time varies based on the routing protocol and the type of failure (link or a node).

Figure 3-6 illustrates an example of convergence.

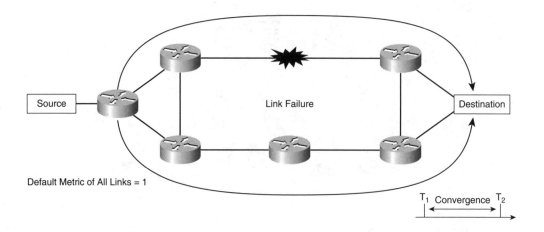

Figure 3-6   *Network convergence.*

In this example, assume a flow from source to destination. When the link fails at time T_1, the best path is affected, which results in traffic loss. At time T_2, the network converges, and the next best path is computed. Traffic resumes and reaches the destination again. The time period when the connectivity was lost, $T_{total} = T_2 - T_1$, is called *convergence.*

Convergence time or the capability to reroute traffic is one of the key issues in any large-scale network. With the recent enhancements in IGPs and fast link-failure detection mechanisms, it is possible for link-state routing protocols to converge in tens of milliseconds.

Key Convergence Elements

The primary goal of the core layer is to switch traffic at very high speeds between the various modular components of the network. The current generation of Cisco switches can route or switch voice and data packets using Layer 3 information without an increase in latency or a loss of capacity. Cisco recommends a routed network core in which the design is composed of a full-mesh equal-cost path routing that uses Layer 3 switching.

Routed cores have numerous advantages, including the following:

- **High availability:** Direct fiber interconnects simplify neighbor-failure detection.

  Deterministic convergence times for any link or node failure in an equal-cost path Layer 3 design of less than 200 ms.

  No potential for Layer 2 loops.

- **Scalability and flexibility:** Lower cost redundancy allows use of the optimal redundant design, which can provide dynamic traffic load balancing with best path selection.

  Structured routing allowing the use of modular design and ease of growth.

- **Simplified management and troubleshooting:** Simplified routing design eases operational support.

  Removal of the need to troubleshoot interactions between Layer 2 and Layer 3 in the core.

  Hardware-based Layer 3 switching ensures dedicated CPU resources for control-plane processing.

  Fewer bandwidth limitations allow for aggressive tuning of control-plane traffic (for example, configuration of hello packet intervals).

Convergence in a core network relies on IGP. Therefore, IGP fast convergence optimization becomes a key factor in optimizing service recovery upon link or node failures.

When optimizing any routing design, you should consider the following elements:

- Failure detection and tuning
- Alternate route computation
- Switching table (Cisco Express Forwarding [CEF]) rewrite

Failure Detection and Tuning

The best practice for core and data center network design uses point-to-point fiber connections for all links between switches. In addition to providing electromagnetic and error protection, fewer distance limitations, and higher capacity, fiber links between switches enable improved fault detection. In a point-to-point fiber connection that uses

Gigabit Ethernet or 10 Gigabit Ethernet, remote node and link loss detection typically is accomplished by using the remote fault detection mechanism implemented as a part of the 802.3z and 802.3ae link negotiation protocols. If a physical link, local or remote transceiver, or remote node fails, the remote fault detection mechanism triggers a link-down condition that then triggers routing and forwarding table recovery. The efficiency and speed of this fault-detection mechanism allows rapid convergence in the core.

Note   See IEEE standards 802.3ae and 802.3z for information about the remote fault operation for Gigabit Ethernet or 10 Gigabit Ethernet, respectively.

Link and node failure detection both play a vital role in fast convergence. Link failure detection should provide speed and reliability/stability. For link types that do not offer prompt failure detection (for example, multipoint Ethernet), the failure detection speed is a function of the OSPF Hello, and hold timers considering OSPF is the IGP configured in the network. In such cases only, it makes sense to tune the OSPF timers. In all other cases, you should consider configuring IP event dampening, which uses a configurable exponential decay mechanism to suppress the effects of excessive interface flapping, and thereby selectively dampening a local interface. Dampening an interface removes the interface from the network until the interface becomes stable. This approach improves stability throughout the network.

Bidirectional Forwarding Detection (BFD) is a new fast hello mechanism for detecting a link or neighbor failure. When BFD is configured, it is not necessary to tune IGP hello and hold timers to an aggressive value.

The following sections discuss IP event dampening, BFD, link debounce, and carrier delay in detail.

IP Event Dampening

When tightly tuning the interface failure-detection mechanisms, a best practice is to configure IP event dampening on every routed interface. IP event dampening provides a mechanism for controlling the rate at which interface state changes are propagated to the routing protocols if a link flaps. IP event dampening operates like other dampening mechanisms, providing a penalty and penalty decay mechanism on link-state transitions. If a rapid series of link-status changes occurs, the penalty value for an interface increases until it exceeds a threshold. Then, no additional interface state changes are propagated to the routing protocols until the penalty value associated with the interface drops below the reuse threshold.

Example 3-2 shows IP event dampening configuration with default values for suppress, reuse, and maximum penalty.

Example 3-2 *IP Event Dampening Configuration*

```
interface GigabitEthernet1/1
description Uplink to Core1
dampening
ip address 10.120.0.205 255.255.255.254
ip ospf dead-interval minimal hello-multiplier 4
logging event link-status
load-interval 30
carrier-delay msec 0
```

To display dampened interfaces on a router, use the **show interface dampening** command in EXEC mode, as demonstrated in Example 3-3.

Example 3-3 *Summary of the Dampening Parameters and Status*

```
lon-n-pe1# show interfaces dampening
TenGigabitEthernet2/0/0 used for QinQ ES20 card facing lon-agg-pe1 (member of MEC
toward VSS)
  Flaps Penalty    Supp ReuseTm    HalfL   ReuseV    SuppV   MaxSTm    MaxP Restart
      0       0    FALSE       0        5     1000     2000       20    16000        0
TenGigabitEthernet2/0/1 used for QinQ ES20 card facing lon-agg-pe2 (member of MEC
toward VSS)
  Flaps Penalty    Supp ReuseTm    HalfL   ReuseV    SuppV   MaxSTm    MaxP Restart
      1       0    FALSE       0        5     1000     2000       20    16000        0
TenGigabitEthernet3/2 connected to lon-c1 T1/2 for PE/CE connection with sub-ints
  Flaps Penalty    Supp ReuseTm    HalfL   ReuseV    SuppV   MaxSTm    MaxP Restart
      0       0    FALSE       0        5     1000     2000       20    16000        0
TenGigabitEthernet4/0/0 L3 connection to N-PE2
  Flaps Penalty    Supp ReuseTm    HalfL   ReuseV    SuppV   MaxSTm    MaxP Restart
      0       0    FALSE       0        5     1000     2000       20    16000        0
TenGigabitEthernet4/0/1 L3 connection to CRS1-P1 TE0/0/0/0
  Flaps Penalty    Supp ReuseTm    HalfL   ReuseV    SuppV   MaxSTm    MaxP Restart
      0       0    FALSE       0        5     1000     2000       20    16000        0
lon-n-pe1#
```

For more information about IP event dampening, refer to the IP event dampening documentation available at
http://www.cisco.com/en/US/docs/ios/12_2s/feature/guide/fsipevdp.html.

BFD

BFD is a detection protocol that provides fast forwarding-path failure detection for all media types, encapsulations, topologies, and the routing protocols (Border Gateway Protocol [BGP], Enhanced Interior Gateway Routing Protocol [EIGRP], Intermediate System-to-Intermediate System [IS-IS], and Open Shortest Path First [OSPF]). BFD provides a low-overhead, short-duration method of detecting failures in the forwarding path between two adjacent routers, including the interfaces, data links, and forwarding planes. By sending rapid failure-detection notices to the routing protocols in the local router to initiate the routing table recalculation process, BFD greatly reduces overall network convergence time. BFD can be enabled at the interface and routing protocol levels.

In addition to fast forwarding-path failure detection, BFD provides a consistent failure-detection method regardless of the media type. This feature allows network administrators to detect forwarding-path failures at a uniform rate, rather than the variable rates detected by different routing protocol hello mechanisms. This feature makes network profiling and planning easier, and provides consistent and predictable convergence times.

Cisco supports BFD asynchronous mode, which depends on the exchange of BFD control packets between two systems to activate and maintain BFD neighbor sessions between routers. For a BFD session to be created, you must configure BFD on both peers. After a BFD session is created, BFD timers are negotiated, and BFD peers begin to send BFD control packets to each other at the negotiated interval.

Figure 3-7 shows a simple network with two routers running OSPF and BFD. The steps for establishing a BFD neighbor relationship, as depicted in the figure, are as follows:

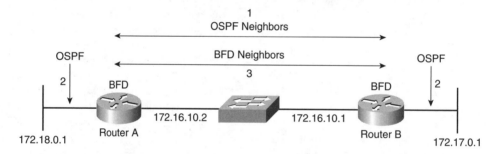

Figure 3-7 *Establishing a BFD neighbor relationship.*

1. OSPF discovers a neighbor.

2. OSPF sends a request to the local BFD process to initiate a BFD neighbor session with the OSPF neighbor router.

3. The BFD neighbor session with the OSPF neighbor router is established.

Figure 3-8 shows what happens when a failure occurs in the network:

1. A failure occurs on a link between two BFD neighbors.

2. The BFD neighbor session with the OSPF neighbor router is torn down.

3. BFD notifies the local OSPF process that the BFD neighbor is no longer reachable.

4. The local OSPF process tears down the OSPF neighbor relationship.

If an alternative path is available, the routers immediately start converging on that path.

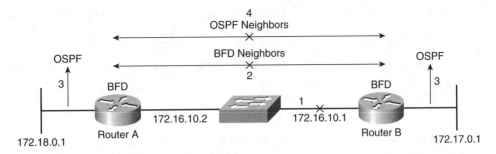

Figure 3-8 *Tearing down an OSPF neighbor relationship.*

After a BFD session is established and timer negations are complete, BFD peers send BFD control packets that act in the same manner as an IGP hello protocol to detect liveliness, except at an accelerated rate. When using BFD, be aware of the following:

■ BFD is a forwarding-path failure-detection protocol. BFD detects a failure, but the routing protocol must take action to bypass a failed peer.

■ Typically, BFD can be used at any protocol layer. However, the Cisco implementation of BFD for Cisco IOS Software Releases 12.2(18)SXE, 12.0(31)S, and 12.4(4)T supports only Layer 3 clients, in particular, the BGP, EIGRP, IS-IS, and OSPF routing protocols.

■ Cisco IOS Software Release 12.2(33)SRC and later support BFD for static routing.

■ Cisco devices use one BFD session for multiple client protocols in the Cisco implementation of BFD for Cisco IOS Releases 12.2(18)SXE, 12.0(31)S, and 12.4(4)T. For example, if a network runs OSPF and EIGRP across the same link to the same peer, only one BFD session is established, and BFD will share session information with both routing protocols.

For more information about BDF, refer to the document *Bidirectional Forwarding Detection* at www. http://tinyurl.com/55q8mw.

Link Debounce Timer

The debounce timer sets the amount of time that firmware waits before it notifies the software that a link is down.

To achieve faster convergence, review the status of the link debounce and carrier-delay configuration. By default, most Gigabit Ethernet and 10 Gigabit Ethernet fiber interfaces operate with a 10-ms debounce timer, which provides optimal link-failure detection. The default debounce timer for 10/100-Mbps Ethernet and all copper links is longer than that for Gigabit Ethernet or 10 Gigabit Ethernet fiber. Therefore, consider deploying high-speed fiber for switch-to-switch links. Reviewing the status of this configuration on all switch-to-switch links to ensure the desired operation is a good practice.

Example 3-4 shows how to review the link debounce and carrier-delay configuration status.

Example 3-4 *Displaying Link Debounce and Carrier-Delay Configuration*

```
DistributionSwitch# show interfaces tenGigabitEthernet 4/2 debounce
Port  Debounce time  Value (ms)
Te4/2  Disable
```

The default and recommended configuration for the debounce timer is "disabled," which results in the minimum time between link failure and notification of this failure to the upper-layer protocols. Table 3-2 lists the time delays that occur before notification of a link-status change.

Table 3-2 *Default Port (Link) Debounce Timer Delay Time*

Port Type	Debounce Timer Disabled	Debounce Timer Enables
Ports operating at 10 Mbps or 100 Mbps	300 ms	3100 ms
Ports operating at 1000 Mbps or 10 Mbps over copper media	300 ms	3100 ms
Ports operating at 1000 Mbps or 10 Mbps over fiber media, except WS-X6502-10GE	10 ms	100 ms
X6502-10GE 10-gigabit ports	1000 ms	3100 ms

Note For more information about the configuration and timer settings of the link debounce timer, refer to www. http://tinyurl.com/qdtenn.

Carrier-Delay Timer

If a link fails, by default there is a 2-second timer that must expire before an interface, and the associated routes are declared as down. If a link goes down and comes back up before the carrier-delay timer expires, the down state is effectively filtered, and the rest of the software on the switch is not aware that a link-down event occurred. The following sections provide guidance for configuring carrier delay on Ethernet and POS interfaces.

Ethernet Interfaces

Configure the carrier-delay timer on the interface to a value of zero (0) to ensure no additional delay in the notification that a link is down. Cisco Catalyst switches use a default value of 0 ms on all Ethernet interfaces for the carrier-delay time to ensure fast link detection. It is a best practice to hard-code the carrier-delay value on critical interfaces with a value of 0 ms to ensure the desired behavior. Example 3-5 shows the configuration of the carrier-delay timer.

Example 3-5 *Carrier-Delay Timer Configuration*

```
interface GigabitEthernet1/1
 description Uplink to Distribution 1
 ip address 10.120.0.205 255.255.255.252
 logging event link-status
 load-interval 30
 carrier-delay msec 0
```

You can confirm the status of carrier delay by looking at the status of the interface via the **show interface** command, as demonstrated in Example 3-6.

Example 3-6 *Confirming Carrier-Delay Status on an Interface*

```
lon-n-pe1# sh int ten 2/0/0
TenGigabitEthernet2/0/0 is up, line protocol is up (connected)
  Hardware is TenGigEther SPA, address is 001d.7198.9500 (bia 001d.7198.9500)
  Description: used for QinQ ES20 card facing lon-agg-pe1 (member of MEC toward
VSS)
  MTU 9216 bytes, BW 10000000 Kbit, DLY 10 usec,
     reliability 255/255, txload 1/255, rxload 1/255
  Encapsulation ARPA, loopback not set
  Keepalive not supported
  Carrier delay is 0 msec
  Full-duplex, 10Gb/s
  input flow-control is on, output flow-control is on
  ARP type: ARPA, ARP Timeout 04:00:00
  Last input 00:00:26, output 00:04:04, output hang never
  Last clearing of "show interface" counters never
  Input queue: 0/75/0/0 (size/max/drops/flushes); Total output drops: 0
  Queueing strategy: fifo
  Output queue: 0/40 (size/max)
  30 second input rate 36000 bits/sec, 69 packets/sec
  30 second output rate 0 bits/sec, 0 packets/sec
  L2 Switched: ucast: 0 pkt, 0 bytes - mcast: 0 pkt, 0 bytes
  L3 in Switched: ucast: 0 pkt, 0 bytes - mcast: 0 pkt, 0 bytes mcast
  L3 out Switched: ucast: 0 pkt, 0 bytes mcast: 0 pkt, 0 bytes
     117400881 packets input, 7855352199 bytes, 0 no buffer
     Received 114 broadcasts (0 multicasts)
     0 runts, 0 giants, 0 throttles
     0 input errors, 0 CRC, 0 frame, 0 overrun, 0 ignored
     0 watchdog, 117400182 multicast, 0 pause input
```

```
      0 input packets with dribble condition detected
      119147 packets output, 13723156 bytes, 0 underruns
      0 output errors, 0 collisions, 2 interface resets
      0 babbles, 0 late collision, 0 deferred
      0 lost carrier, 0 no carrier, 0 pause output
      0 output buffer failures, 0 output buffers swapped out
lon-n-pe1#
```

Note   On Cisco Catalyst 6500 switches, the "LINEPROTO-UPDOWN" message appears when the interface state changes before the expiration of the carrier-delay timer configured via the **carrier delay** command. This behavior is expected and is documented in Cisco defect CSCsh94221.

POS Interfaces

For SONET, carrier delay is an additive function on top of SONET-level holdoff timers. It also acts in the same way the Packet over SONET (POS) triggers act: If the alarm clears before the end of the holdoff period, the interface is not brought down.

The SONET debounce timer is set at 10 seconds (+/- .5 sec) and is required by GR-253 specifications to ensure that a flap period of less than 10 seconds does not occur. This debounce timer does not kick in and clear the defect before the carrier delay activates, unless carrier delay is more than 10 seconds. This leaves a situation where carrier delay is almost always activated and therefore should generally be considered to be rather small when deployed with POS interfaces.

Carrier delay is also added after a alarm is cleared before declaring the interface up. Therefore, the effective delay before the interface comes back up is twice the configured value of the carrier delay. With some interfaces and physical media, this delay is helpful. With POS interfaces, however, you can use and combine a number of triggers and timers to create the desired effect without carrier delay taking such a major role. Based on limited internal testing, a carrier-delay value of 0 to 8 ms is a good value to use when testing this feature. In general, use the POS triggers to absorb any problems and provide the desired holdoff effect, and keep the carrier-delay value small to minimize its effect.

Alternate Route Computation

The most reliable and fastest converging network design uses a tier of redundant switches with redundant equal-cost links. This design using redundant links and equal-cost path routing provides for restoration of traffic flows if either a link or node fails, without having to wait for a routing protocol convergence.

The following factors affect the time that EIGRP, OSPF, or any other routing protocol takes to restore traffic flows within the network:

- The time required to detect the loss of a valid forwarding path

- The time required to determine a new best path (which is partially determined by the number of routers involved in determining the new path or the number of routers that must be informed of the new path before the network can be considered converged)

- The time required to update software and associated CEF hardware forwarding tables with the new routing information

If the switch has redundant equal-cost paths, all of these events are performed locally within the switch and controlled by the internal interaction of software and hardware. If there is no second equal-cost path, EIGRP or OSPF must determine a new route. This process significantly affects network convergence times.

In the case of OSPF, the time required to flood and receive link-state advertisements (LSA) in combination with the time to run the Dijkstra shortest path first (SPF) computation to determine the shortest path tree (SPT) provides a bound on the time required to restore traffic flows. Optimizing the network recovery involves tuning the design of the network to minimize the time and resources required to complete these events.

The optimal OSPF design must improve the convergence time for the OSPF routing protocol. You can use a combination of physical and routing design to affect time to detect a failure and time to update software and hardware forwarding tables. The time to determine a new optimal path is also partially achieved by optimal area and routing designs. However, optimization of the design by itself is not always sufficient to meet convergence requirements. Cisco recommends tuning the OSPF timers and process. OSPF uses a link-state routing algorithm that uses LSAs to propagate information about the links and nodes in the network, and the Dijkstra SPF algorithm to calculate the network topology. Updates to the switches' routing tables involve a process of flooding and receiving updated LSAs, followed by an update of the network topology by the SPF algorithm. The time taken to complete this process depends on the following:

- Number of LSAs

- Number of nodes that need to receive the LSAs

- Time required to transmit the LSAs

- Time required to run the SPF calculation

With the introduction of the new SPF throttle mechanism, the interaction of the throttle timers has been improved to implement an exponential backoff mechanism in the event of multiple triggers for sequential SPF runs.

The throttle timer can be configured with three values:

- *spf-start* (default 5000 ms)

- *spf-hold* (default 10,000 ms)

- *spf-max-wait* (default 10,000 ms)

With the introduction of the these SPF throttle timers, it is now possible to safely reduce the initial SPF timer to a subsecond value and improve the convergence time of the network.

The command to configure the SPF throttle timer is as follows:

timers throttle spf *spf-start spf-hold spf-max-wait*

A typical configuration is as follows:

```
lon-n-pe1# config t
Enter configuration commands, one per line.  End with CNTL/Z.
lon-n-pe1(config)# router ospf 1
lon-n-pe1(config-router)# timers throttle spf 100 100 5000
```

When designing a network to achieve subsecond convergence, the most important of the three timers to modify is the *spf-start*, or the initial wait timer. By reducing this timer, you can significantly reduce the convergence time. It is best not to set this timer to zero (0) because providing a slight wait interval provides a window in which multiple LSA events caused by multiple interface changes can be processed together. Cisco recommends that the wait interval be at least 10 ms (equivalent to the interface debounce timer on Gigabit Ethernet and 10 Gigabit Ethernet fiber links). Configuring a short but nonzero initial wait timer should allow most local interface changes that occur simultaneously to be processed concurrently.

Consider the stability of the network infrastructure when tuning these SPF throttle timers.

If you are a registered user of Cisco.com, you can find more information about the configuration of SPF throttle timers at www. http://tinyurl.com/p6pv36.

Summary

This chapter described the components that are important for effective high availability in extended Layer 2 networks. Effectively implementing and managing these components can help ensure a network that is redundant, resilient, and protected against downtime.

## Chapter 4

MPLS Traffic Engineering

As of this writing, Virtual Private LAN Services (VPLS) and Ethernet over Multiprotocol Label Switching (EoMPLS) technologies are the most appropriate methods for extending a Layer 2 VLAN. In most cases, these technologies require enabling MPLS in the core network. In addition, correlated MPLS features such as traffic engineering (TE) and Fast Reroute (FRR) should be considered for improving network transport.

Understanding MPLS-TE

When IP or Label Distribution Protocol (LDP) is the transport mechanism, traffic always follows the Interior Gateway Protocol (IGP) shortest path and benefits from equal-cost multipath (ECMP) balancing.

MPLS Traffic Engineering (MPLS-TE) is based on a different approach. It relies on source routing, in which the headend of the path creates an end-to-end circuit that is based on several constraints. In addition to shortest path, MPLS-TE allows the following constraints:

- **Explicit path:** Specifies a sequential list of nodes that must be traversed.

- **Affinity path:** Specifies a path affinity that must match the link affinity attribute.

- **Dynamic path:** Computes a shortest path first (SPF) topology over a set of metrics other than IGP metrics.

- **Dynamic path with bandwidth reservation:** Allows reserving the amount of link bandwidth for each MPLS-TE circuit. The headend router determines whether links in the path are able to host circuits. This approach is very useful to build assured circuit topology for sensitive applications like video.

- **Preestablished backup path:** Allows FRR if a failure occurs.

MPLS-TE enables a new type of interface tunnel (called *tunnel LSP* or simply *TE tunnel*) that connects a headend router to a tailend router via the MPLS core.

To create constraint-based LSP, MPLS-TE relies on five main elements:

- **Configuration of additional link attributes, which specify the following:** TE metric (cost) for dynamic topology SPF 32 bits to qualify a link.

  Reservable bandwidth, which decreases dynamically along circuit reservations.

- **Link information distribution through SPF (ISIS-TE or OSPF-TE):** Floods link attributes across all nodes so that the headend router is aware of the network capability to accept a tunnel.

- **Path calculation (CSPF) executed on the headend router:** The headend router computes the best available path to match tunnel constraint configuration such as bandwidth, affinity, explicit path, and priority. May specify multiple options lists.

- **Path setup (RSVP-TE):** The headend router creates the end-to-end LSP using Resource Reservation Protocol (RSVP) signaling, and obtains label allocation along the matching constraints' core path.

- **Forwarding traffic down the tunnel:** There are several ways to forward traffic over the tunnel LSP after the tunnel becomes active. VPLS uses per-virtual forwarding instance/pseudowire (VFI/PW) tunnel allocation, in which VFI and PW are VPLS elements.

MPLS-TE is often deployed in service provider networks. However, large enterprises and public organizations that have deployed MPLS have also found this technology useful.

The FRR option is an attractive feature for data center interconnection because it further decreases the convergence time if a link failure occurs. However, complex core topologies require controlled load repartition. Parallel link bundling to increase intersite bandwidth is difficult to accomplish without a tool such as traffic engineering. The following sections discuss FRR and load repartition in greater detail.

Data center interconnect rarely uses the bandwidth reservation paradigm because its topology is often not highly complex. In addition, the percentage of sensitive traffic lost is low. However, with the availability of Fibre Channel over IP (FCoIP) traffic, the tolerance for loss of sensitive traffic is very low.

Fast Reroute

When protecting the MPLS core links and nodes, it is common to tune the routing protocol (IGP) to achieve a few hundred of milliseconds of convergence time on failures. Nevertheless, even when the SPF initial-wait timer (SPF init) is aggressively reduced, the IGP recovery times are still in the order of magnitude higher when compared to preset techniques like FRR, particularly if you have built a complex MPLS core network in which VPLS nodes, the Network-facing Provider Edges (N-PEs), do not directly interconnect.

FRR relies on a preconfigured backup path that is used immediately if a link or an adjacent node fails. The system executes the repair, called a *local repair*, when it detects this failure. In comparison, IP routing requires recomputation of an alternate path by the rerouting node when it detects a failure.

Load Repartition over the Core

When multiple paths between two N-PEs are not equal in cost, which primarily occurs when the core is not full, meshed, IGP does not allow traffic load balancing. In this case, you can rely exclusively on VLAN load repartition at the edge to balance traffic on two N-PEs and thus on two paths in the core. Alternatively, you can build several MPLS-TE circuits from one N-PE and balance VFI from the N-PE.

Load Repartition over a Parallel-Links Bundle

Repartition of encapsulated traffic is complex because nodes do not have direct access to encapsulated content. Therefore, you should understand the following load-balancing algorithms that most N-PE and core nodes apply to a parallel-links bundle:

- **Basic MPLS load balancing:** The maximum number of load-balancing paths is eight.

  The switching engine on Cisco 7600 series routers and Catalyst 6500 series switches, called the policy feature card (PFC), forwards MPLS labeled packets without explicit configuration. If the packet includes three labels or fewer and the underlying packet is IPv4, the PFC uses the source and destination IPv4 addresses. If the underlying packet is not IPv4 or if it includes more than three labels, the PFC parses down as deep as the fifth or lowest label and uses it for hashing. This stack depth limit is for the Cisco 7600 router and may be different for other devices.

- **MPLS Layer 2 VPN load balancing:** Load balancing is based on the PW label in the MPLS core if the first nibble (4 bits) of the MAC address in the customer Ethernet frame is not the value of 4.

A VFI is considered to be a whole set, and its content is not balanced based on MAC addresses, regardless of the parallel link grooming, equal-cost multipath (ECMP), or EtherChannel (EC). Depending on the line card interfaces used as core links, EC may not be supported. Load repartition over a parallel link bundle with EC and ECMP hashing is executed on the last label of the stack, which points to the VFI. Consequently, when there are few VFIs configured, unequal distribution of traffic might occur across multiple links in the bundle. To overcome such a situation, you can implement MPLS-TE to ensure per-VFI load repartition over multiple links in a bundle.

Implementing MPLS-TE for Traffic Repartition over Parallel Links

This section walks you through the steps required to implement MPLS-TE. Optionally, FRR can be enabled to protect MPLS-TE tunnels.

MPLS-TE can be used to optimize network usage in several ways, but with data center interconnect, a common usage is the controlled load repartition of traffic over bundled links.

Implementing traffic balancing per-VFI over bundled links can be complicated. To help understand the required configuration, consider inter-N-PE connectivity between data centers using a bundle of three links.

The goal is to statically map VFI traffic over a link in the bundle and avoid dynamic allocation that may overload one of the links. This mapping must be effective in normal conditions and even in the case of a link failure.

Figure 4-1 shows a site that uses nodes 1 and 2 to connect using two set of bundled links toward a remote site, which uses nodes 3 and 4.

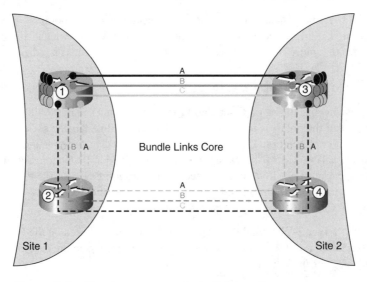

Figure 4-1   *Sites interconnected via link bundles.*

Each node is connected with two other nodes through a bundle of three links (links A, B, and C) to increase intersite bandwidth. Consider the traffic from node 1 to node 3. To allow controlled traffic distribution on the bundle, you have to create three MPLS-TE tunnels from node 1 to node 3 (tunnels A, B, and C). The tunnel A primary path is through the direct link A that connects nodes 1 and 3, and the secondary path is through the three links joining nodes 1, 2, 4, and 3. In normal mode, a VFI attached to tunnel A will use the direct link A joining nodes 1 and 3; other VFIs will use links B or C. If link A between nodes 1 and 3 fails, tunnel A will be rerouted through the secondary path, which is using only type A links, and so will not disturb the VFI using type B or type C.

This behavior differs completely from uncontrolled balancing with ECMP, where, during link A failure, traffic passes through the direct links B or C.

Example 4-1 shows how to set up a TE tunnel from node 1 to node 3 (tunnel 3) through either direct link A when active, or through alternate link A via nodes 2 and 4 when in backup mode.

Example 4-1 *Setting Up MPLS-TE Tunnels*

```
Link A subnet addresses convention are:
 - 10.10.13.0 between node 1 & 3
 - 10.10.12.0 between node 1 & 2
 - 10.10.24.0 between node 2 & 4
 - 10.10.34.0 between node 3 & 4
the last digit is the node number.
```

The following sections document the steps to implement controlled load repartition of traffic over bundled links using MPLS-TE.

Enable TE

Example 4-2 illustrates a configuration that enables TE globally, per interface and under the SPF IGP.

Example 4-2 *Enabling MPLS-TE*

```
mpls traffic-eng tunnels

interface Giga 3/0/0
 ! Description: Core interface
 mpls traffic-eng tunnels

 . . .

router isis
 metric-style wide
 mpls traffic-eng router-id Lo98
 mpls traffic-eng level-1

! or

router ospf 7600
 router-id 10.98.76.1
 mpls traffic-eng router-id Lo98
 mpls traffic-eng area 7600
```

Create MPLS-TE Tunnels and Map Each VFI to a Tunnel LSP

To balance VFI traffic, first create an MPLS-TE tunnel and map this tunnel to a VFI. To attach the VFI, create a PW class in which all VFI options are listed, as shown in Example 4-3.

Example 4-3   *Balancing VFI Traffic*

```
interface Tunnel13
 ip unnumbered Loopback98
 mpls ip

 tunnel destination 10.98.76.3
 tunnel mode mpls traffic-eng
 ! see options in next paragraph

pseudowire-class VPLS-TE-13
 encapsulation mpls
 preferred-path interface Tunnel13
!
l2 vfi VFI-99 manual
 vpn id 99
 neighbor 10.98.76.3 pw-class VPLS-TE-13
 neighbor 10.98.76.4 pw-class ...
```

The **preferred-path** command provides options for strictly or loosely tying a VPLS PW to a TE tunnel. If a PW is strictly tied, whenever the tunnel fails, the PW also goes down. On the other hand, the **loose** option allows PW to be active even when the TE tunnel fails. Therefore, the **loose** option is preferred.

Explicit-Path Option

When the network topology is not too complex, as is generally the case for a data center core, TE can be managed easily through explicit-path configuration.

There are three ways to create an explicit path:

- **next-address:** The **next-address** option includes the following characteristics:
  - Allows listing in hop-by-hop sequence all for nodes or links that the path passes through. Each node or link of the path must be listed.

- In link mode, the next address is a link subnet. In node mode, the next address is the IGP MPLS-TE router ID. So, if multiple parallel links exist between two nodes, the tiebreaker is dynamic balancing.

- The goal of this design is to strictly control traffic repartition over links. In this case, select link mode and use the link subnet address as the next address.

- **next-address loose:** The **next-address loose** option has the following characteristics:

  - Allows specifying an intermediate node that the path passes through. SPF dynamically builds a path before and after this node.

  - The previous address (if any) in the explicit path need not be connected directly to the next IP address.

- **exclude-address:** Excludes an address from subsequent partial-path segments. You can enter the IP address of a link or the router ID of a node.

Example 4-4 shows how to configure explicit-path sequences.

Example 4-4   *Configuring Explicit-Path Sequences*

```
ip explicit-path name A13 enable
 next-address 10.10.13.3
! Primary link to use

ip explicit-path name A13-bck enable
 next-address 10.10.12.2
 next-address 10.10.24.4
 next-address 10.10.34.3
```

Example 4-5 demonstrates how to specify tunnel-path options.

Example 4-5   *Specifying Tunnel-Path Options*

```
interface tunnel13
tunnel mpls traff path-option 1 explicit name A13
tunnel mpls traff path-option 2 explicit name A13-bck
tunnel mpls traff path-option 3 dynamic
```

In Example 4-5, if the direct link A between nodes 1 and 3 is active, the TE LSP and the VFI traffic passes through. If this link goes down, traffic routes through an alternate path A, even if the other direct links are active (B and C). The last path option specifies that if no path A is available, the tunnel is allowed to pass through any other link. If this option had not been enabled, the TE tunnel would have failed.

Adding FRR to Explicit Option

FRR increases the efficiency of rerouting if a failure occurs. This efficiency becomes more apparent in a complex network topology.

To compare the efficiency of FRR with IP rerouting, consider the following cases:

- **IP versus FRR link protection:** When a link failure occurs, FRR reacts in just a few milliseconds to swap primary traffic to the backup tunnel, whereas IP rerouting must wait for the SPF init delay. When the network topology and link type are simple, the SPF init can be lowered to 20 ms or less. In this case, the IP rerouting efficiency is close to that of FRR.

    Configuring FRR is much more complex than configuring IGP fast convergence. Therefore, consider FRR when the core is complex and the IGP SPF init timer cannot be lowered any further without compromising network stability.

- **LDP versus FRR:** Data center interconnect Layer 2 traffic is transported by MPLS and not by IP. Therefore, in this situation, compare IGP + LDP to FRR instead of IP to FRR. IGP+LDP convergence takes some time to rewrite labels and to synchronize IGP and LDP, so IGP+LDP can take upward of tens of milliseconds to converge. On the other hand, FRR ensures convergence in milliseconds. Depending on the application's sensitivity to loss, this reduction in convergence time that FRR provides may be valuable.

- **MPLS-TE RSVP convergence versus FRR:** When MPLS-TE is selected for load repartition, either for path balancing or for bundle balancing, compare RSVP convergence to FRR instead of IGP efficiency to FRR. In this case, regardless of the core topology, RSVP convergence time is much higher than FRR convergence. Therefore, FRR is recommended when MPLS-TE is already deployed for load balancing traffic.

Figure 4-2 shows the implementation of FRR in a square topology.

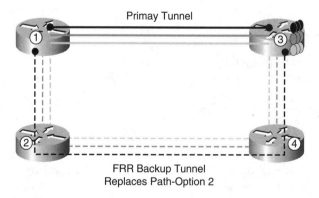

Figure 4-2   *FRR implementation for link protection.*

A backup tunnel for an existing primary tunnel must be configured by using FRR instead of a secondary **path-option**, as shown in previously Example 4-5. The configuration in Example 4-6 shows how to configure a backup tunnel so that it is active and ready for use if a failure occurs.

Example 4-6   *Presetting a Backup Tunnel*

```
interface Tunnel13
 ...
 tunnel mpls traffic-eng fast-reroute

interface Tunnel1243
tunnel mpls traff path-option 2 explicit name A13-bck

Int te3/0/0
! Description: core interface FRR protected
 mpls traffic-eng backup-path Tunnel1243
```

FRR LSP is always active and does not require any recomputation after convergence.

Figure 4-3 illustrates the application of FRR when using core nodes. FRR is typically configured to protect sensitive links, which are most often connecting core routers.

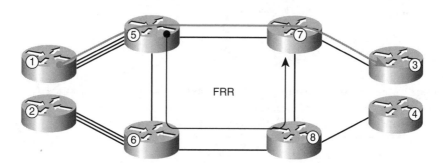

Figure 4-3   *FRR implementation in the core.*

In the preceding configuration examples, FRR was restricted to link protection. This approach is simple and effective because it allows the use of nonprotected dense wavelength-division multiplexing (DWDM) links for data center interconnection while maintaining fast convergence and protection. In addition, FRR can be configured to protect against core node failures. Although it is appealing, the configuration for protection from node failures is complex.

Affinity Option

When the network topology is simple, explicit-path configuration is easy and comprehensive. If this configuration does not provide the desired result, you can use the MPLS-TE feature called *affinity*. This feature provides attributes to every core link and gives the MPLS-TE tunnel an affinity to those attributes.

The affinity is represented by 32-bits per mask. Each bit defines an attribute. These attributes have no predetermined significance and are free for interpretation.

For example, the affinity for link type A could be represented by the value 2 (0x10).

A tunnel that is to be configured on a link type A would need to specify affinity = 0x10, with an optional mask of 0x11. The mask specifies which bits to check when the attribute word has multiple meanings.

MPLS-TE computes path calculation (PCALC) to determine the best path among the type A links. It is a good practice to define a TE-dedicated metric to break a tie among possible paths.

The configuration in Example 4-7 shows how to use affinity to build a tunnel over type A links without having to list every hop via the **explicit-path** option.

Example 4-7 *Using an Affinity*

```
int te3/0/1
 mpls traffic-eng attribute-flags 0x10
 mpls traffic-eng administrative-weight 2


...
interface Tunnel13
 tunnel mpls traffic-eng affinity 0x10 mask 0x11
 tunnel mpls traffic-eng path-option 2 dynamic
 tunnel mpls traffic-eng path-selection metric te
```

Adding FRR to Affinity Option

FRR can be added to the configuration in Example 4-7 to protect a primary tunnel via a backup tunnel built on affinity.

The configuration in Example 4-8 shows how to assign the FRR tunnel the same type A affinity as that of the primary tunnels, and specifies that this backup tunnel must exclude the link that it protects.

Example 4-8 *Adding FRR to Protect the Primary Tunnel*

```
interface Tunnel13
 tunnel mpls traffic-eng affinity 0x10 mask 0x11
 tunnel mpls traff path-option 1 dynamic
```

```
  tunnel mpls traffic-eng fast-reroute

interface Tunnel1243
  tunnel mpls traffic-eng affinity 0x10 mask 0x11
  tunnel mpls traff path-option 2 explicit name RED-exclude13

ip explicit-path name RED-exclude13 enable
  exclude-address 10.10.13.3
int te3/0/0
  mpls traffic-eng backup-path Tunnel1243
```

Summary

Traffic engineering is useful for overcoming limitations of Layer 2 VPN encapsulations, primarily in the areas of load repartition and link bundling. MPLS-TE can be combined with MPLS FRR to achieve fast convergence times.

## Chapter 5

Data Center Interconnect: Architecture Alternatives

This chapter describes design alternatives for removing interdependence of data centers by using spanning-tree isolation techniques.

Data center Layer 2 interconnect solutions that use the Virtual Private LAN Service (VPLS) offer the following key advantages:

- Multisite Layer 2 transport over Layer 3 protected links

- Spanning-tree isolation in the core network that connects remote locations

Several designs exist for data center Layer 2 connectivity because a VPLS device can connect to the aggregation switch in various ways. These designs depend on the following conditions:

- IEEE 802.1Q-in-Q VLAN tag (QinQ) for VLAN scalability

- Monotenant or multitenant data center with local VLAN number overlapping

- Type of aggregation switch with Multichassis EtherChannel (MEC) support, such as a Virtual Switching System (VSS) or a Nexus Virtual PortChannel (vPC)

- Capability of an aggregation switch to execute embedded scripts required to flush MAC addresses

Ensuring a Loop-Free Global Topology: Two Primary Solution Models

The best way to ensure loop-free global topology is to ensure that each data center connects to the VPLS device through only one active link at a time. Depending on the protocol used to ensure this global loop-free topology, the following main models have emerged:

- Multiple Spanning Tree (MST) protocol

■ Active/standby interchassis communication using an Embedded Event Manager (EEM) semaphore in the absence of the Inter-Chassis Communication Protocol (ICCP)

N-PE Using MST for Access to VPLS

In a VPLS model, the node performing the VPLS encapsulation is called the Network Provider Edge (N-PE) device.

One model is to have the N-PE using MST for access to the VPLS. Both N-PEs participate in Spanning Tree Protocol (STP) local to the data center. Two links, one from each N-PE device, connect the data center to the Multiprotocol Label Switching (MPLS)-enabled core network. One of these links is in forwarding mode, and the other is in blocking mode. Which link is in which mode depends on the placement of the MST root bridge.

The MST-based solutions that this book describes are as follows:

■ **MST option 1a—MST in pseudowire (PW):** This IOS-integrated feature can be a viable option if all Layer 2 switches within the data center run MST. Cisco 7600 series platforms with Cisco IOS Software Release 12.2(33)SRC or later offer this feature.

In this solution, an Ethernet over MPLS (EoMPLS) PW relays MST bridge protocol data units (BPDU) between the primary and backup N-PEs. Because both N-PEs participate in local STP, one of the N-PE-to-Agg-PE link is in the forwarding state, and the second link is either in a blocking or down state. This solution also is known as *MST in N-PE using Layer 2 forward protocol.*

■ **MST option 1b—Isolated MST in N-PE:** Consider this solution even in situations in which all Layer 2 switches within the data center do not run the MST protocol. In this solution, MST provides VPLS access control. The N-PEs may enable Rapid Spanning Tree Protocol (RSTP) / MST interoperability, and run MST only on an EtherChannel that connects the primary and backup N-PE.

N-PE Using ICCP Emulation for Access to VPLS

In this model, the N-PE nodes are required to synchronize their state. This chassis-level synchronization is achieved via the EEM semaphore protocol. The N-PE using ICCP emulation for access to VPLS model (also known as *N-PE using semaphore concept for active/standby access to VPLS core*) relies on local synchronization of the active/standby state on the primary and backup N-PEs to ensure backup and recovery.

In this solution, the backup VPLS node tracks a dedicated IP address on the primary N-PE. This IP address is called a primary semaphore (P-semaphore). If the backup N-PE cannot reach the P-semaphore, the backup N-PE enables its PW by using an EEM script.

The EEM semaphore concept and scripts are identical, regardless of the various EEM-based solution options. However, depending on the data center design, there are several options for performing MAC address flushing:

- **EEM option 2—VPLS:** An N-PE device participates in local STP. EEM manages VPLS PW redundancy, and local STP controls the edge links.

- **EEM option 3—H-VPLS:** An N-PE device participates in the local STP and uses QinQ to scale VPLS. A control-plane link on the N-PE participates in local STP. EEM manages the data-plane links and VPLS pseudowire (PW) redundancy.

- **EEM option 4a—Multi-domain H-VPLS:** An N-PE device does not participate in the local STP and uses Hierarchical VPLS (H-VPLS). This option requires an EEM script on aggregation switches to adapt to topology changes and flush MAC addresses. EEM also controls the data-plane links and VPLS PW redundancy.

- **EEM option 4b—Multi-domain H-VPLS with dedicated U-PE:** An N-PE does not participate in the local STP and uses H-VPLS. A User-facing Provider Edge (U-PE) switch exists between the N-PE and the data center to flush MAC addresses. Due to the insertion of a U-PE switch, there is no affect on the distribution device. EEM scripts are required on the intermediate U-PE switch instead of the aggregation switches as in option 4a.

- **EEM option 5a—Multi-domain H-VPLS with MEC:** An N-PE connects to the data center via a Multichassis EtherChannel (MEC) toward the virtual switching system (VSS) on Cisco Catalyst 6500 series switches or a Nexus 7000 virtual PortChannel (vPC) system. EEM manages VPLS PW redundancy, and Link Aggregation Control Protocol (LACP) controls the MEC at the edge.

- **EEM option 5b—Multi-domain H-VPLS with MEC and VLAN load balancing:** N-PE connects to the data center via MEC toward the VSS or a Nexus 7000 vPC system. EEM manages VPLS PW redundancy, and load-balanced LACP controls the MEC at the edge. Aggregation switches require EEM scripts for MAC address flushing.

- **EEM option 5c—Multidomain H-VPLS with MEC and VLAN Load-Balancing:** PWs on Active and Standby VPLS Nodes in UP/UP State: Options 5a and 5b are highly scalable solutions for multi-tenants. In option 5c, the PWs on the primary and backup N-PEs are in UP-UP state. This design enables faster convergence time because the backup PW is always up and ready for use.

Data Center Interconnect Design Alternatives: Summary and Comparison

Table 5-1 summarizes and compares the options for implementing data center interconnect. This information can assist enterprises or application service providers select an appropriate solution based on requirements such as scalability, ease of implementation, and data center STP type.

Table 5-1   *Options for Data Center Interconnect*

Type	MST		EEM / Semaphore					
Option	1a	1b	2	3	4a	4b	5a	5b and 5c
Description	MST in PW	Isolated MST	VPLS	H-VPLS	Multidomain H-VPLS	Multidomain H-VPLS with dedicated U-PE	Multidomain H-VPLS with MEC	Multidomain H-VPLS with MEC and VLAN load balancing
Domain	Enterprise	Enterprise	Enterprise	Enterprise	Multitenant (ASP/Enterprise)	Multitenant (ASP/Enterprise)	Multitenant (ASP/Enterprise)	Multitenant (ASP/Enterprise)
DC STP type	Only MST (1 instance)	RSTP	RSTP/MST	RSTP/MST	Any	RSTP/MST	Any	Any
Solution complexity	Low	Low	Average	Medium	Medium	High	Average	Medium
Ease of implementation	Straightforward (native)	Average	Average	Medium	Medium	High	Average	Medium
Scalability	Medium (hundreds of VLANs) 1 dynamic VFI per VLAN)	Low (5 to 30 VLANs) 1 static VFI per VLAN	Low (5 to 30 VLANs) 1 static VFI per VLAN	Medium (max 1000 VLANs) 1 VFI per QinQ	High (any number of VLANs) 1 semaphore/script per access block	High (any number of VLANs) 1 semaphore/script per access block	Very high (any number of VLANs) 1 semaphore/script per N-PE	High (any number of VLANs) 1 semaphore/script per access block
Local VLAN overlapping	No	No	No	No	Yes	Yes (at N-PE level)	Yes	Yes

Table 5-1   *Options for Data Center Interconnect*

Type	MST		EEM / Semaphore					
Intrusive on DC	Medium (N-PE participates to local MST)	High (N-PE is the root bridge of DC for cross-connected VLANs)	Medium (N-PE participates in local STP)	Medium (N-PE participates in local STP)	Low (requires a simple script into distribution)	None	None	Low (requires a simple script into distribution)
IOS native	Yes 12.2(33)SRC1 or later IOS release	Partially (requires small additional scripts)	Requires EEM scripts in N-PE	Requires EEM scripts in N-PE	Requires EEM scripts in N-PE and in distribution switches	Requires EEM scripts in N-PE and in U-PE	Requires EEM scripts in N-PE	Requires EEM scripts in N-PE and in distribution switches
N-PE platform	Cisco 7600	Cisco 7600	Cisco 7600	Cisco 7600	Cisco 7600	Cisco 7600	Cisco 7600	Cisco 7600

Cisco 7600 routers were used as N-PEs during validation of all these solutions. However, these solutions do work with other platforms such as Cisco Cat6500 series switches and ASR9000 as N-PE.

Type	MST		EEM / Semaphore					
Requires additional control-plane links	No	No	No	Yes (TCN link to distribution and inter-N-PE B-link)	Yes (E-link to trigger distribution script)	Yes (only between U-PE and N-PE, not toward distribution)	No	Yes (E-link to trigger distribution script)

## Chapter 6

Case Studies for Data Center Interconnect

Data center interconnect (DCI) is attracting attention because it is one of the pillars of generalizing the concept of virtualization across data centers. Both new server middleware usages, which offer clustering for high availability or flexibility for servers' virtual organization (VMotion), and more traditional requirements for physical server migration increasingly require a capability to extend VLANs (Layer 2 bridging, L2) across data center sites.

This chapter examines two deployments that implement DCI using Virtual Private LAN Service (VPLS) technology. One deployment is a large government organization (GOV) that provides internal networking and data center solutions. The other is an application service provider (OUT) that hosts servers and provides applications to a large customer base.

Case Study 1: Large Government Organization

GOV is a large government organization that provides networking solutions and data center infrastructure to several other government entities.

Challenges

To increase the availability of key applications, GOV's IT department decided several years ago to implement a server cluster strategy. This strategy provided good application redundancy and scalability and significantly improved GOV's capability to recover from server and operating system failures.

However, to benefit from new networking features, the implementations required cluster members to reside in the same network subnet. In addition, clusters relied on heartbeats that must run in a dedicated VLAN. To take advantage of current cluster technologies, GOV had to extend most VLANs within each data center.

Furthermore, GOV needed to improve its high-availability capabilities. In addition to handling server and operating system failures, clustering had to provide solutions for situations such as partial data center power failures and site inaccessibility. Addressing these requirements meant extending clusters across multiple sites.

Like many other data centers, GOV's data centers also began to encounter physical constraints. Insufficient power, limited space, and inadequate cooling posed insolvable issues with server physical organization and operation, which led to GOV not even being able to install a new cluster member when application performance required it.

Solution

To address these issues, GOV determined that it required a solution that included a multi-site VLAN extension.

The initial solution was a Spanning Tree Protocol (STP) design that controlled four data centers in a global switching domain. GOV carefully followed best practices for L2 design, but the optical topology of the sites' interconnection was unable to match standard STP recommendations; dual hub-and-spoke topology and dense wavelength-division multiplexing (DWDM) protection are considered a must for STP. In addition, the size of the STP domain started to increase above any common implementation.

GOV operated its networks using this design for 1 year. During this time, several small failures occurred, which led to unpredicted results. In one instance, for example, a link failure did not report the loss of signal, leading STP to slow convergence. Every heartbeat over every data center timed out; consequently, all clusters experienced a split-brain situation. Resynchronization took more than 1 hour to recover. During this time, all critical applications stopped operating. Other small failures had similar catastrophic effects. As a result, GOV contacted Cisco for recommendations about how to strengthen its network.

Working in partnership with the GOV networking team, the server cluster vendor, and an external consulting team, Cisco recommended a VPLS solution as described in this book.

The solution team also determined to provide Multiprotocol Label Switching (MPLS) features, such as Virtual Routing and Forwarding (VRF), to provide user-group security segmentation, and traffic engineering, to better manage link loads.

After thorough testing and a pilot phase, the solution was deployed in three GOV data centers. A fourth data center was added soon afterward, and the solution is running successfully.

Figure 6-1 illustrates the new GOV solution.

To build the L3-VPN network and the 10-Gbps MPLS core, GOV selected a Cisco Catalyst 6500 switch with a 67xx line card. This approach allows the easy deployment of VRF within the aggregation layer. L3-VPN extends to all data centers and toward user sites.

To enable the MPLS Traffic-Engineering (TE) feature, the routing protocol had to be link-state-based, so the choice was reduced to either Open Shortest Path First (OSPF) or Intermediate System-to-Intermediate System (IS-IS) routing. In a network of this size,

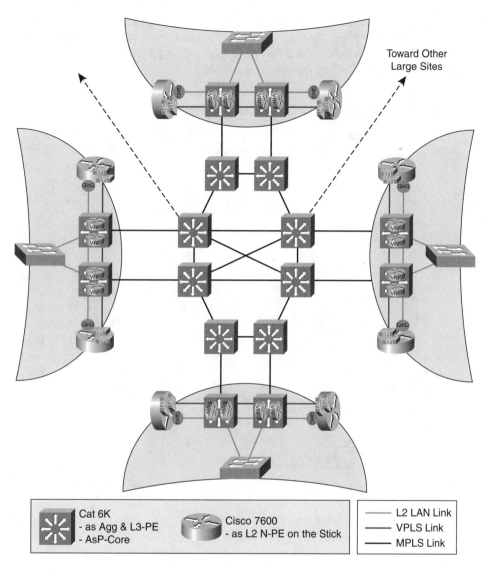

Figure 6-1   *Global VPLS architecture.*

IS-IS and OSPF offer quite similar capabilities, but IS-IS allows a clear demarcation with existing OSPF routing that simplifies deployment. GOV selected IS-IS as its MPLS core routing protocol.

Routing fast convergence is set with a target of a few hundred of milliseconds. Bidirectional Forwarding Detection (BFD) is used to detect long-distance link failure, which allows the system to react in approximately .5 seconds to any nonforwarding link. (GOV plans to include the MPLS Fast-ReRoute [FRR] function in future implementations, with the objective of achieving even more convergence on clear link failures.)

To implement the VLAN extension design using VPLS, the most advanced Network Provider Edge (N-PE) node was the Cisco 7600. Because Cisco 7600 Ethernet Service (ES) cards were not yet available at that time, GOV selected a SIP-600 card to provide 10 Gbps. (An ES card would be the right choice now.)

GOV selected Hierarchical-VPLS (H-VPLS) with Embedded Event Manager (EEM) scripts to provide STP isolation and long-distance link protection.

Four data centers required a VLAN extension to allow cluster extension. The solution included the Cisco 7600 N-PE on a stick. Figure 6-2 illustrates the concept of a "node on a stick."

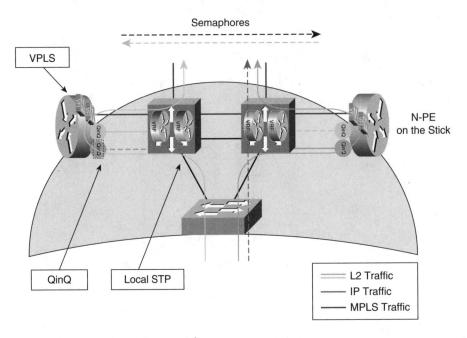

Figure 6-2 *VPLS N-PE on a stick.*

VPLS technology was quite new at the time of implementation. The "on a stick" design allowed GOV to avoid the insertion of new devices with the new Cisco IOS Software and new features along the existing L3 path. Because of this, VPLS failure would affect only L2 traffic, not IP traffic.

L2 traffic first passes in a bridge fashion through the aggregation Cisco Catalyst switch, and then is encapsulated in VPLS by the Cisco 7600 N-PE and pushed back to the Cisco Catalyst switch via a MPLS L3 port. Then traffic flows to the MPLS core.

The Cisco 7600 N-PE uses the 67xx LAN card toward the edge. Each ingress port is then encapsulated into a dual VLAN tag using the IEEE 802.1Q-in-Q VLAN tag (QinQ) feature before being forwarded to VPLS. This QinQ encapsulation enables scalability to any number of VLANs. However, QinQ requires the careful management of overlapping inter-VLAN MAC addressees. This issue is analyzed in depth in Chapter 11, "Additional Design Considerations."

Enterprises should avoid extending network services such as firewalls or load balancers across data centers. In addition, good data center design uses different Hot Standby Router Protocol (HSRP) groups in each data center. These rules were implemented with GOV, where VLAN extension is strictly reserved for issues with multiple data center clusters and not used for other requirements.

In addition, LAN ports are protected from a data-plane storm using *storm control for broadcast and multicast*, which allows deployments to avoid the propagation of flooding across sites. This issue is also analyzed in depth in Chapter 11.

To enable N-PE backup, GOV deployed EEM scripting. The deployment did not include the Ethernet Virtual Circuit (EVC) feature because LAN port types do not allow it.

VLAN load repartition is performed at the edge by using two 10-Gbps edge ports, with per-VLAN cost balancing.

To manage core load repartition over multiple paths, MPLS-TE was deployed, with each virtual forwarding instance (VFI) targeted to a different path.

Case Study 2: Large Outsourcer for Server Migration and Clustering

OUT is an outsourcer that has deployed L2 DCI.

Challenges

Outsourcers such as OUT require the capability to easily perform add and move on request by individual servers. In addition, space, cooling, and power issues require the frequent reorganization of data centers. Flexibility is therefore a master word for outsourcing services. With the arrival on the market of dynamic server virtualization (VMotion), outsourcers can now operate servers more dynamically and with increased flexibility. Flexibility to move servers requires VLAN extension, but outsourcers are well aware of the strong limitations of L2 bridging in terms of resiliency. VPLS is perceived as a solution that combines flexibility with high availability.

Solution

Figure 6-3 illustrates the new OUT virtualized data center.

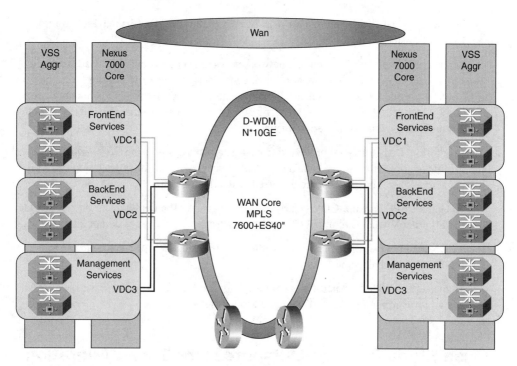

Figure 6-3   *Multisite virtualized data center.*

The OUT DCI network was designed to include ten sites interconnected through 10 Gbps over DWDM links.

Outsourcers have strong scalability requirements and must therefore deploy hardened and flexible solutions. Choosing the correct architecture is important. The best choice for N-PE redundancy will be available in the future and will use Inter-Chassis Communication Protocol (ICCP) with multichassis Link Aggregation Control Protocol (mLACP). An EEM-based solution allows immediate deployment and is adaptable to any design topology.

OUT selected the Cisco 7600 with ES40 10-Gbps card to simultaneously perform H-VPLS, VRF, and core routing functions.

OUT chose H-VPLS with EEM for node redundancy. EEM offers a large panel of options detailed in Chapter 9, "EEM-Based Deployment Models." OUT selected multiple options based on the site architecture:

■ EEM option 5 was selected for green-field data centers with Nexus virtual PortChannel (vPC) or with Virtual Switching System (VSS).

■ EEM option 4 was selected for existing data centers.

■ EEM option 3 was considered, but not yet deployed, for a very old-fashioned data center that does not support scripting into aggregation switches.

OUT considered connections to customer-owned data centers, mainly for migration purposes, but also for cluster extension. Because customer aggregation switches cannot be modified, it was decided to insert a physical small switch (User Provider Edge [U-PE]) per distant customer to perform the MAC-flush script on behalf; this is EEM option 4b, which is also described in this book.

One of the main issues comes from the multitenant aspect of the design. OUT offers its customers hosting for either applications or dedicated physical servers, and sometimes offers dedicated full DC zones. To create secure data centers, OUT selected the Nexus-based virtual data center (VDC) to ensure separation between front-end and back-end areas and to provide management-area isolation. A single VDC is shared between multiple customers, and connection to the 7600 N-PE uses one 10-Gbps port per VDC.

The initial plan was to create one VFI per VDC. This approach would have allowed easy scalability because N-PE would be transparent to the aggregation VLAN. However, sharing the same QinQ bridging domain between customers could result in the overlapping of MAC addresses.

While waiting for future MACinMAC encapsulation (802.1ah), which will be performed at ingress by an ES40 card, it has been decided to allocate one QinQ bridge domain per large customer, and one QinQ domain gathers smaller customers. To accomplish such a dynamic allocation, the Selective QinQ option will be intensively used. This feature allows OUT to identify a set of customer VLANs and encapsulate them in one core VLAN that will be transported using VPLS. Such dynamic encapsulation is a good compromise between scalability and security.

OUT evaluated standard EEM options. However, to improve its convergence timing, OUT asked Cisco to tune scripts to allow active and standby pseudowires in the UP/UP condition. (That is, the alternate path is up and ready but not forwarding traffic until backup.) This configuration is accomplished by tuning the EEM script that inserts and removes the bridge domain condition from the ingress port service instance. To avoid the need to modify the script each time a new customer is inserted, OUT created a set of preprovisioned VFIs.

Load repartition is a key element of the design. With load repartition, multiple parallel links are used to increase intersite throughput. With the Cisco 7600, a VFI is considered as a whole set, and its content is not balanced based on MAC addresses, whether the parallel link uses equal-cost multipath (ECMP) routing or EtherChannel. Load repartition over a parallel links bundle is executed blindly on the last label of the stack, which is the pseudowire (PW) pointing to the remote VFI. Because granularity is per VFI, balancing is poor when the number of VFIs is low, and one link could easily be overloaded while others are almost empty. To avoid this situation, MPLS-TE was implemented to ensure controlled balancing for each VFI.

Figure 6-4 illustrates an efficient way to control balancing on a link bundle.

The approach illustrated in Figure 6-4 ensures that, in normal mode, traffic coming into an N-PE at 10 Gbps can find a 10-Gbps path toward the next hop, even in link-failure conditions. Link-overload conditions could occur with complex traffic patterns or if a node fails, so standard DiffServ queuing is applied to protect key traffic. MPLS-TE is also offering measure of end-to-end traffic over the core, which provides a view of traffic patterns so that paths can be adjusted if needed.

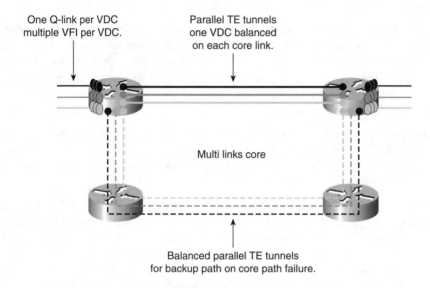

One Q-link per VDC
multiple VFI per VDC.

Parallel TE tunnels
one VDC balanced
on each core link.

Multi links core

Balanced parallel TE tunnels
for backup path on core path failure.

Figure 6-4   *Link bundle balancing using MPLS-TE.*

Summary

VPLS with N-PE redundancy allows customers to flatten the bridging domain over multiple data centers by using the strongest technology currently available. This approach benefits both the server and application layers because it enables flexibility and availability for

- High-availability extended server clusters

- Virtual machines

- Migration

This flexibility does inherently include some caveats, however:

- The solution is complex and introduces constraints at the networking layer.

- Extension of the broadcast domain might present some storm risk.

Balancing the risks and benefits between implementing VLAN extension and a lack of flexibility for servers led these organizations to select VPLS.

## Chapter 7

Data Center Multilayer Infrastructure Design

A data center is home to the computational power, storage, and applications that support an enterprise business. The data center infrastructure is central to the IT architecture, from which all content is sourced or passes through. It is critical to properly plan the data center infrastructure design, and to carefully consider performance, resiliency, and scalability.

Data center design should also address flexibility to enable quickly deploying and supporting new services. Designing a flexible architecture that efficiently supports new applications can provide a significant competitive advantage. Such a design requires solid initial planning and thoughtful consideration of port density, access layer uplink bandwidth, true server capacity, oversubscription, and various other factors.

The data center network design is based on a proven layered approach, which has been tested and improved over several years in some of the largest data center implementations. The layered approach provides the basic foundation of a data center design that improves scalability, performance, flexibility, resiliency, and maintenance. Figure 7-1 shows the basic layered design.

The data center includes the following layers:

- **Core layer:** Provides the high-speed packet-switching backplane for all flows that pass in to and out of the data center. The core layer provides connectivity to multiple aggregation modules and provides a resilient Layer 3 routed fabric with no single point of failure. The core layer runs an interior routing protocol, such as Open Shortest Path First (OSPF) or Enhanced Interior Gateway Routing Protocol (EIGRP), and load balances traffic between the campus core and aggregation layers by using Cisco Express Forwarding (CEF)-based hashing algorithms.

- **Aggregation layer:** Provides important functions, such as service module integration, Layer 2 domain definitions, spanning-tree processing, and default gateway redundancy. Server-to-server multitier traffic flows through the aggregation layer and can use services such as firewall and server load balancing to optimize and secure applications. The smaller icons within the aggregation layer switch in Figure 7-1 represent the integrated service modules. These modules provide services, such as content switching, firewall, Secure Sockets Layer (SSL) offload, intrusion detection, network analysis, and more.

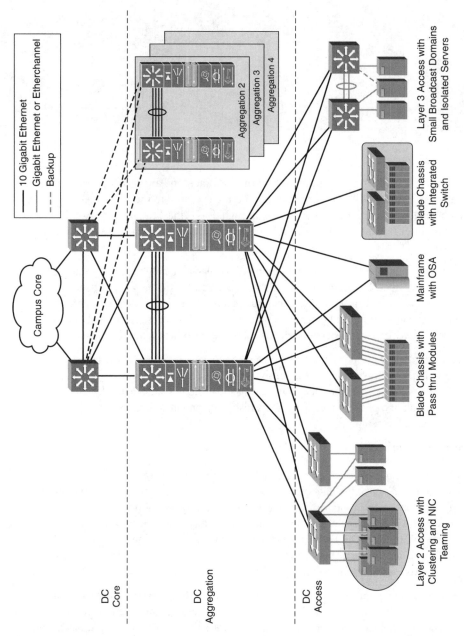

Figure 7-1   *Data center multilayer topology.*

- **Access layer:** This layer is where the servers physically attach to the network. The server components consist of one rack unit (1RU) servers, blade servers with integral switches, blade servers with pass-through cabling, clustered servers, and mainframes with Open Systems Adapters (OSA). The access layer network infrastructure consists of modular switches, fixed configuration 1RU or 2RU switches, and integral blade server switches. Switches provide both Layer 2 and Layer 3 topologies, fulfilling the various servers' broadcast domain or administrative requirements.

Note For detailed information about each of the three layers of the data center design and their functions, refer to the Cisco Data Center Infrastructure 2.5 Design Guide at http://tinyurl.com/27rscs.

Network Staging for Design Validation

The validated network design consists of data centers that interconnect via the enterprise core network. Each data center is built based on the multilayer design described in the preceding section. Each data center includes dual Network Provider Edge (N-PE) routers in addition to core, aggregation, and access layers.

Figure 7-2 shows the data center interconnect (DCI) topology.

Note The topology diagram refers to London, San Jose, and Singapore data centers. These names were selected to reflect remote locations or represent geographically dispersed locations and are not meant to imply the actual distances between these locations. The data centers were collocated in a lab with back-to-back fiber connections.

A Microsoft server cluster is implemented via three servers located within each data center. Two VLANs were provisioned for connectivity to public and private networks. These VLANs were then extended across data centers via pseudowire schemes, as described in Chapters 8 to 10, which cover the Multiple Spanning Tree (MST)-, Embedded Event Manager (EEM) - and generic routing encapsulation (GRE)-based deployment models.

End-to-end service validation was performed by using traffic tools to generate IP unicast, multicast, and simulated voice traffic on the network.

A variety of health checks were performed, including memory and CPU utilization, tracebacks, memory alignment errors, deviations in number of routes and mroutes, interface errors, line card status, and syslog messages. These checks were performed during every stage of network provisioning and before and after inducing errors and failures to determine the convergence of traffic and robustness of the various deployment models.

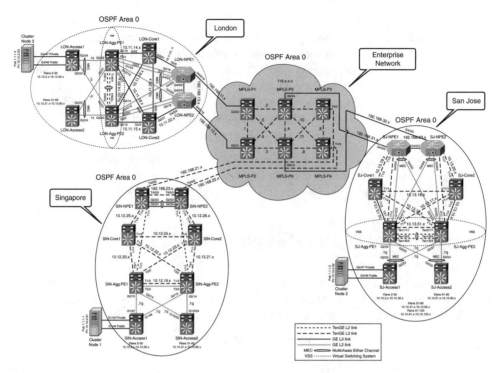

Figure 7-2   *Data center interconnect topology.*

Hardware and Software

Table 7-1 provides information about the hardware and software that was used in validating MST-, EEM- and GRE-based solutions.

Table 7-1   *Hardware and Software Device Information*

Hardware Platform	Role	DRAM	Cisco IOS Version	Line Cards / Interfaces
Cisco 7600 RSP720-3CXL-GE	N-PE	RP: 2GB SP: 2GB	12.2(33)SRC1	WS-X6724-SFP 7600-ES20-GE3C WS-X6704-10GE
Catalyst 6500 Sup720-3BXL	*N-PE	RP: 2GB SP: 2GB	12.2(33)SRC1	WS-X6724-SFP SIP-400 with 1GigE port adapter WS-X6704-10GE
Catalyst 6500 Sup720-3BXL	Enterprise Core	RP: 1GB SP: 1GB	12.2(33)SXH1	WS-X6724-SFP WS-X6704-10GE

Table 7-1   *Hardware and Software Device Information*

Hardware Platform	Role	DRAM	Cisco IOS Version	Line Cards / Interfaces
Catalyst 6500 Sup720-3BXL	DC core	RP: 1GB SP: 1GB	12.2(33)SXH 1	WS-X6724-SFP WS-X6704-10GE
Catalyst 6500 Sup720-3BXL VS-S720-10G	DC aggregation	RP: 1GB SP: 1GB	12.2(33)SXH 1 12.2(33)SXH2a (for VSS)	WS-X6704-10GE WS-X6724-SFP ACE20-MOD-K9
Catalyst 6500 Sup720-3BXL	DC access	RP: 1GB SP: 1GB	12.2(33)SXH1	WS-X6724-SFP
Catalyst 4948	DC access	256 MB	12.2(40)SG	WS-X4548-GB-RJ45
Catalyst 3750G	DC access	256 MB	12.2(37)SE	WS-C3750-24P WS-C3750E-24P

Cisco Catalyst 6500 switch was used as N-PEs in the VPLSoGRE solutions described in Chapter 10, "GRE-Based Deployment Models for Interconnecting Data Centers."

Convergence Tests

Convergence testing was performed to measure convergence times for voice, unicast, and multicast traffic during various link and node failures. Convergence was measured from the data source to the receiver (end-to-end network convergence). During convergence, packet loss was determined for each flow. For example, a packet rate of 1000 packets per second (pps) corresponds to 1-millisecond (ms) convergence time for each packet dropped.

Traffic Flow

Even though three data centers are used in all designs that this book documents, only the London and San Jose data centers were used for convergence tests. Unidirectional traffic flows were provisioned across these two locations.

For each unicast, multicast, and voice traffic type, there were 58 unidirectional flows from London to San Jose and 60 unidirectional flows from San Jose to London.

Convergence tests were performed with these three traffic types enabled simultaneously. Therefore, there were a total of 174 unidirectional traffic flows from London to San Jose and 180 unidirectional traffic flows from San Jose to London.

Traffic Rate

Table 7-2 documents the traffic rates used to determine convergence numbers for all solutions that this book presents.

Table 7-2   *Traffic Types/Rates Used for Convergence Testing*

	Voice	Unicast	Multicast
	[1]The G711A codec was used for voice traffic		[2]120 multicast groups with one source and one receiver per group
Packet size (bytes)	128	128	128
Forwarding rate	50 pps; 1 packet every 20 ms	1000 pps	100 pps
London to San Jose transmission rate	2900 pps (2.97 Mbps)	58,000 pps (59.39 Mbps)	5800 pps (5.93 Mbps)
San Jose to London transmission rate	3000 pps (3.07 Mbps)	60,000 pps (61.44 Mbps)	6000 pps (6.14 Mbps)

Traffic Profile

Table 7-3 lists the traffic flows from the London to San Jose data centers, and Table 7-4 lists the traffic flows from from the San Jose to London data centers. There were 118 unidirectional flows total (58 from London to San Jose and 60 from San Jose to London).

Table 7-3   *Traffic Flows from Intra-VLAN 4–61 London to San Jose*

Voice Stream No.	Traffic Generator (TG) Source Port	TG Destination Port	Source Switch Port	Destination Switch Port	Source VLAN	Source IP	Destination VLAN		Destination IP	Traffic Rate (in pps)	Frame Size (in bytes)
1	3/1	3/3	lon-a1 g4/17	sj-a1 g4/17	4	10.10.4.71	4	—	10.10.4.72	50	128
...	...	...	...	...	...	...	...	—	...	...	...
58	3/1	3/3	lon-a1 g4/17	sj-a1 g4/17	61	10.10.61.71	61	—	10.10.61.72	50	128

Multicast Stream No.	TG Source Port	TG Destination Port	Source Switch Port	Destination Switch Port	Source VLAN	Source IP	Destination VLAN	IGMP Group	Destination IP	Traffic Rate (in pps)	Frame Size (in bytes)
1	3/1	3/3	lon-a1 g4/17	sj-a1 g4/17	4	10.10.4.61	4	239.254.4.4	10.10.4.62	100	128

Table 7-3 *Traffic Flows from Intra-VLAN 4–61 London to San Jose*

Multicast Stream No.	TG Source Port	TG Destination Port	Source Switch Port	Destination Switch Port	Source VLAN	Source IP	Destination VLAN	IGMP Group	Destination IP	Traffic Rate (in pps)	Frame Size (in bytes)
...	...	...	...	...	...	...	...	...	...	...	...
58	3/1	3/3	lon-a1 g4/17	sj-a1 g4/17	61	10.10.61.61	61	239.254.4.61	10.10.61.62	100	128

Unicast Stream No.	TG Source Port	TG Destination Port	Source Switch Port	Destination Switch Port	Source VLAN	Source IP	Destination VLAN		Destination IP	Traffic Rate (in pps)	Frame Size (in bytes)
1	3/1	3/3	lon-a1 g4/17	sj-a1 g4/17	4	10.10.4.51	4	—	10.10.4.52	1000	128
...	...	...	...	...	...	...	...	—	...	...	...
58	3/1	3/3	lon-a1 g4/17	sj-a1 g4/17	61	10.10.4.51	61	—	10.10.61.52	1000	128

Table 7-4 *Traffic Flows from Intra-VLAN 201–260 San Jose to London*

Voice Stream No.	TG Source Port	TG Destination Port	Source Switch Port	Destination Switch Port	Source VLAN	Source IP	Destination VLAN		Destination IP	Traffic Rate (in pps)	Frame Size (in bytes)
1	3/4	3/2	sj-a2 g2/17	Lon-a2 g2/17	201	10.30.1.72	201	—	10.30.1.71	50	128
...	...	...	...	...	...	...	...	—	...	...	...
60	3/4	3/2	sj-a2 g2/17	lon-a2 g2/17	260	10.30.60.72	260	—	10.30.60.71	50	128

Multicast Stream No.	TG Source Port	TG Destination Port	Source Switch Port	Destination Switch Port	Source VLAN	Source IP	Destination VLAN	IGMP Group	Destination IP	Traffic Rate (in pps)	Frame Size (in bytes)
1	3/4	3/2	sj-a2 g2/17	lon-a2 g2/17	201	10.30.1.62	201	239.254.4.62	10.30.1.61	100	128
...	...	...	...	...	...	...	...	...	...	...	...
60	3/4	3/2	sj-a2 g2/17	lon-a2 g2/17	260	10.30.60.62	260	239.254.4.121	10.30.60.61	100	128

Table 7-4   *Traffic Flows from Intra-VLAN 201–260 San Jose to London (continued)*

Unicast Stream No.	TG Source Port	TG Destination Port	Source Switch Port	Destination Switch Port	Source VLAN	Source IP	Destination VLAN		Destination IP	Traffic Rate (in pps)	Frame Size (in bytes)
1	3/4	3/2	sj-a2 g2/17	lon-a2 g2/17	201	10.30.1.52	201	—	10.30.1.51	1000	128
…	…	…	…	…	…	…	…	—	…	…	…
60	3/4	3/2	sj-a2 g2/17	lon-a2 g2/17	260	10.30.60.52	260	—	10.30.60.51	1000	128

Summary

This chapter provided an overview of the Cisco recommended multitier design for data centers. This design provides performance, resiliency, and scalability. This design was used to create the network topology that was used to validate a DCI solution based on MST-, EEM-, and GRE-based deployment models.

## Chapter 8

MST-Based Deployment Models

This chapter describes two Multiple Spanning Tree (MST)-based deployment models:

- **MST in N-PE:** This solution requires that MST protocol be configured on all Layer 2 devices in the local data center. In addition, the Spanning Tree Protocol (STP) root bridge placement must be moved from the aggregation to the WAN edge layer. This design achieves load balancing across the primary and backup N-PE by tuning the STP cost on a per-MST-instance basis. VLANs are split between two MST instances to achieve equal distribution of the application or organization traffic.

- **Isolated MST in N-PE:** This solution allows organizations to continue the use of Rapid Spanning Tree Protocol (RSTP) configured on the aggregation and access layer devices within the data center. However, this solution requires the placement of STP root in the WAN edge layer. This design achieves load balancing across the primary and backup Network-facing Provider Edge (N-PE) by altering the STP cost on per-VLAN basis.

In both of these MST-based models, the pseudowires (PW) on the primary and the backup N-PEs are in up/up state, and the global loop in the topology is avoided by blocking appropriate VLANs on the dot1q trunk link between N-PE and aggregation via the use of STP. Both solutions rely on the inter-aggregation switch dot1q trunk link to be up and forwarding for all VLANs. Cisco recommends that you configure an EtherChannel distributed across different line cards to protect this inter-aggregation switch link from fiber or line card failures.

MST in N-PE: MST Option 1a

MST in N-PE, also known as MST in PW using Layer 2 forwarding protocol, is available on Cisco 7600 platforms running Cisco IOS Software Release 12.2(33)SRC or later. The key aspect of this feature is the capability to create a PW tunnel to carry only the MST bridge protocol data units (BPDU) between the primary and backup N-PE within the data center through the Multiprotocol Label Switching (MPLS) cloud. This special PW is not blocked by STP nor used to forward any data packets. However, this feature requires that the access network be designed so that one of the N-PEs is always the root of MST.

In this solution, each data center is a separate MST region, and STP between data centers is isolated via the Virtual Private LAN Service (VPLS) core. MST instance 1 and 2 are created, and all odd VLANs are assigned to MST instance 1 and all even VLANs to MST instance 2. In addition, MST instance priority on both N-PEs in the data center is configured so that N-PE1 becomes the root bridge for MST instance 1, and N-PE2 becomes the root bridge for MST instance 2.

> **Note**   In MST, only one BPDU is sent for all MST instances configured on the switch. This single BPDU carries all mappings between MST instances and the member VLANs.
>
> You must configure multiple MST instances because, in MST, the STP cost can be applied only on a per-MST-instance basis and not on a per-VLAN basis as with Rapid Per-VLAN STP (RPVST). Configuration of the appropriate STP cost per MST instance ensures that certain VLANs are blocked on the dot1q trunk between the N-PE and the aggregation switch and the inter-aggregation dot1q trunk is always forwarding all VLANs, thus avoiding a loop in the topology and providing a mechanism to load balance VLANs between the two N-PE/aggregation trunk links.

Figure 8-1 shows N-PE1 and N-PE2 are configured as the MST root bridges for instance 1 and 2, respectively, and VLANs are assigned to these MST instances. For example, VLAN 10 (V10) is mapped to MST instance 1, and VLAN 20 (V20) is mapped to instance 2.

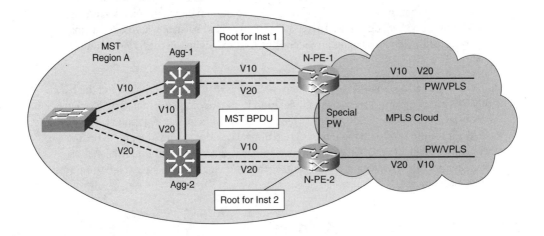

Figure 8-1   *VPLS with N-PE redundancy using MST in N-PE.*

It is very important to manipulate STP costs on the inter-N-PE and aggregation link to block one of the two uplinks from the aggregation layer to the WAN edge layer. In this way, VLAN 10 forwards via the link between Agg-1 and N-PE1, and VLAN 20 forwards on link between Agg-2 and N-PE2. Manipulating STP cost provides the capability to load balance traffic at Layer 2 by forwarding odd VLANs toward N-PE1 and even VLANs toward N-PE2, thus avoiding an STP loop.

In this solution, every N-PE is configured as the root bridge and backup root bridge for each MSTP instance. This configuration requires that the root and backup root bridge be moved from the aggregation to the WAN edge layer. In addition, STP mode MST also might have to be configured on all Layer 2 switches that are not running MST.

Note   This book emphasizes load balancing based on odd and even VLANs solely for the sake of simplicity and to assist with understanding. A better approach is to use a VLAN range (for example, VLAN 10 to 100 and from 101 to 200). This approach reduces typographical errors when the requirement is to configure hundreds of VLANs.

When a broadcast packet for a user VLAN (for example, VLAN 5) arrives from the VPLS cloud at N-PE1, the packet is not flooded to N-PE2 for two reasons:

■   The inter-N-PE EtherChannel does not carry that VLAN.

■   Flooding that packet to Agg-1 and then to Agg-2 does not send it back to N-PE2 because the link between Agg-2 and N-PE2 blocks that VLAN.

A primary advantage of this feature is the unrestricted support of various access topologies, such as hub-and-spoke or rings access. The inter-N-PE PW can be established through the MPLS/VPLS network, so this design does not require that both N-PEs be collocated within the same data center. Also, with the deployment of MST in all the Layer 2 devices in the access and aggregation layers within the entire data center, Cisco IOS Software Release 12.2(33)SRC1 supports MAC-withdrawal message over VPLS. Due to this MAC-withdrawal feature, if an N-PE experiences an STP topology change, it sends the MAC-withdrawal message to remote N-PEs over the PWs, thus allowing the remote N-PE to purge its content-addressable memory (CAM) table.

In this solution, all PWs on the primary and backup N-PEs are active. If the link between N-PE1 and Agg-1 goes down, the link between Agg-2 and N-PE2 forwards traffic for all the VLANs after STP convergence. For devices that are not running Cisco IOS Software Release 12.2(33)SRC1, Embedded Event Manager (EEM) scripts must be configured so that the N-PE shuts down its local link to the aggregation switch when VPLS link from that N-PE goes down, thus avoiding black-holing traffic.

Configuring MST in PW is a two-step process:

Step 1.   Define the special PW using the **forward permit l2protocol all** command:

l2 vfi *vfi_name* manual

        vpn id *vpn_id*

        forward permit l2protocol all

        neighbor *IP address of peer N-PE* encapsulation mpls

        !

        end

Step 2.   Connect this PW to the native VLAN (usually VLAN 1) to carry the untagged MST BPDUs:

        interface vlan 1

         xconnect vfi *vfi_name*

        !

        end

The following modules support the configuration of an Ethernet over MPLS (EoMPLS) PW tunnel to carry MSTP BPDUs:

- SIP-400

- SIP-600

- ES-20

Implementing MST in N-PE: MST Option 1a Design

In this solution, all PWs on N-PE1 and N-PE2 routers are active. Blocking of VLANs (loop avoidance) is performed on the links between the N-PEs and aggregation switches via STP cost associated with multiple MST instances.

Figure 8-2 provides a configuration overview of the various links and the nodes.

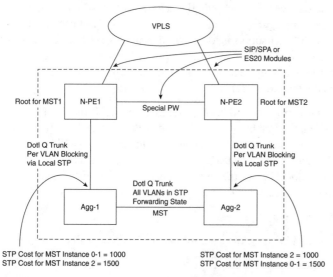

Figure 8-2   *Implementing MST in PW: Configuration overview.*

The following provides snippets of configuration from N-PE and aggregation devices and output from various **show** commands:

Step 1.   Determine the existing STP root bridge priority for all VLANs that are required to be extended across data centers using the **show spanning-tree vlan 7** command. For example:

```
lon-n-pe1# sh spanning-tree vlan 7


MST0
   Spanning tree enabled protocol mstp
   Root ID    Priority    8192
              Address     001d.7198.8fc0
              Cost        0
              Port        3329 (Port-channel1)
              Hello Time  2 sec  Max Age 20 sec  Forward Delay 15 sec


   Bridge ID  Priority    16384   (priority 16384 sys-id-ext 0)
              Address     001d.7198.9500
              Hello Time  2 sec  Max Age 20 sec  Forward Delay 15 sec


Interface          Role Sts Cost      Prio.Nbr Type
---------------    ---  ---  ------    --------  ------------------
Gi2/1              Desg FWD 20000      128.257   P2p Bound(PVST)


lon-n-pe1#
```

Step 2.   Configure STP mode MST on N-PE1. Configure N-PE1 as the root bridge for MST instance 0 and 1 by reducing the bridge priority to a value lower than the value found in Step 1. Similarly, configure N-PE2 as the root bridge for MST instance 2. Assign all odd VLANs to MST instance 1 and all even VLANs to MST instance 2. Lower the priority for MST instances 0–2 such that N-PE1 becomes the backup root bridge for all the even VLANs and N-PE2 the backup root bridge for all odd VLANs.

N-PE1 Configuration	**N-PE2 Configuration**
spanning-tree mode mst	spanning-tree mode mst
!	!
spanning-tree mst configuration	spanning-tree mst configuration
name lon-datacenter	name lon-datacenter
revision 10	revision 10

instance 1 vlan 1, 3, 5, 7, 9, 11, 13,
  15, 17, 19, 21, 23, 25, 27, 29 ...
	instance 1 vlan 1, 3, 5, 7, 9, 11, 13, 15,
	  17, 19, 21, 23, 25, 27, 29 ...

instance 2 vlan 2, 4, 6, 8, 10, 12, 14,
  16, 18, 20, 22, 24, 26, 28, 30 ...
	instance 2 vlan 2, 4, 6, 8, 10, 12, 14,
	  16, 18, 20, 22, 24, 26, 28, 30 ...

!	!
spanning-tree mst 0-1 priority 8192	spanning-tree mst 0-1 priority 16384
spanning-tree mst 2 priority 16384	spanning-tree mst 2 priority 8192
!	!
vlan 2-61,201-260	vlan 2-61,201-260

Step 3.   Verify MST configuration on the both the N-PEs:

```
! On N-PE1:

lon-n-pe1# show spanning-tree mst detail


##### MST0     vlans mapped:   62-200,261-300,302,304-4094
Bridge         address 001d.7198.9500  priority   8192  (8192 sysid 0)
Root           this switch for the CIST
Operational    hello time 2 , forward delay 15, max age 20, txholdcount 6
Configured     hello time 2 , forward delay 15, max age 20, max hops  20


GigabitEthernet2/1 of MST0 is designated forwarding
Port info          port id     128.257       priority  128  cost 20000
Designated root    address 001d.7198.9500    priority  8192 cost    0
Design. regional root address 001d.7198.9500 priority  8192 cost    0
Designated bridge      address 001d.7198.9500 priority  8192 port
   id   128.257
Timers: message expires in 0 sec, forward delay 0, forward transitions 1
Bpdus sent 11083, received 4


BRIDGE4/132 of MST0 is designated forwarding
```

```
Port info        port id      128.900  priority   128  cost      200
Designated root address 001d.7198.9500 priority   8192 cost        0
Design. regional root address 001d.7198.9500 priority 8192 cost     0
Designated bridge address 001d.7198.9500 priority 8192 port id 128.900
Timers: message expires in 0 sec, forward delay 0, forward transitions 23
Bpdus sent 30369, received 18330


BRIDGE4/196 of MST0 is designated forwarding
Port info              port id      128.964  priority  128  cost 200
Designated root        address 001d.7198.9500  priority  8192  cost  0
Design. regional root address 001d.7198.9500  priority  8192  cost  0
Designated bridge      address 001d.7198.9500  priority  8192  port
  id  128.964
Timers: message expires in 0 sec, forward delay 0, forward transitions 24
Bpdus sent 30416, received 11409


##### MST1     vlans mapped:    1,3,5,7,9,11,13,15,17,19,21,23,25,27,29
   31,33,35,37,39,41,43,45,47,49,51,53,55,57
   59,61,201,203,205,207,209,211,213,215,217
   219,221,223,225,227,229,231,233,235,237
   239,241,243,245,247,249,251,253,255,257,259,301,303
Bridge        address 001d.7198.9500  priority   8193  (8192 sysid 1)
Root          this switch for MST1


GigabitEthernet2/1 of MST1 is designated forwarding
  Port info           port id      128.257  priority 128  cost      20000
Designated root    address 001d.7198.9500 priority 8193 cost         0
Designated bridge address 001d.7198.9500 priority 8193 port id 128.257
Timers: message expires in 0 sec, forward delay 0, forward transitions 1
Bpdus (MRecords) sent 11083, received 4


BRIDGE4/132 of MST1 is designated forwarding
Port info          port id      128.900 priority 128 cost      200
Designated root    address 001d.7198.9500 priority 8193 cost        0
Designated bridge address 001d.7198.9500 priority 8193 port id 128.900
Timers: message expires in 0 sec, forward delay 0, forward transitions 23
```

```
Bpdus (MRecords) sent 30369, received 18329


BRIDGE4/196 of MST1 is designated forwarding
Port info              port id      128.964   priority   128 cost 200
Designated root        address 001d.7198.9500  priority  8193 cost    0
Designated bridge      address 001d.7198.9500  priority  8193 port
  id  128.964
Timers: message expires in 0 sec, forward delay 0, forward transitions 24
Bpdus (MRecords) sent 30416, received 11408


##### MST2    vlans mapped:   2,4,6,8,10,12,14,16,18,20,22,24,26,28,30
   32,34,36,38,40,42,44,46,48,50,52,54,56,58
   60,202,204,206,208,210,212,214,216,218,220
   222,224,226,228,230,232,234,236,238,240
   242,244,246,248,250,252,254,256,258,260
Bridge      address 001d.7198.9500  priority    16386 (16384
  sysid 2)
Root        address 001d.7198.8fc0  priority   8194  (8192 sysid 2)
            port    BR4/132         cost      200    rem hops 19


GigabitEthernet2/1 of MST2 is designated forwarding
Port info              port id      128.257  priority    128
  cost   20000
Designated root        address 001d.7198.8fc0  priority  8194   cost 200
Designated bridge      address 001d.7198.9500  priority 16386  port
  id  128.257
Timers: message expires in 0 sec, forward delay 0, forward transitions 1
Bpdus (MRecords) sent 11083, received 4


BRIDGE4/132 of MST2 is root forwarding
Port info              port id      128.900  priority    128
  cost    200
Designated root        address 001d.7198.8fc0  priority  8194   cost   0
Designated bridge      address 001d.7198.8fc0  priority  8194   port
  id  128.900
Timers: message expires in 4 sec, forward delay 0, forward transitions 22
Bpdus (MRecords) sent 30369, received 18329


BRIDGE4/196 of MST2 is designated forwarding
```

```
Port info          port id      128.964  priority   128   cost  200

Designated root    address 001d.7198.8fc0  priority  8194  cost  200

Designated bridge  address 001d.7198.9500  priority  16386  port
  id   128.964

Timers: message expires in 0 sec, forward delay 0, forward transitions 24

Bpdus (MRecords) sent 30416, received 11408


lon-n-pe1#

lon-n-pe1# show running-config interface gig 2/1

Building configuration...


Current configuration : 384 bytes

!

interface GigabitEthernet2/1

 description L2 to Agg-1

 switchport

 switchport trunk encapsulation dot1q

 switchport trunk allowed vlan 1-61,201-260

 switchport mode trunk

 switchport nonegotiate

 mtu 9216

 logging event link-status

 logging event spanning-tree status

 storm-control broadcast level 5.00

 storm-control multicast level 5.00

 spanning-tree portfast trunk

 spanning-tree link-type point-to-point

end

lon-n-pe1# show spanning-tree vlan 7


MST1

  Spanning tree enabled protocol mstp

  Root ID    Priority    8193

             Address     001d.7198.9500

             This bridge is the root

             Hello Time   2 sec  Max Age 20 sec  Forward Delay 15 sec


  Bridge ID  Priority    8193    (priority 8192 sys-id-ext 1)
```

```
                    Address        001d.7198.9500

                    Hello Time    2 sec  Max Age 20 sec  Forward Delay 15 sec


   Interface              Role Sts Cost      Prio.Nbr Type
   _____. __ _. ____. ____ _____

   Gi2/1                  Desg FWD 20000     128.257  P2p

   BR4/132                Desg FWD 200       128.900  P2p

   BR4/196                Desg FWD 200       128.964  P2p


   lon-n-pe1#

   ! On N-PE2:

   lon-n-pe2#  show spanning-tree mst detail


   ##### MST0    vlans mapped:   62-200,261-300,302,304-4094

   Bridge       address 001d.7198.8fc0  priority       16384 (16384
     sysid 0)

   Root         address 001d.7198.9500  priority       8192  (8192 sysid 0)

                port  BR4/132           path cost      0

   Regional Root address 001d.7198.9500 priority       8192   (8192 sysid 0)

                                        internal cost 200      rem hops 19

   Operational hello time 2 , forward delay 15, max age 20, txholdcount 6

   Configured  hello time 2 , forward delay 15, max age 20, max hops   20


   GigabitEthernet2/2 of MST0 is designated forwarding

   Port info              port id      128.258  priority       128
     cost      20000

   Designated root        address 001d.7198.9500  priority  8192  cost 0

   Design. regional root address 001d.7198.9500  priority  8192  cost 200

   Designated bridge      address 001d.7198.8fc0  priority  16384 port
     id  128.258

   Timers: message expires in 0 sec, forward delay 0, forward transitions 4

   Bpdus sent 11707, received 49
```

```
BRIDGE4/132 of MST0 is root forwarding
Port info                port id       128.900  priority  128
   cost        200
Designated root        address 001d.7198.9500  priority  8192  cost  0
Design. regional root  address 001d.7198.9500  priority  8192  cost  0
Designated bridge      address 001d.7198.9500  priority  8192  port
   id  128.900
Timers: message expires in 5 sec, forward delay 0, forward transitions 32
Bpdus sent 31817, received 19251


BRIDGE4/196 of MST0 is designated forwarding
Port info                port id       128.964  priority    128
   cost 200
Designated root        address 001d.7198.9500  priority    8192 cost  0
Design. regional root  address 001d.7198.9500  priority    8192 cost 200
Designated bridge      address 001d.7198.8fc0  priority  16384 port
   id  128.964
Timers: message expires in 0 sec, forward delay 0, forward transitions 45
Bpdus sent 31868, received 11415


##### MST1    vlans mapped:    1,3,5,7,9,11,13,15,17,19,21,23,25,27,29
   31,33,35,37,39,41,43,45,47,49,51,53,55,57
   59,61,201,203,205,207,209,211,213,215,217
   219,221,223,225,227,229,231,233,235,237
   239,241,243,245,247,249,251,253,255,257
   259,301,303
Bridge        address 001d.7198.8fc0  priority    16385 (16384
   sysid 1)
Root          address 001d.7198.9500  priority    8193  (8192 sysid 1)
                  port    BR4/132        cost      200    rem hops 19


GigabitEthernet2/2 of MST1 is designated forwarding
Port info             port id       128.258  priority    128  cost
   20000
Designated root       address 001d.7198.9500  priority    8193  cost 200
Designated bridge     address 001d.7198.8fc0  priority  16385  port
   id  128.258
```

```
Timers: message expires in 0 sec, forward delay 0, forward transitions 4
Bpdus (MRecords) sent 11707, received 45


BRIDGE4/132 of MST1 is root forwarding
Port info               port id       128.900  priority    128  cost 200
Designated root       address 001d.7198.9500  priority   8193  cost  0
Designated bridge     address 001d.7198.9500  priority   8193  port
  id   128.900
Timers: message expires in 5 sec, forward delay 0, forward transitions 23
Bpdus (MRecords) sent 31817, received 19251


BRIDGE4/196 of MST1 is designated forwarding
Port info               port id       128.964  priority    128  cost 200
Designated root       address 001d.7198.9500  priority   8193  cost 200
Designated bridge     address 001d.7198.8fc0  priority  16385  port
  id   128.964
Timers: message expires in 0 sec, forward delay 0, forward transitions 35
Bpdus (MRecords) sent 31868, received 11415


##### MST2    vlans mapped:   2,4,6,8,10,12,14,16,18,20,22,24,26,28,30
  32,34,36,38,40,42,44,46,48,50,52,54,56,58
  60,202,204,206,208,210,212,214,216,218,220
  222,224,226,228,230,232,234,236,238,240
  242,244,246,248,250,252,254,256,258,260
Bridge       address 001d.7198.8fc0  priority   8194  (8192 sysid 2)
Root         this switch for MST2


GigabitEthernet2/2 of MST2 is designated forwarding
Port info               port id       128.258  priority    128  cost 20000
Designated root       address 001d.7198.8fc0 priority   8194  cost  0
Designated bridge     address 001d.7198.8fc0 priority   8194  port
  id   128.258
Timers: message expires in 0 sec, forward delay 0, forward transitions 4
Bpdus (MRecords) sent 11707, received 45
```

```
BRIDGE4/132 of MST2 is designated forwarding
Port info          port id         128.900   priority  128  cost  200
Designated root    address 001d.7198.8fc0   priority  8194 cost    0
Designated bridge  address 001d.7198.8fc0   priority  8194 port
  id  128.900
Timers: message expires in 0 sec, forward delay 0, forward transitions 32
Bpdus (MRecords) sent 31817, received 19251

BRIDGE4/196 of MST2 is designated forwarding
Port info          port id         128.964   priority  128  cost  200
Designated root    address 001d.7198.8fc0   priority  8194  cost    0
Designated bridge  address 001d.7198.8fc0   priority  8194  port
  id  128.964
Timers: message expires in 0 sec, forward delay 0, forward transitions 44
Bpdus (MRecords) sent 31868, received 11415


lon-n-pe2#
lon-n-pe2# show running-config interface gig 2/2
Building configuration...


Current configuration : 374 bytes
!
interface GigabitEthernet2/2
 description L2 to Agg-2
 switchport
 switchport trunk encapsulation dot1q
 switchport trunk allowed vlan 1-61,201-260
 switchport mode trunk
 switchport nonegotiate
 mtu 9216
 load-interval 30
 storm-control broadcast level 5.00
 storm-control multicast level 5.00
 spanning-tree portfast trunk
 spanning-tree link-type point-to-point
end
lon-n-pe2# show spanning-tree vlan 7
```

```
MST1
   Spanning tree enabled protocol mstp
   Root ID    Priority    8193
              Address     001d.7198.9500
              Cost        200
              Port        900 (BRIDGE4/132)
              Hello Time   2 sec  Max Age 20 sec  Forward Delay 15 sec


   Bridge ID  Priority    16385  (priority 16384 sys-id-ext 1)
              Address     001d.7198.8fc0
              Hello Time   2 sec  Max Age 20 sec  Forward Delay 15 sec


Interface             Role Sts Cost     Prio.Nbr Type
_____   __ __. _____.  ____ _____

Gi2/2                 Desg FWD 20000    128.258  P2p
BR4/132               Root FWD 200      128.900  P2p
BR4/196               Desg FWD 200      128.964  P2p


lon-n-pe2#
```

Step 4.   Ensure that all Layer 2 switches in the local data center are running MST. If they are not, configure spanning-tree mode MST and allocate all odd VLANs to MST instance 1 and all even VLANs to MST instance 2 on all the aggregation PEs and access switches:

```
! On Agg-1 , Agg-2, Access-1, and Access-2:
spanning-tree mode mst
!
spanning-tree mst configuration
name lon-datacenter
revision 10
instance 1 vlan 1, 3, 5, 7, 9, 11, 13, 15, 17, 19, 21, 23, 25, 27, 29
..
instance 2 vlan 2, 4, 6, 8, 10, 12, 14, 16, 18, 20, 22, 24, 26, 28,
30 ..
!
vlan 2-61,201-260
```

Step 5. On the link between both N-PEs and aggregation switches, configure the following:

a. Increase the STP cost on the aggregation switch link connected to N-PE such that all odd VLANs in MST instance 1 forward via Agg-1 to N-PE1 and all even VLANs in MST instance 2 forward through Agg-2 and N-PE2 link. Configure a higher cost on the aggregation switch link connected to N-PE so that regardless of the bandwidth of the inter-aggregation switch link, the inter-aggregation switch link always is in forwarding mode for all VLANs.

As per the N-PE to aggregation switch interface configuration that follows, STP cost for MST instance 1 on Agg-1 has been set to 1000, and the STP cost for MST instance 2 is 1500. On Agg-2, the STP cost of 1000 has been configured for MST instance 2 and 1500 for MST instance 1.

a. STP point-to-point link.

b. Storm control; broadcast and multicast on the N-PE side of the link. For threshold guidelines, see Chapter 11, "Additional Data Center Interconnect Design Considerations."

Agg-1 Configuration	Agg-2 Configuration
interface GigabitEthernet2/19	interface GigabitEthernet2/18
description L2 connection to lon-n-pe1	description L2 connection to lon-n-pe2
switchport	switchport
switchport trunk encapsulation dot1q	switchport trunk encapsulation dot1q
switchport trunk allowed vlan 1-61,201-260	switchport trunk allowed vlan 1-61,201-260
switchport mode trunk	switchport mode trunk
switchport nonegotiate	switchport nonegotiate
mtu 9216	mtu 9216
logging event link-status	logging event link-status
logging event spanning-tree status	logging event spanning-tree status
spanning-tree link-type point-to-point	spanning-tree link-type point-to-point
spanning-tree mst 0-1 cost 1000	spanning-tree mst 2 cost 1000
spanning-tree mst 2 cost 1500	spanning-tree mst 0-1 cost 1500

Step 6. Verify the STP configuration on both of the aggregation switches and confirm that the inter-aggregation switch link forwards all VLANs:

```
! On Agg-1:

lon-agg-1#  show spanning-tree interface Port-channel 1


Mst Instance          Role Sts Cost      Prio.Nbr Type

_____    __  _. ____.  ____  _____
```

```
MST0                     Desg FWD 1           128.1665 P2p

MST1                     Desg FWD 1           128.1665 P2p

MST2                     Root FWD 1           128.1665 P2p
```

lon-agg-1# show spanning-tree vlan7


```
MST1

  Spanning tree enabled protocol mstp

  Root ID    Priority     8193

             Address      001d.7198.9500

             Cost         1000

             Port         147 (GigabitEthernet2/19)

             Hello Time   2 sec  Max Age 20 sec  Forward Delay 15 sec


  Bridge ID  Priority     32769  (priority 32768 sys-id-ext 1)

             Address      001c.b126.d000

             Hello Time   2 sec  Max Age 20 sec  Forward Delay 15 sec


Interface          Role Sts Cost      Prio.Nbr Type

---------------- -- -- ----- ---- ------------

Gi2/19             Root FWD 1000      128.147  P2p

Gi2/22             Desg FWD 20000     128.150  P2p

Po1                Desg FWD 1          128.1665 P2p
```

! On Agg-2:

lon-agg-2# show spanning-tree interface Port-channel 1


```
Mst Instance       Role Sts Cost      Prio.Nbr Type

---------------- -- -- ----- ---- ------------

MST0               Root FWD 1          128.1665 P2p

MST1               Root FWD 1          128.1665 P2p

MST2               Desg FWD 1          128.1665 P2p
```


lon-agg-2# show spanning-tree vlan 7


```
MST1

  Spanning tree enabled protocol mstp

  Root ID    Priority     8193
```

```
                    Address       001d.7198.9500

                    Cost          1001

                    Port          1665 (Port-channel1)

                    Hello Time    2 sec  Max Age 20 sec  Forward Delay 15 sec


          Bridge ID  Priority     32769  (priority 32768 sys-id-ext 1)

                     Address      001c.b144.4c00

                     Hello Time   2 sec  Max Age 20 sec  Forward Delay 15 sec


Interface          Role Sts Cost      Prio.Nbr Type

---------------    --- --- -------    -------- --------

Gi2/18             Altn BLK 1500      128.146  P2p

Gi2/21             Desg FWD 20000     128.149  P2p

Po1                Root FWD 1         128.1665 P2p
```

From the output of **show spanning-tree vlan 7**, you can see that the spanning
tree blocks odd VLANs on the link between N-PE2 and Agg-2. Also, all
VLANs are in forwarding state on the inter-aggregation switch link. This configuration provides per-MST instance VLAN load balancing and avoids Layer
2 loop.

Step 7. Configure Open Shortest Path First (OSPF) Protocol on the N-PE routers:

```
router ospf 1

 router-id 11.11.11.11

 log-adjacency-changes

 auto-cost reference-bandwidth 10000

 area 0 authentication message-digest

 timers throttle spf 100 100 5000

 timers throttle lsa 100 100 5000

 timers lsa arrival 80

 ...

 distribute-list 1 in GigabitEthernet2/6

 bfd all-interfaces

 mpls ldp sync

 !


lon-n-pe1# show ip ospf 1

Routing Process "ospf 1" with ID 11.11.11.11

 Start time: 00:00:50.580, Time elapsed: 06:14:40.996
```

Supports only single TOS(TOS0) routes

Supports opaque LSA

Supports Link-local Signaling (LLS)

Supports area transit capability

Event-log enabled, Maximum number of events: 1000, Mode: cyclic

Router is not originating router-LSAs with maximum metric

Initial SPF schedule delay 100 msecs

Minimum hold time between two consecutive SPFs 100 msecs

Maximum wait time between two consecutive SPFs 5000 msecs

Incremental-SPF disabled

Initial LSA throttle delay 100 msecs

Minimum hold time for LSA throttle 100 msecs

Maximum wait time for LSA throttle 5000 msecs

Minimum LSA arrival 80 msecs

LSA group pacing timer 240 secs

Interface flood pacing timer 33 msecs

Retransmission pacing timer 66 msecs

Number of external LSA 1. Checksum Sum 0x00D71C

Number of opaque AS LSA 0. Checksum Sum 0x000000

Number of DCbitless external and opaque AS LSA 0

Number of DoNotAge external and opaque AS LSA 0

Number of areas in this router is 1. 1 normal 0 stub 0 nssa

Number of areas transit capable is 0

External flood list length 0

IETF NSF helper support enabled

Cisco NSF helper support enabled

BFD is enabled

Reference bandwidth unit is 10000 mbps

  Area BACKBONE(0)

     Number of interfaces in this area is 6 (2 loopback)

     Area has message digest authentication

     SPF algorithm last executed 00:55:35.412 ago

     SPF algorithm executed 68 times

     Area ranges are

     Number of LSA 22. Checksum Sum 0x099D4E

     Number of opaque link LSA 0. Checksum Sum 0x000000

```
                    Number of DCbitless LSA 0

                    Number of indication LSA 0

                    Number of DoNotAge LSA 0

                    Flood list length 0


lon-n-pe1# show ip ospf neighbor


Neighbor ID      Pri   State         Dead Time    Address
   Interface
116.5.200.77       0   FULL/  -      00:00:39     192.168.11.7
   GigabitEthernet4/0/19
12.12.12.12        0   FULL/  -      00:00:37     192.168.13.6
   GigabitEthernet4/0/0
13.13.13.13        0   FULL/  -      00:00:35     10.11.21.3
   GigabitEthernet2/6


lon-n-pe1# show cdp neighbors


Capability Codes: R - Router, T - Trans Bridge, B - Source Route Bridge
              S - Switch, H - Host, I - IGMP, r - Repeater, P -
              Phone
Device ID        Local Intrfce    Holdtme    Capability  Platform
   Port ID
lon-n-pe2        Gig 4/0/0        150         R S I      CISCO7604
   Gig 4/0/0
lon-agg-1        Gig 2/1          144         R S I      WS-
   C6509- Gig 2/19
lon-core1        Gig 2/6          151         R S I      WS-
   C6506  Gig 3/21
mpls-p1          Gig 4/0/19       149         R S I      WS-
   C6506  Gig 2/22
```

Step 8. Configure MPLS, virtual forwarding instance (VFI), and switched virtual interface (SVI) on N-PE1 and N-PE2. The output from the **show mpls l2transport vc** command displays the MPLS virtual circuit (VC) transport information. MST in PW is implemented with a separate VFI: bpdu-pw. Redundancy in the VPLS domain relies on an MPLS mechanism. Each N-PE will have an alternate MPLS path, or an EEM policy can be used at each N-PE to shut down its link to the local aggregation switch when the VPLS link is down:

```
! On N-PE1:
lon-n-pe1#
```

```
!
...
mpls ldp neighbor 10.76.70.12 targeted ldp
mpls ldp neighbor 10.76.70.21 targeted ldp
mpls ldp neighbor 10.76.70.22 targeted ldp
mpls ldp neighbor 10.76.70.31 targeted ldp
mpls ldp neighbor 10.76.70.32 targeted ldp
mpls ldp tcp pak-priority
mpls ldp session protection
no mpls ldp advertise-labels
mpls ldp advertise-labels for 76
mpls label protocol ldp
!
xconnect logging pseudowire status
!
access-list 76 permit 10.76.0.0 0.0.255.255
! VFI for MST in PW
l2 vfi bpdu-pw manual
 vpn id 1
 forward permit l2protocol all
 neighbor 10.76.100.12 encapsulation mpls
! VFI for VLAN 7
l2 vfi lon-pe1-7 manual
 vpn id 7
 neighbor 10.76.100.32 encapsulation mpls
 neighbor 10.76.100.31 encapsulation mpls
 neighbor 10.76.100.22 encapsulation mpls
 neighbor 10.76.100.21 encapsulation mpls
!
!
interface Vlan7
 mtu 9216
 no ip address
 xconnect vfi lon-pe1-7
!
lon-n-pe1# show mpls l2transport vc
```

```
Local intf      Local circuit           Dest address    VC ID  Status
—————.  ————————————— ————————. —————

VFI bpdu-pw     VFI                     10.76.100.11    1      UP

VFI lon-pe2-7   VFI                     10.76.100.21    7      UP

VFI lon-pe2-7   VFI                     10.76.100.22    7      UP

VFI lon-pe2-7   VFI                     10.76.100.31    7      UP

VFI lon-pe2-7   VFI                     10.76.100.32    7      UP


Lon-n-pe1#

lon-n-pe1#  show running-config interface gig 4/0/19

!

interface GigabitEthernet4/0/19

 description L3 connection to MPLS P router

   dampening

 mtu 9216

 ip address 192.168.11.5 255.255.255.0

 ip ospf message-digest-key 1 md5 lab

 ip ospf network point-to-point

 load-interval 30

 carrier-delay msec 0

 mls qos trust dscp

 mpls ip

 bfd interval 100 min_rx 100 multiplier 3

end

! On N-PE2:

lon-n-pe2#

! VFI for MST in PW

l2 vfi bpdu-pw manual

 vpn id 1

 forward permit l2protocol all

 neighbor 10.76.100.11 encapsulation mpls  << lon-n-pe1

!

l2 vfi lon-pe2-7 manual

 vpn id 7

 neighbor 10.76.100.32 encapsulation mpls  << sj-n-pe2

 neighbor 10.76.100.31 encapsulation mpls  << sj-n-pe1
```

```
       neighbor 10.76.100.22 encapsulation mpls   << sin-n-pe2

       neighbor 10.76.100.21 encapsulation mpls   << sin-n-pe1

      !

      !

     interface Vlan7

      mtu 9216

      no ip address

      xconnect vfi lon-pe2-7

      !

     lon-n-pe2# show mpls l2transport vc
```

Local intf	Local circuit	Dest address	VC ID	Status
VFI bpdu-pw	VFI	10.76.100.11	1	UP
VFI lon-pe2-7	VFI	10.76.100.21	7	UP
VFI lon-pe2-7	VFI	10.76.100.22	7	UP
VFI lon-pe2-7	VFI	10.76.100.31	7	UP
VFI lon-pe2-7	VFI	10.76.100.32	7	UP

```
     Lon-n-pe2#
```

Step 9.   Configure object tracking using EEM. Use the **show running-config | begin event manager** command to display EEM applets configured:

```
     lon-n-pe1#

     !

     process-max-time 50

     !

     track 20 interface GigabitEthernet4/0/0 line-protocol

     !

     track 21 interface GigabitEthernet4/0/19 line-protocol

     !

     track 25 list boolean or

      object 20

      object 21

      delay up 90
```

```
lon-n-pe1# show running-config | begin event manager
event manager applet DOWN_Gig2/1
event track 25 state down
 action 1.0 cli command "enable"
 action 2.0 cli command "config t"
 action 3.0 cli command "int Gig 2/1 "
 action 4.0 cli command "shut"
 action 5.0 syslog msg "EEM has shut Gig 2/1 "
event manager applet UP_Gig2/1
 event track 25 state up
 action 1.0 cli command "enable"
 action 2.0 cli command "config t"
 action 3.0 cli command "int Gig2/1"
 action 4.0 cli command "no shut"
 action 5.0 syslog msg "EEM has unshut Gig2/1"
event manager applet DOWN_GIG2/1-boot
 event timer cron name "_EEMinternalname6" cron-entry "@reboot"
 action 1.0 cli command "enable"
 action 2.0 cli command "config t"
 action 3.0 cli command "interface Gig 2/1 "
 action 4.0 cli command "shutdown"
 action 5.0 syslog msg "EEM has shut Gig 2/1 "
!
end
```

Pertaining to the highlighted line of output, when an N-PE router reloads, power to the LAN modules is enabled before the WAN modules power on. In this situation, LAN interfaces are enabled before interfaces on the WAN modules become active. After the LAN interfaces become active, spanning tree converges and puts the interface between N-PE and aggregation switch in forwarding mode. Therefore, traffic is black-holed because the WAN interfaces might still be in down state or the path to the core network might not be available via the N-PE that was reloaded. An EEM reboot applet ensures that the LAN interfaces are in shut state until the WAN interfaces configured with the **track** command become active after the router initializes completely.

Convergence Tests

The traffic profile outlined in Chapter 7, "Data Center Multilayer Infrastructure Design," was used to determine end-to-end convergence for unidirectional voice, unicast, and multicast traffic. Links and nodes were failed to simulate network failures.

Table 8-1 shows results of various nodes and links failures. Convergence numbers (max and min) are in seconds.

Table 8-1   *Convergence Numbers for Link and Node Failures for MST in PW Solution*

| | | | | Traffic Direction | | | |
| | | | | LON → SJ | | SJ → LON | |
Failure Type	Action	VLAN	Traffic Type	Max	Min	Max	Min
Reload N-PE1	Reload	'Odd VLAN	Voice	3.92	3.84	3.78	3.76
			Unicast	3.91	3.87	3.77	3.75
			Multicast	6.37	4.06	6.61	3.93
		Even VLAN	Voice	0.14	0.12	0.00	0.00
			Unicast	0.14	0.14	0.00	0.00
			Multicast	0.15	0.13	0.00	0.00
	Restore	Odd VLAN	Voice	0.44	0.02	0.73	0.73
			Unicast	0.43	0.16	0.71	0.18
			Multicast	8.43	0.92	5.47	2.45
		Even VLAN	Voice	0.00	0.73	0.02	0.02
			Unicast	0.00	0.00	0.00	0.00
			Multicast	0.00	0.00	0.00	0.00
Reload N-PE2	Reload	Odd VLAN	Voice	0.02	0.02	0.02	0.02
			Unicast	0.00	0.00	0.00	0.00
			Multicast	0.01	0.00	0.02	0.02
		'Even VLAN	Voice	3.76	3.66	3.76	3.74
			Unicast	3.73	3.68	3.74	3.72
			Multicast	6.30	4.18	6.00	3.84
	Restore	Odd VLAN	Voice	0.02	0.02	0.02	0.02
			Unicast	0.00	0.00	0.00	0.00
			Multicast	0.10	0.00	0.03	0.02
		Even VLAN	Voice	1.18	0.62	1.34	1.28
			Unicast	1.15	0.62	1.32	0.72
			Multicast	4.68	0.97	6.04	0.96
Reload Agg-1	Reload	Odd VLAN	Voice	0.50	0.02	0.50	0.50
			Unicast	0.47	0.47	0.48	0.48
			Multicast	4.59	2.49	1.21	0.67
		Even VLAN	Voice	0.02	0.02	0.02	0.02
			Unicast	0.00	0.00	0.00	0.00
			Multicast	0.03	0.01	0.03	0.01
	Restore	Odd VLAN	Voice	0.06	0.02	0.04	0.04
			Unicast	0.03	0.02	0.00	0.00
			Multicast	2.89	0.76	2.00	0.02
		Even VLAN	Voice	0.02	0.02	0.04	0.04
			Unicast	0.00	0.00	0.00	0.00
			Multicast	0.01	0.00	0.02	0.02

Table 8-1   *Convergence Numbers for Link and Node Failures for MST in PW Solution*

Failure Type	Action	VLAN	Traffic Type	Traffic Direction			
				LON → SJ		SJ → LON	
				Max	Min	Max	Min
Reload Agg-2	Reload	Odd VLAN	Voice	0.46	0.00	0.00	0.00
			Unicast	0.00	0.00	0.00	0.00
			Multicast	0.00	0.00	0.00	0.00
		Even VLAN	Voice	0.48	0.46	0.46	0.46
			Unicast	0.47	0.46	0.46	0.46
			Multicast	4.53	1.76	7.06	0.79
	Restore	Odd VLAN	Voice	0.02	0.00	0.02	0.02
			Unicast	0.00	0.00	0.00	0.00
			Multicast	0.00	0.00	0.01	0.01
		Even VLAN	Voice	0.06	0.02	0.02	0.02
			Unicast	0.04	0.04	0.01	0.01
			Multicast	1.74	0.28	1.07	0.02
Fail L2 link between N-PE1 and Agg-1	Shut	Odd VLAN	Voice	0.90	0.87	0.30	0.24
			Unicast	0.89	0.89	0.30	0.23
			Multicast	5.55	0.97	2.60	0.56
		Even VLAN	Voice	0.00	0.24	0.00	0.00
			Unicast	0.00	0.00	0.00	0.00
			Multicast	0.01	0.00	0.02	0.01
	No shut	Odd VLAN	Voice	0.28	0.02	0.36	0.26
			Unicast	0.29	0.20	0.33	0.18
			Multicast	4.29	0.46	3.32	0.28
		Even VLAN	Voice	0.02	0.02	0.02	0.02
			Unicast	0.00	0.00	0.00	0.00
			Multicast	0.01	0.00	0.00	0.00
Fail L2 link between N-PE2 and Agg-2	Shut	Odd VLAN	Voice	0.58	0.00	0.02	0.02
			Unicast	0.00	0.00	0.00	0.00
			Multicast	0.02	0.00	0.01	0.01
		Even VLAN	Voice	0.62	0.58	0.60	0.58
			Unicast	0.59	0.57	0.58	0.56
			Multicast	5.75	2.26	5.94	2.25
	No shut	Odd VLAN	Voice	0.02	0.02	0.00	0.00
			Unicast	0.00	0.00	0.00	0.00
			Multicast	0.01	0.00	0.01	0.01
		Even VLAN	Voice	0.64	0.40	0.72	0.72
			Unicast	0.63	0.41	0.71	0.63
			Multicast	6.86	1.52	2.74	1.03
Fail L2 link between Agg-1 and Agg-2	Shut	Odd VLAN	Voice	0.00	0.00	0.00	0.00
			Unicast	0.00	0.00	0.00	0.00
			Multicast	0.01	0.00	0.00	0.00
		Even VLAN	Voice	0.00	0.00	0.00	0.00
			Unicast	0.00	0.00	0.00	0.00
			Multicast	0.01	0.00	0.01	0.01
	No shut	Odd VLAN	Voice	0.00	0.00	0.00	0.00
			Unicast	0.00	0.00	0.00	0.00
			Multicast	0.01	0.00	0.00	0.00
		Even VLAN	Voice	0.00	0.00	0.00	0.00
			Unicast	0.00	0.00	0.00	0.00
			Multicast	0.01	0.00	0.01	0.01

Table 8-1   *Convergence Numbers for Link and Node Failures for MST in PW Solution*

Failure Type	Action	VLAN	Traffic Type	Traffic Direction			
				LON → SJ		SJ → LON	
				Max	Min	Max	Min
Fail WAN link facing core on N-PE1	Shut	Odd VLAN	Voice	0.56	0.04	0.54	0.46
			Unicast	0.53	0.51	0.51	0.43
			Multicast	2.48	1.37	0.52	0.44
		Even VLAN	Voice	0.02	0.02	0.04	0.04
			Unicast	0.00	0.00	0.00	0.00
			Multicast	0.01	0.00	0.01	0.01
	No shut	Odd VLAN	Voice	0.02	0.02	0.02	0.02
			Unicast	0.00	0.00	0.00	0.00
			Multicast	3.60	0.17	0.02	0.02
		Even VLAN	Voice	0.02	0.02	0.02	0.02
			Unicast	0.00	0.00	0.00	0.00
			Multicast	0.01	0.00	0.02	0.02
Fail WAN link facing core on N-PE2	Shut	Odd VLAN	Voice	0.06	0.02	0.02	0.02
			Unicast	0.01	0.01	0.01	0.00
			Multicast	0.02	0.00	0.01	0.01
		Even VLAN	Voice	0.62	0.56	0.54	0.50
			Unicast	0.61	0.56	0.54	0.27
			Multicast	3.44	0.61	0.54	0.27
	No shut	Odd VLAN	Voice	0.02	0.02	0.04	0.04
			Unicast	0.01	0.00	0.00	0.00
			Multicast	0.02	0.00	0.01	0.01
		Even VLAN	Voice	0.02	0.02	0.12	0.10
			Unicast	0.00	0.00	0.06	0.06
			Multicast	3.12	0.14	0.07	0.07
Fail both WAN links on N-PE1	Shut	'Odd VLAN	Voice	3.88	0.04	3.98	3.98
			Unicast	3.86	3.85	3.99	3.99
			Multicast	6.54	4.81	7.42	4.28
		Even VLAN	Voice	0.02	0.02	0.04	0.04
			Unicast	0.02	0.02	0.01	0.01
			Multicast	0.01	0.00	0.02	0.02
	No shut	Odd VLAN	Voice	0.26	0.06	0.54	0.54
			Unicast	0.26	0.06	0.54	0.26
			Multicast	4.25	0.35	4.51	0.58
		Even VLAN	Voice	0.54	0.00	0.00	0.00
			Unicast	0.00	0.00	0.00	0.00
			Multicast	0.01	0.00	0.00	0.00
Fail both WAN links on N-PE2	Shut	Odd VLAN	Voice	0.02	0.02	0.04	0.02
			Unicast	0.00	0.00	0.00	0.00
			Multicast	0.01	0.00	0.00	0.00
		'Even VLAN	Voice	2.86	2.82	2.86	2.86
			Unicast	2.84	2.84	2.84	2.84
			Multicast	2.85	2.84	4.76	4.56
	No shut	Odd VLAN	Voice	0.06	0.02	0.02	0.02
			Unicast	0.01	0.00	0.00	0.00
			Multicast	0.02	0.01	0.00	0.00
		Even VLAN	Voice	0.43	0.08	0.50	0.46
			Unicast	0.44	0.10	0.48	0.12
			Multicast	5.28	0.86	2.62	0.85

Table 8-1 *Convergence Numbers for Link and Node Failures for MST in PW Solution*

Failure Type	Action	VLAN	Traffic Type	Traffic Direction			
				LON → SJ		SJ → LON	
				Max	Min	Max	Min
Clear entire routing table on both N-PEs	Clear	Odd VLAN	Voice	0.02	0.02	0.00	0.00
			Unicast	0.00	0.00	0.00	0.00
			Multicast	0.00	0.00	0.01	0.01
		Even VLAN	Voice	0.00	0.00	0.00	0.00
			Unicast	0.00	0.00	0.00	0.00
			Multicast	0.01	0.00	0.01	0.01
Clear entire dynamic MAC address table on both N-PEs	Clear	Odd VLAN	Voice	0.00	0.00	0.00	0.00
			Unicast	0.00	0.00	0.00	0.00
			Multicast	0.01	0.00	0.00	0.00
		Even VLAN	Voice	0.00	0.00	0.00	0.00
			Unicast	0.00	0.00	0.00	0.00
			Multicast	0.01	0.00	0.01	0.01
Fail L3 links between N-PEs	Shut	Odd VLAN	Voice	0.00	0.00	0.00	0.00
			Unicast	0.00	0.00	0.00	0.00
			Multicast	0.01	0.00	0.00	0.00
		Even VLAN	Voice	0.00	0.00	0.00	0.00
			Unicast	0.00	0.00	0.00	0.00
			Multicast	0.01	0.00	0.01	0.01
	No shut	Odd VLAN	Voice	0.00	0.00	0.00	0.00
			Unicast	0.00	0.00	0.00	0.00
			Multicast	0.01	0.00	0.01	0.00
		Even VLAN	Voice	0.00	0.00	0.00	0.00
			Unicast	0.00	0.00	0.00	0.00
			Multicast	0.01	0.00	0.01	0.01

[1] If the EoMPLS PW carrying MST BPDUs between the N-PEs fails, MST convergence within the local data center takes longer because of the delay in propagation of topology-change notification. Cisco defect number CSCsk85658 documents this issue.

Cluster Server Tests

Event logs are captured from the Event Viewer of the Microsoft cluster server. The logs are in the reverse order, showing the last event first. It is best to view the time stamps when analyzing these logs.

Table 8-2 shows the event logs from the Event Viewer of the Microsoft cluster server.

Table 8-2   *Event Logs for MST in PW (Option 1a)*

Test Case	Time in Seconds	Event Logs with Time Stamps from Microsoft Server			
Power off both N-PEs	123	12/16/2008	3:47:48 PM	CAMP3-SERVER2	The cluster service brought the resource group "ClusterGroup" online.
		12/16/2008	3:46:09 PM	CAMP3-SERVER2	The cluster service is attempting to bring online the resource group "Cluster Group."
		12/16/2008	3:46:09 PM	CAMP3-SERVER2	Cluster node CAMP3-SERVER3 was removed from the active server cluster membership. Cluster service may have been stopped on the node, the node may have failed, or the node may have lost communication with the other active server cluster nodes.
		12/16/2008	3:45:47 PM	CAMP3-SERVER2	The node lost communication with cluster node 'CAMP3-SERVER3' on network 'public.'
		12/16/2008	3:45:45 PM	CAMP3-SERVER2	The node lost communication with cluster node 'CAMP3-SERVER3' on network 'private(1).'
Power off access switch	120	12/16/2008	6:24:19 PM	CAMP3-SERVER2	The cluster service brought the resource group "Cluster Group" online.
		12/16/2008	6:22:49 PM	CAMP3-SERVER2	The cluster service is attempting to bring online the resource group "Cluster Group."
		12/16/2008	6:22:49 PM	CAMP3-SERVER2	Cluster node CAMP3-SERVER3 was removed from the active server cluster membership. Cluster service may have been stopped on the node, the node may have failed, or the node may have lost communication with the other active server cluster nodes.
		12/16/2008	6:22:27 PM	CAMP3-SERVER2	The node lost communication with cluster node 'CAMP3-SERVER3' on network 'private(1).'
		12/16/2008	6:22:27 PM	CAMP3-SERVER2	The node lost communication with cluster node 'CAMP3-SERVER3' on network 'public.'
		12/16/2008	6:22:19 PM	CAMP3-SERVER1	The node lost communication with cluster node 'CAMP3-SERVER3' on network 'private(1).'
		12/16/2008	6:22:19 PM	CAMP3-SERVER1	The node lost communication with cluster node 'CAMP3-SERVER3' on network 'public.'

Table 8-2   *Event Logs for MST in PW (Option 1a)*

Test Case	Time in Seconds	Event Logs with Time Stamps from Microsoft Server			
Power off active node	125	12/16/2008	5:54:19 PM	CAMP3-SERVER2	The cluster service brought the resource group "Cluster Group" online.
		12/16/2008	5:52:44 PM	CAMP3-SERVER2	The cluster service is attempting to bring online the resource group "ClusterGroup."
		12/16/2008	5:52:44 PM	CAMP3-SERVER2	Cluster node CAMP3-SERVER3 was removed from the active server cluster membership. Cluster service may have been stopped on the node, the node may have failed, or the node may have lost communication with the other active server cluster nodes.
		12/16/2008	5:52:22 PM	CAMP3-SERVER2	The node lost communication with cluster node 'CAMP3-SERVER3' on network 'private(1).'
		12/16/2008	5:52:22 PM	CAMP3-SERVER2	The node lost communication with cluster node 'CAMP3-SERVER3' on network 'public.'
		12/16/2008	5:52:14 PM	CAMP3-SERVER1	The node lost communication with cluster node 'CAMP3-SERVER3' on network 'private(1).'
		12/16/2008	5:52:14 PM	CAMP3-SERVER1	The node lost communication with cluster node 'CAMP3-SERVER3' on network 'public.'
Private VLAN N-PE reload	6	12/16/2008	5:35:23 PM	CAMP3-SERVER2	Cluster network 'private(1)' is operational (up). All available server cluster nodes attached to the network can communicate using it.
		12/16/2008	5:35:20 PM	CAMP3-SERVER3	The node (re)established communication with cluster node 'CAMP3-SERVER2' on network 'private(1).'
		12/16/2008	5:35:20 PM	CAMP3-SERVER3	The node (re)established communication with cluster node 'CAMP3-SERVER1' on network 'private(1).'
		12/16/2008	5:35:14 PM	CAMP3-SERVER3	The node lost communication with cluster node 'CAMP3-SERVER2' on network 'private(1).'
		12/16/2008	5:35:14 PM	CAMP3-SERVER3	The node lost communication with cluster node 'CAMP3-SERVER1' on network 'private(1).'

Table 8-2 *Event Logs for MST in PW (Option 1a)*

Test Case	Time in Seconds	Event Logs with Time Stamps from Microsoft Server			
Unplug active server	125	12/16/2008	5:54:19 PM	CAMP3-SERVER2	The cluster service brought the resource group "Cluster Group" online.
		12/16/2008	5:52:44 PM	CAMP3-SERVER2	The cluster service is attempting to bring online the resource group "Cluster Group."
		12/16/2008	5:52:44 PM	CAMP3-SERVER2	Cluster node CAMP3-SERVER3 was removed from the active server cluster membership. Cluster service might have been stopped on the node, the node might have failed, or the node might have lost communication with the other active server cluster nodes.
		12/16/2008	5:52:22 PM	CAMP3-SERVER2	The node lost communication with cluster node 'CAMP3-SERVER3' on network 'public.'
		12/16/2008	5:52:14 PM	CAMP3-SERVER1	The node lost communication with cluster node 'CAMP3-SERVER3' on network 'public.'
Establish L2 connectivity	No convergence	12/16/2008	6:36:03 PM	CAMP3-SERVER2	The cluster service service entered the running state.
		12/16/2008	6:36:02 PM	CAMP3-SERVER2	Cluster service successfully joined the server cluster CLUSTER-MNS.
		12/16/2008	6:35:44 PM	CAMP3-SERVER2	The node (re)established communication with cluster node 'CAMP3-SERVER3' on network 'public.'
		12/16/2008	6:35:44 PM	CAMP3-SERVER2	The node (re)established communication with cluster node 'CAMP3-SERVER3' on network 'private(1).'
		12/16/2008	6:35:43 PM	CAMP3-SERVER2	The node (re)established communication with cluster node 'CAMP3-SERVER1' on network 'public.'
		12/16/2008	6:35:43 PM	CAMP3-SERVER2	The node (re)established communication with cluster node 'CAMP3-SERVER1' on network 'private(1).'
		12/16/2008	6:35:35 PM	CAMP3-SERVER2	The cluster service service was successfully sent a start control.

VPLS with N-PE Redundancy Using RPVST with Isolated MST in N-PE: MST Option 1b

Today, most data centers still use legacy Per-VLAN Spanning Tree Plus (PVST+) or Rapid PVST (RPVST). Therefore, it is practical to continue with the deployment of Rapid PVST within the data center and configure MST only on the N-PE routers.

The first model, MST in PW, requires that all Layer 2 switches that belong to the STP domain migrate to MST mode. However, this isolated MST in N-PE solution provides the flexibility of having the existing Layer 2 switches run in the existing STP mode.

Using an isolated MST instance in the N-PE devices is a simple way to provide redundancy and ensure a loop-free Layer 2 topology while maintaining topology synchronization between the Layer 2 domains.

This approach uses three key features of MST:

■ Capability to map multiple VLANs in a single STP instance

■ Capability to be inserted as one logical switch in the local data center Layer 2 domain

■ The independence between the control plane for link blocking and the data plane for the user data VLAN

Figure 8-3 shows VPLS with N-PE redundancy using RPVST with isolated MST in N-PE.

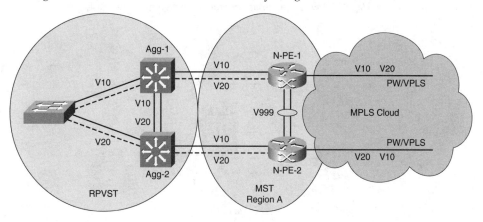

Figure 8-3 *RPVST within the data center with isolated MST in N-PE (MST option 1b).*

This solution allows network managers to deploy the solution without major changes in spanning-tree configuration on existing Layer 2 devices. Organizations can continue the use of 802.1d (PVST+) or 802.1w (RPVST) as the local STP and take advantage of MST and RPVST interaction to load balance traffic at Layer 2 by forwarding a different set of VLANs on two separate links.

In this deployment, only N-PE1 and N-PE2 run MST. For VLANs that require extension across data centers, N-PE1 and N-PE2 must be configured as STP root bridges. The EtherChannel link in Figure 8-3 carries only one VLAN that is not associated with a VPLS VFI. The sole purpose of this VLAN is to allow N-PE1 and N-PE2 to form an MST0 instance and appear as a virtual bridge to the Layer 2 switches in the RSTP domain. With Agg-1 and Agg-2 running RPVST, the link between N-PE1 and Agg-1 or N-PE2 and Agg-2 blocks VLANs depending on the STP cost. When a broadcast packet for a specific user VLAN arrives from the VPLS cloud at N-PE1, the packet is prevented from looping because it is not flooded to N-PE2 for the following reasons:

■ The inter-N-PE EtherChannel does not carry that VLAN.

■ Flooding that packet to Agg-1, then to Agg-2, does not send it back to N-PE2 because the link between Agg-2 and N-PE2 is blocking that VLAN.

The advantage of MST0 on N-PE1 and N-PE2 and RPVST on the aggregation switches is
per-VLAN load balancing across the links between N-PEs and the aggregation switches.

Also in this setup, all PWs on both N-PEs are active, and there are no direct PWs
between N-PE1 and N-PE2. If the link between N-PE1 and Agg-1 goes down, the link
between Agg-2 and N-PE2 forwards all VLANs after STP convergence. Using EEM, the
N-PE shuts down its local link to the aggregation switch when the VPLS link from that
N-PE goes down.

Both N-PEs belong to the isolated MST region. MST instance 0 is perceived as one logical switch by the local STP within the data center, as shown in Figure 8-4.

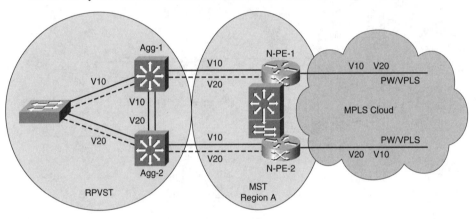

Figure 8-4   *Logical view of RSTP within the data center with isolated MST in N-PE.*

The interoperation point between RPVST and MST is on the N-PE side of the N-PE and
aggregation switch links. However, this interaction requires the placement of the root and
backup root bridges within the MST region. Also, you need to manipulate the per-VLAN
link cost to load balance Layer 2 traffic across redundant links. With only one link for a
VLAN in forwarding state toward the VPLS core, a global loop is avoided. A key requirement for achieving this behavior is to ensure that the inter-N-PE link does not carry
VLANs that are to be extended. That is, VLANs to be extended across data centers
should not be allowed on the inter-N-PE link. In addition, the link between Agg-1 and
Agg-2 should be forwarding all VLANs.

Note   A main constraint of this solution is the root bridge assignment. This shift in STP
root and backup root placement is required only for those VLANs that are to be extended
across geographically dispersed data centers.

EEM Scripting to Complement Isolated MST Solution

MST is only aware of the redundant links within the edge of the data center. The protocol is not aware of the VPLS topology because of STP isolation in the VPLS core.

You must enable the following main elements to maintain topology synchronization between MST and VPLS:

- WAN access failure with remote N-PE and remote N-PE to aggregation link failure must be reported to MST to force a topology change within the data center. Notification of these failures enables the backup path causing the alternate aggregation link to transition to forwarding state. Also, MAC addresses must be flushed to start the MAC address learning via flooding process and avoid black-holing traffic until these addresses time out (max timeout of 300 seconds based on default CAM aging timer).

   EEM scripts monitor the status of the WAN links and bring down the primary aggregation link if WAN connectivity is not available.

- The isolated MST concept works on the fact that the links between N-PE and aggregation devices are alternatively forwarding/blocking VLANs. This forwarding and blocking of VLANs on the inter N-PE and aggregation device links is controlled by the inter-N-PE link that must always be in forwarding mode. Take care to protect the inter-N-PE from failures. Cisco recommends that this inter-N-PE link be configured as an EtherChannel and preferably distributed on different line cards. To add to the robustness of the solution, in addition to the EtherChannel, an EEM script can be deployed on the backup N-PE as a protection from EtherChannel failures.

- After a failure, the alternate node becomes active, and remote data centers learn local MAC addresses through this backup node. When the primary node boots and becomes operational, flushing of MAC addresses must be induced via an EEM script.

Note   MAC address flushing becomes an issue for unidirectional traffic or for asymmetric flows. Bidirectional traffic and TCP flows are not sensitive to this flush requirement. Therefore, an EEM script is not mandatory, but it is recommended.

This isolated MST in N-PE solution is intended for enterprises that require extending approximately 30 VLANs across geographically dispersed data centers. N-PE routers are required to participate in local STP, so VLAN overlapping in multitenant environments is not possible.

Even though MST is the main protocol that controls forwarding and blocking access to VPLS, EEM scripts are required to control and ensure topology-change synchronization between VPLS and local STP domains. In some conditions, MAC addresses might not be flushed due to asymmetric flows, which could lead to slow convergence if a failure occurs.

If the requirement is to extend more than 30 VLANs across remote locations, or faster convergence, you can use the next set of EEM-based solutions. These EEM-based solutions are also appropriate because they facilitate a smooth transition to Ethernet access with IEEE 802.1Q-in-Q VLAN tag (QinQ) and finally QinQ with Virtual Switching System (VSS) in the aggregation layer.

Implementing RPVST in a Data Center with Isolated MST in N-PE (MST Option 1b) Design

In this solution, all PWs on N-PE1 and N-PE2 are active and blocking of VLANs (loop avoidance) is done by local STP. In this design, it is important that the access switches be dual-homed to both the aggregation switches.

Figure 8-5 provides a configuration overview of the various links and the nodes.

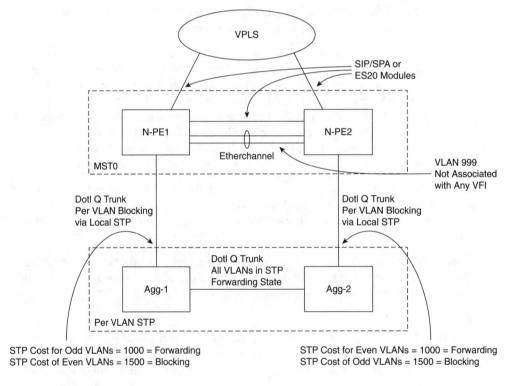

Figure 8-5   *Implementing isolated MST in N-PE (MST option 1b): Configuration overview.*

The following provides snippets of configuration from N-PE and aggregation devices and output from various **show** commands

Step 1.   Determine the existing STP root bridge priority for all VLANs that are required to be extended across data centers. You can verify this information with the **show spanning-tree vlan 7** command.

Step 2.   Configure STP mode MST on N-PE1 and N-PE2 and make them the root bridges for MST instance 0 by reducing the bridge priority to a value lower than value found in Step 1.

On both N-PEs, create only those VLANs that are required to be extended across remote locations. In addition, create the VLAN essential for MST instance 0; in this case, VLAN 999 was selected. Any dummy VLAN number can be used rather than 999 so long as that VLAN is not used for user traffic:

On N-PE1	On N-PE2
```spanning-tree mode mst```	```spanning-tree mode mst```
```!```	```!```
```spanning-tree mst configuration```	```spanning-tree mst configuration```
```name lon-datacenter```	```name lon-datacenter```
```revision 10```	```revision 10```
```!```	```!```
```spanning-tree mst 0 priority 16384```	```spanning-tree mst 0 priority 8192```
```!```	```!```
```vlan 2-61,201-260,999```	```vlan 2-61,201-260,999```

Step 3.   Verify MST configuration on the both N-PEs:

```
! On N-PE1:

lon-n-pe1# show spanning-tree mst


##### MST0     vlans mapped:    1-4094
Bridge         address 001d.7198.9500 priority    16384 (16384
  sysid 0)
Root           address 001d.7198.8fc0 priority     8192 (8192 sysid 0)
               port    Po1          path cost     0
Regional Root address 001d.7198.8fc0 priority     8192 (8192 sysid 0)
                                     internal cost 10000
  rem hops 19
Operational   hello time 2 , forward delay 15, max age 20, txholdcount 6
Configured    hello time 2 , forward delay 15, max age 20, max hops 20
```

```
Interface          Role Sts Cost      Prio.Nbr Type
---------- -- --- ---- ---- ------------
Gi2/1              Desg FWD 20000      128.257  P2p Bound(PVST)
Po1                Root FWD 10000      128.3329 P2p
```

lon-n-pe1# **show spanning-tree mst 0 detail**

```
##### MST0     vlans mapped:   1-4094
Bridge         address 001d.7198.9500  priority   16384 (16384
  sysid 0)
Root           address 001d.7198.8fc0  priority    8192 (8192 sysid 0)
               port    Gi2/1             path cost   20008
Regional Root this switch
Operational hello time 2 , forward delay 15, max age 20, txholdcount 6
Configured  hello time 2 , forward delay 15, max age 20, max hops 20


GigabitEthernet2/1 of MST0 is root forwarding
Port info              port id     128.257  priority    128
  cost       20000
Designated root        address 001d.7198.8fc0  priority   8192  cost  8
Design. regional root address 001c.b126.d000  priority  32769  cost  0
Designated bridge      address 001c.b126.d000  priority  32769  port
  id  128.147
Timers: message expires in 4 sec, forward delay 0, forward transitions 2
Bpdus sent 14185, received 15654


Port-channel1 of MST0 is designated forwarding
Port info              port id     128.3329  priority    128
  cost       10000
Designated root        address 001d.7198.8fc0  priority   8192  cost
  20008
Design. regional root address 001d.7198.9500  priority  16384  cost  0
Designated bridge      address 001d.7198.9500  priority  16384  port
  id 128.3329
Timers: message expires in 0 sec, forward delay 0, forward transitions 1
Bpdus sent 97, received 0
```

```
lon-n-pe1#

lon-n-pe1# show spanning-tree interface gig 2/1

Mst Instance          Role Sts Cost       Prio.Nbr Type
————————.  ——  —.  ————.  ————  ———————————

MST0                  Desg FWD 20000      128.257  P2p Bound(PVST)
lon-n-pe1#

lon-n-pe1# show running-config interface gig 2/1

Building configuration...

Current configuration : 384 bytes
!
interface GigabitEthernet2/1
 description L2 to Agg-1
 switchport
 switchport trunk encapsulation dot1q
 switchport trunk allowed vlan 1-61,201-260
 switchport mode trunk
 switchport nonegotiate
 mtu 9216
 logging event link-status
 logging event spanning-tree status
 storm-control broadcast level 5.00
 storm-control multicast level 5.00
 spanning-tree portfast trunk
 spanning-tree link-type point-to-point
end

lon-n-pe1# show spanning-tree vlan 7

MST0
  Spanning tree enabled protocol mstp
  Root ID    Priority    8192
             Address     001d.7198.8fc0
             Cost        0
             Port        3329 (Port-channel1)
             Hello Time   2 sec  Max Age 20 sec  Forward Delay 15 sec
```

```
 Bridge ID  Priority    16384  (priority 16384 sys-id-ext 0)
            Address     001d.7198.9500
            Hello Time  2 sec  Max Age 20 sec  Forward Delay 15 sec


Interface          Role Sts Cost      Prio.Nbr Type
---------------    -- --. -----.  ---- ------------

Gi2/1              Desg FWD 20000     128.257  P2p Bound(PVST)


lon-n-pe1#
! On N-PE2:
lon-n-pe2#  show spanning-tree mst


##### MST0    vlans mapped:   1-4094
Bridge       address 001d.7198.8fc0  priority    8192  (8192 sysid 0)
Root         this switch for the CIST
Operational hello time 2 , forward delay 15, max age 20, txholdcount 6
Configured  hello time 2 , forward delay 15, max age 20, max hops  20


Interface          Role Sts Cost      Prio.Nbr Type
--------- -- --. -----.  ---- ------------

Gi2/2              Desg FWD 20000     128.258  P2p Bound(PVST)
Po1                Desg FWD 10000     128.3329 P2p


lon-n-pe2#  show spanning-tree mst 0 detail


##### MST0    vlans mapped:   1-4094
Bridge       address 001d.7198.8fc0  priority    8192  (8192 sysid 0)
Root         this switch for the CIST
Operational hello time 2 , forward delay 15, max age 20, txholdcount 6
Configured  hello time 2 , forward delay 15, max age 20, max hops  20


GigabitEthernet2/2 of MST0 is designated forwarding
Port info              port id      128.258  priority    128
  cost      20000
Designated root       address 001d.7198.8fc0  priority    8192  cost 0
Design. regional root address 001d.7198.8fc0  priority    8192  cost  0
Designated bridge     address 001d.7198.8fc0  priority    8192  port
  id  128.258
```

```
Timers: message expires in 0 sec, forward delay 0, forward transitions 1
Bpdus sent 77233, received 4492


Port-channel1 of MST0 is designated forwarding
Port info               port id      128.3329  priority    128
   cost      10000
Designated root        address 001d.7198.8fc0 priority   8192  cost 0
Design. regional root  address 001d.7198.8fc0 priority   8192  cost  0
Designated bridge      address 001d.7198.8fc0 priority   8192  port
   id 128.3329
Timers: message expires in 0 sec, forward delay 0, forward transitions 1
Bpdus sent 80, received 8


lon-n-pe2#

lon-n-pe2# show spanning-tree interface gig 2/2


Mst Instance          Role Sts Cost      Prio.Nbr Type
----------------- -- -- ---- ---- ---------------
MST0                  Desg FWD 20000     128.258  P2p Bound(PVST)
lon-n-pe2#

lon-n-pe2# show running-config interface gig 2/2
Building configuration...


Current configuration : 374 bytes
!
interface GigabitEthernet2/2
 description L2 to Agg-2
 switchport
 switchport trunk encapsulation dot1q
 switchport trunk allowed vlan 1-61,201-260
 switchport mode trunk
 switchport nonegotiate
 mtu 9216
 load-interval 30
 storm-control broadcast level 5.00
 storm-control multicast level 5.00
 spanning-tree portfast trunk
 spanning-tree link-type point-to-point
```

```
end
lon-n-pe2# show spanning-tree vlan 7


MST0
  Spanning tree enabled protocol mstp
  Root ID    Priority    8192
             Address     001d.7198.8fc0
             This bridge is the root
             Hello Time   2 sec  Max Age 20 sec  Forward Delay 15 sec


  Bridge ID  Priority    8192   (priority 8192 sys-id-ext 0)
             Address     001d.7198.8fc0
             Hello Time   2 sec  Max Age 20 sec  Forward Delay 15 sec


Interface        Role Sts Cost      Prio.Nbr Type
---------------- ---- --- --------- -------- --------------------
Gi2/2            Desg FWD 20000     128.258  P2p Bound(PVST)


lon-n-pe2#
```

Step 4. Configure a distributed EtherChannel for the Layer 2 links between the two
N-PE routers. Allow only VLAN 999 (any non-VFI VLAN) for MST instance
0 on this EtherChannel.

On N-PE1

```
lon-n-pe1# show run int port-channel 1
Building configuration...

Current configuration : 161 bytes
!
interface Port-channel1
 description Inter N-PE link
 switchport
 switchport access vlan 999
 switchport mode access
 mtu 9216
 logging event link-status
 logging event spanning-tree status
end

lon-n-pe1# show run interface gig 2/4
Building configuration...

Current configuration : 215 bytes
!
```

On N-PE2

```
lon-n-pe2# show run int port-channel 1
Building configuration...

Current configuration : 161 bytes
!
interface Port-channel1
 description Inter N-PE link
 switchport
 switchport access vlan 999
 switchport mode access
 mtu 9216
 logging event link-status
 logging event spanning-tree status
end

lon-n-pe2# show run interface gig 2/4
Building configuration...

Current configuration : 215 bytes
!
```

On N-PE1	On N-PE2
``	```

```
interface GigabitEthernet2/4
 description LAN etherchannel interface to
   lon-n-pe2
 switchport
 switchport access vlan 999
 switchport mode access
 mtu 9216
 logging event link-status
 logging event spanning-tree status
 channel-group 1 mode on
end

lon-n-pe1# show run interface gig 2/5
Building configuration...

Current configuration : 215 bytes
!
interface GigabitEthernet2/5
 description LAN etherchannel interface to
   lon-n-pe2
 switchport
 switchport access vlan 999
 switchport mode access
 mtu 9216
 logging event link-status
 logging event spanning-tree status
 channel-group 1 mode on
end
```

```
interface GigabitEthernet2/4
 description LAN etherchannel interface to
   lon-n-pe1
 switchport
 switchport access vlan 999
 switchport mode access
 mtu 9216
 logging event link-status
 logging event spanning-tree status
 channel-group 1 mode on
end

lon-n-pe2# show run interface gig 2/5
Building configuration...

Current configuration : 215 bytes
!
interface GigabitEthernet2/5
 description LAN etherchannel interface to
   lon-n-pe1
 switchport
 switchport access vlan 999
 switchport mode access
 mtu 9216
 logging event link-status
 logging event spanning-tree status
 channel-group 1 mode on
end
```

Step 5. Configure RPVST on both the aggregation PEs for per-VLAN load balancing. The configuration for both Agg-1 and Agg-2 is as follows:

```
spanning-tree mode rapid-pvst
!
vlan 2-61,201-260
```

Step 6. On the link between both N-PEs and aggregation switches, configure the following:

a. The dot1q trunk between the N-PE and aggregation switch should allow only those VLANs that are to be extended across the data centers; otherwise, N-PE becomes the STP root for all VLANs that are allowed on this trunk connection.

b. Increase the STP cost so that all odd VLANs forward via Agg-1 to N-PE1 and even VLANs forward through Agg-2 and N-PE2. Configure higher cost so that, regardless of the bandwidth of the inter-aggregation switch link, the inter-aggregation switch link is always in forwarding mode for all the VLANs. In the following configuration on N-PE1, the STP cost for all odd VLANs has been increased to 1000, and the STP cost for even VLANs has been increased to 1500. On N-PE2, the STP cost of 1000 has been configured for all even VLANs and 1500 for all odd VLANs.

c. STP point-to-point link.

d. Storm control; broadcast and multicast on the N-PE side of the link. For threshold guidelines, see Chapter 11.

On N-PE1	On N-PE2
interface GigabitEthernet2/1	interface GigabitEthernet2/2
description L2 to Agg-1	description L2 to Agg-2
switchport	switchport
switchport trunk encapsulation dot1q	switchport trunk encapsulation dot1q
switchport trunk allowed vlan 1-61, 201-260	switchport trunk allowed vlan 1-61, 201-260
switchport mode trunk	switchport mode trunk
switchport nonegotiate	switchport nonegotiate
mtu 9216	mtu 9216
logging event link-status	logging event link-status
logging event spanning-tree status	logging event spanning-tree status
storm-control broadcast level 5.00	storm-control broadcast level 5.00
storm-control multicast level 5.00	storm-control multicast level 5.00
spanning-tree portfast trunk	spanning-tree portfast trunk
spanning-tree link-type point-to-point	spanning-tree link-type point-to-point
end	end

On Agg-1	On Agg-2
`interface GigabitEthernet2/19`	`interface GigabitEthernet2/18`
` description L2 connection to lon-n-pe1`	` description L2 connection to lon-n-pe2`
` switchport`	` switchport`
` switchport trunk encapsulation dot1q`	` switchport trunk encapsulation dot1q`
` switchport trunk allowed vlan 1-61,201-` `  260`	` switchport trunk allowed vlan 1-61,201-` `  260`
` switchport mode trunk`	` switchport mode trunk`
` switchport nonegotiate`	` switchport nonegotiate`
` mtu 9216`	` mtu 9216`
` logging event link-status`	` logging event link-status`
` logging event spanning-tree status`	` logging event spanning-tree status`
` spanning-tree link-type point-to-point`	` spanning-tree link-type point-to-point`
` spanning-tree vlan` `1,3,5,7,9,11,13,15,17,19,21,23,25,27,29,...` `.... cost 1000`	` spanning-tree vlan` `2,4,6,8,10,12,14,16,18,20,22,24,26,28,` `30,...... cost 1000`
` spanning-tree vlan` `2,4,6,8,10,12,14,16,18,20,22,24,26,28,30,..` `.... cost 1500`	` spanning-tree vlan` `3,5,7,9,11,13,15,17,19,21,23,25,27,` `29,......... cost 1500`
`end`	`end`

Step 7.   Verify STP configuration on both the aggregation switches and confirm that the appropriate links forward and block VLANs as expected.

On Agg-1, all odd VLANs are in forwarding state, and all even VLANs are in blocking state:

```
lon-agg-1# show spanning-tree interface gig 2/19
```

```
Vlan               Role Sts Cost     Prio.Nbr Type
---------------    ---- --- -------  -------- ---------------
VLAN0001           Altn BLK 1000     128.147  P2p Peer(STP)
VLAN0002           Altn BLK 1500     128.147  P2p Peer(STP)
VLAN0003           Root FWD 1000     128.147  P2p Peer(STP)
VLAN0004           Altn BLK 1500     128.147  P2p Peer(STP)
VLAN0005           Root FWD 1000     128.147  P2p Peer(STP)
VLAN0006           Altn BLK 1500     128.147  P2p Peer(STP)
VLAN0007           Root FWD 1000     128.147  P2p Peer(STP)
VLAN0008           Altn BLK 1500     128.147  P2p Peer(STP)
VLAN0009           Root FWD 1000     128.147  P2p Peer(STP)
```

```
VLAN0010              Altn BLK 1500      128.147  P2p Peer(STP)
VLAN0011              Root FWD 1000      128.147  P2p Peer(STP)
VLAN0012              Altn BLK 1500      128.147  P2p Peer(STP)
VLAN0013              Root FWD 1000      128.147  P2p Peer(STP)
VLAN0014              Altn BLK 1500      128.147  P2p Peer(STP)
VLAN0015              Root FWD 1000      128.147  P2p Peer(STP)
VLAN0016              Altn BLK 1500      128.147  P2p Peer(STP)
VLAN0017              Root FWD 1000      128.147  P2p Peer(STP)
VLAN0018              Altn BLK 1500      128.147  P2p Peer(STP)
VLAN0019              Root FWD 1000      128.147  P2p Peer(STP)
...
...
...

lon-agg-1# show spanning-tree int gig 2/23


Vlan                  Role Sts Cost      Prio.Nbr Type
--------------------- ---- --- --------- -------- --------------------
VLAN0001              Root FWD 4         128.151  P2p
VLAN0002              Root FWD 4         128.151  P2p
VLAN0003              Desg FWD 4         128.151  P2p
VLAN0004              Root FWD 4         128.151  P2p
VLAN0005              Desg FWD 4         128.151  P2p
VLAN0006              Root FWD 4         128.151  P2p
VLAN0007              Desg FWD 4         128.151  P2p
VLAN0008              Root FWD 4         128.151  P2p
VLAN0009              Desg FWD 4         128.151  P2p
VLAN0010              Root FWD 4         128.151  P2p
VLAN0011              Desg FWD 4         128.151  P2p
VLAN0012              Root FWD 4         128.151  P2p
VLAN0013              Desg FWD 4         128.151  P2p
VLAN0014              Root FWD 4         128.151  P2p
VLAN0015              Desg FWD 4         128.151  P2p
VLAN0016              Root FWD 4         128.151  P2p
VLAN0017              Desg FWD 4         128.151  P2p
VLAN0018              Root FWD 4         128.151  P2p
VLAN0019              Desg FWD 4         128.151  P2p
...
...
...
```

On Agg-2, all even VLANs are in forwarding state, and all odd VLANs are in blocking state:

lon-agg-2# show spanning-tree interface gig 2/18

```
Vlan                Role Sts Cost     Prio.Nbr Type
–––––––––––. –– –. ––––. –––– ––––––––––––

VLAN0001            Root FWD 4        128.146  P2p Peer(STP)
VLAN0002            Root FWD 1000     128.146  P2p Peer(STP)
VLAN0003            Altn BLK 1500     128.146  P2p Peer(STP)
VLAN0004            Root FWD 1000     128.146  P2p Peer(STP)
VLAN0005            Altn BLK 1500     128.146  P2p Peer(STP)
VLAN0006            Root FWD 1000     128.146  P2p Peer(STP)
VLAN0007            Altn BLK 1500     128.146  P2p Peer(STP)
VLAN0008            Root FWD 1000     128.146  P2p Peer(STP)
VLAN0009            Altn BLK 1500     128.146  P2p Peer(STP)
VLAN0010            Root FWD 1000     128.146  P2p Peer(STP)
VLAN0011            Altn BLK 1500     128.146  P2p Peer(STP)
VLAN0012            Root FWD 1000     128.146  P2p Peer(STP)
VLAN0013            Altn BLK 1500     128.146  P2p Peer(STP)
VLAN0014            Root FWD 1000     128.146  P2p Peer(STP)
VLAN0015            Altn BLK 1500     128.146  P2p Peer(STP)
VLAN0016            Root FWD 1000     128.146  P2p Peer(STP)
VLAN0017            Altn BLK 1500     128.146  P2p Peer(STP)
VLAN0018            Root FWD 1000     128.146  P2p Peer(STP)
VLAN0019            Altn BLK 1500     128.146  P2p Peer(STP)
...
...
...
```

lon-agg-2# sh spanning-tree interface gig2/23

```
Vlan                    Role Sts Cost      Prio.Nbr Type
---------------.  -- --. -----.  ----  ------------
VLAN0001                Desg FWD 4         128.151  P2p
VLAN0002                Desg FWD 4         128.151  P2p
VLAN0003                Root FWD 4         128.151  P2p
VLAN0004                Desg FWD 4         128.151  P2p
VLAN0005                Root FWD 4         128.151  P2p
VLAN0006                Desg FWD 4         128.151  P2p
VLAN0007                Root FWD 4         128.151  P2p
VLAN0008                Desg FWD 4         128.151  P2p
VLAN0009                Root FWD 4         128.151  P2p
VLAN0010                Desg FWD 4         128.151  P2p
VLAN0011                Root FWD 4         128.151  P2p
VLAN0012                Desg FWD 4         128.151  P2p
VLAN0013                Root FWD 4         128.151  P2p
VLAN0014                Desg FWD 4         128.151  P2p
VLAN0015                Root FWD 4         128.151  P2p
VLAN0016                Desg FWD 4         128.151  P2p
VLAN0017                Root FWD 4         128.151  P2p
VLAN0018                Desg FWD 4         128.151  P2p
VLAN0019                Root FWD 4         128.151  P2p
...
...
...
```

From the preceding configuration example, you can see that spanning tree blocks even VLANs on the link between N-PE1 and Agg-1 and odd VLANs on the link between N-PE2 and Agg-2. Also, all VLANs are in forwarding state on the inter-aggregation switch link. This configuration provides per-VLAN load balancing and at the same times avoids a Layer 2 loop.

Step 8.   Configure OSPF on the N-PE routers:

```
router ospf 1
 router-id 11.11.11.11
 log-adjacency-changes
 auto-cost reference-bandwidth 10000
 area 0 authentication message-digest
 timers throttle spf 100 100 5000
 timers throttle lsa 100 100 5000
 timers lsa arrival 80
 ...
```

```
    distribute-list 1 in GigabitEthernet2/6
    bfd all-interfaces
    mpls ldp sync
  !


lon-n-pe1# show ip ospf 1
  Routing Process "ospf 1" with ID 11.11.11.11
  Start time: 00:02:32.568, Time elapsed: 01:30:13.904
  Supports only single TOS(TOS0) routes
  Supports opaque LSA
  Supports Link-local Signaling (LLS)
  Supports area transit capability
  Event-log enabled, Maximum number of events: 1000, Mode: cyclic
  Router is not originating router-LSAs with maximum metric
  Initial SPF schedule delay 100 msecs
  Minimum hold time between two consecutive SPFs 100 msecs
  Maximum wait time between two consecutive SPFs 5000 msecs
  Incremental-SPF disabled
  Initial LSA throttle delay 100 msecs
  Minimum hold time for LSA throttle 100 msecs
  Maximum wait time for LSA throttle 5000 msecs
  Minimum LSA arrival 80 msecs
  LSA group pacing timer 240 secs
  Interface flood pacing timer 33 msecs
  Retransmission pacing timer 66 msecs
  Number of external LSA 1. Checksum Sum 0x00E9DA
  Number of opaque AS LSA 0. Checksum Sum 0x000000
  Number of DCbitless external and opaque AS LSA 0
  Number of DoNotAge external and opaque AS LSA 0
  Number of areas in this router is 1. 1 normal 0 stub 0 nssa
  Number of areas transit capable is 0
  External flood list length 0
  IETF NSF helper support enabled
  Cisco NSF helper support enabled
  BFD is enabled
  Reference bandwidth unit is 10000 mbps
    Area BACKBONE(0)
```

```
            Number of interfaces in this area is 6 (2 loopback)

            Area has message digest authentication

            SPF algorithm last executed 00:40:52.952 ago

            SPF algorithm executed 75 times

            Area ranges are

            Number of LSA 84. Checksum Sum 0x2844BB

            Number of opaque link LSA 0. Checksum Sum 0x000000

            Number of DCbitless LSA 0

            Number of indication LSA 0

            Number of DoNotAge LSA 0

            Flood list length 0
```

lon-n-pe1# show ip ospf neighbor

```
Neighbor ID      Pri   State          Dead Time    Address    Interface
116.5.200.77      0    FULL/ -        00:00:32     192.168.11.7
GigabitEthernet4/0/19
12.12.12.12       0    FULL/ -        00:00:34     192.168.13.6
GigabitEthernet4/0/0
13.13.13.13       0    FULL/ -        00:00:33     10.11.21.3
GigabitEthernet2/6
```

lon-n-pe1# show cdp neighbors

```
Capability Codes: R - Router, T - Trans Bridge, B - Source Route Bridge
                  S - Switch, H - Host, I - IGMP, r - Repeater, P -
                  Phone
```

```
Device ID       Local Intrfce   Holdtme   Capability   Platform   Port ID
campus3-223sw8   Gig 1/2         145       S I          WS-C2950T Fas 0/2
lon-n-pe2        Gig 2/5         179       R S I        CISCO7604 Gig 2/5
lon-n-pe2        Gig 2/4         179       R S I        CISCO7604 Gig 2/4
lon-n-pe2        Gig 4/0/0       169       R S I        CISCO7604 Gig 4/0/0
```

```
lon-agg-1        Gig 2/1       167    R S I    WS-C6509- Gig 2/19

lon-core1        Gig 2/6       165    R S I    WS-C6506  Gig 3/21

mpls-p1          Gig 4/0/19    157    R S I    WS-C6506  Gig 2/22
```

Step 9.   Configure MPLS, VFI, and SVI on N-PE1 and N-PE2. The output from the
show mpls l2transport vc command displays the MPLS VC transport information.

Redundancy in the VPLS domain relies on an MPLS mechanism. Each N-PE can
have an alternate MPLS path, or an EEM policy can be used at each N-PE to
shut down its link to the local aggregation switch when the VPLS link is down:

```
! On N-PE1:

lon-n-pe1#

!

...

mpls ldp neighbor 10.76.70.12 targeted ldp

mpls ldp neighbor 10.76.70.21 targeted ldp

mpls ldp neighbor 10.76.70.22 targeted ldp

mpls ldp neighbor 10.76.70.31 targeted ldp

mpls ldp neighbor 10.76.70.32 targeted ldp

mpls ldp tcp pak-priority

mpls ldp session protection

no mpls ldp advertise-labels

mpls ldp advertise-labels for 76

mpls label protocol ldp

!

xconnect logging pseudowire status

!

access-list 76 permit 10.76.0.0 0.0.255.255

!

!

lon-n-pe1# show bfd neighbors


OurAddr        NeighAddr       LD/RD  RH/RS  Holddown(mult)  State   Int
```

```
192.168.13.5  192.168.13.6   1/1   Up        0   (3 )   Up
  Gi4/0/0
192.168.11.5  192.168.11.7   2/1   Up        0   (3 )   Up
  Gi4/0/19


! VFI for VLAN 7
l2 vfi lon-pe1-7 manual
 vpn id 7
 neighbor 10.76.100.32 encapsulation mpls
 neighbor 10.76.100.31 encapsulation mpls
 neighbor 10.76.100.22 encapsulation mpls
 neighbor 10.76.100.21 encapsulation mpls
!
!
interface Vlan7
 mtu 9216
 no ip address
 xconnect vfi lon-pe1-7
!
lon-n-pe1# show mpls l2transport vc 7


Local intf      Local circuit        Dest address     VC ID    Status
----------.     ----------------     ----------.      ------ -
VFI lon-pe1-7   VFI                  10.76.100.21     7   UP
VFI lon-pe1-7   VFI                  10.76.100.22     7   UP
VFI lon-pe1-7   VFI                  10.76.100.31     7   UP
VFI lon-pe1-7   VFI                  10.76.100.32     7   UP


lon-n-pe1#
lon-n-pe1# show running-config interface gig 4/0/19
!
interface GigabitEthernet4/0/19
```

```
 description L3 connection to MPLS P router
 dampening
 mtu 9216
 ip address 192.168.11.5 255.255.255.0
 ip ospf message-digest-key 1 md5 lab
 ip ospf network point-to-point
 load-interval 30
 carrier-delay msec 0
 mls qos trust dscp
 mpls ip
 bfd interval 100 min_rx 100 multiplier 3
end
! On N-PE2:
lon-n-pe2#
!
l2 vfi lon-pe2-7 manual
 vpn id 7
 neighbor 10.76.100.32 encapsulation mpls
 neighbor 10.76.100.31 encapsulation mpls
 neighbor 10.76.100.22 encapsulation mpls
 neighbor 10.76.100.21 encapsulation mpls
 !
 !
interface Vlan7
 mtu 9216
 no ip address
 xconnect vfi lon-pe2-7
 !
lon-n-pe2#  show mpls l2transport vc 7


Local intf      Local circuit        Dest address    VC ID      Status
-------         --------------       --------        -------     -------
VFI lon-pe2-7   VFI                  10.76.100.21    7           UP
VFI lon-pe2-7   VFI                  10.76.100.22    7           UP
```

```
VFI lon-pe2-7   VFI                10.76.100.31    7            UP
VFI lon-pe2-7   VFI                10.76.100.32    7            UP
Lon-n-pe2#
! On N-PE1 in San Jose data center:
sj-n-pe1#
!
l2 vfi sj-pe1-vlan7 manual
 vpn id 7
 neighbor 10.76.100.22 encapsulation mpls
 neighbor 10.76.100.12 encapsulation mpls
 neighbor 10.76.100.11 encapsulation mpls
 neighbor 10.76.100.21 encapsulation mpls
!
interface Vlan7
 mtu 9216
 no ip address
 xconnect vfi sj-pe1-vlan7
!
sj-n-pe1# show mpls l2transport vc 7


Local intf     Local circuit       Dest address    VC ID       Status
------------.  ---------------- --------.  -------

VFI sj-pe1-vlan7  \
                  VFI             10.76.100.11    7            UP
VFI sj-pe1-vlan7  \
                  VFI             10.76.100.12    7            UP
VFI sj-pe1-vlan7  \
                  VFI             10.76.100.21    7            UP
VFI sj-pe1-vlan7  \
                  VFI             10.76.100.22    7            UP
!
```

Step 10.   Configure object tracking using EEM. Use the **show running-config | begin event manager** command to display EEM applets configured:

```
lon-n-pe1#
!
process-max-time 50
!
track 20 interface GigabitEthernet4/0/0 line-protocol
!
track 21 interface GigabitEthernet4/0/19 line-protocol
!
track 25 list boolean or
 object 20
 object 21
 delay up 90


lon-n-pe1# show running-config | begin event manager
event manager applet DOWN_Gig2/1
 event track 25 state down
 action 1.0 cli command "enable"
 action 2.0 cli command "config t"
 action 3.0 cli command "int Gig 2/1 "
 action 4.0 cli command "shut"
 action 5.0 syslog msg "EEM has shut Gig 2/1 "
event manager applet UP_Gig2/1
 event track 25 state up
 action 1.0 cli command "enable"
 action 2.0 cli command "config t"
 action 3.0 cli command "int Gig2/1"
 action 4.0 cli command "no shut"
 action 5.0 syslog msg "EEM has unshut Gig2/1"
event manager applet DOWN_GIG2/1-boot
 event timer cron name "_EEMinternalname6" cron-entry "@reboot"
 action 1.0 cli command "enable"
 action 2.0 cli command "config t"
 action 3.0 cli command "interface Gig 2/1 "
 action 4.0 cli command "shutdown"
 action 5.0 syslog msg "EEM has shut Gig 2/1 "
!
end
```

Pertaining to the highlighted line of output, when an N-PE router reloads, power to the LAN modules is enabled before WAN modules power on. In this situation, LAN interfaces are enabled before interfaces on the WAN modules become active. After the LAN interfaces become active, spanning tree converges and puts the interface between the N-PE and aggregation switch in forwarding mode. Therefore, traffic is black-holed because the WAN interfaces may still be in down state, or the path to the core network might not be available via the N-PE that was reloaded. An EEM reboot applet ensures that the LAN interfaces are in shut state until the IP route configured in the **track** command is reachable after the router initializes completely.

Convergence Tests

The traffic profile outlined in Chapter 7 was used to determine end-to-end convergence for unidirectional voice, unicast, and multicast traffic. Links and nodes failed to simulate network failures.

Table 8-3 shows results of various node and link failures for the isolated MST and in N-PE solution. Convergence numbers (max and min) are in seconds.

Table 8-3   *Convergence Numbers for Link and Node Failures for the Isolated MST in N-PE: MST Option 1b Solution*

| | | | | Traffic Direction | | | |
| | | | | LON → SJ | | SJ → LON | |
Failure Type	Action	VLAN	Traffic Type	Max	Min	Max	Min
Reload SJ N-PE1	Reload	Odd VLAN	Voice	3.82	0.02	3.80	3.78
			Unicast	3.79	3.79	3.78	3.72
			Multicast	5.66	3.82	5.27	3.86
		Even VLAN	Voice	0.02	0.02	0.02	0.02
			Unicast	0.00	0.00	0.00	0.00
			Multicast	0.03	0.01	0.01	0.01
	Restore	Odd VLAN	Voice	0.02	0.02	0.02	0.02
			Unicast	0.01	0.01	0.01	0.01
			Multicast	1.16	0.08	0.62	0.59
		Even VLAN	Voice	0.00	0.02	0.00	0.00
			Unicast	0.00	0.00	0.00	0.00
			Multicast	0.00	0.00	0.00	0.00
Reload N-PE2	*Reload	Odd VLAN	Voice	13.07	12.91	13.04	13.04
			Unicast	13.05	12.89	13.06	12.84
			Multicast	13.45	13.06	13.13	12.85
		Even VLAN	Voice	16.95	16.93	16.88	16.84
			Unicast	16.94	16.92	16.88	16.82
			Multicast	17.61	17.05	16.92	16.83
	Restore	Odd VLAN	Voice	0.02	0.02	0.02	0.02
			Unicast	0.00	0.00	0.00	0.00
			Multicast	0.01	0.01	0.01	0.01
		Even VLAN	Voice	0.04	0.04	0.16	0.16
			Unicast	0.01	0.01	0.15	0.01
			Multicast	2.21	0.92	2.45	0.84

Table 8-3 *Convergence Numbers for Link and Node Failures for the Isolated MST in N-PE: MST Option 1b Solution*

Failure Type	Action	VLAN	Traffic Type	Traffic Direction LON → SJ Max	LON → SJ Min	SJ → LON Max	SJ → LON Min
Reload SJ Agg-1	Reload	Odd VLAN	Voice	0.92	0.92	1.36	1.34
			Unicast	0.92	0.92	1.35	1.35
			Multicast	2.00	0.93	3.39	1.58
		Even VLAN	Voice	0.00	0.00	0.02	0.00
			Unicast	0.00	0.00	0.00	0.00
			Multicast	0.00	0.00	0.01	0.00
	Restore	Odd VLAN	Voice	0.10	0.02	0.06	0.02
			Unicast	0.05	0.05	0.03	0.01
			Multicast	2.07	1.14	1.90	0.08
		Even VLAN	Voice	0.04	0.04	0.02	0.02
			Unicast	0.00	0.00	0.00	0.00
			Multicast	0.02	0.02	0.00	0.00
Reload SJ Agg-2	Reload	Odd VLAN	Voice	0.02	0.02	0.00	0.00
			Unicast	0.00	0.00	0.00	0.00
			Multicast	0.00	0.00	0.00	0.00
		Even VLAN	Voice	0.68	0.68	1.48	1.48
			Unicast	0.68	0.68	1.48	1.48
			Multicast	2.59	0.68	1.83	1.47
	Restore	Odd VLAN	Voice	0.02	0.02	0.02	0.02
			Unicast	0.00	0.00	0.00	0.00
			Multicast	0.00	0.00	0.00	0.00
		Even VLAN	Voice	0.20	0.20	0.20	0.20
			Unicast	0.19	0.19	0.18	0.18
			Multicast	1.94	0.39	1.42	0.31
Fail L2 link between SJ N-PE1 and Agg-1	Shut	Odd VLAN	Voice	0.60	0.56	0.58	0.52
			Unicast	0.58	0.57	0.57	0.56
			Multicast	1.16	0.57	2.57	0.57
		Even VLAN	Voice	0.02	0.02	0.02	0.00
			Unicast	0.00	0.00	0.00	0.00
			Multicast	0.01	0.00	0.01	0.00
	No shut	Odd VLAN	Voice	0.02	0.00	0.02	0.00
			Unicast	0.01	0.01	0.02	0.01
			Multicast	0.97	0.03	0.32	0.07
		Even VLAN	Voice	0.00	0.00	0.00	0.00
			Unicast	0.00	0.00	0.00	0.00
			Multicast	0.01	0.00	0.01	0.00
Fail L2 link between SJ N-PE2 and Agg-2	Shut	Odd VLAN	Voice	0.02	0.02	0.02	0.00
			Unicast	0.00	0.00	0.00	0.00
			Multicast	0.01	0.01	0.01	0.01
		Even VLAN	Voice	0.44	0.40	0.44	0.34
			Unicast	0.42	0.42	0.42	0.37
			Multicast	1.26	0.57	2.41	0.36
	No shut	Odd VLAN	Voice	0.02	0.00	0.02	0.00
			Unicast	0.00	0.00	0.00	0.00
			Multicast	0.01	0.00	0.01	0.00
		Even VLAN	Voice	0.04	0.00	0.02	0.00
			Unicast	0.01	0.01	0.01	0.01
			Multicast	0.90	0.06	2.11	0.02

Table 8-3 *Convergence Numbers for Link and Node Failures for the Isolated MST in N-PE: MST Option 1b Solution*

Failure Type	Action	VLAN	Traffic Type	Traffic Direction			
				LON → SJ		SJ → LON	
				Max	Min	Max	Min
Fail One L2 physical link between SJ N-PE1 and N-PE2	Shut	Odd VLAN	Voice	0.02	0.00	0.02	0.00
			Unicast	0.00	0.00	0.00	0.00
			Multicast	0.01	0.00	0.01	0.00
		Even VLAN	Voice	0.02	0.00	0.00	0.00
			Unicast	0.00	0.00	0.00	0.00
			Multicast	0.01	0.00	0.01	0.00
	No shut	Odd VLAN	Voice	0.02	0.02	0.02	0.00
			Unicast	0.00	0.00	0.00	0.00
			Multicast	0.01	0.00	0.01	0.01
		Even VLAN	Voice	0.02	0.02	0.02	0.00
			Unicast	0.00	0.00	0.00	0.00
			Multicast	0.01	0.00	0.01	0.01
Fail L3 link between SJ N-PE1 and N-PE2	Shut	Odd VLAN	Voice	0.02	0.02	0.02	0.00
			Unicast	0.00	0.00	0.00	0.00
			Multicast	0.01	0.01	0.01	0.01
		Even VLAN	Voice	0.02	0.02	0.02	0.00
			Unicast	0.00	0.00	0.00	0.00
			Multicast	0.01	0.01	0.01	0.01
	No shut	Odd VLAN	Voice	0.02	0.02	0.02	0.00
			Unicast	0.00	0.00	0.00	0.00
			Multicast	0.01	0.01	0.01	0.01
		Even VLAN	Voice	0.02	0.02	0.02	0.00
			Unicast	0.00	0.00	0.00	0.00
			Multicast	0.01	0.01	0.01	0.01
Fail L2 link between SJ Agg-1 and Agg-2	Shut	Odd VLAN	Voice	0.02	0.02	0.02	0.00
			Unicast	0.00	0.00	0.00	0.00
			Multicast	0.01	0.01	0.01	0.01
		Even VLAN	Voice	0.02	0.00	0.02	0.00
			Unicast	0.00	0.00	0.00	0.00
			Multicast	0.01	0.01	0.01	0.01
	No shut	Odd VLAN	Voice	0.02	0.00	0.02	0.00
			Unicast	0.00	0.00	0.00	0.00
			Multicast	0.01	0.00	0.01	0.01
		Even VLAN	Voice	0.02	0.00	0.02	0.00
			Unicast	0.00	0.00	0.00	0.00
			Multicast	0.01	0.00	0.01	0.01
Fail WAN link facing core on SJ N-PE1	Shut	Odd VLAN	Voice	0.82	0.74	0.84	0.80
			Unicast	0.80	0.75	0.82	0.77
			Multicast	0.80	0.75	0.96	0.90
		Even VLAN	Voice	0.02	0.02	0.02	0.00
			Unicast	0.00	0.00	0.00	0.00
			Multicast	0.01	0.01	0.01	0.01
	No shut	Odd VLAN	Voice	0.04	0.02	0.02	0.00
			Unicast	0.02	0.00	0.00	0.00
			Multicast	0.02	0.00	0.01	0.01
		Even VLAN	Voice	0.02	0.02	0.02	0.00
			Unicast	0.00	0.00	0.00	0.00
			Multicast	0.01	0.00	0.01	0.01

Table 8-3 *Convergence Numbers for Link and Node Failures for the Isolated MST in N-PE: MST Option 1b Solution*

| | | | | Traffic Direction | | | |
| | | | | LON → SJ | | SJ → LON | |
Failure Type	Action	VLAN	Traffic Type	Max	Min	Max	Min
Fail WAN link facing core on SJ N-PE2	Shut	Odd VLAN	Voice	0.02	0.02	0.02	0.00
			Unicast	0.00	0.00	0.00	0.00
			Multicast	0.01	0.01	0.01	0.00
		Even VLAN	Voice	0.10	0.04	0.34	0.28
			Unicast	0.07	0.07	0.34	0.24
			Multicast	0.08	0.06	0.35	0.24
	No shut	Odd VLAN	Voice	0.02	0.00	0.02	0.00
			Unicast	0.00	0.00	0.00	0.00
			Multicast	0.00	0.00	0.01	0.00
		Even VLAN	Voice	0.00	0.00	0.02	0.00
			Unicast	0.00	0.00	0.00	0.00
			Multicast	0.01	0.00	0.01	0.00
Fail both WAN links on SJ N-PE1	Shut	Odd VLAN	Voice	2.04	1.88	2.04	1.90
			Unicast	2.02	1.90	2.03	1.90
			Multicast	4.15	2.59	2.57	1.98
		Even VLAN	Voice	0.02	0.02	0.02	0.00
			Unicast	0.00	0.00	0.00	0.00
			Multicast	0.01	0.00	0.01	0.01
	No shut	Odd VLAN	Voice	0.12	0.12	0.00	0.00
			Unicast	0.13	0.13	0.02	0.01
			Multicast	2.12	0.58	0.56	0.08
		Even VLAN	Voice	0.00	0.00	0.00	0.00
			Unicast	0.00	0.00	0.00	0.00
			Multicast	0.01	0.01	0.01	0.01
Fail both WAN links on SJ N-PE2	Shut	Odd VLAN	Voice	0.00	0.00	0.00	0.00
			Unicast	0.00	0.00	0.00	0.00
			Multicast	0.00	0.00	0.00	0.00
		Even VLAN	Voice	2.68	2.68	2.52	2.52
			Unicast	2.69	2.69	2.52	2.52
			Multicast	2.71	2.69	2.52	2.52
	No shut	Odd VLAN	Voice	0.00	0.12	0.02	0.02
			Unicast	0.00	0.00	0.00	0.00
			Multicast	0.00	0.00	0.01	0.01
		Even VLAN	Voice	0.16	0.16	0.18	0.12
			Unicast	0.17	0.16	0.16	0.11
			Multicast	1.53	0.66	1.03	0.68
Clear CEF adjacencies on SJ N-PE1	Clear	Odd VLAN	Voice	0.00	0.00	0.02	0.00
			Unicast	0.00	0.00	0.00	0.00
			Multicast	0.00	0.00	0.01	0.00
		Even VLAN	Voice	0.02	0.00	0.02	0.00
			Unicast	0.00	0.00	0.00	0.00
			Multicast	0.00	0.00	0.01	0.00

Table 8-3   *Convergence Numbers for Link and Node Failures for the Isolated MST in N-PE: MST Option 1b Solution*

Failure Type	Action	VLAN	Traffic Type	Traffic Direction			
				LON → SJ		SJ → LON	
				Max	Min	Max	Min
Clear CEF adjacencies on SJ N-PE2	Clear	Odd VLAN	Voice	0.00	0.00	0.02	0.00
			Unicast	0.00	0.00	0.00	0.00
			Multicast	0.01	0.01	0.01	0.00
		Even VLAN	Voice	0.02	0.00	0.02	0.00
			Unicast	0.00	0.00	0.00	0.00
			Multicast	0.01	0.01	0.01	0.00
Clear entire routing table on SJ N-PE1	Clear	Odd VLAN	Voice	0.02	0.02	0.02	0.00
			Unicast	0.00	0.00	0.00	0.00
			Multicast	0.01	0.01	0.37	0.00
		Even VLAN	Voice	0.02	0.02	0.02	0.00
			Unicast	0.00	0.00	0.00	0.00
			Multicast	0.01	0.01	0.01	0.00
Clear entire routing table on SJ N-PE2	Clear	Odd VLAN	Voice	0.02	0.00	0.02	0.00
			Unicast	0.00	0.00	0.00	0.00
			Multicast	0.01	0.01	0.01	0.01
		Even VLAN	Voice	0.02	0.00	0.04	0.00
			Unicast	0.00	0.00	0.00	0.00
			Multicast	0.01	0.01	0.01	0.01
Clear dynamic MAC address table on SJ N-PE1	Clear	Odd VLAN	Voice	0.02	0.02	0.02	0.00
			Unicast	0.00	0.00	0.00	0.00
			Multicast	0.01	0.00	0.01	0.01
		Even VLAN	Voice	0.02	0.02	0.02	0.00
			Unicast	0.00	0.00	0.00	0.00
			Multicast	0.01	0.00	0.01	0.01
Clear dynamic MAC address table on SJ N-PE2	Clear	Odd VLAN	Voice	0.02	0.02	0.02	0.00
			Unicast	0.00	0.00	0.00	0.00
			Multicast	0.01	0.01	0.01	0.00
		Even VLAN	Voice	0.02	0.02	0.02	0.00
			Unicast	0.00	0.00	0.00	0.00
			Multicast	0.01	0.01	0.01	0.00

[1]Because of a timing issue between MST and RPVST interaction, high convergence times may be observed while reloading the spanning-tree root bridge in the MST region. Cisco defect number CSCsq90624 documents this issue.

Cluster Server Tests

Event logs are captured from the Event Viewer of the Microsoft cluster server. The logs are in the reverse order, showing the last event first. It is best to view the time stamps when analyzing these logs.

Table 8-4 shows event logs from the Event Viewer of the Microsoft cluster server.

Table 8-4   *Event Logs for Isolated MST in N-PE: MST Option 1b*

Test Case	Time in Seconds	Event Logs with Time Stamps from Microsoft Server			
Establish L2 connectivity	No convergence	4/13/2008	15:20:19 AM	CAMP3-SERVER2	The time service is now synchronizing the system time with the time source camp3-server1.camp3.com (ntp.d|10.10.5.102:123->1.1.1.1:123).
		4/13/2008	15:20:18 AM	CAMP3-SERVER2	The time provider NtpClient is currently receiving valid time data from camp3-server1.camp3.com (ntp.d|10.10.5.102:123->1.1.1.1:123).
		4/13/2008	15:10:29 AM	CAMP3-SERVER1	The node (re)established communication with cluster node 'CAMP3-SERVER2' on network 'public.'
		4/13/2008	15:10:29 AM	CAMP3-SERVER3	The node (re)established communication with cluster node 'CAMP3-SERVER2' on network 'public.'
Shut down both N-PEs	70	4/13/2008	12:17:35 PM	CAMP3-SERVER1	The cluster service brought the resource group "Cluster Group" online.
		4/13/2008	12:16:25 PM	CAMP3-SERVER3	The node lost communication with cluster node 'CAMP3-SERVER2' on network 'private 2(1).'
		4/13/2008	12:16:25 PM	CAMP3-SERVER3	The node lost communication with cluster node 'CAMP3-SERVER2' on network 'public.'
		4/13/2008	12:16:25 PM	CAMP3-SERVER3	The node lost communication with cluster node 'CAMP3-SERVER2' on network 'private(1).'
		4/13/2008	12:16:47 PM	CAMP3-SERVER1	The cluster service is attempting to bring online the resource group "Cluster Group."
		4/13/2008	12:16:47 PM	CAMP3-SERVER1	Cluster node CAMP3-SERVER2 was removed from the active server cluster membership. Cluster service may have been stopped on the node, the node may have failed, or the node may have lost communication with the other active server cluster nodes.
		4/13/2008	12:16:25 PM	CAMP3-SERVER1	The node lost communication with cluster node 'CAMP3-SERVER2' on network 'private 2(1).'
		4/13/2008	12:16:25 PM	CAMP3-SERVER1	The node lost communication with cluster node 'CAMP3-SERVER2' on network 'public.'
		4/13/2008	12:16:25 PM	CAMP3-SERVER1	The node lost communication with cluster node 'CAMP3-SERVER2' on network 'private(1).'

Table 8-4 *Event Logs for Isolated MST in N-PE: MST Option 1b*

Test Case	Time in Seconds	Event Logs with Time Stamps from Microsoft Server			
Power off access switch	70	4/13/2008	11:44:56 AM	CAMP3-SERVER1	The cluster service brought the resource group "Cluster Group" online.
		4/13/2008	11:43:46 AM	CAMP3-SERVER3	The node lost communication with cluster node 'CAMP3-SERVER2' on network 'public.'
		4/13/2008	11:43:46 AM	CAMP3-SERVER3	The node lost communication with cluster node 'CAMP3-SERVER2' on network 'private(1).'
		4/13/2008	11:43:46 AM	CAMP3-SERVER3	The node lost communication with cluster node 'CAMP3-SERVER2' on network 'private 2(1).'
		4/13/2008	11:44:09 AM	CAMP3-SERVER1	The cluster service is attempting to bring online the resource group "Cluster Group."
		4/13/2008	11:44:09 AM	CAMP3-SERVER1	Cluster node CAMP3-SERVER2 was removed from the active server cluster membership. Cluster service may have been stopped on the node, the node may have failed, or the node may have lost communication with the other active server cluster nodes.
		4/13/2008	11:43:46 AM	CAMP3-SERVER1	The node lost communication with cluster node 'CAMP3-SERVER2' on network 'public.'
		4/13/2008	11:43:46 AM	CAMP3-SERVER1	The node lost communication with cluster node 'CAMP3-SERVER2' on network 'private(1).'
		4/13/2008	11:43:46 AM	CAMP3-SERVER1	The node lost communication with cluster node 'CAMP3-SERVER2' on network 'private 2(1).'

Table 8-4   *Event Logs for Isolated MST in N-PE: MST Option 1b*

Test Case	Time in Seconds	Event Logs with Time Stamps from Microsoft Server			
		4/13/2008	11:36:07 AM	CAMP3-SERVER3	The cluster service brought the resource group "Cluster Group" online.
		4/13/2008	11:35:32 AM	CAMP3-SERVER3	The time provider NtpClient is currently receiving valid time data from camp3-server1.camp3.com (ntp.d|10.10.5.103:123->10.10.2.81:123).
		4/13/2008	11:35:09 AM	CAMP3-SERVER1	Cluster node CAMP3-SERVER2 was removed from the active server cluster membership. Cluster service may have been stopped on the node, the node may have failed, or the node may have lost communication with the other active server cluster nodes.
		4/13/2008	11:32:37 AM	CAMP3-SERVER1	The node lost communication with cluster node 'CAMP3-SERVER2' on network 'public.'
		4/13/2008	11:32:37 AM	CAMP3-SERVER1	The node lost communication with cluster node 'CAMP3-SERVER2' on network 'private(1).'
Shut down active node	240	4/13/2008	11:32:37 AM	CAMP3-SERVER1	The node lost communication with cluster node 'CAMP3-SERVER2' on network 'private 2(1).'
		4/13/2008	11:32:37 AM	CAMP3-SERVER3	The node lost communication with cluster node 'CAMP3-SERVER2' on network 'public.'
		4/13/2008	11:32:37 AM	CAMP3-SERVER3	The node lost communication with cluster node 'CAMP3-SERVER2' on network 'private(1).'
		4/13/2008	11:32:37 AM	CAMP3-SERVER3	The node lost communication with cluster node 'CAMP3-SERVER2' on network 'private 2(1).'
		4/13/2008	11:32:26 AM	CAMP3-SERVER3	The cluster service is attempting to bring online the resource group "Cluster Group."
		4/13/2008	11:31:57 AM	CAMP3-SERVER2	The process Explorer.EXE has initiated the shutdown of computer CAMP3-SERVER2 on behalf of user CAMP3\Administrator for the following reason: Other (Planned) Reason Code: 0x85000000 Shutdown Type: shutdown Comment: datas

Table 8-4   *Event Logs for Isolated MST in N-PE: MST Option 1b*

Test Case	Time in Seconds	Event Logs with Time Stamps from Microsoft Server			
Private VLAN N-PE reload	3	4/13/2008	3:28:18 PM	CAMP3-SERVER2	The node (re)established communication with cluster node 'CAMP3-SERVER3' on network 'private(1).'
		4/13/2008	3:28:16 PM	CAMP3-SERVER2	The node lost communication with cluster node 'CAMP3-SERVER3' on network 'private(1).'
		4/13/2008	3:28:13 PM	CAMP3-SERVER2	The node (re)established communication with cluster node 'CAMP3-SERVER1' on network 'private(1).'
		4/13/2008	3:28:10 PM	CAMP3-SERVER2	The node lost communication with cluster node 'CAMP3-SERVER1' on network 'private(1).'
Unplug active server	88	4/13/2008	11:55:33 AM	CAMP3-SERVER1	The cluster service brought the resource group "Cluster Group" online.
		4/13/2008	11:54:21 AM	CAMP3-SERVER3	The node lost communication with cluster node 'CAMP3-SERVER2' on network 'public.'
		4/13/2008	11:54:04 AM	CAMP3-SERVER3	The node lost communication with cluster node 'CAMP3-SERVER2' on network 'private(1).'
		4/13/2008	11:54:27 AM	CAMP3-SERVER1	The cluster service is attempting to bring online the resource group "Cluster Group."
		4/13/2008	11:54:27 AM	CAMP3-SERVER1	Cluster node CAMP3-SERVER2 was removed from the active server cluster membership. Cluster service may have been stopped on the node, the node may have failed, or the node may have lost communication with the other active server cluster nodes.
		4/13/2008	11:54:22 AM	CAMP3-SERVER1	The node lost communication with cluster node 'CAMP3-SERVER2' on network 'public.'
		4/13/2008	11:54:05 AM	CAMP3-SERVER1	The node lost communication with cluster node 'CAMP3-SERVER2' on network 'private(1).'

Summary

This chapter described "MST in pseudowire" and "isolated MST in N-PE" solutions along with configuration details for implementing these solutions when MPLS is enabled in the core network. For related information, see Chapter 11.

EEM-Based Deployment Models

In the Multiple Spanning Tree (MST)-based solutions described in Chapter 8, "MST-Based Deployment Models," redundant access to Virtual Private LAN Service (VPLS) nodes is achieved via the use of Spanning Tree Protocol (STP) to manage the state of links that connect aggregation switches toward the VPLS node, the Network-facing Provider Edge (N-PE).

This chapter describes a solution that provides a combination of high availability in terms of link and node redundancy, scalability based on 802.1Q in 802.1Q (QinQ) technology, and overlapping VLANs.

This chapter also describes various Embedded Event Manager (EEM)-based solutions that provide N-PE redundancy. It discusses deployment scenarios in which pseudowires (PW) on the primary and backup N-PEs are in up/down state or up/up state. The chapter also explains the naming conventions for physical and loopback interfaces used throughout these solutions.

N-PE Redundancy Using the Semaphore Protocol: Overview

In the absence of the Inter-Chassis Communication Protocol (ICCP), state synchronization of VPLS nodes is accomplished by a set of validated scripts executed in IOS by the EEM. (Chapter 12, "VPLS PE Redundancy Using Inter-Chassis Communication Protocol," discusses VPLS N-PE node redundancy using ICCP in detail.) Synchronization of the EEM scripts is achieved by using a semaphore concept.

Before considering the details of EEM-based solutions, it is important to understand the semaphore concept and how EEM is leveraged to achieve ICCP in the absence of the protocol available today.

Figure 9-1 illustrates the concept of node synchronization.

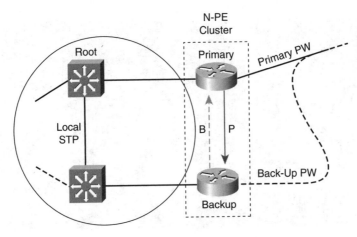

Figure 9-1   *Active/standby VPLS node synchronization.*

The EEM semaphore concept in N-PEs applies to the following VPLS implementations. These implementations are explained in detail in subsequent sections of this chapter:

■ **EEM option 2—VPLS:** An N-PE device participates in local STP. EEM manages VPLS PW redundancy, and the local STP controls the edge links.

■ **EEM option 3—H-VPLS:** An N-PE device participates in the local STP and uses QinQ to scale VPLS. A control-plane link on the N-PE participates in local STP. EEM manages the data-plane links and VPLS PW redundancy.

■ **EEM option 4a—Multidomain H-VPLS:** An N-PE device does not participate in the local STP and uses Hierarchical VPLS (H-VPLS). This option requires an EEM script on aggregation switches to adapt to topology changes and flush MAC addresses. EEM also controls the data-plane links and VPLS PW redundancy.

■ **EEM option 4b—Multidomain H-VPLS with Dedicated U-PE:** An N-PE does not participate in the local STP and uses H-VPLS. A U-PE switch is deployed between the N-PE and the customer edge (CE) device to flush MAC addresses. The insertion of a U-PE switch prevents disruption to the distribution device from configuration changes. EEM scripts are required on the intermediate U-PE switch instead of the aggregation switches as in option 4a.

■ **EEM option 5a—Multidomain H-VPLS with MEC:** An N-PE connects to the data center via Multichassis EtherChannel (MEC) toward the Virtual Switching System (VSS) or toward a Nexus 7000 virtual PortChannel (vPC) system. EEM manages VPLS PW redundancy, and Link Aggregation Control Protocol (LACP) controls the MEC at the edge.

■ **EEM option 5b—Multidomain H-VPLS with MEC and VLAN Load Balancing:** An N-PE connects to the data center via MEC toward the VSS or toward a Nexus 7000 vPC system. EEM manages VPLS PW redundancy, and load-balanced LACP controls the MEC at the edge. Aggregation switches require EEM scripts to flush MAC addresses.

■ **EEM option 5c—Multidomain H-VPLS with MEC and VLAN Load Balancing: PWs on Active and Standby VPLS Nodes in Up/Up State:** Options 5a and 5b are highly scalable solutions for multitenants. In option 5c, the PWs on the primary and backup N-PEs are in up-up state. This design enables faster convergence time because the backup PW is always up and ready for use.

Figure 9-1 uses a top-down arrow between the primary and backup N-PEs to illustrate the primary semaphore (P-semaphore). A bottom-up arrow indicates the backup semaphore (B-semaphore). A dotted line indicates that a semaphore drawing is down or in standby state. A solid line indicates that a semaphore is active or in up state.

In each of the EEM-based designs, semaphores play a major role in synchronizing the states between primary and backup N-PEs to achieve redundancy at the chassis level. They facilitate a dual handshake mechanism between both N-PEs in the data center, which prevents active/active state and thus avoids loops within the global topology.

Semaphore Definition

Originally, a semaphore was designed as a system to convey information based on moving items, such as two flags or lights. Various positions of these items convey information.

Figure 9-2 illustrates the semaphore concept.

Figure 9-2 *Semaphore using flags.*

Invented by Edsger Dijkstra, a semaphore in computer science is a common method for protecting shared resources. In multiprogramming environments such as UNIX systems, semaphores provide a technique for synchronizing activities in which multiple processes compete for the same set of resources. A process that requires the resource checks the semaphore to determine the resource's status. Depending on the value found, the process can use the resource or will find that it's already in use and must wait for some time before trying again, thus avoiding deadlocks.

This semaphore concept is used with EEM to provide node redundancy. One of the N-PEs, the VPLS edge device, is designated as *primary*, and the second N-PE is designated as *backup*. As long as the PW on the primary node is active, the backup PW remains in standby mode. If the primary node fails, the semaphore flags the failure, causing an EEM script to activate the backup PW.

Semaphore Theory Application

Semaphores are event indicators that actively monitor that states of the primary and backup VPLS nodes. Semaphores use the IP routing protocol to advertise the states of the primary and backup VPLS nodes to N-PEs. P- and B-semaphores are simply dedicated loopback interfaces on an N-PE. EEM tracks the reachability of the B-semaphore on the primary N-PE and the P-semaphore on the backup N-PE.

Primary and backup N-PEs are synchronized through advertisement of these loopback interfaces by the core Interior Gateway Protocol (IGP). The goal is to ensure that the backup node activates upon failure of the primary N-PE while preventing any active/active state that would lead to a bridging loop.

As long as the P-semaphore is active and is reachable by the backup node, the backup or the standby PW will be set in shut state. Therefore, there is one PW active at any given time, and Layer 2 loops cannot exist even at the global topology.

N-PE Redundancy Using Semaphore Protocol: Details

The semaphore concept is used with EEM to achieve state synchronization between the primary and the standby VPLS nodes.

Figure 9-3 shows the finite state machine of the redundancy protocol using EEM semaphore.

The following sections describe the operational model of the EEM semaphore and its finite state machine in normal and in failure conditions.

VPLS PWs in Normal Mode

Primary N-PE routers in each data center are fully meshed. They also have PWs to the backup nodes in other data centers. Conversely, the backup N-PEs only have PWs to the primary N-PEs. There are no PWs configured between the backup N-PEs. This connectivity arrangement between primary and backup N-PE nodes provides a loop-free global topology.

Finite State Machine

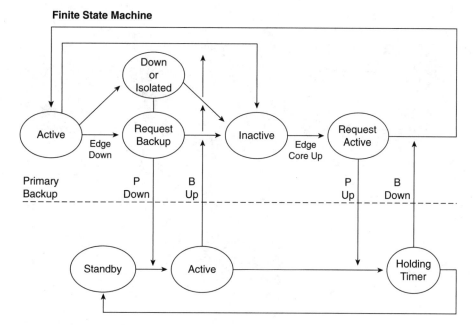

Figure 9-3 *EEM semaphore protocol finite state machine.*

Figure 9-4 shows the topology of all PWs connecting primary and backup nodes between multiple sites.

When the P-semaphore on the primary node is active, the backup node is forced to be in standby mode. This status is acknowledged via B-semaphore in shut state. Therefore, the B-semaphore in down state allows the primary node to be active.

Figure 9-5 shows the state of semaphores and PW topology in normal mode.

Normal mode can be analyzed from the perspective of each node as follows:

- **From the primary N-PE perspective:** In normal mode, the PW from the primary N-PE in one data center to the primary N-PE in other data center is active.

  In normal mode, the PW from the primary N-PE to the backup N-PE is in ready mode (not active) waiting for the backup N-PE to take action. Per RFC 3985, a PW must be activated on both sides to become active. In normal state, the backup PW is always in no shut on the primary N-PE side; however, on the backup N-PE, the same PW is in admin shut state.

- **From the backup N-PE perspective:** In normal mode, the backup PW to the remote end's primary N-PE is in admin shut state.

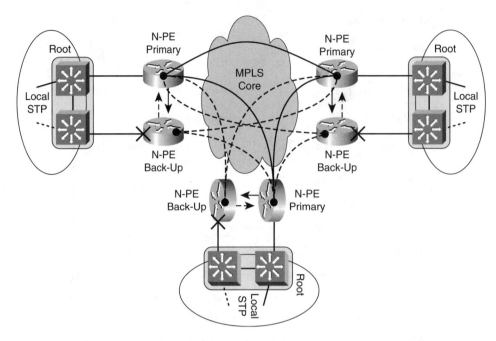

Figure 9-4   *Partially meshed PW topology.*

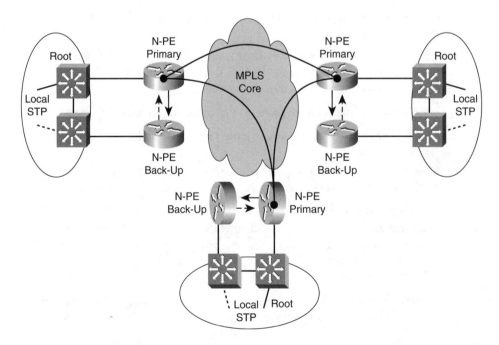

Figure 9-5   *EEM semaphore protocol in normal mode.*

PWs on the backup N-PEs are cross-connected (xconnected) to only the primary virtual forwarding instance (VFI) of remote sites into the same VFI that owns the primary PW, thus enabling split-horizon protection for loop avoidance.

Primary N-PE Failure

If a primary node fails, its semaphore goes down. The backup node detects this situation. A primary node failure is detected by the backup node. When a primary node fails, its semaphore will go down, too, and this will be detected by the backup node.

A P-semaphore may go down due to several reasons, including the following:

- The N-PE node is down.

- The N-PE node is isolated from the VPLS core.

- The loopback interface has been shut down by the local EEM script, which can occur for a number of reasons, including the following:

    - The active N-PE node cannot reach the core, so the local EEM script shut down the P-semaphore.

    - The primary PW goes down because the loopback IP address on the remote primary N-PE where the PW terminates is unreachable.

- The backup node raises its B-semaphore to force the primary N-PE to become inactive.

- The backup node is active.

- The backup node cannot reach the P-semaphore.

Figure 9-6 shows a backup N-PE providing connectivity to remote data centers after a primary node failure.

EEM must also take other actions, such as flush MAC addresses, when the backup node becomes active.

Primary N-PE Recovers After the Failure

After a failure, the primary node will complete initialization and become ready. The EEM semaphore protocol is capable of preemption, where the backup node will give away its active role and go back in backup mode once the primary node becomes active.

The following sequence of events occurs when primary node initializes after a failure:

1. The primary N-PE goes through the initialization process and becomes ready.

2. As soon as the node has completely initialized, the primary N-PE detects that the B-semaphore is up and therefore stays in standby mode.

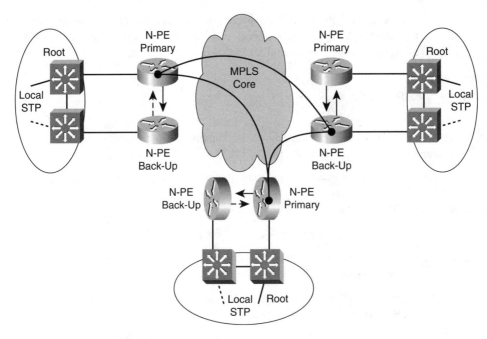

Figure 9-6   *Active PW topology after primary node failure.*

3.   To regain active state, the primary N-PE raises the P-semaphore. The core IGP announces this route to the backup node.

4.   After the backup node learns the P-semaphore route, it starts a configurable delay timer to ensure the stability of the primary node.

5.   When the delay timer expires

    a.   The backup node admin shuts the PW.

    b.   The backup node shuts down B-semaphore to allow the primary node to become active.

With this series of events, the primary and backup N-PEs return to the normal mode of operation. The dual handshake mechanism in the EEM semaphore protocol is thoughtfully designed such that one node is always in the backup mode. At any given time, both the N-PEs will not be in active/active state, thus avoiding a loop.

Implementing a Semaphore

As discussed in the preceding section, a semaphore is a loopback IP address that is advertised through the core IGP that allows a node to track its N-PE peer status and take action on state change using EEM scripting.

Figure 9-7 shows semaphore configuration in IOS.

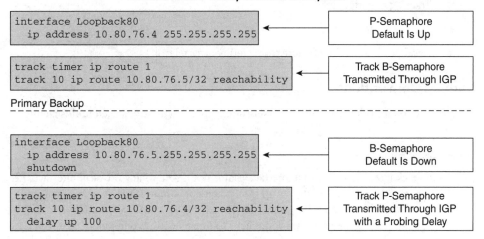

N-PE – Primary and Backup Nodes
Set and Track P-semaphore & B-Semaphore

```interface Loopback80 ip address 10.80.76.4 255.255.255.255```	P-Semaphore Default Is Up
```track timer ip route 1 track 10 ip route 10.80.76.5/32 reachability```	Track B-Semaphore Transmitted Through IGP

Primary Backup

``interface Loopback80
  ip address 10.80.76.5.255.255.255.255
  shutdown```
	B-Semaphore
	Default Is Down

```track timer ip route 1 track 10 ip route 10.80.76.4/32 reachability delay up 100```	Track P-Semaphore Transmitted Through IGP with a Probing Delay

Figure 9-7 *Semaphore definition.*

EEM / Semaphore Scripts

VPLS redundancy relies on EEM scripts managing three loopback interfaces. In this chapter, the tracking mechanisms are defined as follows:

- **LDP neighbor always active:** Track loopback 70

- **Semaphore to check if other N-PE is active:** Track loopback 80

- **PW ID used to shut/no shut VPLS PWs:** Track loopback 90

The redundant N-PEs in the data centers are synchronized using semaphoring, and EEM takes action when the semaphore state changes.

The following are the four main actions that have to be executed by the EEM scripts:

- Manage local semaphore

- Manage PW state

- Trigger topology-change notification (TCN) within the data center

- Inform management system of state change (syslog / trap / ...)

In all the EEM-based options, the only major difference is the way how N-PE triggers TCN. In addition to these semaphore scripts, additional scripts may also have to be added for the following:

- Track aggregation links

- Track core links

- Reset N-PE node state to active or standby after reboot

Naming Conventions

This section introduces the IP addressing and naming conventions used in this chapter.

Loopback Definitions

A loopback interface is a virtual interface that is not linked to any physical interface. In other words, the interface is always up state when not administratively shut down, and therefore is used for establishing neighbor relationships by protocol for stability. The list that follows defines the necessary loopbacks to implement the semaphore protocol:

- **Loopback 0—OSPF protocol router ID:** OSPF uses the largest IP address configured on the interfaces as its router ID. If the interface associated with this IP address is ever unavailable, or if the address is removed, the OSPF process must recalculate a new router ID and flood all its routing information out its interfaces. If a loopback interface is configured with an IP address, OSPF defaults to using this IP address as its router ID, even if other interfaces have larger IP addresses. Because loopback interfaces never go down, greater stability throughout the OSPF network is achieved.

- **Loopback 70—LDP protocol source:** Used as common source IP address for targeted-LDP sessions of all PWs.

A common practice for load repartition is to use one PW peer ID for all even VLANs and a second peer ID for all odd VLANs, as described in the list that follows, via loopback 90 and loopback 91 interfaces:

- **Loopback 90 and loopback 91:** Targeted-LDP protocol peer IDs. Lo90 is dedicated to the PW that carries even VLANs. Lo91 is dedicated to the PW that carries odd VLANs.

  Used as IP address for PWs.

  EEM scripts will alternatively shut or activate these loopbacks to enable or disable PWs.

  All VFIs belonging to the same backup group (that is, that use the same semaphore) use the same PW peer ID.

  In normal mode, even and odd VLANs are split between the primary and backup N-PE. Therefore, the status of these loopback interfaces is normally the opposite, except during failure mode.

- **Loopback 80:** EEM semaphore protocol for even VLANs

- **Loopback 81:** EEM semaphore protocol for odd VLANs

Each backup domain is associated with its own semaphore. The IP addresses of loopback 80 and loopback 81 interfaces are advertised to the VPLS peers by the core IGP. Only one semaphore is required when protecting a node in a situation where the links to aggregation are already protected by either local STP or via Multichassis EtherChannel (VSS or Nexus vPC). In situations where the links to aggregation are also to be protected by semaphoring concept, one pair (semaphore / PW peer ID) must be created per backup domain.

The backup domain is a set of ingress N-PE links that are associated with the same semaphore. This configuration allows the use of single N-PE for multiple independent bridging domains, each of which has its own backup mechanism. For example, in EEM semaphore designs, two domains have been created, one for odd VLANs and the second for even VLANs. When the primary link for odd VLANs fails, only odd VLANs will be backed up.

Each N-PE must advertise its availability to its backup peer:

- Loopback 80 on the primary N-PE node is called P-semaphore for all the even VLANs.

- Loopback 80 on the backup N-PE node is called B-semaphore for all the even VLANs.

- Loopback 81 on the primary N-PE node is called P-semaphore for all the odd VLANs.

- Loopback 81 on the backup N-PE node is called B-semaphore for all the odd VLANs.

Both of these loopback interfaces are advertised via the core IGP.

EEM scripts ensure that both P-semaphore and B-semaphore are in the opposite administrative state.

Node Definitions

The following list outlines the link- and node-naming conventions used in this chapter:

- **N-PE is a VPLS or H-VPLS device:**

    - **I-link:** N-PE edge link configured as dot1q

    - **Q-link:** N-PE edge link configured as QinQ

    - **B-link:** Inter-N-PE link

    - **E-link:** (E-semaphore) Signaling link between N-PE and aggregation to force EEM synchronization

- **U-PE is an optional physical device inserted between the N-PE and aggregation switch:**

    - **U-link:** U-PE edge link

- **EB-link:** Signaling link between N-PE and U-PE to force EEM synchronization

- **UB-link:** Inter-U-PE link

VPLS with N-PE Redundancy Using EEM Semaphore: EEM Option 2

This solution provides the simplest implementation of VPLS node redundancy. Organizations can deploy this solution today and later migrate to scalable solutions that are described in this chapter if they need to extend a large number of VLANs across geographically dispersed data centers.

This solution is extremely flexible and can be adapted to any data center topology while providing scalability. Redeployment of STP root and backup root bridges is not required, and this solution is fully compatible with the use of VSS technology in the distribution layer.

The positioning of this solution is similar to the "MST in N-PE" solution, and is intended for enterprises that require extension of approximately 30 VLANs across remote locations. In this solution, instead of MST, the EEM semaphore protocol is used to synchronize N-PEs. Also, the N-PEs must participate in local STP. Therefore, VLAN overlapping in a multitenant environment is not possible.

Figure 9-8 shows node and protocol positioning for this solution.

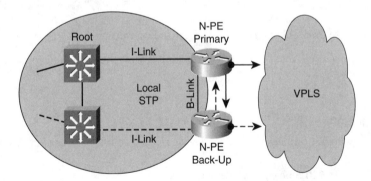

Figure 9-8   *VPLS with N-PE redundancy using EEM semaphore.*

The local STP domain is decoupled from the VPLS domain, and both STP and VPLS use independent mechanisms for redundancy. Aggregation switches and I-links are protected using local STP, and N-PEs and core links are protected using EEM semaphore.

Unlike the MST-based solution, the global loop avoidance does not depend on the local STP. Instead, the EEM semaphore manages active/standby access to the VPLS domain, thus avoiding a loop. Because each cross-connected VLAN maps to a VFI, per-LAN load repartition all the way from the aggregation to the core links becomes easy.

Control Plane

The key point that delivers scalability and availability of this solution is the independence of domains. To accomplish this, there are three independent control planes:

- **Spanning tree:** Interfaces connecting N-PEs to aggregation switches (I-links) participate in local STP, which is already deployed in the data center.

  Spanning-tree bridge protocol data units (BPDUs) are not transmitted over VPLS.

  Inter-N-PE link (B-link) is used to generate topology changes toward local STP when N-PE active/standby state changes.

- **VPLS:** P- and B-semaphores allow active/standby state between primary and backup N-PE nodes.

  For load-balancing purposes, two semaphore pairs are configured, one for active/standby and one for standby/active.

- **MPLS core:** LDP and IGP protocols are enabled in the core.

Data Plane

Every VLAN within the data center that needs to be extended to remote locations through VPLS is associated with a unique VFI. This VFI connects to other data center VFIs with partially meshed PWs. In this way, the VFI in a primary node (primary VFI) connects all other data centers' primary and backup VFIs. But the VFI of a backup node (backup VFI) is connected *only* to all other data center primary VFIs.

All VLANs are load balanced on the I-links, and the choice of balancing is per odd and even VLANs. Associated VFIs are load balanced on both N-PEs, and PW load balancing is achieved on the core links. In the case of equal-cost multipath into the core, PWs are load balanced based on destination N-PE / VFI number, which is nothing but the destination VLAN.

Theory of Operation

This section analyses EEM option 2 behavior in normal and failure states.

Normal Mode

In normal mode, the I-link1 between the N-PE1 and Agg-1 forwards all odd VLANs, and the I-link2 between N-PE2 and Agg-2 forwards all the even VLANs. At the same time, I-link1 blocks all even VLANs, and I-link2 blocks all the odd VLANs.

All the edge VLANs to be cross-connected are created on the N-PEs and allowed on the B-link. During normal operation, there is no traffic on the B-link.

For every edge VLAN to be cross-connected, an SVI (interface VLAN) and a VFI is created on the N-PE. The VFI on the active N-PE is connected using the active PW to the VFI at other remote sites. The VFI on the standby N-PE is not connected.

Consider the following analysis of normal mode from the perspective of both primary and backup nodes:

- **From primary N-PE perspective:** In normal mode, the PW from the primary N-PE in one data center to the primary N-PE in the other data center is active.

    The PW from the primary N-PE to the backup N-PE in the other data center is in ready mode, waiting for the backup N-PE to take action. A backup action is always taken by a backup node, not by a primary node.

- **From backup N-PE perspective:** In normal mode, the backup PW is in admin shut state.

    The PW is ready, but not active, to be connected to the primary node on the remote side.

    There is no PW from the backup node toward another backup node, to prevent a transient loop.

Figure 9-9 shows active links and PW when the EEM option 2 solution is in normal mode.

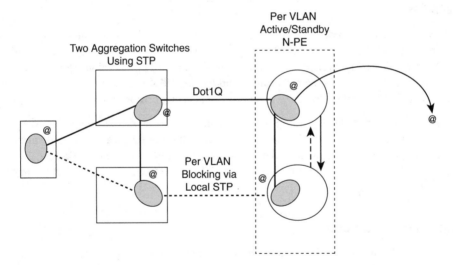

Figure 9-9   *EEM option 2: Normal mode.*

Failure Conditions

Several failure conditions might occur, including the following:

- Aggregation switch failure

- I-link failure

- Primary N-PE failure

- Backup N-PE failure

- B-link failure

- Main core link (MPLS) failure

- All core links failure on primary N-PE (node isolation)

- All core links failure on backup N-PE

The following are protocols for recovery mechanisms that react to the preceding failures:

- Edge spanning tree for aggregation switch, I-link, or B-link failures

- EEM semaphores for N-PE node failure or node isolation

- LDP for core link failure without isolation

Primary N-PE Node Failure

When the primary N-PE fails or gets isolated from the core, its P-semaphore is no longer advertised by the core IGP.

Figure 9-10 shows active links and the PW with EEM option 2 solution, when in node failure recovery.

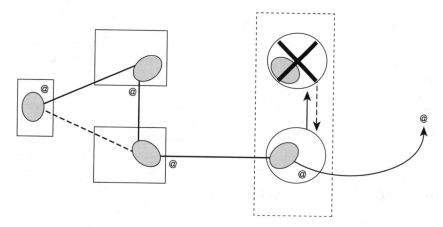

Figure 9-10   *EEM option 2: Primary N-PE node failure.*

As soon as the backup N-PE node detects that the primary node is down, it enables the backup PWs, which are connected to the primary N-PE nodes at other remote sites.

In addition, to prevent an active/active state, the backup N-PE raises B-semaphore, thus preventing primary N-PE from becoming active.

Figure 9-11 shows a configuration example of an EEM script. This script accomplishes action when the EEM semaphore protocol detects that the primary node is down.

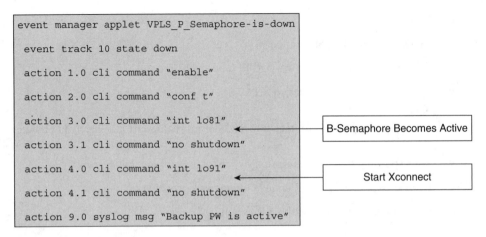

Figure 9-11 *EEM semaphore protocol script for primary down.*

When the primary PW goes down because of primary node failure, all the MAC address-es associated with this PW get flushed from the MAC address learning table at the remote ends. Also, the local STP transitions the backup I-link from blocking state to for-warding state, generating a topology-change notification (TCN) toward aggregation switches to facilitate learning of the new Layer 2 path.

Primary N-PE Node Recovers After the Failure

When the primary node initializes and becomes ready, it receives a B-semaphore route and therefore stays in standby mode. The primary N-PE raises the P-semaphore, which is announced by the core IGP. After the backup node learns the P-semaphore route, it starts a delay timer (configured to 100 sec). The traffic continues to forward through the backup PWs until this delay timer expires. However, the local STP converges toward the primary N-PE. At this time, traffic uses the B-link as an interim path. When the delay timer expires, the backup node disables the backup PW by shutting down the B-semaphore loopback inter-face. This action allows the primary node to become active and thus return to normal state.

N-PE Routers: Hardware and Software

Table 9-1 compares the hardware and software that can be used for N-PE nodes. Cisco 7600 routers were used as N-PEs for all the MST- and EEM-based solutions that this book describes.

Implementing VPLS with N-PE Redundancy Using EEM Semaphore Design

The EEM option 2 solution requires a square topology between N-PEs and aggregation switches. The PWs on N-PE1 and N-PE2 are in active or standby state and are managed by EEM scripts. Blocking of VLANs (loop avoidance) is done at the aggregation layer by local STP.

Figure 9-12 provides a configuration overview of the various links and the nodes for one data center. Other data centers are similarly configured.

Table 9-1   *Hardware and Software for N-PE Nodes*

Cisco 7600 Router	Cisco Catalyst 6500
Interfaces on SIP or ES modules are required for connectivity toward the VPLS core.	Interfaces on SIP modules are required for connectivity toward the VPLS core.
Interfaces on any fiber-based 67xx LAN or ES modules can be used for connectivity toward the edge (that is, connectivity to aggregation switches).	Interfaces on any fiber-based 67xx LAN modules can be used for connectivity toward the edge (that is, connectivity to aggregation switches).
Interface on any fiber-based 67xx LAN module.	Interface on any fiber based 67xx LAN module.
Cisco IOS 12.2(33)SRC1.	Cisco IOS 12.2(33)SXI.

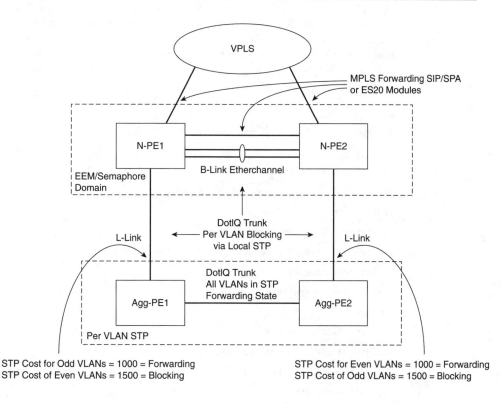

Figure 9-12   *Implementing EEM option 2: Configuration overview.*

The following list provides snippets of configuration from N-PE and aggregation devices and output from various **show** commands to show the configuration of the EEM option 2 solution:

Step 1.   STP root and backup root assignment remains unchanged. This solution leverages the STP mode and the root bridge placement configured in the data center.

On Agg-1	On Agg-2
`lon-agg-1#`	`lon-agg-2#`
`!`	`!`
`spanning-tree mode rapid-pvst`	`spanning-tree mode rapid-pvst`
`spanning-tree vlan 1,3,5,7,9,11,13,15,17...`	`spanning-tree vlan 2,4,6,8,10,12,14.....`
`priority 8192`	`priority 8192`
`spanning-tree vlan 2,4,6,8,10,12,14, 16....`	`spanning-tree vlan 1,3,5,7,9,11,13,15....`
`priority 16384`	`priority 16384`

Step 2.   Configure I-links (links between N-PEs and aggregation switches) as dot1q trunks to allow all VLANs to be extended across data centers. Placement of the local STP root bridge will simply determine which I-link is forwarding and which one is blocking VLANs. In the following case, all odd VLANs that are to be extended across the data centers are forwarded via N-PE1, and the even VLANs are forwarded via N-PE2:

```
! On Agg-1:
lon-agg-1#  show running-config interface gig 2/19
!
interface GigabitEthernet2/19
 description L2 connection to lon-n-pe1
 switchport
 switchport trunk encapsulation dot1q
 switchport trunk allowed vlan 2-61,201-260
 switchport mode trunk
 switchport nonegotiate
 mtu 9216
 logging event link-status
 logging event spanning-tree status
 spanning-tree link-type point-to-point
 spanning-tree guard root
 spanning-tree vlan 1,3,5,7,9,11,13,15,17,19,21,23,25,27,29,.....cost 1000
 spanning-tree vlan
```

```
 2,4,6,8,10,12,14,16,18,20,22,24,26,28,30,.....cost 1500
end
! On N-PE1:
interface GigabitEthernet2/1
 description L2 to Agg-1
 switchport
 switchport trunk encapsulation dot1q
 switchport trunk allowed vlan 2-61,201-260
 switchport mode trunk
 switchport nonegotiate
 mtu 9216
 logging event link-status
 logging event spanning-tree status
 storm-control broadcast level 5.00
 storm-control multicast level 5.00
 spanning-tree link-type point-to-point
 spanning-tree vlan 1,3,5,7,9,11,13,15,17,19,21,23,25,27,29,.....cost 1000
 spanning-tree vlan
2,4,6,8,10,12,14,16,18,20,22,24,26,28,30,.....cost 1500
! On Agg-2:
lon-agg-2#  show running-config interface gig 2/19
 !
interface GigabitEthernet2/18
 description L2 connection to lon-n-pe2
 switchport
 switchport trunk encapsulation dot1q
 switchport trunk allowed vlan 1-61,201-260
 switchport mode trunk
 switchport nonegotiate
 mtu 9216
 logging event link-status
 logging event spanning-tree status
 spanning-tree link-type point-to-point
 spanning-tree vlan 2,4,6,8,10,12,14,16,18,20,22,24,26,28,30,......
  cost 1000
 spanning-tree vlan 1,3,5,7,9,11,13,15,17,19,21,23,25,27,29,.......
  cost 1500
```

```
                 end
                 ! On N-PE2:
                 interface GigabitEthernet2/2
                  description L2 to Agg-2
                  switchport
                  switchport trunk encapsulation dot1q
                  switchport trunk allowed vlan 2-61,201-260
                  switchport mode trunk
                  switchport nonegotiate
                  mtu 9216
                  logging event link-status
                  logging event spanning-tree status
                  storm-control broadcast level 5.00
                  storm-control multicast level 5.00
                  spanning-tree link-type point-to-point
                  spanning-tree vlan 1,3,5,7,9,11,13,15,17,19,21,23,25,27,29,.....cost
                    1500
                  spanning-tree vlan
                  2,4,6,8,10,12,14,16,18,20,22,24,26,28,30,.....cost 1000
```

Step 3.   Display the status of spanning tree for VLAN 7 on both the N-PEs.

On N-PE1	On N-PE2
lon-n-pe1# **show spanning-tree vlan 7**	lon-n-pe2# **show spanning-tree vlan 7**

```
VLAN0007                              VLAN0007
  Spanning tree enabled protocol rstp   Spanning tree enabled protocol rstp
  Root ID    Priority    8192          Root ID    Priority    8192
             Address     001c.b126.d007           Address     001c.b126.d007
             Cost        1000                     Cost        1003
             Port        257                      Port        3329 (Port-
(GigabitEthernet2/1)                  channel1)
             Hello Time   2 sec   Max Age          Hello Time   2 sec   Max Age
20 sec   Forward Delay 15 sec         20 sec   Forward Delay 15 sec


  Bridge ID  Priority    61447  (priority   Bridge ID  Priority    61447  (priority
61440 sys-id-ext 7)                   61440 sys-id-ext 7)
             Address     001d.7198.9500           Address     001d.7198.8fc0
             Hello Time   2 sec   Max Age          Hello Time   2 sec   Max Age
#
```

On N-PE1			On N-PE2		
20 sec Forward Delay 15 sec			20 sec Forward Delay 15 sec		
Aging Time 300			Aging Time 300		
Interface	Role Sts Cost		Interface	Role Sts Cost	
Prio.Nbr Type			Prio.Nbr Type		
—————————. —— —. ————. — —— ———————————————			—————————. —— —. ————. — ——— ——————————————		
Gi2/1	Root FWD 1000		Gi2/2	Altn BLK 1500	
128.257 P2p			128.258 P2p		
Po1	Desg FWD 3		Po1	Root FWD 3	
128.3329 P2p			128.3329 P2p		
lon-n-pe1#			lon-n-pe2#		

Step 4. On the N-PEs, create VLANs that are to be extended across data centers and configure the B-links (inter-N-PE links) as dot1q trunks. Even though an EtherChannel is configured in this example, it is not a requirement:

```
! On N-PE1:
vlan 2-61,201-260
!
interface Port-channel1
 switchport
 switchport trunk encapsulation dot1q
 switchport mode trunk
 mtu 9216
 logging event bundle-status
 logging event link-status
 logging event spanning-tree status

!
interface GigabitEthernet2/4
 description LAN etherchannel interface to lon-n-pe2
 switchport
 switchport trunk encapsulation dot1q
 switchport mode trunk
 mtu 9216
 logging event link-status
```

```
  logging event spanning-tree status
  channel-group 1 mode on
 !
 interface GigabitEthernet2/5
  description LAN etherchannel interface to lon-n-pe2
  switchport
  switchport trunk encapsulation dot1q
  switchport mode trunk
  mtu 9216
  logging event link-status
  logging event spanning-tree status
  channel-group 1 mode on
 ! On N-PE2:
 vlan 2-61,201-260
 !
 interface Port-channel1
  switchport
  switchport trunk encapsulation dot1q
  switchport mode trunk
  mtu 9216
  logging event bundle-status
  logging event link-status
  logging event spanning-tree status
 !
 interface GigabitEthernet2/4
  description LAN etherchannel interface to lon-n-pe1
  switchport
  switchport trunk encapsulation dot1q
  switchport mode trunk
  mtu 9216
  logging event link-status
  logging event spanning-tree status
  channel-group 1 mode on
 !
 interface GigabitEthernet2/5
  description LAN etherchannel interface to lon-n-pe1
  switchport
```

```
      switchport trunk encapsulation dot1q
      switchport mode trunk
      mtu 9216
      logging event link-status
      logging event spanning-tree status
      channel-group 1 mode on
```

Step 5.   Configure OSPF on all N-PE routers:

```
! On N-PE1:
router ospf 1
 ...
  timers throttle spf 100 100 5000
  timers throttle lsa 100 100 5000
  timers lsa arrival 80
 ...
  bfd all-interfaces
  mpls ldp sync
 !

lon-n-pe1# show ip ospf 1
 Routing Process "ospf 1" with ID 11.11.11.11
 Start time: 00:00:51.832, Time elapsed: 05:05:54.500
 Supports only single TOS(TOS0) routes
 Supports opaque LSA
 Supports Link-local Signaling (LLS)
 Supports area transit capability
 Event-log enabled, Maximum number of events: 1000, Mode: cyclic
 Router is not originating router-LSAs with maximum metric
 Initial SPF schedule delay 100 msecs
 Minimum hold time between two consecutive SPFs 100 msecs
 Maximum wait time between two consecutive SPFs 5000 msecs
 Incremental-SPF disabled
 Initial LSA throttle delay 100 msecs
 Minimum hold time for LSA throttle 100 msecs
 Maximum wait time for LSA throttle 5000 msecs
 Minimum LSA arrival 80 msecs
 LSA group pacing timer 240 secs
```

```
Interface flood pacing timer 33 msecs

Retransmission pacing timer 66 msecs

Number of external LSA 0. Checksum Sum 0x000000

Number of opaque AS LSA 0. Checksum Sum 0x000000

Number of DCbitless external and opaque AS LSA 0

Number of DoNotAge external and opaque AS LSA 0

Number of areas in this router is 1. 1 normal 0 stub 0 nssa

Number of areas transit capable is 0

External flood list length 0

IETF NSF helper support enabled

Cisco NSF helper support enabled

BFD is enabled

Reference bandwidth unit is 10000 mbps

    Area BACKBONE(0)

        Number of interfaces in this area is 4

        Area has message digest authentication

        SPF algorithm last executed 00:25:43.076 ago

        SPF algorithm executed 174 times

        Area ranges are

        Number of LSA 84. Checksum Sum 0x2A96B9

        Number of opaque link LSA 0. Checksum Sum 0x000000

        Number of DCbitless LSA 0

        Number of indication LSA 0

        Number of DoNotAge LSA 0

        Flood list length 0


lon-n-pe1#  show ip ospf neighbor


Neighbor ID      Pri    State           Dead Time    Address
Interface
12.12.12.12        0    FULL/   -       00:00:33     192.168.13.6
GigabitEthernet4/0/0
116.5.200.77       0    FULL/   -       00:00:35     192.168.11.7
GigabitEthernet4/0/19
13.13.13.13        0    FULL/   -       00:00:33     10.11.21.3
GigabitEthernet2/6
```

```
lon-n-pe1# show cdp neighbors

Capability Codes: R - Router, T - Trans Bridge, B - Source Route Bridge

                  S - Switch, H - Host, I - IGMP, r - Repeater,

                  P - Phone


Device ID         Local Intrfce  Holdtme   Capability  Platform
                                                       Port ID

campus3-223sw8    Gig 1/2        131            S I     WS-C2950T
                                                       Fas 0/2

lon-n-pe2         Gig 4/0/0      149          R S I     CISCO7604 Gig
                                                       4/0/0

lon-n-pe2         Gig 2/5        167          R S I     CISCO7604 Gig
                                                       2/5

lon-n-pe2         Gig 2/4        167          R S I     CISCO7604
                                                       Gig 2/4

lon-agg-1         Gig 2/1        134          R S I     WS-C6509- Gig
                                                       2/19

lon-core1         Gig 2/6        158          R S I     WS-C6506- Gig
                                                       3/21

mpls-p1           Gig 4/0/19     159          R S I     WS-C6506- Gig
                                                       2/22

lon-n-pe1#
```

Step 6. Configure MPLS, VFI, and SVI on N-PE1 and N-PE2. The output from the **show mpls l2transport vc** command displays the MPLS virtual circuit transport information.

Create one VFI per VLAN, which is xconnected to the primary and backup nodes in other data centers. Taking VLAN 7 as an example, under normal mode, traffic from VLAN 7 forwards via N-PE1 because N-PE1 is the primary node for VLAN 7. You might note that VFI for VLAN 7 on N-PE1 is xconnected using PW toward the primary and backup N-PEs of all other data centers. On N-PE2, which is the backup node for VLAN 7, VFI for VLAN 7 xconnects only to all the primary nodes in other data centers:

```
! On N-PE1:

lon-n-pe1#

...

!

mpls ldp neighbor 10.76.70.12 targeted ldp

mpls ldp neighbor 10.76.70.21 targeted ldp
```

```
mpls ldp neighbor 10.76.70.22 targeted ldp

mpls ldp neighbor 10.76.70.31 targeted ldp

mpls ldp neighbor 10.76.70.32 targeted ldp

mpls ldp tcp pak-priority

mpls ldp session protection

no mpls ldp advertise-labels

mpls ldp advertise-labels for 76

mpls label protocol ldp

xconnect logging pseudowire status

!

access-list 76 permit 10.76.0.0 0.0.255.255

!

lon-n-pe1#  show bfd neighbors


OurAddr        NeighAddr      LD/RD   RH/RS   Holddown(mult)   State   Int

192.168.13.5   192.168.13.6   1/1     Up           0    (3 )    Up  Gi4/0/0

192.168.11.5   192.168.11.7   9/1     Up           0    (3 )    Up  Gi4/0/19

lon-n-pe1#


! VFI for VLAN 7

l2 vfi VFI-7 manual

 vpn id 7

 neighbor 10.76.91.21 encapsulation mpls

 neighbor 10.76.91.32 encapsulation mpls

 neighbor 10.76.91.31 encapsulation mpls

 neighbor 10.76.91.22 encapsulation mpls

!

!

interface Vlan7

 mtu 9216

 no ip address

 xconnect vfi VFI-7

end
```

```
lon-n-pe1#  show mpls l2transport vc 7


Local intf     Local circuit          Dest address    VC ID
Status
——————·  ——————————————  ———————·  ————
————

VFI VFI-7      VFI                    10.76.91.21     7  UP
VFI VFI-7      VFI                    10.76.91.22     7  DOWN
VFI VFI-7      VFI                    10.76.91.31     7  UP
VFI VFI-7      VFI                    10.76.91.32     7  DOWN
lon-n-pe1#
! On N-PE2:
l2 vfi VFI-7 manual
 vpn id 7
 neighbor 10.76.91.31 encapsulation mpls
 neighbor 10.76.91.21 encapsulation mpls
!
interface Vlan7
 mtu 9216
 no ip address
xconnect vfi VFI-7


lon-n-pe2#  show mpls l2transport vc 7


Local intf     Local circuit          Dest address    VC ID
Status
——————·  ——————————————  ———————·  ————
————

VFI VFI-7      VFI                    10.76.91.21     7  DOWN
VFI VFI-7      VFI                    10.76.91.31     7  DOWN
lon-n-pe2#
```

Step 7.   Configure object tracking using EEM. Use the **show running-config | begin event manager** command to display EEM applets that are configured.

N-PE1 is the primary node for odd VLANs. N-PE2 is the primary node for even VLANs. In addition, each N-PE1 is the backup node for even VLANs, and N-PE2 is the backup node for odd VLANs. Therefore, the configurations for each are similar, and the configuration for one can be derived from the configuration of the other:

```
! On N-PE1:
lon-n-pe1#
!
track timer ip route 1
!
track 10 ip route 10.76.80.12 255.255.255.255 reachability
 delay up 100
!
track 11 ip route 10.76.81.12 255.255.255.255 reachability
!
track 110 interface GigabitEthernet4/0/19 line-protocol
 delay down 5 up 60
!
lon-n-pe1# show running-config | begin event manager
event manager applet VPLS_EVEN-VLAN_P_semaphore-is-down
 event track 10 state down
 action 1.0 cli command "enable"
 action 2.0 cli command "conf t"
 action 3.0 cli command "int lo80"
 action 3.1 cli command "no shut"
 action 4.0 cli command "int lo90"
 action 4.1 cli command "no shut"
 action 9.0 syslog msg "Backup PW is active"
event manager applet VPLS_EVEN-VLAN_P_semaphore-is-up
 event track 10 state up
 action 1.0 cli command "enable"
 action 2.0 cli command "conf t"
 action 3.0 cli command "int lo90"
 action 3.1 cli command "shut"
 action 4.0 cli command "int lo80"
```

```
 action 4.1 cli command "shut"
 action 9.0 syslog msg "Backup PW is shutdown"
event manager applet VPLS_ODD-VLAN_B_semaphore-is-up
 event track 11 state up
 action 1.0 cli command "enable"
 action 2.0 cli command "conf t"
 action 4.0 cli command "int lo91"
 action 4.1 cli command "shutdown"
 action 5.1 cli command "do clear mac-address-table dynamic"
 action 9.0 syslog msg "Backup N-PE is Active, Force Primary in
   Standby"
event manager applet VPLS_ODD-VLAN_B_semaphore-is-down
 event track 11 state down
 action 1.0 cli command "enable"
 action 2.0 cli command "conf t"
 action 4.0 cli command "int lo91"
 action 4.1 cli command "no shut"
 action 9.0 syslog msg "Backup N-PE has become Standby, Primary runs
   Active"
event manager applet Backup-node_ready
 event track 110 state up
 action 1.0 cli command "enable"
 action 2.0 cli command "conf t"
 action 3.0 cli command "track 10 ip route 10.76.80.12 255.255.255.255
   reachability"
 action 3.1 cli command "delay up 100"
 action 9.0 syslog msg "Backup node is operational"
   event manager applet Backup-node_not_ready
 event track 110 state down
 action 1.0 cli command "enable"
 action 2.0 cli command "conf t"
 action 3.0 cli command "no track 10"
 action 4.0 cli command "int lo90"
 action 4.1 cli command "shut"
 action 5.0 cli command "int lo80"
 action 5.1 cli command "shut"
 action 9.0 syslog msg "Backup node not operational"
```

```
!
event manager history size events 20
event manager history size traps 20
end


lon-n-pe1# show ip interface brief | inc Loopback
Loopback0                 11.11.11.11      YES NVRAM   up              up
Loopback70                10.76.70.11      YES NVRAM   up              up
Loopback80                10.76.80.11      YES NVRAM   administratively
                                                      down down
Loopback81                10.76.81.11      YES NVRAM   up              up
Loopback90                10.76.90.11      YES NVRAM   administratively
                                                      down down
Loopback91                10.76.91.11      YES NVRAM   up              up
lon-n-pe1#
```

Convergence Tests

The traffic profile outlined in Chapter 7, "Data Center Multilayer Infrastructure Design,"
was used to determine end-to-end convergence for unidirectional voice, unicast, and multicast traffic. Links and nodes failed to simulate network failures.

Table 9-2 shows results of various node and link failures. Convergence numbers (max and
min) are in seconds.

Table 9-2 *Convergence Numbers for Link and Node Failures for VPLS with N-PE
Redundancy Using EEM Semaphore: EEM Option 2 Solution*

| | | | | Traffic Direction | | | |
| | | | | LON → SJ | | SJ → LON | |
Failure Type	Action	VLAN	Traffic Type	Max	Min	Max	Min
Fail N-PE1	Reload	Odd VLAN	Voice	3.72	3.62	4.28	4.24
			Unicast	3.73	3.63	4.28	4.26
			Multicast	5.17	4.3	4.45	4.27
		Even VLAN	Voice	0.00	0.00	0.00	0.00
			Unicast	0.00	0.00	0.00	0.00
			Multicast	0.00	0.00	0.00	0.00
	Restore	Odd VLAN	Voice	1.64	1.58	1.74	1.6
			Unicast	1.63	1.6	1.71	1.61
			Multicast	2.38	1.64	2.24	1.65
		Even VLAN	Voice	0.00	0.00	0.00	0.00
			Unicast	0.00	0.00	0.00	0.00
			Multicast	0.00	0.00	0.00	0.00

Table 9-2 *Convergence Numbers for Link and Node Failures for VPLS with N-PE Redundancy Using EEM Semaphore: EEM Option 2 Solution*

Failure Type	Action	VLAN	Traffic Type	Traffic Direction			
				LON → SJ		SJ → LON	
				Max	Min	Max	Min
Fail N-PE2	Reload	Odd VLAN	Voice	0.00	0.00	0.00	0.00
			Unicast	0.00	0.00	0.00	0.00
			Multicast	0.00	0.00	0.00	0.00
		Even VLAN[1,2]	Voice	8.14	8.02	8.14	8.06
			Unicast	8.13	8.03	8.13	8.06
			Multicast	8.91	8.1	8.87	8.16
	Restore	Odd VLAN	Voice	0.00	0.00	0.00	0.00
			Unicast	0.00	0.00	0.00	0.00
			Multicast	0.00	0.00	0.00	0.00
		Even VLAN	Voice	1.06	0.56	1.10	0.66
			Unicast	1.03	0.59	1.08	0.66
			Multicast	2.25	1.04	1.70	1.08
Fail Agg-1	Reload	Odd VLAN	Voice	0.50	0.48	0.98	0.86
			Unicast	0.49	0.48	0.97	0.85
			Multicast	1.17	0.64	1.75	1.12
		Even VLAN	Voice	0.00	0.00	0.00	0.00
			Unicast	0.00	0.00	0.00	0.00
			Multicast	0.00	0.00	0.00	0.00
	Restore	Odd VLAN	Voice	0.66	0.48	0.26	0.14
			Unicast	0.66	0.51	0.27	0.16
			Multicast	1.44	1.30	0.43	0.37
		Even VLAN	Voice	0.00	0.00	0.00	0.00
			Unicast	0.00	0.00	0.00	0.00
			Multicast	0.00	0.00	0.00	0.00
Fail Agg-2	Reload	Odd VLAN	Voice	0.00	0.00	0.00	0.00
			Unicast	0.00	0.00	0.00	0.00
			Multicast	0.00	0.00	0.00	0.00
		Even VLAN	Voice	0.86	0.82	1.86	1.20
			Unicast	0.84	0.82	1.82	1.23
			Multicast	1.34	0.86	4.93	1.77
	Restore	Odd VLAN	Voice	0.00	0.00	0.00	0.00
			Unicast	0.00	0.00	0.00	0.00
			Multicast	0.00	0.00	0.00	0.00
		Even VLAN	Voice	0.54	0.48	0.44	0.04
			Unicast	0.51	0.49	0.44	0.04
			Multicast	1.46	0.49	1.02	0.12

Table 9-2 *Convergence Numbers for Link and Node Failures for VPLS with N-PE Redundancy Using EEM Semaphore: EEM Option 2 Solution*

Failure Type	Action	VLAN	Traffic Type	Traffic Direction			
				LON → SJ		SJ → LON	
				Max	Min	Max	Min
Fail MPLS links on N-PE1	Shut MPLS core-facing link	Odd VLAN	Voice	0.30	0.20	0.26	0.08
			Unicast	0.29	0.23	0.25	0.08
			Multicast	1.22	0.28	0.25	0.08
		Even VLAN	Voice	0.00	0.00	0.00	0.00
			Unicast	0.00	0.00	0.00	0.00
			Multicast	0.00	0.00	0.00	0.00
	Shut inter-N-PE MPLS link	Odd VLAN	Voice	1.20	1.08	1.18	1.12
			Unicast	1.18	1.11	1.18	1.12
			Multicast	1.88	1.28	1.98	1.23
		Even VLAN	Voice	0.00	0.00	0.00	0.00
			Unicast	0.00	0.00	0.00	0.00
			Multicast	0.00	0.00	0.00	0.00
	Restore inter-N-PE MPLS link	Odd VLAN	Voice	0.20	0.16	0.26	0.12
			Unicast	0.18	0.16	0.24	0.13
			Multicast	0.11	0.19	0.24	0.13
		Even VLAN	Voice	0.00	0.00	0.00	0.00
			Unicast	0.00	0.00	0.00	0.00
			Multicast	0.00	0.00	0.00	0.00
	Restore MPLS core-facing link	Odd VLAN	Voice	0.86	0.78	0.92	0.84
			Unicast	0.85	0.78	0.91	0.86
			Multicast	1.65	0.88	1.63	0.97
		Even VLAN	Voice	0.00	0.00	0.00	0.00
			Unicast	0.00	0.00	0.00	0.00
			Multicast	0.00	0.00	0.00	0.00
Fail MPLS links on N-PE2	Shut MPLS core-facing link	Odd VLAN	Voice	0.00	0.00	0.00	0.00
			Unicast	0.00	0.00	0.00	0.00
			Multicast	0.00	0.00	0.00	0.00
		Even VLAN	Voice	0.24	0.12	0.10	0.04
			Unicast	0.23	0.14	0.09	0.06
			Multicast	0.96	0.21	0.09	0.06
	Shut inter-N-PE MPLS link	Odd VLAN	Voice	0.00	0.00	0.00	0.00
			Unicast	0.00	0.00	0.00	0.00
			Multicast	0.00	0.00	0.00	0.00
		Even VLAN	Voice	0.84	0.8	0.92	0.86
			Unicast	0.85	0.81	0.90	0.85
			Multicast	1.32	0.9	1.24	0.88
	Restore inter-MPLS N-PE link	Odd VLAN	Voice	0.00	0.00	0.00	0.00
			Unicast	0.00	0.00	0.00	0.00
			Multicast	0.00	0.00	0.00	0.00
		Even VLAN	Voice	1.20	1.14	1.24	1.14
			Unicast	1.18	1.15	1.23	1.15
			Multicast	1.98	1.21	1.23	1.15
	Restore MPLS core-facing link	Odd VLAN	Voice	0.00	0.00	0.00	0.00
			Unicast	0.00	0.00	0.00	0.00
			Multicast	0.00	0.00	0.00	0.00
		Even VLAN	Voice	1.26	1.20	1.28	1.24
			Unicast	1.25	1.22	1.27	1.25
			Multicast	1.81	1.23	1.64	1.27

Table 9-2 *Convergence Numbers for Link and Node Failures for VPLS with N-PE Redundancy Using EEM Semaphore: EEM Option 2 Solution*

Failure Type	Action	VLAN	Traffic Type	Traffic Direction			
				LON → SJ		SJ → LON	
				Max	Min	Max	Min
Fail link between N-PE1 and N-PE2	Shut	Odd VLAN	Voice	0.00	0.00	0.00	0.00
			Unicast	0.00	0.00	0.00	0.00
			Multicast	0.00	0.00	0.00	0.00
		Even VLAN	Voice	0.00	0.00	0.00	0.00
			Unicast	0.00	0.00	0.00	0.00
			Multicast	0.00	0.00	0.00	0.00
	Restore	Odd VLAN	Voice	0.00	0.00	0.00	0.00
			Unicast	0.00	0.00	0.00	0.00
			Multicast	0.00	0.00	0.00	0.00
		Even VLAN	Voice	0.00	0.00	0.00	0.00
			Unicast	0.00	0.00	0.00	0.00
			Multicast	0.00	0.00	0.00	0.00
Fail Link between Agg-1 and Agg-2	Shut a link in PortChannel	Odd VLAN	Voice	0.04	0.00	0.34	0.00
			Unicast	0.03	0.00	0.33	0.00
			Multicast	0.02	0.00	0.33	0.00
		Even VLAN	Voice	0.00	0.00	0.00	0.00
			Unicast	0.00	0.00	0.00	0.00
			Multicast	0.00	0.00	0.00	0.00
	Restore a member link in PortChannel	Odd VLAN	Voice	0.02	0.00	0.18	0.00
			Unicast	0.03	0.00	0.17	0.00
			Multicast	0.03	0.00	0.17	0.00
		Even VLAN	Voice	0.00	0.00	0.00	0.00
			Unicast	0.00	0.00	0.00	0.00
			Multicast	0.00	0.00	0.00	0.00
	Shut down PortChannel	Odd VLAN	Voice	0.00	0.00	0.00	0.00
			Unicast	0.00	0.00	0.00	0.00
			Multicast	0.00	0.00	0.00	0.00
		Even VLAN	Voice	0.00	0.00	0.00	0.00
			Unicast	0.00	0.00	0.00	0.00
			Multicast	0.00	0.00	0.00	0.00
	Restore PortChannel	Odd VLAN	Voice	0.00	0.00	0.00	0.00
			Unicast	0.00	0.00	0.00	0.00
			Multicast	0.00	0.00	0.00	0.00
		Even VLAN	Voice	0.00	0.00	0.00	0.00
			Unicast	0.00	0.00	0.00	0.00
			Multicast	0.00	0.00	0.00	0.00
Clear IP routing table on N-PEs	Clear all IP routes from the N-PE routing table	Odd VLAN	Voice	0.00	0.00	0.00	0.00
			Unicast	0.00	0.00	0.00	0.00
			Multicast	0.00	0.00	0.00	0.00
		Even VLAN	Voice	0.00	0.00	0.00	0.00
			Unicast	0.00	0.00	0.00	0.00
			Multicast	0.00	0.00	0.00	0.00
Clear dynamic MAC address table on the SJ N-PE1	Clear	Odd VLAN	Voice	0.00	0.00	0.00	0.00
			Unicast	0.00	0.00	0.00	0.00
			Multicast	0.00	0.00	0.00	0.00
		Even VLAN	Voice	0.00	0.00	0.00	0.00
			Unicast	0.00	0.00	0.00	0.00
			Multicast	0.00	0.00	0.00	0.00

Cluster Server Tests

Event logs are captured from the Event Viewer of the Microsoft cluster server. The logs are in the reverse order, showing the last event first. It is best to view the time stamps when analyzing these logs.

Table 9-3 shows the event logs from the Event Viewer of the Microsoft cluster server.

Table 9-3 *Event Logs for VPLS with N-PE Redundancy Using EEM Semaphore: EEM Option 2*

Server Test	Time in Seconds	Event Logs with Time Stamps from Microsoft Server			
Power off both N-PEs	83	6/25/2008	11:21:45 PM	CAMP3-SERVER2	The cluster service brought the resource group "Cluster Group" online.
		6/25/2008	11:20:44 PM	CAMP3-SERVER2	The cluster service is attempting to bring online the resource group "Cluster Group."
		6/25/2008	11:20:44 PM	CAMP3-SERVER2	Cluster node CAMP3-SERVER3 was removed from the active server cluster membership. Cluster service may have been stopped on the node, the node may have failed, or the node may have lost communication with the other active server cluster nodes.
		6/25/2008	11:20:22 PM	CAMP3-SERVER2	The node lost communication with cluster node 'CAMP3-SERVER3' on network 'public.'
		6/25/2008	11:20:22 PM	CAMP3-SERVER2	The node lost communication with cluster node 'CAMP3-SERVER3' on network 'private(1).'
		6/25/2008	9:18:54 PM	CAMP3-SERVER1	The cluster service brought the resource group "Cluster Group" online.
		6/25/2008	9:18:37 PM	CAMP3-SERVER2	The cluster service service entered the running state.
		6/25/2008	9:18:37 PM	CAMP3-SERVER2	Cluster service successfully joined the server cluster CLUSTER-MNS.
		6/25/2008	9:18:21 PM	CAMP3-SERVER2	The node (re)established communication with cluster node 'CAMP3-SERVER1' on network 'public.'
		6/25/2008	9:18:21 PM	CAMP3-SERVER2	The node (re)established communication with cluster node 'CAMP3-SERVER1' on network 'private(1).'
		6/25/2008	9:18:21 PM	CAMP3-SERVER2	The node (re)established communication with cluster node 'CAMP3-SERVER1' on network 'public.'

Table 9-3 *Event Logs for VPLS with N-PE Redundancy Using EEM Semaphore: EEM Option 2*

Server Test	Time in Seconds	Event Logs with Time Stamps from Microsoft Server			
Power off access switch	239	6/25/2008	9:18:21 PM	CAMP3-SERVER2	The node (re)established communication with cluster node 'CAMP3-SERVER1' on network 'private(1).'
		6/25/2008	9:18:21 PM	CAMP3-SERVER1	The interface for cluster node 'CAMP3-SERVER2' on network 'private(1)' is operational (up). The node can communicate with all other available cluster nodes on the network.
		6/25/2008	9:18:21 PM	CAMP3-SERVER1	The interface for cluster node 'CAMP3-SERVER2' on network 'public' is operational (up). The node can communicate with all other available cluster nodes on the network.
		6/25/2008	9:18:20 PM	CAMP3-SERVER1	The node (re)established communication with cluster node 'CAMP3-SERVER2' on network 'private(1).'
		6/25/2008	9:18:20 PM	CAMP3-SERVER1	The node (re)established communication with cluster node 'CAMP3-SERVER2' on network 'public.'
		6/25/2008	9:17:24 PM	CAMP3-SERVER1	The cluster service is attempting to bring online the resource group "Cluster Group."
		6/25/2008	9:17:24 PM	CAMP3-SERVER1	Cluster node CAMP3-SERVER3 was removed from the active server cluster membership. Cluster service may have been stopped on the node, the node may have failed, or the node may have lost communication with the other active server cluster nodes.
		6/25/2008	9:14:56 PM	CAMP3-SERVER2	The node lost communication with cluster node 'CAMP3-SERVER3' on network 'private(1).'
		6/25/2008	9:14:56 PM	CAMP3-SERVER2	The node lost communication with cluster node 'CAMP3-SERVER3' on network 'public.'
		6/25/2008	9:14:55 PM	CAMP3-SERVER1	The node lost communication with cluster node 'CAMP3-SERVER3' on network 'private(1).'
		6/25/2008	9:14:55 PM	CAMP3-SERVER1	The node lost communication with cluster node 'CAMP3-SERVER3' on network 'public.'

Table 9-3 *Event Logs for VPLS with N-PE Redundancy Using EEM Semaphore: EEM Option 2*

Server Test	Time in Seconds	Event Logs with Time Stamps from Microsoft Server			
Power off active node	186	6/25/2008	10:27:57 PM	CAMP3-SERVER1	The cluster service brought the resource group "Cluster Group" online.
		6/25/2008	10:27:36 PM	CAMP3-SERVER1	The registration of DNS name cluster-mns.camp3.com for resource 'Cluster Name' over adapter 'public' failed for the following reason: This operation returned because the timeout period expired.
		6/25/2008	10:26:50 PM	CAMP3-SERVER1	Cluster node CAMP3-SERVER3 was removed from the active server cluster membership. Cluster service may have been stopped on the node, the node may have failed, or the node may have lost communication with the other active server cluster nodes.
		6/25/2008	10:24:52 PM	CAMP3-SERVER2	The node lost communication with cluster node 'CAMP3-SERVER3' on network 'private(1).'
		6/25/2008	10:24:52 PM	CAMP3-SERVER2	The node lost communication with cluster node 'CAMP3-SERVER3' on network 'public.'
		6/25/2008	10:24:51 PM	CAMP3-SERVER1	The node lost communication with cluster node 'CAMP3-SERVER3' on network 'private(1).'
		6/25/2008	10:24:51 PM	CAMP3-SERVER1	The node lost communication with cluster node 'CAMP3-SERVER3' on network 'public.'
Private VLAN N-PE reload	3	6/25/2008	10:03:47 PM	CAMP3-SERVER1	The node (re)established communication with cluster node 'CAMP3-SERVER3' on network 'private(1).'
		6/25/2008	10:03:45 PM	CAMP3-SERVER3	The node (re)established communication with cluster node 'CAMP3-SERVER1' on network 'private(1).'
		6/25/2008	10:03:44 PM	CAMP3-SERVER1	The node lost communication with cluster node 'CAMP3-SERVER3' on network 'private(1).'
		6/25/2008	10:03:41 PM	CAMP3-SERVER3	The node lost communication with cluster node 'CAMP3-SERVER1' on network 'private(1).'

Table 9-3   *Event Logs for VPLS with N-PE Redundancy Using EEM Semaphore: EEM Option 2*

Server Test	Time in Seconds	Event Logs with Time Stamps from Microsoft Server		
Unplug active server	196	6/25/2008	8:28:44 PM	CAMP3-SERVER1	The cluster service brought the resource group "Cluster Group" online.
		6/25/2008	8:27:57 PM	CAMP3-SERVER1	The cluster service is attempting to bring online the resource group "Cluster Group."
		6/25/2008	8:27:57 PM	CAMP3-SERVER1	Cluster node CAMP3-SERVER3 was removed from the active server cluster membership. Cluster service may have been stopped on the node, the node may have failed, or the node may have lost communication with the other active server cluster nodes.
		6/25/2008	8:27:57 PM	CAMP3-SERVER1	Cluster node CAMP3-SERVER2 was removed from the active server cluster membership. Cluster service may have been stopped on the node, the node may have failed, or the node may have lost communication with the other active server cluster nodes.
		6/25/2008	8:27:44 PM	CAMP3-SERVER1	The node lost communication with cluster node 'CAMP3-SERVER2' on network 'public.'
		6/25/2008	8:27:44 PM	CAMP3-SERVER1	The node lost communication with cluster node 'CAMP3-SERVER2' on network 'private(1).'
		6/25/2008	8:27:33 PM	CAMP3-SERVER1	The node lost communication with cluster node 'CAMP3-SERVER3' on network 'public.'
		6/25/2008	8:25:28 PM	CAMP3-SERVER2	The node lost communication with cluster node 'CAMP3-SERVER3' on network 'private(1).'
		6/25/2008	8:25:28 PM	CAMP3-SERVER1	The node lost communication with cluster node 'CAMP3-SERVER3' on network 'private(1).'

Table 9-3 *Event Logs for VPLS with N-PE Redundancy Using EEM Semaphore: EEM Option 2*

Server Test	Time in Seconds	Event Logs with Time Stamps from Microsoft Server			
Establish L2 connectivity	No convergence	6/25/2008	11:06:50 PM	CAMP3-SERVER1	The cluster service service entered the running state.
		6/25/2008	11:06:50 PM	CAMP3-SERVER1	Cluster service successfully joined the server cluster CLUSTER-MNS.
		6/25/2008	11:06:48 PM	CAMP3-SERVER1	The node (re)established communication with cluster node 'CAMP3-SERVER2' on network 'private(1).'
		6/25/2008	11:06:48 PM	CAMP3-SERVER1	The node (re)established communication with cluster node 'CAMP3-SERVER3' on network 'private(1).'
		6/25/2008	10:47:38 PM	CAMP3-SERVER1	The node lost communication with cluster node 'CAMP3-SERVER3' on network 'private(1).'
		6/25/2008	10:47:38 PM	CAMP3-SERVER1	The node lost communication with cluster node 'CAMP3-SERVER3' on network 'public.'
		6/25/2008	10:47:37 PM	CAMP3-SERVER1	The node lost communication with cluster node 'CAMP3-SERVER2' on network 'public.'
		6/25/2008	10:47:37 PM	CAMP3-SERVER1	The node lost communication with cluster node 'CAMP3-SERVER2' on network 'private(1).'
		6/25/2008	10:47:26 PM	CAMP3-SERVER1	The cluster service is attempting to bring online the resource group "Cluster Group."

H-VPLS with N-PE Redundancy Using EEM Semaphore: EEM Option 3

H-VPLS with N-PE redundancy using EEM semaphore (referred to as EEM option 3) is a highly scalable solution and includes the use of Hierarchical VPLS (H-VPLS) in addition to the EEM option 2 solution.

This solution is highly scalable because it allows a large number of VLANs to be extended across remote sites and eliminates cumbersome and lengthy configuration as required in MST-based and in EEM option 2 solutions.

Use of VPLS implies the creation of one VFI per VLAN that is to be xconnected. When the requirement is to extend a large number of VLANs, it is not feasible to create one VFI per VLAN because this situation leads to a huge configuration file. With the introduction of QinQ, only one VFI is required toward all the other data centers per QinQ VLAN, thus allowing this solution to scale up to 1000 VLANs.

However, this solution requires VPLS node participation in the local STP control plane.

Most enterprises use one only VLAN domain in their data center. Therefore, N-PEs participating in local STP is not a problem. However, when the requirement is for a data center to present several independent domains, referenced as multitenant, this implementation may not be applicable, because VLAN number overlapping between domains in a multitenant environment is not possible.

VPLS autodiscovery using the Border Gateway Protocol (BGP) feature enables each VPLS node (N-PE routers) to discover other N-PE routers that are part of the same VPLS domain. Autodiscovery also automatically detects when N-PE routers are added to or removed from the VPLS domain. You no longer need to manually change configuration when a N-PE router is added or removed from the VPLS domain. However, autodiscovery implies that BGP is enabled in the network and all N-PE routers are to be connected in a full-mesh fashion.

With EEM option 3, QinQ VLAN (also known as the core VLAN) is cross-connected using only one VFI toward all the other remote data centers. The N-PE router performs QinQ encapsulation or adds a QinQ outer tag to the received dot1q traffic on the Q-link (port facing the edge on the N-PE to aggregation link) before forwarding the traffic via the VFI.

The Q-link interface on the N-PE side can either be a LAN port on 67xx module or an interface on an ES module:

- **LAN port:** Selective QinQ is not supported, so only one QinQ tag can be added per port.

- **ES module interface:** Selective QinQ is supported, which allows the configuration of multiple "service instances" mapped to multiple QinQ VLANs. This feature enables distribution of VLANs across multiple EVCs and load repartition of traffic flows on the core links.

QinQ link cannot participate in local STP and therefore cannot generate TCNs during topology change. To circumvent the inability of the QinQ link to transport BPDUs, this solution requires an additional link called the TCN link, which allows N-PEs to participate in local STPs. The two links that this solution requires between N-PEs and aggregation switches are as follows:

- **Q-link:** High-speed link (1gig, 10gig, or EtherChannel) for data traffic, used for VLAN cross-connect

- **TCN-link:** This link does not forward any data but does carry broadcast traffic. This link is used for control-plane traffic, allowing the N-PE router to generate TCN during a VPLS topology change.

This solution is appropriate for enterprise customers that require hundreds of VLANs to be extended across geographically dispersed data centers. Besides scalability, the key solution positioning is that this design does not require any changes to the aggregation switches.

Figure 9-13 illustrates the H-VPLS with N-PE redundancy using the EEM semaphore: EEM option 3 solution.

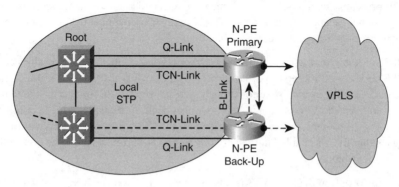

Figure 9-13 *H-VPLS with N-PE Redundancy using EEM semaphore: EEM option 3.*

In the EEM option 3 solution, N-PEs participate in local STP only via the B-link (inter-N-PE link) and TCN-link, both configured as dot1q trunks. The B-link is managed by the primary node and is in shut state when the primary N-PE is either down or in standby mode. To notify data center devices of changes in the VPLS topology, the primary N-PE changes B-link status by simply executing shut/no shut. This action generates an STP topology change message that will be flooded toward the data center. On the N-PE routers, when an interface on a LAN module is used for connection to aggregation switches, QinQ tagging can be achieved only on a per-port basis. This restriction implies that all traffic on the Q-link is encapsulated into only one core VLAN. Therefore, VLAN load repartition can be done only on a per-port basis with one semaphore protection per port.

When using the ES module-facing edge, load repartition becomes easy via selective QinQ. VLANs are groomed into two VFIs, where one VFI can be active for a certain set of VLANs, and a second VFI can be a backup for another set of VLANs. This configuration requires two semaphores, one for each VFI.

In this solution, the core VLANs imposed by QinQ are as follows:

- **N-PE1:** 3001 for odd VLANs grooming into VFI 3001

    3004 for even VLANs acting as backup for N-PE2 core VLAN 3002 into VFI 3002

- **N-PE2:** 3002 for even VLANs grooming into VFI 3002

    3003 for odd VLANs acting as backup for N-PE1 core VLAN 3001 into VFI 3001

Even though a VPLS core ensures that these core VLANs are locally significant, Cisco recommends the use of unique core VLAN numbers on N-PE1 and N-PE2 within the data center. These core VLANs must not be allowed on the B-link because the B-link is restricted to edge STP.

Control Plane

In addition to QinQ, the independence of STP, VPLS, and MPLS core domains also provide scalability and availability of this solution. To accomplish this, there are three independent control planes:

- **Spanning tree:** TCN links connecting N-PEs to aggregation switches that participate in local STP (RPVSTP, MST, and PVSTP), which is already deployed in the data center.

  Spanning-tree BPDUs are not transmitted over VPLS.

  The inter-N-PE link (B-link) generates topology changes toward local STP via TCN-link when the N-PE active/standby state changes.

- **VPLS:** P- and B-semaphores allow active/standby state between primary and backup N-PE nodes.

  For load balancing, two semaphore pairs are configured, one for active/standby and one for standby/active.

- **MPLS core:** LDP and IGP protocols are enabled in the core.

Data Plane

VPLS and STP data plane are interrelated because STP is used to mainly report EEM semaphore state changes.

Incoming traffic on a Q-link is encapsulated into either of the two core VLANs. Selective QinQ is configured, and odd VLANs and even VLANs are split into two different core VLANs. These core VLANs are attached to two core VFIs, and each VFI is connected to other data center VFIs with partially meshed PWs.

Associated VFIs are load-balanced on both N-PEs, and PW load-balancing is achieved on the core links. In the case of equal-cost multipath into core, PWs are load-balanced based on destination N-PE/VCID, which is the destination VLAN.

Theory of Operation

This section analyzes EEM option 3 behavior in normal and failure states.

Normal Mode

In normal mode, odd VLANs on N-PE1 are connected to an active VFI while the active VFI associated with even VLANs is on N-PE2. All edge VLANs to be cross-connected are created on both the N-PEs and allowed on TCN-link and B-link, both configured as dot1q trunks. The TCN- and the B-link are provisioned for signaling only and do not carry user traffic.

Several failure conditions may occur, including the following:

■   Aggregation switch failure

■   Q-link failure

■   Primary N-PE failure

■   Backup N-PE failure

■   Main core link (MPLS) failure

■   All core links failure on the primary N-PE (node isolation)

■   All core links failure on the backup N-PE

The following are the main recovery mechanisms that react to these failures:

■   EEM semaphore for aggregation switch or Q-link or B-link failures

■   EEM semaphores for N-PE node failure or node isolation

■   LDP for core link failure without isolation

Primary N-PE Node or Q-Link Failure

Consider the following analysis of what happens when a primary node fails or becomes
isolated from a data center because of its Q-link failure.

Figure 9-14 shows the link and PW state after a node or edge link failure.

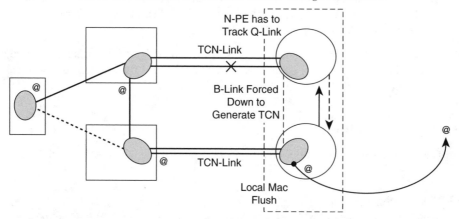

Figure 9-14   *EEM option 3 redundancy: Q-link failure.*

If the Q-link goes down, either because of link or aggregation switch failure, the primary
N-PE is unable to reach the local data center. EEM determines this failure and reacts by
shutting down its own P-semaphore, requesting the backup node to become active. The
primary N-PE also shuts down its own primary PW to force MAC address flushing at the
remote sites.

The backup node activates its backup PW toward the primary nodes of other remote data centers via unshutting the PW-ID loopback interface. In addition, to prevent an active/active state, the backup N-PE raises its own B-semaphore, thus preventing the primary N-PE from becoming active.

When the primary node shuts down its B-link, the backup TCN-link transitions to STP forwarding mode, thereby generating an STP TCN. The TCN flushes MAC addresses within the local data center devices, forcing them to learn a new Layer 2 path.

Even though the failure scenario described is related to Q-link failure, the behavior of the EEM semaphore protocol during primary node failure or when the primary node becomes isolated from the MPLS core is identical.

When a primary N-PE gets isolated from the MPLS core, EEM script tracking connectivity to the core will detect this failure and will shut down its Q-link, leading itself to go into backup mode as just described.

Figure 9-15 shows the process of generating a TCN. In normal condition, the B-link is in forwarding mode. Shutting this link down will indirectly trigger generation of a TCN.

```
event manager applet VPLS_B_Semaphore-is-up

event track 10 state up

action 1.0 cli command "enable"

action 2.0 cli command "conf t"

action 4.0 cli command "int lo90"        ◄──────  Stop Xconnect

action 4.1 cli command "shutdown"

action 5.0 cli command "int g1/1"        ◄──────  Shut B-link to generate TCN

action 5.1 cli command "shutdown"

action 9.0 syslog msg "Backup N-PE is Active, Force Primary in Standby"
```

Example of EEM Script on Primary N-PE Transitioning to Standby Mode

Figure 9-15 *EEM option 3: TCN generation during topology change.*

Primary N-PE Node or Q-Link Recovers After the Failure

When the primary N-PE becomes ready (for example, because the Q-link is up, the core is reachable, or the N-PE initializes and becomes ready), the primary N-PE perceives that the B-semaphore is up and remains in standby state. Before becoming active, the primary N-PE raises its P-semaphore to request preemption of the primary role. After the backup N-PE learns the P-semaphore route that the core IGP announces, it starts a delay timer (the recommended value is 100 sec). The traffic continues to forward through the backup PWs via the backup Q-link until the delay time expires. When the delay timer expires, the backup node disables the backup PW by shutting its PW-ID loopback interface. The backup node will also shut down its B-semaphore to allow the primary node to become active and return to normal state. The primary N-PE will unshut the B-link, which generates the TCN through the TCN-link toward the data center.

N-PE Routers: Hardware and Software

Table 9-4 compares the hardware and software that can be used for N-PE nodes. Cisco 7600 routers were used as N-PEs for all the MST- and EEM-based solutions that this book describes. In this solution, selective QinQ with two EVCs was configured using ES20 modules facing the aggregation.

Table 9-4   *Hardware and Software for N-PE Nodes*

Cisco 7600 Router	Cisco Catalyst 6500
Interfaces on SIP or ES modules are required for connectivity toward the VPLS core.	Interface on SIP module is required for connectivity toward the VPLS core.
ES module: Selective QinQ. 67xx module: Plain QinQ tagging, one QinQ tag per port.	ES module: Not supported. 67xx module: Plain QinQ tagging, one QinQ tag per port.
Interface on 67xx or ES module.	Interface on 67xx LAN module.
Interface on any fiber-based 67xx LAN module.	Interface on 67xx LAN module.
Cisco IOS 12.2(33)SRC1.	Cisco IOS 12.2(33)SXI.

Implementing H-VPLS with N-PE Redundancy Using EEM Semaphore Design

This EEM option 3 solution requires a square topology between N-PEs and aggregation switches. PWs on N-PE1 and N-PE2 are in active or standby state and are managed by EEM scripts.

Figure 9-16 provides a configuration overview of the various links and the nodes.

The following provides snippets of configuration from N-PE and aggregation devices and output from various **show** commands for verification:

Step 1.   Configure the core IGP, MPLS, and targeted LDP as documented in the section "VPLS with N-PE Redundancy Using EEM Semaphore: EEM Option 2."

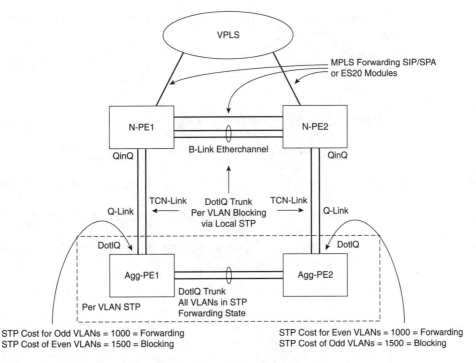

Figure 9-16 *Implementing EEM option 3: Configuration overview.*

Step 2.   This solution leverages the STP mode and the root bridge placement that are configured on the aggregation devices in the data center. The STP root and backup root assignment remains unchanged. The following example shows spanning-tree configuration on aggregation switches.

On Agg-1	On Agg-2
| ```
lon-agg-1#
!
spanning-tree mode rapid-pvst
spanning-tree vlan
1,3,5,7,9,11,13,15,17... priority 8192
spanning-tree vlan 2,4,6,8,10,12,14,
16.... priority 16384
``` | ```
lon-agg-2#
!
spanning-tree mode rapid-pvst
spanning-tree vlan
2,4,6,8,10,12,14.....priority 8192
spanning-tree vlan
1,3,5,7,9,11,13,15....priority 16384
``` |

The following example shows the spanning-tree output for VLAN 7 on both aggregation switches:

```
! On Agg-1:
lon-agg-1# show spanning-tree vlan 7


VLAN0007
  Spanning tree enabled protocol rstp
  Root ID    Priority    8199
             Address     001c.b126.d000
             This bridge is the root
             Hello Time   2 sec  Max Age 20 sec  Forward Delay 15 sec

  Bridge ID  Priority    8199    (priority 8192 sys-id-ext 7)
             Address     001c.b126.d000
             Hello Time   2 sec  Max Age 20 sec  Forward Delay 15 sec
             Aging Time 300


Interface            Role Sts Cost      Prio.Nbr Type
------------------- --- --- ----- ---- -------------------

Gi2/1                Desg FWD 4         128.129  P2p Edge
Gi2/19               Desg FWD 4         128.147  P2p
Gi2/22               Desg FWD 4         128.150  P2p
Po1                  Desg FWD 3         128.1665 P2p


lon-agg-1#
! On Agg-2:
lon-agg-2# show spanning-tree vlan 7


VLAN0007
  Spanning tree enabled protocol rstp
  Root ID    Priority    8199
             Address     001c.b126.d000
             Cost        3
             Port        1665 (Port-channel1)
             Hello Time   2 sec  Max Age 20 sec  Forward Delay 15 sec

  Bridge ID  Priority    16391   (priority 16384 sys-id-ext 7)
             Address     001c.b144.4c00
             Hello Time   2 sec  Max Age 20 sec  Forward Delay 15 sec
             Aging Time 300


Interface            Role Sts Cost      Prio.Nbr Type
------------------- --- --- ----- ---- -------------------

Gi2/1                Desg FWD 4         128.129  P2p Edge
```

```
Gi2/18              Desg FWD 4           128.146  P2p
Gi2/21              Desg FWD 4           128.149  P2p
Po1                 Root FWD 3           128.1665 P2p


lon-agg-2#
```

Step 3.   Display spanning tree output for VLAN 7 from both N-PEs:

```
On N-PE1:
```

lon-n-pe1# **show spanning-tree vlan 7**

```
VLAN0007
  Spanning tree enabled protocol rstp
  Root ID    Priority    8199
             Address     001c.b126.d000
             Cost        1000
             Port        257 (GigabitEthernet2/1)
             Hello Time   2 sec  Max Age 20 sec  Forward Delay 15 sec


  Bridge ID  Priority    61447  (priority 61440 sys-id-ext 7)
             Address     001d.7198.9500
             Hello Time   2 sec  Max Age 20 sec  Forward Delay 15 sec
             Aging Time 300


Interface            Role Sts Cost       Prio.Nbr Type
---------------- ---- --- ---------- -------- ---------------
Gi2/1                Root FWD 1000        128.257  P2p
Po1                  Desg FWD 3           128.3329 P2p


lon-n-pe1#
! On N-PE2:
```

lon-n-pe2# **show spanning-tree vlan 7**

```
VLAN0007
  Spanning tree enabled protocol rstp
  Root ID    Priority    8199
             Address     001c.b126.d000
             Cost        1003
             Port        3329 (Port-channel1)
             Hello Time   2 sec  Max Age 20 sec  Forward Delay 15 sec


  Bridge ID  Priority    61447  (priority 61440 sys-id-ext 7)
             Address     001d.7198.8fc0
             Hello Time   2 sec  Max Age 20 sec  Forward Delay 15 sec
             Aging Time 300
```

```
Interface              Role Sts Cost     Prio.Nbr Type
---------------. -- -. -------. ---- --------------

Gi2/2                  Altn BLK 1500     128.258  P2p
Po1                    Root FWD 3        128.3329 P2p


lon-n-pe2#
```

Step 4. Create QinQ VLANs on both N-PEs. Configure selective QinQ on the Q-links between N-PEs and aggregation switches and ensure that these core VLANs are not allowed on the B-link (inter-N-PE link) or the TCN-links (link between N-PE and aggregation).

On N-PE1	On N-PE2

```
vlan 3001
name H-
VPLS_Primary_core_VLAN_for_odd_vlans
vlan 3004
name H-
VPLS_Backup_core_VLAN_for_even_vlans
!
!
lon-n-pe1# show running-config interface gig 4/0/2
!
interface GigabitEthernet4/0/2
 description - Q-link - QinQ ES20
 mtu 9216
 logging event link-status
 ip arp inspection limit none
 no ip address
 load-interval 30
 mls qos trust dscp
 service instance 3001 ethernet
encapsulation dot1q 3,5,7,9,11,13,
15,17,19,21,23,.....bridge-domain 3001
 !
 service instance 3004 ethernet
encapsulation dot1q 2,4,6,8,10,12,14,
16,18,20,22,24.....bridge-domain 3004
 !
end
```

```
vlan 3002
name H-
VPLS_Primary_core_VLAN_for_even_vlans
vlan 3003
name H-VPLS_Backup_core_VLAN_for_odd_vlans
!
!
lon-n-pe2# show running-config interface gig 4/0/2
!
interface GigabitEthernet4/0/2
 description Q-link - QinQ ES20
 mtu 9216
 logging event link-status
 ip arp inspection limit none
 no ip address
 load-interval 30
 mls qos trust dscp
 service instance 3002 ethernet
encapsulation dot1q 2,4,6,8,10,12,14,
16,18,20,22,24.....bridge-domain 3002
 !
 service instance 3003 ethernet
encapsulation dot1q 3,5,7,9,11,13,
15,17,19,21,23,.....bridge-domain 3003
 !
end
```

On Agg-1

```
lon-agg-1# show running-config interface gig 2/1
!
interface GigabitEthernet2/1
 description QinQ connection to lon-n-pe1
 switchport
 switchport trunk encapsulation dot1q
 switchport trunk allowed vlan 2-61,201-
   260
 switchport mode trunk
 switchport nonegotiate
 mtu 9216
 logging event link-status
 logging event spanning-tree status
 load-interval 30
 spanning-tree portfast trunk
 spanning-tree link-type point-to-point
end
```

On Agg-2

```
lon-agg-2# show running-config interface gig 2/1
!
interface GigabitEthernet2/1
 description QinQ connection to lon-n-pe2
 switchport
 switchport trunk encapsulation dot1q
 switchport trunk allowed vlan 1-61,201-
   260
 switchport mode trunk
 switchport nonegotiate
 mtu 9216
 logging event link-status
 logging event spanning-tree status
 load-interval 30
 spanning-tree portfast trunk
 spanning-tree link-type point-to-point
end
```

Step 5. Configure the TCN-link between N-PEs and aggregation switches and allow VLANs that are to be extended to remote data centers.

On N-PE1

```
lon-n-pe1# show running-config interface gig 2/1
!
interface GigabitEthernet2/1
 description L2 to Agg-1 - non forwarding
interface, used only for TCN signaling
 switchport
 switchport trunk encapsulation dot1q
 switchport trunk allowed vlan 1-61,201-
   260
 switchport mode trunk
 switchport nonegotiate
 mtu 9216
 logging event link-status
 logging event spanning-tree status
 load-interval 30
 storm-control broadcast level 5.00
 storm-control multicast level 5.00
 spanning-tree link-type point-to-point
 spanning-tree vlan
1,3,5,7,9,11,13,...cost 1000
 spanning-tree vlan 2,4,6,8,10,12,...cost
   1500
end
```

On N-PE2

```
lon-n-pe2# show running-config interface gig 2/2
!
interface GigabitEthernet2/2
 description L2 to Agg-2 - non forwarding
interface, used only for TCN signaling
 switchport
 switchport trunk encapsulation dot1q
 switchport trunk allowed vlan 2-61,201-
   260
 switchport mode trunk
 switchport nonegotiate
 mtu 9216
 logging event link-status
 logging event spanning-tree status
 load-interval 30
 storm-control broadcast level 5.00
 storm-control multicast level 5.00
 spanning-tree link-type point-to-point
 spanning-tree vlan
1,3,5,7,9,11,13,...cost 1500
 spanning-tree vlan 2,4,6,8,10,12,...cost
   1000
end
```

On Agg-1	On Agg-2

```
lon-agg-1# show running-config interface gig 2/19
!
interface GigabitEthernet2/19
 description L2 connection to lon-n-pe1
for Q-in-Q TCN link
 switchport
 switchport trunk encapsulation dot1q
 switchport trunk allowed vlan 2-61,201-
   260
 switchport mode trunk
 switchport nonegotiate
 mtu 9216
 logging event link-status
 logging event spanning-tree status
 spanning-tree link-type point-to-point
end
```

```
lon-agg-2# show running-config interface gig 2/18
!
interface GigabitEthernet2/18
 description L2 connection to lon-n-pe2
for Q-in-Q TCN link
 switchport
 switchport trunk encapsulation dot1q
 switchport trunk allowed vlan 1-61,201-
   260
 switchport mode trunk
 switchport nonegotiate
 mtu 9216
 logging event link-status
 logging event spanning-tree status
 spanning-tree link-type point-to-point
end
```

Step 6. Configure the B-link (inter-N-PE link) and do not allow QinQ VLANs on the trunk:

```
! On N-PE1:
interface Port-channel1
 description LAN etherchannel interface to lon-n-pe2  - non forwarding
interface, used only for TCN signaling
 switchport
 switchport trunk encapsulation dot1q
 switchport trunk allowed vlan 2-61,201-260
 switchport mode trunk
 mtu 9216
 logging event link-status
 logging event spanning-tree status
!
interface GigabitEthernet2/4
 description LAN etherchannel interface to lon-n-pe2  - non forwarding
interface, used only for TCN signaling
 switchport
 switchport trunk encapsulation dot1q
 switchport trunk allowed vlan 2-61,201-260
 switchport mode trunk
 mtu 9216
```

```
 logging event link-status

 logging event spanning-tree status

 channel-group 1 mode on

!

interface GigabitEthernet2/5

 description LAN etherchannel interface to lon-n-pe2  - non forwarding
interface, used only for TCN signaling

 switchport

 switchport trunk encapsulation dot1q

 switchport trunk allowed vlan 2-61,201-260

 switchport mode trunk

 mtu 9216

 logging event link-status

 logging event spanning-tree status

 channel-group 1 mode on

! On N-PE2:

interface Port-channel1

 description LAN etherchannel interface to lon-n-pe1  - non forwarding
interface, used only for TCN signaling

 switchport

 switchport trunk encapsulation dot1q

 switchport trunk allowed vlan 2-61,201-260

 switchport mode trunk

 mtu 9216

 logging event link-status

 logging event spanning-tree status

!

interface GigabitEthernet2/4

 description LAN etherchannel interface to lon-n-pe1  - non forwarding
interface, used only for TCN signaling

 switchport

 switchport trunk encapsulation dot1q

 switchport trunk allowed vlan 2-61,201-260

 switchport mode trunk

 mtu 9216

 logging event link-status

 logging event spanning-tree status
```

```
channel-group 1 mode on
!
interface GigabitEthernet2/5
 description LAN etherchannel interface to lon-n-pe1  - non forwarding
 interface, used only for TCN signaling
 switchport
 switchport trunk encapsulation dot1q
 switchport trunk allowed vlan 2-61,201-260
 switchport mode trunk
 mtu 9216
 logging event link-status
 logging event spanning-tree status
 channel-group 1 mode on
```

Step 7.   Configure MPLS, VFI, and SVI on N-PE1 and N-PE2. The output from the
show mpls l2transport vc command displays the MPLS virtual circuit transport information.

On N-PE1	On N-PE2

<pre>lon-n-pe1#
!
l2 vfi VFI-Even manual
 vpn id 3002
 neighbor 10.76.90.32 encapsulation mpls
 neighbor 10.76.90.22 encapsulation mpls
!
l2 vfi VFI-Odd manual
 vpn id 3001
 neighbor 10.76.91.31 encapsulation mpls
 neighbor 10.76.91.22 encapsulation mpls
 neighbor 10.76.91.21 encapsulation mpls
 neighbor 10.76.91.32 encapsulation mpls
 	
lon-n-pe1#
...
!
mpls ldp neighbor 10.76.70.12 targeted ldp
mpls ldp neighbor 10.76.70.21 targeted ldp
mpls ldp neighbor 10.76.70.22 targeted ldp
mpls ldp neighbor 10.76.70.31 targeted ldp
mpls ldp neighbor 10.76.70.32 targeted ldp
mpls ldp tcp pak-priority
mpls ldp session protection</pre>
	<pre>lon-n-pe2#
	!
	l2 vfi VFI-Even manual
	 vpn id 3002
	 neighbor 10.76.90.21 encapsulation mpls
	 neighbor 10.76.90.22 encapsulation mpls
	 neighbor 10.76.90.31 encapsulation mpls
	 neighbor 10.76.90.32 encapsulation mpls
	!
	l2 vfi VFI-Odd manual
	 vpn id 3001
	 neighbor 10.76.91.21 encapsulation mpls
	 neighbor 10.76.91.31 encapsulation mpls
	
	lon-n-pe2#
	...
	!
	mpls ldp neighbor 10.76.70.11 targeted ldp
	mpls ldp neighbor 10.76.70.21 targeted ldp
	mpls ldp neighbor 10.76.70.22 targeted ldp
	mpls ldp neighbor 10.76.70.31 targeted ldp
	mpls ldp neighbor 10.76.70.32 targeted ldp
	mpls ldp tcp pak-priority
	mpls ldp session protection</pre>

On N-PE1	On N-PE2

```
no mpls ldp advertise-labels
mpls ldp advertise-labels for 76
mpls label protocol ldp
xconnect logging pseudowire status
!
access-list 76 permit 10.76.0.0 0.0.255.255
!
lon-n-pe1#


lon-n-pe1#
!
interface Vlan3001
 description Primary Core QinQ VLAN - used
to transport Odd edge VLAN
 mtu 9216
 no ip address
 xconnect vfi VFI-Odd
!
interface Vlan3004
 description Backup Core QinQ VLAN - used to
transport Even edge VLAN
 mtu 9216
 no ip address
 xconnect vfi VFI-Even


lon-n-pe1# show mpls l2 vc


Local intf     Local circuit
Dest address   VC ID       Status
——————·  ————————————  —
——————·  ————  ————

VFI VFI-Even   VFI
10.76.90.22    3002        DOWN
VFI VFI-Even   VFI
10.76.90.32    3002        DOWN
VFI VFI-Odd    VFI
10.76.91.21    3001        UP
VFI VFI-Odd    VFI
10.76.91.22    3001        DOWN
VFI VFI-Odd    VFI
10.76.91.31    3001        UP
VFI VFI-Odd    VFI
10.76.91.32    3001        DOWN
lon-n-pe1#
```

```
no mpls ldp advertise-labels
mpls ldp advertise-labels for 76
mpls label protocol ldp
xconnect logging pseudowire status
!
access-list 76 permit 10.76.0.0 0.0.255.255
!
lon-n-pe1#


lon-n-pe2#
!
interface Vlan3002
 description Primary Core QinQ VLAN - used
to transport Even edge VLAN
 mtu 9216
 no ip address
 xconnect vfi VFI-Even
!
interface Vlan3003
 description Backup Core QinQ VLAN - used to
transport odd edge VLAN
 mtu 9216
 no ip address
 xconnect vfi VFI-odd


lon-n-pe2# show mpls l2 vc


Local intf     Local circuit
Dest address   VC ID       Status
——————·  ————————————  —
——————·  ————  ————

VFI VFI-Even   VFI
10.76.90.21    3002        DOWN
VFI VFI-Even   VFI
10.76.90.22    3002        UP
VFI VFI-Even   VFI
10.76.90.31    3002        DOWN
VFI VFI-Even   VFI
10.76.90.32    3002        UP
VFI VFI-Odd    VFI
10.76.91.21    3001        DOWN
VFI VFI-Odd    VFI
10.76.91.31    3001        DOWN
lon-n-pe2#
```

Step 8.　Configure object tracking using EEM to manage semaphore and TCN-link. Use the **show running-config | begin event manager** command to display EEM applets that are configured:

```
! On N-PE1:
lon-n-pe1#
!
process-max-time 50
!
track timer ip route 1
!
track 10 ip route 10.76.80.12 255.255.255.255 reachability
 delay up 100
!
track 11 ip route 10.76.81.12 255.255.255.255 reachability
!
track 20 interface GigabitEthernet4/0/2 line-protocol
!
track 25 list boolean or
 object 110
 object 112
 delay up 40
!
track 110 interface GigabitEthernet4/0/19 line-protocol
 delay down 5 up 60
!
track 112 interface GigabitEthernet4/0/0 line-protocol
!
lon-n-pe1# show running-config | begin event manager
event manager applet VPLS_EVEN-VLAN_P_semaphore-is-down
 event track 10 state down
 action 1.0 cli command "enable"
 action 2.0 cli command "conf t"
 action 3.0 cli command "int lo80"
 action 3.1 cli command "no shut"
 action 4.0 cli command "int lo90"
 action 4.1 cli command "no shut"
 action 9.0 syslog msg "Backup PW is active"
event manager applet VPLS_EVEN-VLAN_P_semaphore-is-up
 event track 10 state up
```

```
action 1.0 cli command "enable"

action 2.0 cli command "conf t"

action 3.0 cli command "int lo90"

action 3.1 cli command "shut"

action 4.0 cli command "int lo80"

action 4.1 cli command "shut"

action 9.0 syslog msg "Backup PW is shutdown"

event manager applet VPLS_ODD-VLAN_B_semaphore-is-up

event track 11 state up

action 1.0 cli command "enable"

action 2.0 cli command "conf t"

action 4.0 cli command "int lo91"

action 4.1 cli command "shut"

action 5.0 cli command "int port-channel 1"

action 5.1 cli command "shut"

action 9.0 syslog msg "Backup N-PE is Active, Force Primary in
    Standby"

event manager applet VPLS_ODD-VLAN_B_semaphore-is-down

event track 11 state down

action 1.0 cli command "enable"

action 2.0 cli command "conf t"

action 4.0 cli command "int lo91"

action 4.1 cli command "no shut"

action 5.0 cli command "int port-channel1"

action 5.1 cli command "no shut"

action 9.0 syslog msg "Backup N-PE has become Standby, Primary runs
    Active"

event manager applet Track_Aggregation_link_failure

event track 20 state down

action 1.0 cli command "enable"

action 2.0 cli command "conf t"

action 3.0 cli command "int lo91"

action 3.1 cli command "shut"

action 4.0 cli command "int lo81"

action 4.1 cli command "shut"

action 5.0 cli command "int port-channel 1"

action 5.1 cli command "shut"

action 9.0 syslog msg "Aggregation link is failing, Force Primary
    in Standby"

event manager applet Track_Aggregation_link_recovery
```

```
    event track 20 state up
    action 1.0 cli command "enable"
    action 2.0 cli command "conf t"
    action 4.0 cli command "int lo81"
    action 4.1 cli command "no shut"
    action 9.0 syslog msg "Aggregation link as recover, Primary requests
      to become active"
event manager applet Backup-node_ready
    event track 110 state up
    action 1.0 cli command "enable"
    action 2.0 cli command "conf t"
    action 3.0 cli command "track 10 ip route 10.76.80.12 255.255.255.255
      reachability"
    action 3.1 cli command "delay up 100"
    action 9.0 syslog msg "Backup node is operational"
event manager applet Backup-node_not_ready
    event track 110 state down
    action 1.0 cli command "enable"
    action 2.0 cli command "conf t"
    action 3.0 cli command "no track 10"
    action 4.0 cli command "int lo90"
    action 4.1 cli command "shut"
    action 5.0 cli command "int lo80"
    action 5.1 cli command "shut"
    action 9.0 syslog msg "Backup node not operational"
event manager applet WAN_Interfaces_Down
    event track 25 state down
    action 1.0 cli command "enable"
    action 2.0 cli command "config t"
    action 3.0 cli command "interface gi4/0/2"
    action 4.0 cli command "shut"
    action 9.0 syslog msg "Both WAN interfaces are down. Shutting down
      QinQ link"
event manager applet WAN_Either_Interface_up
    event track 25 state up
    action 1.0 cli command "enable"
    action 2.0 cli command "config t"
    action 3.0 cli command "interface gi4/0/2"
```

```
    action 4.0 cli command "no shut"
    action 9.0 syslog msg "One WAN interface is up. Unshutting QinQ link"
    !
  event manager history size events 20
  event manager history size traps 20
  end
```

Convergence Tests

The traffic profile outlined in Chapter 7 was used to determine end-to-end convergence for unidirectional voice, unicast, and multicast traffic. Links and nodes were failed to simulate network failures.

Table 9-5 shows results of various node and link failures. Convergence numbers (max and min) are in seconds.

Table 9-5 *Convergence Results for Link and Node Failures for H-VPLS with N-PE Redundancy Using EEM Semaphore: EEM Option 3 Solution*

Failure Type	Action	VLAN	Traffic Type	Traffic Direction			
				LON → SJ		SJ → LON	
				Max	Min	Max	Min
Fail N-PE1	Reload	Odd VLAN	Voice	1.22	1.20	1.22	1.20
			Unicast	1.23	1.21	1.23	1.21
			Multicast	1.59	1.36	1.22	1.21
		Even VLAN	Voice	0.00	0.00	0.00	0.00
			Unicast	0.00	0.00	0.00	0.00
			Multicast	0.00	0.00	0.00	0.00
	Restore	Odd VLAN	Voice	1.16	1.12	1.16	1.12
			Unicast	1.15	1.12	1.15	1.13
			Multicast	2.85	1.35	1.15	1.13
		Even VLAN	Voice	0.00	0.00	0.00	0.00
			Unicast	0.00	0.00	0.00	0.00
			Multicast	0.00	0.00	0.00	0.00
Fail N-PE2	Reload	Odd VLAN	Voice	0.00	0.00	0.00	0.00
			Unicast	0.00	0.00	0.00	0.00
			Multicast	0.00	0.00	0.00	0.00
		Even VLAN	Voice	1.30	1.26	1.30	1.26
			Unicast	1.29	1.27	1.29	1.28
			Multicast	1.50	1.32	1.29	1.28
	Restore	Odd VLAN	Voice	0.00	0.00	0.00	0.00
			Unicast	0.00	0.00	0.00	0.00
			Multicast	0.00	0.00	0.00	0.00
		Even VLAN	Voice	0.62	0.60	0.66	0.64
			Unicast	0.61	0.60	0.66	0.65
			Multicast	1.10	0.70	0.66	0.65

Table 9-5   *Convergence Results for Link and Node Failures for H-VPLS with N-PE Redundancy Using EEM Semaphore: EEM Option 3 Solution*

Failure Type	Action	VLAN	Traffic Type	Traffic Direction			
				LON → SJ		SJ → LON	
				Max	Min	Max	Min
Fail Agg-1	Reload	Odd VLAN	Voice	1.64	1.60	1.68	1.64
			Unicast	1.63	1.60	1.65	1.65
			Multicast	2.10	1.79	2.41	1.82
		Even VLAN	Voice	0.00	0.00	0.00	0.00
			Unicast	0.00	0.00	0.00	0.00
			Multicast	0.00	0.00	0.00	0.00
	Restore	Odd VLAN[1,2]	Voice	10.36	10.30	9.66	9.60
			Unicast	10.32	10.01	9.62	9.62
			Multicast	12.11	10.64	13.87	10.96
		Even VLAN	Voice	0.00	0.00	0.00	0.00
			Unicast	0.00	0.00	0.00	0.00
			Multicast	0.00	0.00	0.00	0.00
Fail Agg-2	Reload	Odd VLAN	Voice	0.00	0.00	0.00	0.00
			Unicast	0.00	0.00	0.00	0.00
			Multicast	0.00	0.00	0.00	0.00
		Even VLAN[1,2]	Voice	7.30	7.26	7.30	7.26
			Unicast	7.28	7.28	7.28	7.28
			Multicast	11.11	7.50	7.29	7.28
	Restore	Odd VLAN	Voice	0.00	0.00	0.00	0.00
			Unicast	0.00	0.00	0.00	0.00
			Multicast	0.00	0.00	0.00	0.00
		Even VLAN	Voice	3.04	2.90	5.00	4.24
			Unicast	3.03	2.93	4.98	4.21
			Multicast	7.77	5.21	7.17	5.06
Fail MPLS links core facing on N-PE1	Shut MPLS core-facing link	Odd VLAN	Voice	0.14	0.10	0.10	0.08
			Unicast	0.12	0.11	0.10	0.09
			Multicast	0.12	0.11	0.10	0.08
		Even VLAN	Voice	0.00	0.00	0.00	0.00
			Unicast	0.00	0.00	0.00	0.00
			Multicast	0.00	0.00	0.00	0.00
	Shut inter-N-PE MPLS link	Odd VLAN	Voice	1.26	1.24	1.26	1.24
			Unicast	1.25	1.24	1.26	1.25
			Multicast	3.27	1.33	1.26	1.25
		Even VLAN	Voice	0.00	0.00	0.00	0.00
			Unicast	0.00	0.00	0.00	0.00
			Multicast	0.00	0.00	0.00	0.00
	Restore inter-N-PE MPLS link	Odd VLAN	Voice	1.94	1.92	2.28	2.26
			Unicast	1.93	1.92	2.29	2.28
			Multicast	1.98	1.93	2.31	2.21
		Even VLAN	Voice	0.00	0.00	0.00	0.00
			Unicast	0.00	0.00	0.00	0.00
			Multicast	0.00	0.00	0.00	0.00
	Restore MPLS core-facing link	Odd VLAN	Voice	0.62	0.60	0.68	0.64
			Unicast	0.61	0.60	0.66	0.65
			Multicast	1.43	1.41	0.66	0.65
		Even VLAN	Voice	0.00	0.00	0.00	0.00
			Unicast	0.00	0.00	0.00	0.00
			Multicast	0.00	0.00	0.00	0.00

Table 9-5   *Convergence Results for Link and Node Failures for H-VPLS with N-PE Redundancy Using EEM Semaphore: EEM Option 3 Solution*

Failure Type	Action	VLAN	Traffic Type	Traffic Direction LON → SJ Max	Min	SJ → LON Max	Min
Fail MPLS links core facing on N-PE2	Shut MPLS core-facing link	Odd VLAN	Voice	0.00	0.00	0.00	0.00
			Unicast	0.00	0.00	0.00	0.00
			Multicast	0.00	0.00	0.00	0.00
		Even VLAN	Voice	0.14	0.10	0.10	0.08
			Unicast	0.11	0.10	0.10	0.09
			Multicast	0.11	0.10	0.10	0.09
	Shut inter-N-PE MPLS link	Odd VLAN	Voice	0.00	0.00	0.00	0.00
			Unicast	0.00	0.00	0.00	0.00
			Multicast	0.00	0.00	0.00	0.00
		Even VLAN	Voice	1.10	1.08	1.12	1.10
			Unicast	1.11	1.09	1.11	1.10
			Multicast	1.24	1.18	1.11	1.10
	Restore inter-N-PE MPLS link	Odd VLAN	Voice	0.00	0.00	0.00	0.00
			Unicast	0.00	0.00	0.00	0.00
			Multicast	0.00	0.00	0.00	0.00
		Even VLAN	Voice	1.12	1.10	1.28	1.24
			Unicast	1.11	1.10	1.27	1.26
			Multicast	1.11	1.10	1.27	1.17
	Restore MPLS core-facing link	Odd VLAN	Voice	0.00	0.00	0.00	0.00
			Unicast	0.00	0.00	0.00	0.00
			Multicast	0.00	0.00	0.00	0.00
		Even VLAN	Voice	0.70	0.68	0.74	0.72
			Unicast	0.69	0.68	0.74	0.72
			Multicast	3.57	1.01	0.74	0.72
Fail link between N-PE1 and N-PE2	Shut	Odd VLAN	Voice	0.00	0.00	0.00	0.00
			Unicast	0.00	0.00	0.00	0.00
			Multicast	0.00	0.00	0.00	0.00
		Even VLAN	Voice	0.00	0.00	0.00	0.00
			Unicast	0.00	0.00	0.00	0.00
			Multicast	0.00	0.00	0.00	0.00
	Restore	Odd VLAN	Voice	0.00	0.00	0.00	0.00
			Unicast	0.00	0.00	0.00	0.00
			Multicast	0.00	0.00	0.00	0.00
		Even VLAN	Voice	0.00	0.00	0.00	0.00
			Unicast	0.00	0.00	0.00	0.00
			Multicast	0.00	0.00	0.00	0.00

Table 9-5 *Convergence Results for Link and Node Failures for H-VPLS with N-PE Redundancy Using EEM Semaphore: EEM Option 3 Solution*

| | | | | Traffic Direction | | | |
| | | | | LON → SJ | | SJ → LON | |
Failure Type	Action	VLAN	Traffic Type	Max	Min	Max	Min
Fail link between Agg-1 and Agg-2	Shut a link in PortChannel	Odd VLAN	Voice	0.00	0.00	0.00	0.00
			Unicast	0.00	0.00	0.00	0.00
			Multicast	0.00	0.00	0.00	0.00
		Even VLAN	Voice	0.00	0.00	0.00	0.00
			Unicast	0.00	0.00	0.00	0.00
			Multicast	0.00	0.00	0.00	0.00
	Restore a member link in PortChannel	Odd VLAN	Voice	0.00	0.00	0.00	0.00
			Unicast	0.00	0.00	0.00	0.00
			Multicast	0.00	0.00	0.00	0.00
		Even VLAN	Voice	0.00	0.00	0.00	0.00
			Unicast	0.00	0.00	0.00	0.00
			Multicast	0.00	0.00	0.00	0.00
	Shut down PortChannel	Odd VLAN	Voice	0.00	0.00	0.00	0.00
			Unicast	0.00	0.00	0.00	0.00
			Multicast	0.00	0.00	0.00	0.00
		Even VLAN	Voice	0.00	0.00	0.00	0.00
			Unicast	0.00	0.00	0.00	0.00
			Multicast	0.00	0.00	0.00	0.00
	Restore PortChannel	Odd VLAN	Voice	0.00	0.00	0.00	0.00
			Unicast	0.00	0.00	0.00	0.00
			Multicast	0.00	0.00	0.00	0.00
		Even VLAN	Voice	0.00	0.00	0.00	0.00
			Unicast	0.00	0.00	0.00	0.00
			Multicast	0.00	0.00	0.00	0.00
Clear core-facing routes on N-PEs	Clear routes learned from the core from the N-PE routing table	Odd VLAN	Voice	0.00	0.00	0.00	0.00
			Unicast	0.00	0.00	0.00	0.00
			Multicast	0.00	0.00	0.00	0.00
		Even VLAN	Voice	0.00	0.00	0.00	0.00
			Unicast	0.00	0.00	0.00	0.00
			Multicast	0.00	0.00	0.00	0.00
Clear IP routing table on N-PEs	Clear all IP routes from the N-PE routing table	Odd VLAN	Voice	0.00	0.00	0.00	0.00
			Unicast	0.00	0.00	0.00	0.00
			Multicast	0.00	0.00	0.00	0.00
		Even VLAN	Voice	0.00	0.00	0.00	0.00
			Unicast	0.00	0.00	0.00	0.00
			Multicast	0.00	0.00	0.00	0.00
Clear dynamic MAC address table on SJ N-PE1	Clear	Odd VLAN	Voice	0.00	0.00	0.00	0.00
			Unicast	0.00	0.00	0.00	0.00
			Multicast	0.00	0.00	0.00	0.00
		Even VLAN	Voice	0.00	0.00	0.00	0.00
			Unicast	0.00	0.00	0.00	0.00
			Multicast	0.00	0.00	0.00	0.00

[1]Under certain conditions, especially when using a P-core, a node may delay new PW LDP label advertisement toward peers until a background timer, currently hard-coded to 10 seconds, expires. When this situation occurs, a PW may not be activated before 10 seconds. Cisco defect CSCso99838 documents this issue.

[2]Under normal conditions, when N-PE routers advertise labels to new peers, convergence of unicast traffic takes approximately 2 seconds.

Server Cluster Tests

Event logs are captured from the Event Viewer of the Microsoft cluster server. The logs are in the reverse order, showing the last event first. It is best to view the time stamps when analyzing these logs.

Table 9-6 shows the event logs from the Event Viewer of the Microsoft cluster server.

Table 9-6 *Event Logs for H-VPLS with N-PE Redundancy Using EEM Semaphore: EEM Option 3*

Test Case	Time (Seconds)	Event Logs with Time Stamps from Microsoft Server			
Establish L2 connectivity between Microsoft server nodes	0	6/24/2008	6:59:35 PM	CAMP3-SERVER2	The node (re)established communication with cluster node 'CAMP3-SERVER1' on network 'public.'
		6/24/2008	6:59:35 PM	CAMP3-SERVER2	The node (re)established communication with cluster node 'CAMP3-SERVER1' on network 'private(1).'
		6/24/2008	6:59:35 PM	CAMP3-SERVER2	The node (re)established communication with cluster node 'CAMP3-SERVER3' on network 'public.'
		6/24/2008	6:59:35 PM	CAMP3-SERVER2	The node (re)established communication with cluster node 'CAMP3-SERVER3' on network 'private(1).'
		6/24/2008	6:59:30 PM	CAMP3-SERVER3	The node (re)established communication with cluster node 'CAMP3-SERVER2' on network 'private(1).'
		6/24/2008	6:59:30 PM	CAMP3-SERVER3	The node (re)established communication with cluster node 'CAMP3-SERVER2' on network 'public.'
		6/24/2008	6:59:30 PM	CAMP3-SERVER1	The node (re)established communication with cluster node 'CAMP3-SERVER2' on network 'public.'
		6/24/2008	6:59:30 PM	CAMP3-SERVER1	The node (re)established communication with cluster node 'CAMP3-SERVER2' on network 'private(1).'
		6/24/2008	6:53:57 PM	CAMP3-SERVER3	The interface for cluster node 'CAMP3-SERVER1' on network 'private(1)' is operational (up). The node can communicate with all other available cluster nodes on the network.
		6/24/2008	6:53:55 PM	CAMP3-SERVER3	The interface for cluster node 'CAMP3-SERVER1' on network 'public' is operational (up). The node can communicate with all other available cluster nodes on the network.
		6/24/2008	6:54:14 PM	CAMP3-SERVER1	The start type of the cluster service service was changed from demand start to auto start.
		6/24/2008	6:54:04 PM	CAMP3-SERVER1	The cluster service service entered the running state.
		6/24/2008	6:54:04 PM	CAMP3-SERVER1	Cluster service successfully joined the server cluster CLUSTER-MNS.

Table 9-6 *Event Logs for H-VPLS with N-PE Redundancy Using EEM Semaphore: EEM Option 3*

Test Case	Time (Seconds)	Event Logs with Time Stamps from Microsoft Server			
Shut down both N-PEs in a data center	70	6/20/2008	6:31:00 PM	CAMP3-SERVER2	The cluster service brought the resource group "Cluster Group" online.
		6/20/2008	6:30:30 PM	CAMP3-SERVER2	The time provider NtpClient is currently receiving valid time data from camp3-server1.camp3.com (ntp.d|172.25.196.29:123->1.1.1.1:123).
		6/20/2008	6:30:13 PM	CAMP3-SERVER2	The cluster service is attempting to bring online the resource group "Cluster Group."
		6/20/2008	6:30:13 PM	CAMP3-SERVER2	Cluster node CAMP3-SERVER3 was removed from the active server cluster membership. Cluster service may have been stopped on the node, the node may have failed, or the node may have lost communication with the other active server cluster nodes.
		6/20/2008	6:29:50 PM	CAMP3-SERVER2	The node lost communication with cluster node 'CAMP3-SERVER3' on network 'public.'
		6/20/2008	6:29:50 PM	CAMP3-SERVER2	The node lost communication with cluster node 'CAMP3-SERVER3' on network 'private(1).'
Power off access switch	88	6/20/2008	5:30:22 PM	CAMP3-SERVER2	The cluster service brought the resource group "Cluster Group" online.
		6/20/2008	5:29:50 PM	CAMP3-SERVER2	The time provider NtpClient is currently receiving valid time data from camp3-server1.camp3.com (ntp.d|172.25.196.29:123->1.1.1.1:123).
		6/20/2008	5:29:16 PM	CAMP3-SERVER2	The cluster service is attempting to bring online the resource group "Cluster Group."
		6/20/2008	5:29:16 PM	CAMP3-SERVER2	Cluster node CAMP3-SERVER3 was removed from the active server cluster membership. Cluster service may have been stopped on the node, the node may have failed, or the node may have lost communication with the other active server cluster nodes.
		6/20/2008	5:28:53 PM	CAMP3-SERVER2	The node lost communication with cluster node 'CAMP3-SERVER3' on network 'public.'
		6/20/2008	5:28:53 PM	CAMP3-SERVER2	The node lost communication with cluster node 'CAMP3-SERVER3' on network 'private(1).'
		6/20/2008	5:28:54 PM	CAMP3-SERVER1	The node lost communication with cluster node 'CAMP3-SERVER3' on network 'private(1).'
		6/20/2008	5:28:54 PM	CAMP3-SERVER1	The node lost communication with cluster node 'CAMP3-SERVER3' on network 'public.'

Table 9-6 *Event Logs for H-VPLS with N-PE Redundancy Using EEM Semaphore: EEM Option 3*

Test Case	Time (Seconds)	Event Logs with Time Stamps from Microsoft Server			
		6/20/2008	1:23:58 PM	CAMP3-SERVER3	The cluster service brought the resource group "Cluster Group" online.
		6/20/2008	1:23:02 PM	CAMP3-SERVER2	Cluster node CAMP3-SERVER1 was removed from the active server cluster membership. Cluster service may have been stopped on the node, the node may have failed, or the node may have lost communication with the other active server cluster nodes.
Shut down active node	164	6/20/2008	1:21:13 PM	CAMP3-SERVER2	The node lost communication with cluster node 'CAMP3-SERVER1' on network 'public.'
		6/20/2008	1:21:13 PM	CAMP3-SERVER2	The node lost communication with cluster node 'CAMP3-SERVER1' on network 'private(1).'
		6/20/2008	1:21:14 PM	CAMP3-SERVER3	The node lost communication with cluster node 'CAMP3-SERVER1' on network 'private(1).'
		6/20/2008	1:21:14 PM	CAMP3-SERVER3	The node lost communication with cluster node 'CAMP3-SERVER1' on network 'public.'
		6/23/2008	6:47:27 PM	CAMP3-SERVER3	The node (re)established communication with cluster node 'CAMP3-SERVER2' on network 'private(1).'
Private VLAN N-PE reload	5	6/23/2008	6:47:26 PM	CAMP3-SERVER3	The node (re)established communication with cluster node 'CAMP3-SERVER1' on network 'private(1).'
		6/23/2008	6:47:21 PM	CAMP3-SERVER3	The node lost communication with cluster node 'CAMP3-SERVER1' on network 'private(1).'
		6/23/2008	6:47:21 PM	CAMP3-SERVER3	The node lost communication with cluster node 'CAMP3-SERVER2' on network 'private(1).'
		6/20/2008	7:19:14 PM	CAMP3-SERVER2	The cluster service brought the resource group "Cluster Group" online.
		6/20/2008	7:18:44 PM	CAMP3-SERVER2	The time provider NtpClient is currently receiving valid time data from camp3-server1.camp3.com (ntp.d|172.25.196.29:123->1.1.1.1:123).
		6/20/2008	7:18:35 PM	CAMP3-SERVER2	The cluster service is attempting to bring online the resource group "Cluster Group."
Unplug Active Server	60	6/20/2008	7:18:35 PM	CAMP3-SERVER2	Cluster node CAMP3-SERVER3 was removed from the active server cluster membership. Cluster service may have been stopped on the node, the node may have failed, or the node may have lost communication with the other active server cluster nodes.
		6/20/2008	7:18:21 PM	CAMP3-SERVER2	The node lost communication with cluster node 'CAMP3-SERVER3' on network 'public.'
		6/20/2008	7:18:14 PM	CAMP3-SERVER2	The node lost communication with cluster node 'CAMP3-SERVER3' on network 'private(1).'

Multidomain H-VPLS with N-PE Redundancy: EEM Option 4a

This highly scalable solution called "multidomain H-VPLS with N-PE redundancy: EEM option 4a" is widely deployed by outsourcers and offers many of the key features required for large-scale data center interconnectivity. There is total independence between the N-PE and aggregation layer, VLAN overlapping is supported because N-PE routers do not participate in local STP, and scalability is achieved via QinQ tagging. These advantages make this solution attractive to data centers with multiple domains, such as application service providers (ASPs) and large enterprises that function as service providers. However, MAC address overlapping can be an issue in some implementations. See the "QinQ MAC Overlapping" section in Chapter 11, "Additional Design Considerations," for design considerations.

Figure 9-17 illustrates the EEM option 4a solution.

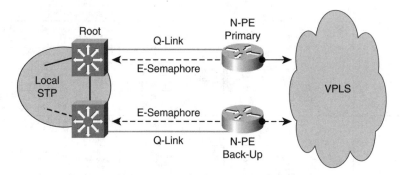

Figure 9-17 *Multidomain H-VPLS with N-PE redundancy using E-semaphore: EEM option 4a*

In the EEM option 4a solution, N-PE routers do not participate in the local STP. Nevertheless, N-PE still is required to communicate VPLS topology changes to the local data center. To circumvent the inability of QinQ link to transport BPDUs, this solution utilizes an additional link called an *E-link*.

E-link, also called the edge semaphore, is used as the control-plane link to trigger an EEM script on the aggregation switch. The function of this EEM script on the aggregation switch is to simply flush the local MAC address table. There are several ways to trigger a topology change in the aggregation layer. However, to maintain compatibility with most of the deployed aggregation switches, MAC address flushing is achieved by flapping the dedicated physical E-link between N-PEs and aggregation switches.

This solution requires two physical links between N-PEs and aggregation switches:

- **Q-link:** High-speed link (1gig, 10gig, or EtherChannel) for data traffic, used for VLAN cross-connect. The Q-link interface on the N-PE side can either be a LAN port on a 67xx module or an interface on an ES module:

  - **LAN port:** Selective QinQ is not supported, and only one QinQ tag can be added per port.

  - **ES module:** Selective QinQ is supported, which allows the configuration of multiple "service instances" mapped to multiple QinQ VLANs. Selective QinQ enables distribution of VLANs across multiple EVCs and load repartition of traffic flows on the core links.

- **E-link:** This link does not forward data and does not carry any broadcast traffic. It is used for control-plane traffic to trigger MAC address flushing on aggregation switches.

In this solution, QinQ VLAN (also known as core VLAN) is cross-connected using only one VFI toward all the other remote data centers. The N-PE router performs QinQ encapsulation or adds a QinQ outer tag to the received dot1q traffic on the Q-link (port facing the edge on the N-PE to aggregation link) before forwarding the traffic via VFI.

EEM scripts are used for protection against N-PE node failure, Q-link failure including the edge aggregation node failure, and N-PE node isolation from the VPLS core. The following actions are taken when the backup node detects primary VPLS node failure or when the primary node is unable to accomplish xconnection:

- Semaphore and PW management, both identical to all EEM-based solutions.

- MAC address flushing is executed by an EEM script in the aggregation switches, triggered by a flapping E-link.

Control Plane

The key point that delivers scalability and availability of this solution is the independence of domains. To accomplish this, there are three independent control planes:

- **Spanning tree:** N-PE routers do not participate in local STP.

  Spanning-tree BPDUs are not transmitted over VPLS.

  The Q-link is configured for *PortFast trunk* and *BPDU filter enable* on the aggregation side.

  Local data center MAC address flushing is executed by EEM script via E-semaphore.

- **VPLS:** P- and B-semaphores allow active/standby state between the primary and backup N-PE nodes.

  For load balancing, two semaphore pairs are configured, one for active/standby and one for standby/active.

- **MPLS core:** LDP and IGP protocols are enabled in the core.

Data Plane

Incoming traffic on the Q-link is encapsulated into one or two core VLANs. Selective QinQ is configured, and odd and even VLANs are split into two different core VLANs. These core VLANs are attached to two core VFIs, and each VFI is connected to other data center VFIs with partially meshed PWs. In this way, the primary VFI is connected to all other data centers' primary and backup VPLS nodes; however, the backup VFI is connected only to all other data centers' primary VPLS nodes. Associated VFIs are load balanced on both N-PEs, and PW load balancing is achieved on the core links. When equal-cost multipath connectivity into the core exists, PWs are load balanced based on the destination N-PE/VCID, which is the destination VLAN.

Theory of Operation

This section analyzes EEM option 4a behavior in normal and failure states.

Normal Mode

In normal mode, odd VLANs on N-PE1 are connected to an active VFI while the active VFI associated with even VLANs is on N-PE2. All edge VLANs to be cross-connected are created on both the N-PEs. The E-link is provisioned for signaling only and does not carry any traffic.

In this solution, failure conditions include the following:

■ Aggregation switch failure

■ Q-link failure

■ Primary N-PE failure

■ Backup N-PE failure

■ Main core link (MPLS) failure

■ All core links failure on primary N-PE (node isolation)

■ All core links failure on backup N-PE

Three main recovery mechanisms to react to these failures are as follows:

■ E-semaphore to trigger MAC address flushing on aggregation

■ EEM semaphores for N-PE node failure or node isolation

■ LDP for core link failure without isolation

Primary N-PE Node or Q-Link Failure

Consider the following analysis of the condition when a primary node loses connectivity to the VPLS domain, either because it is down or because it becomes isolated from the data center or the MPLS core.

Figure 9-18 shows the link and PW state after a primary node or edge link failure in EEM option 4a.

When the Q-link goes down, either because of link or aggregation switch failure, the primary N-PE is unable to reach the local data center. EEM determines this failure and reacts by shutting its own P-semaphore and makes a request via the EEM semaphore protocol to the backup node to become active. The primary N-PE also shuts down its own primary PW to force MAC address flushing on the remote sites.

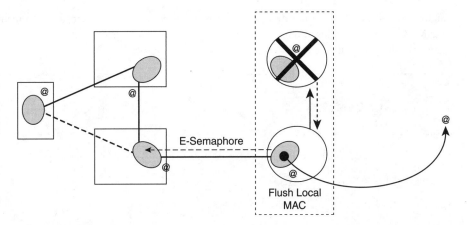

Figure 9-18   *N-PE node or Q-link failure.*

The backup node activates its backup PW toward the primary nodes of other remote data centers via unshutting of the PW-ID loopback interface. In addition, to prevent an active/active state, the backup N-PE raises its own B-semaphore, thus preventing the primary N-PE from becoming active.

Now, MAC addresses within the local data center devices must be flushed for the new path to be learned. The backup node flaps (shut/no shut) the E-link that triggers a script in the aggregation switch forcing it to flush local MAC addresses.

Even though the described failure scenario is related to Q-link failure, the behavior of the EEM semaphore protocol during primary node failure or when the primary node becomes isolated from the MPLS core is identical.

When a primary N-PE gets isolated from the MPLS core, EEM script tracking connectivity to the core will detect this failure and will shut down its Q-link, leading itself to go into backup mode as described.

Primary N-PE Node or Q-Link Recovery After the Failure

When the primary node initializes and becomes ready, either because the Q-link came back up or because the core is now reachable, it receives a B-semaphore route and therefore stays in standby state. The primary N-PE then raises its P-semaphore, which is announced by the core IGP. After the backup node learns the P-semaphore route, it starts a delay timer (recommended value is 100 sec). The traffic continues to forward through the backup PWs via the backup Q-link until this delay timer expires. When the delay timer expires, the backup node disables the backup PW by shutting down its PW-ID loopback interface and its B-semaphore to allow the primary node to become active and return to normal state.

Figure 9-19 shows the configuration on the primary node requesting aggregation to manage MAC address flushing when it changes the state to active. This request is made via flapping (shut/no shut) the E-link, in this case interface gig 2/1.

```
event manager applet VPLS_ODD-VLAN_B_Semaphore-is-down

event track 11 state down

action 1.0 cli command "enable"

action 2.0 cli command "conf t"

action 4.0 cli command "int lo91"              Start Xconnect

action 4.1 cli command "no shutdown"

action 5.0 cli command "int gig 2/1"

action 5.1 cli command "shutdown"              Request aggregation mac-flush

action 5.2 cli command "no shutdown"

action 9.0 syslog msg "Backup N-PE has become Standby, Primary is Active"
```

Figure 9-19   *E-semaphore trigger on N-PE side.*

Figure 9-20 shows the EEM script on the aggregation switch. When the N-PE flaps the E-link, as shown in Figure 9-19, the EEM script running on the aggregation detects the change in interface state and flushes local MAC addresses.

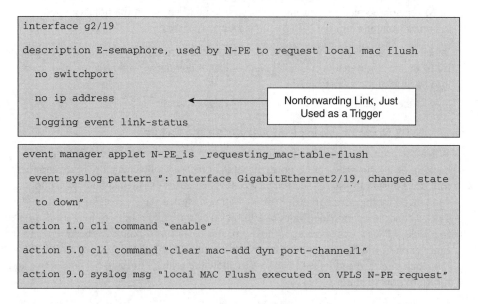

```
interface g2/19

description E-semaphore, used by N-PE to request local mac flush

  no switchport

  no ip address                     Nonforwarding Link, Just
                                     Used as a Trigger
  logging event link-status
```

```
event manager applet N-PE_is _requesting_mac-table-flush

 event syslog pattern ": Interface GigabitEthernet2/19, changed state

  to down"

action 1.0 cli command "enable"

action 5.0 cli command "clear mac-add dyn port-channel1"

action 9.0 syslog msg "local MAC Flush executed on VPLS N-PE request"
```

Figure 9-20   *EEM script on aggregation switch for MAC address flushing.*

The primary and the backup N-PE flap their E-link triggering EEM script to perform MAC address flushing on both the aggregation switches. This flushing of MAC address-es does not cause any disruption to the load-balanced traffic.

N-PE Routers: Hardware and Software

Table 9-7 compares the hardware and software that can be used for N-PE nodes. Cisco 7600 routers were used as N-PEs for all the MST- and EEM-based solutions that this book describes. In this solution, selective QinQ with two EVCs was configured using ES20 modules facing the aggregation. Also, the aggregation switches must support an EEM script that can be trigged on a specific syslog message or on the link state.

Table 9-7 *Hardware and Software for N-PE Nodes*

Cisco 7600 Router	Cisco Catalyst 6500
Interfaces on SIP or ES modules are required for connectivity toward the VPLS core.	Interface on SIP module is required for connectivity toward the VPLS core.
ES module: Selective QinQ. 67xx module: Plain QinQ tagging, one QinQ tag per port.	ES module: Not supported. 67xx module: Plain QinQ tagging, one QinQ tag per port.
Interface on any 67xx LAN or ES module; does not carry any traffic.	Interface on 67xx LAN module; does not carry any traffic.
Cisco IOS 12.2(33)SRC1.	Cisco IOS 12.2(33)SXI.

Implementing Multidomain H-VPLS with N-PE Redundancy Using EEM Semaphore Design

The EEM option 4a solution requires a square topology between N-PEs and aggregation switches. PWs on N-PE1 and N-PE2 are in active or standby state and are managed by EEM scripts.

Figure 9-21 provides a configuration overview of the various links and the nodes.

The following list provides snippets of configuration from N-PE and aggregation devices and output from various **show** commands for verification:

Step 1.   Configure the core IGP, MPLS, and targeted LDP as documented under the VPLS with N-PE redundancy using EEM Semaphore: EEM option 2 solution.

Step 2.   This solution leverages the STP mode and the root bridge placement that are configured on the aggregation devices in the data center. The STP root and backup root assignment remains unchanged. The following example shows spanning tree configuration on aggregation switches.

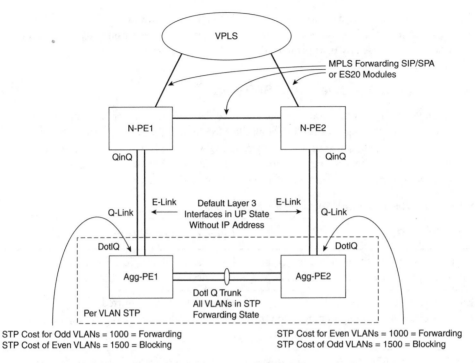

Figure 9-21   *Implementing EEM option 4a: Configuration overview.*

On Agg-1	On Agg-2
| ```
lon-agg-1#
!
spanning-tree mode rapid-pvst
spanning-tree vlan
1,3,5,7,9,11,13,15,17... priority 8192
spanning-tree vlan 2,4,6,8,10,12,14,
  16.... priority 16384
``` | ```
lon-agg-2#
!
spanning-tree mode rapid-pvst
spanning-tree vlan
2,4,6,8,10,12,14.....priority 8192
spanning-tree vlan
1,3,5,7,9,11,13,15....priority 16384
``` |

Step 2.   Show spanning-tree output for VLAN 7 from both the aggregation switches:

On Agg-1:

lon-agg-1# show spanning-tree vlan 7

VLAN0007
    Spanning tree enabled protocol rstp
    Root ID   Priority   8199
               Address   001c.b126.d000
               This bridge is the root

```
                  Hello Time   2 sec  Max Age 20 sec  Forward Delay 15 sec


   Bridge ID  Priority    8199    (priority 8192 sys-id-ext 7)
              Address      001c.b126.d000
              Hello Time   2 sec  Max Age 20 sec  Forward Delay 15 sec
              Aging Time 300


Interface           Role Sts Cost      Prio.Nbr Type
_ _ _ _ _ _ _ _ _ _ . _ _  _ . _ _ _ _ . _ _ _ _  _ _ _ _ _ _ _ _ _ _ _ _

Gi2/1                Desg FWD 4         128.129  P2p Edge
Gi2/22               Desg FWD 4         128.150  P2p
Po1                  Desg FWD 3         128.1665 P2p


lon-agg-1#
! On Agg-2:
lon-agg-2# show spanning-tree vlan 7


VLAN0007
   Spanning tree enabled protocol rstp
   Root ID     Priority    8199
               Address     001c.b126.d000
               Cost        3
               Port        1665 (Port-channel1)
               Hello Time   2 sec  Max Age 20 sec  Forward Delay 15 sec


   Bridge ID  Priority    16391  (priority 16384 sys-id-ext 7)
              Address      001c.b144.4c00 .
              Hello Time   2 sec  Max Age 20 sec  Forward Delay 15 sec
              Aging Time 300


Interface           Role Sts Cost      Prio.Nbr Type
_ _ _ _ _ _ _ _ _ _ . _ _  _ . _ _ _ _ . _ _ _ _  _ _ _ _ _ _ _ _ _ _ _ _

Gi2/1                Desg FWD 4         128.129  P2p Edge
Gi2/21               Desg FWD 4         128.149  P2p
Po1                  Root FWD 3         128.1665 P2p


lon-agg-2#
```

Step 3.   Create QinQ VLANs on both the N-PEs. Configure one SVI per QinQ VLAN
and connect it to VFI. Configure selective QinQ on the Q-links between
N-PEs and aggregation switches for VLAN load repartition.

On N-PE1	On N-PE2

```
vlan 3001
name H-
VPLS_Primary_core_VLAN_for_odd_vlans
vlan 3004
name H-
VPLS_Backup_core_VLAN_for_even_vlans
!
interface Vlan3001
 description Primary Core QinQ VLAN - used
   to transport Odd edge VLAN
 mtu 9216
 no ip address
 xconnect vfi VFI-Odd
 !
interface Vlan3004
 description Backup Core QinQ VLAN - used
   to transport Even edge VLAN
 mtu 9216
 no ip address
 xconnect vfi VFI-Even
 !
l2 vfi VFI-Even manual
 vpn id 3002
 neighbor 10.76.90.22 encapsulation mpls
 neighbor 10.76.90.32 encapsulation mpls
 !
l2 vfi VFI-Odd manual
 vpn id 3001
 neighbor 10.76.91.21 encapsulation mpls
 neighbor 10.76.91.22 encapsulation mpls
 neighbor 10.76.91.31 encapsulation mpls
 neighbor 10.76.91.32 encapsulation mpls
 !
mpls ldp neighbor 10.76.70.12 targeted ldp
mpls ldp neighbor 10.76.70.21 targeted ldp
mpls ldp neighbor 10.76.70.22 targeted ldp
mpls ldp neighbor 10.76.70.31 targeted ldp
mpls ldp neighbor 10.76.70.32 targeted ldp
mpls ldp tcp pak-priority
mpls ldp session protection
no mpls ldp advertise-labels
```

```
vlan 3002
name H-
VPLS_Primary_core_VLAN_for_even_vlans
vlan 3003
name H-VPLS_Backup_core_VLAN_for_odd_vlans
!
interface Vlan3002
 description Primary Core QinQ VLAN - used
   to transport Even edge VLAN
 mtu 9216
 no ip address
 xconnect vfi VFI-Even
 !
interface Vlan3003
 description Backup Core QinQ VLAN - used
   to transport Odd edge VLAN
 mtu 9216
 no ip address
 xconnect vfi VFI-Odd
 !
l2 vfi VFI-Even manual
 vpn id 3002
 neighbor 10.76.90.21 encapsulation mpls
 neighbor 10.76.90.22 encapsulation mpls
 neighbor 10.76.90.31 encapsulation mpls
 neighbor 10.76.90.32 encapsulation mpls
 !
l2 vfi VFI-Odd manual
 vpn id 3001
 neighbor 10.76.91.21 encapsulation mpls
 neighbor 10.76.91.31 encapsulation mpls
 !
mpls ldp neighbor 10.76.70.11 targeted ldp
mpls ldp neighbor 10.76.70.21 targeted ldp
mpls ldp neighbor 10.76.70.22 targeted ldp
mpls ldp neighbor 10.76.70.31 targeted ldp
mpls ldp neighbor 10.76.70.32 targeted ldp
mpls ldp tcp pak-priority
mpls ldp session protection
no mpls ldp advertise-labels
mpls ldp advertise-labels for 76
```

On N-PE1

```
mpls ldp advertise-labels for 76
mpls label protocol ldp
xconnect logging pseudowire status
!
access-list 76 permit 10.76.0.0
0.0.255.255
!
lon-n-pe1#


lon-n-pe1# show running-config interface gig 4/0/2
!
interface GigabitEthernet4/0/2
 description - Q-link - QinQ ES20
 mtu 9216
 logging event link-status
 ip arp inspection limit none
 no ip address
 load-interval 30
 mls qos trust dscp
 service instance 3001 ethernet
encapsulation dot1q 3,5,7,9,11,13,
  15,17,19,21,23,.....
bridge-domain 3001
 !
 service instance 3004 ethernet
encapsulation dot1q 2,4,6,8,10,12,14,
  16,18,20,22,24.....
bridge-domain 3004
 !
end
```

On N-PE2

```
mpls label protocol ldp
xconnect logging pseudowire status
!
access-list 76 permit 10.76.0.0
0.0.255.255
!
lon-n-pe2#


lon-n-pe2# show running-config interface gig 4/0/2
!
interface GigabitEthernet4/0/2
 description Q-link - QinQ ES20
 mtu 9216
 logging event link-status
 ip arp inspection limit none
 no ip address
 load-interval 30
 mls qos trust dscp
 service instance 3002 ethernet
encapsulation dot1q 2,4,6,8,10,12,14,
  16,18,20,22,24.....
bridge-domain 3002
 !
 service instance 3003 ethernet
encapsulation dot1q 3,5,7,9,11,13,
  15,17,19,21,23,.....
bridge-domain 3003
 !
end
```

On Agg-1

```
lon-agg-1# show running-config interface gig 2/1
!
interface GigabitEthernet2/1
 description QinQ connection to lon-n-pe1
 switchport
 switchport trunk encapsulation dot1q
 switchport trunk allowed vlan 2-61,201-
  260
 switchport mode trunk
 switchport nonegotiate
 mtu 9216
```

On Agg-2

```
lon-agg-2# show running-config interface gig 2/1
!
interface GigabitEthernet2/1
 description QinQ connection to lon-n-pe2
 switchport
 switchport trunk encapsulation dot1q
 switchport trunk allowed vlan 1-61,201-
  260
 switchport mode trunk
 switchport nonegotiate
 mtu 9216
```

On Agg-1	On Agg-2
logging event link-status	logging event link-status
logging event spanning-tree status	logging event spanning-tree status
load-interval 30	load-interval 30
spanning-tree portfast trunk	spanning-tree portfast trunk
spanning-tree link-type point-to-point	spanning-tree link-type point-to-point
end	end

Step 4. The output from the **show mpls l2transport vc** command displays the MPLS virtual circuit transport information.

In normal mode, N-PE1 connects the VFI associated with all odd VLANs toward the primary nodes in remote sites. The backup PW are in down state and are ready for activation by the EEM during failure:

```
! On N-PE1:

lon-n-pe1# show mpls l2 vc


Local intf      Local circuit           Dest address    VC ID
Status

_ _ _ _ _ _ .   _ _ _ _ _ _ _ _ _ _ _   _ _ _ _ _ _ .   _ _ _ _ _
_ _ _ _

VFI VFI-Even    VFI                     10.76.90.22     3002
DOWN
VFI VFI-Even    VFI                     10.76.90.32     3002
DOWN
VFI VFI-Odd     VFI                     10.76.91.21     3001
UP
VFI VFI-Odd     VFI                     10.76.91.22     3001
DOWN
VFI VFI-Odd     VFI                     10.76.91.31     3001
UP
VFI VFI-Odd     VFI                     10.76.91.32     3001
DOWN
lon-n-pe1#

! On N-PE2:

lon-n-pe2# show mpls l2 vc
```

```
Local intf        Local circuit           Dest address     VC ID
Status

— — — — —.        — — — — — — — — —      — — — — —.  — — — — —  —

VFI VFI-Even      VFI                     10.76.90.21      3002
DOWN

VFI VFI-Even      VFI                     10.76.90.22      3002
UP

VFI VFI-Even      VFI                     10.76.90.31      3002
DOWN

VFI VFI-Even      VFI                     10.76.90.32      3002
UP

VFI VFI-Odd       VFI                     10.76.91.21      3001
DOWN

VFI VFI-Odd       VFI                     10.76.91.31      3001
DOWN

lon-n-pe2#
```

Step 5. Configure an E-link between N-PEs and aggregation switches. This interface does not forward any traffic and is tracked via an EEM script on the aggregation switches for MAC address flushing.

On N-PE1

```
interface GigabitEthernet2/1
 description connected to lon-agg-1 gi2/19
E-link for Q-in-Q
 no ip address
!
End
```

On N-PE2

```
interface GigabitEthernet2/2
 description connected to lon-agg-2 gi2/18
E-link for Q-in-Q
 no ip address
!
end
```

On Agg-1

```
interface GigabitEthernet2/19
 description connected to lon-n-pe1 gi2/1
E-link for Q-in-Q
 no ip address
 load-interval 30
!
End
```

On Agg-2

```
interface GigabitEthernet2/18
 description connected to lon-n-pe2 gi2/2
E-link for Q-in-Q
 no ip address
 load-interval 30
!
end
```

Step 6. Configure object tracking using EEM. Use the **show running-config | begin event manager** command to display EEM applets that are configured.

N-PE1 is the primary node for odd VLANs. N-PE2 is the primary node for even VLANs. In addition, each N-PE1 is the backup node for even VLANs, and N-PE2 is the backup node for odd VLANs. Therefore, the configurations for each are similar, and the configuration for one can be derived from the configuration of the other:

```
! On N-PE1:
process-max-time 50
!
track timer ip route 1
!
track 10 ip route 10.76.80.12 255.255.255.255 reachability
 delay up 100
!
track 11 ip route 10.76.81.12 255.255.255.255 reachability
!
track 20 interface GigabitEthernet4/0/2 line-protocol
!
track 25 list boolean or
 object 110
 object 112
 delay up 40
!
track 110 interface GigabitEthernet4/0/19 line-protocol
 delay down 5 up 60
!
track 112 interface GigabitEthernet4/0/0 line-protocol
!

event manager applet VPLS_EVEN-VLAN_P_semaphore-is-down
 event track 10 state down
 action 1.0 cli command "enable"
 action 2.0 cli command "conf t"
 action 3.0 cli command "int lo80"
 action 3.1 cli command "no shut"
 action 4.0 cli command "int lo90"
 action 4.1 cli command "no shut"
 action 5.0 cli command "int gi2/1"
 action 5.1 cli command "shut"
 action 5.2 cli command "no shut"
 action 9.0 syslog msg "Backup PW is active"
```

```
event manager applet VPLS_EVEN-VLAN_P_semaphore-is-up
 event track 10 state up
 action 1.0 cli command "enable"
 action 2.0 cli command "conf t"
 action 3.0 cli command "int lo90"
 action 3.1 cli command "shut"
 action 4.0 cli command "int lo80"
 action 4.1 cli command "shut"
 action 5.0 cli command "int gi2/1"
 action 5.1 cli command "shut"
 action 5.2 cli command "no shut"
 action 9.0 syslog msg "Backup PW is shutdown"
event manager applet VPLS_ODD-VLAN_B_semaphore-is-up
 event track 11 state up
 action 1.0 cli command "enable"
 action 2.0 cli command "conf t"
 action 4.0 cli command "int lo91"
 action 4.1 cli command "shut"
 action 9.0 syslog msg "Backup N-PE is Active, Force Primary in
Standby"
event manager applet VPLS_ODD-VLAN_B_semaphore-is-down
 event track 11 state down
 action 1.0 cli command "enable"
 action 2.0 cli command "conf t"
 action 4.0 cli command "int lo91"
 action 4.1 cli command "no shut"
 action 9.0 syslog msg "Backup N-PE has become Standby, Primary runs
Active"
event manager applet Track_Aggregation_link_failure
 event track 20 state down
 action 1.0 cli command "enable"
 action 2.0 cli command "conf t"
 action 3.0 cli command "int lo91"
 action 3.1 cli command "shut"
 action 4.0 cli command "int lo81"
 action 4.1 cli command "shut"
 action 9.0 syslog msg "Aggregation link is failing, Force Primary
   in Standby"
```

```
event manager applet Track_Aggregation_link_recovery
 event track 20 state up
 action 1.0 cli command "enable"
 action 2.0 cli command "conf t"
 action 4.0 cli command "int lo81"
 action 4.1 cli command "no shut"
 action 9.0 syslog msg "Aggregation link as recover, Primary requests
   to become active"
event manager applet WAN_links_down
 event track 25 state down
 action 1.0 cli command "enable"
 action 2.0 cli command "conf t"
 action 3.0 cli command "inter gi4/0/2"
 action 3.1 cli command "shut"
 action 9.0 syslog msg "Both WAN Links are down. Shutting down Q Link"
event manager applet Oneofthe_WAN_Link_is_UP
 event track 25 state up
 action 1.0 cli command "enable"
 action 2.0 cli command "conf t"
 action 3.0 cli command "inter gi4/0/2"
 action 3.1 cli command "no shut"
 action 9.0 syslog msg "One of the WAN link is up. Bring up Q link"
event manager applet Backup-node_ready
 event track 110 state up
 action 1.0 cli command "enable"
 action 2.0 cli command "conf t"
 action 3.0 cli command "track 10 ip route 10.76.80.12 255.255.255.255
   reachability"
 action 3.2 cli command "delay up 100"
 action 9.0 syslog msg "Backup node is operational"
event manager applet Backup-node_not_ready
 event track 110 state down
 action 1.0 cli command "enable"
 action 2.0 cli command "configure t"
 action 3.0 cli command "no track 10"
 action 4.0 cli command "int lo90"
```

```
        action 4.1 cli command "shut"

        action 5.0 cli command "int lo80"

        action 5.1 cli command "shut"

        action 9.0 syslog msg "Backup node not operational"

    !

    event manager history size events 20

    event manager history size traps 20

    end
```

Step 7. Configure EEM on the aggregation switch to flush the MAC address table when requested by N-PE via flapping the E-link:

```
! On Agg-1:

process-max-time 50

!

event manager applet E-link-Monitor-Down

 event syslog pattern "%LINK-3-UPDOWN: Interface GigabitEthernet2/19,
changed state to down"

 action 1.0 cli command "enable"

 action 2.0 cli command "clear mac-address-table dynamic"

 action 3.0 syslog msg "E-link with N-PE1 is down. Execute Local MAC
    address flush"

!
```

Convergence Tests

The traffic profile outlined in Chapter 7 was used to determine end-to-end convergence for unidirectional voice, unicast, and multicast traffic. Links and nodes failed to simulate network failures.

Table 9-8 shows results of various node and link failures. Convergence numbers (max and min) are in seconds.

Table 9-8 *Convergence Numbers for Link and Node Failures for Multidomain H-VPLS with N-PE Redundancy Using EEM Semaphore: EEM Option 4a Solution*

Failure Type	Action	VLAN	Traffic Type	Traffic Direction			
				LON → SJ		SJ → LON	
				Max	Min	Max	Min
Reload N-PE1	Reload	Odd VLAN	Voice	1.70	1.70	1.74	1.74
			Unicast	1.70	1.70	1.73	1.73
			Multicast	1.71	1.69	1.74	1.74
		Even VLAN	Voice	0.02	0.02	0.02	0.02
			Unicast	0.00	0.00	0.00	0.00
			Multicast	0.01	0.00	0.01	0.01
	Restore	Odd VLAN[1,2]	Voice	5.14	5.14	8.40	8.40
			Unicast	5.14	5.14	8.41	8.41
			Multicast	11.47	8.53	8.55	8.41
		Even VLAN	Voice	0.02	0.02	0.00	0.00
			Unicast	0.00	0.00	0.00	0.00
			Multicast	0.31	0.00	0.26	0.00
Reload N-PE2	Reload	Odd VLAN	Voice	0.02	0.02	0.00	0.00
			Unicast	0.00	0.00	0.00	0.00
			Multicast	0.00	0.00	0.00	0.00
		Even VLAN	Voice	1.52	1.50	1.54	1.54
			Unicast	1.52	1.52	1.54	1.54
			Multicast	1.52	1.51	1.54	1.54
	Restore	Odd VLAN	Voice	0.04	0.02	0.00	0.00
			Unicast	0.01	0.01	0.00	0.00
			Multicast	0.04	0.00	0.00	0.00
		Even VLAN[1,2]	Voice	3.42	3.36	6.20	6.20
			Unicast	3.39	3.38	6.21	6.21
			Multicast	7.52	6.32	6.24	6.21
Reload Agg-1	Reload	Odd VLAN	Voice	3.11	3.04	3.06	3.06
			Unicast	3.06	3.06	3.06	3.06
			Multicast	5.49	3.92	5.63	5.46
		Even VLAN	Voice	0.00	0.00	0.00	0.00
			Unicast	0.00	0.00	0.00	0.00
			Multicast	0.04	0.00	0.04	0.01
	Restore	Odd VLAN[1,2]	Voice	2.98	2.92	4.74	4.54
			Unicast	2.96	2.94	4.74	4.53
			Multicast	12.43	6.70	7.01	6.91
		Even VLAN	Voice	0.20	0.18	0.00	0.00
			Unicast	0.19	0.00	0.00	0.00
			Multicast	0.19	0.00	0.01	0.01
Reload Agg-2	Reload	Odd VLAN	Voice	0.00	0.00	0.02	0.02
			Unicast	0.00	0.00	0.00	0.00
			Multicast	0.01	0.00	0.01	0.01
		Even VLAN	Voice	3.08	3.26	3.08	3.08
			Unicast	3.07	3.07	3.07	3.07
			Multicast	5.58	3.10	7.08	3.15
	Restore	Odd VLAN	Voice	0.00	0.00	0.02	0.02
			Unicast	0.00	0.00	0.00	0.00
			Multicast	0.00	0.00	0.00	0.00
		Even VLAN[1,2]	Voice	6.62	6.14	6.50	6.32
			Unicast	6.61	6.17	6.51	6.30
			Multicast	11.13	7.64	8.49	7.31

Table 9-8 *Convergence Numbers for Link and Node Failures for Multidomain H-VPLS with N-PE Redundancy Using EEM Semaphore: EEM Option 4a Solution*

Failure Type	Action	VLAN	Traffic Type	Traffic Direction LON → SJ Max	Min	SJ → LON Max	Min
Fail L2 link between N-PE1 and Agg-1	Shut	Odd VLAN	Voice	2.50	2.46	2.46	2.46
			Unicast	2.47	2.47	2.47	2.47
			Multicast	2.48	2.46	2.47	2.47
		Even VLAN	Voice	0.00	0.00	0.00	0.00
			Unicast	0.00	0.00	0.00	0.00
			Multicast	0.00	0.00	0.00	0.00
	No shut	Odd VLAN	Voice	0.62	0.6	0.63	0.63
			Unicast	0.6	0.6	0.63	0.63
			Multicast	3.39	2.86	0.63	0.63
		Even VLAN	Voice	0.00	0.00	0.00	0.00
			Unicast	0.00	0.00	0.00	0.00
			Multicast	0.00	0.00	0.00	0.00
Fail L2 link between N-PE2 and Agg-2	Shut	Odd VLAN	Voice	0.02	0.02	0.02	0.02
			Unicast	0.00	0.00	0.00	0.00
			Multicast	0.01	0.00	0.02	0.01
		Even VLAN	Voice	2.64	2.62	2.64	2.64
			Unicast	2.63	2.62	2.63	2.63
			Multicast	3.46	2.80	2.65	2.64
	No shut	Odd VLAN	Voice	0.02	0.02	0.02	0.02
			Unicast	0.00	0.00	0.00	0.00
			Multicast	0.00	0.00	0.02	0.02
		Even VLAN	Voice	1.28	1.26	1.30	1.30
			Unicast	1.27	1.27	1.28	1.28
			Multicast	4.10	1.67	1.30	1.30
Fail L2 link between Agg-1 and Agg-2	Shut	Odd VLAN	Voice	0.00	0.00	0.00	0.00
			Unicast	0.00	0.00	0.00	0.00
			Multicast	0.00	0.00	0.00	0.00
		Even VLAN	Voice	0.00	0.00	0.00	0.00
			Unicast	0.00	0.00	0.00	0.00
			Multicast	0.00	0.00	0.00	0.00
	No shut	Odd VLAN	Voice	0.00	0.00	0.00	0.00
			Unicast	0.00	0.00	0.00	0.00
			Multicast	0.00	0.00	0.00	0.00
		Even VLAN	Voice	0.00	0.00	0.00	0.00
			Unicast	0.00	0.00	0.00	0.00
			Multicast	0.00	0.00	0.00	0.00
Fail WAN link facing core on N-PE1	Shut	Odd VLAN	Voice	0.10	0.06	0.06	0.06
			Unicast	0.07	0.07	0.06	0.06
			Multicast	0.08	0.07	0.07	0.07
		Even VLAN	Voice	0.00	0.00	0.00	0.00
			Unicast	0.00	0.00	0.00	0.00
			Multicast	0.00	0.00	0.00	0.00
	No shut	Odd VLAN	Voice	0.02	0.02	0.02	0.02
			Unicast	0.01	0.01	0.00	0.00
			Multicast	0.02	0.01	0.02	0.02
		Even VLAN	Voice	0.02	0.02	0.02	0.02
			Unicast	0.00	0.00	0.00	0.00
			Multicast	0.01	0.00	0.00	0.00

Table 9-8 *Convergence Numbers for Link and Node Failures for Multidomain H-VPLS with N-PE Redundancy Using EEM Semaphore: EEM Option 4a Solution*

Failure Type	Action	VLAN	Traffic Type	LON → SJ		SJ → LON	
				Max	Min	Max	Min
Fail WAN link facing core on N-PE2	Shut	Odd VLAN	Voice	0.02	0.02	0.00	0.00
			Unicast	0.00	0.00	0.00	0.00
			Multicast	0.01	0.00	0.01	0.01
		Even VLAN	Voice	0.08	0.04	0.06	0.06
			Unicast	0.06	0.06	0.06	0.06
			Multicast	0.07	0.05	0.07	0.07
	No shut	Odd VLAN	Voice	0.00	0.00	0.02	0.02
			Unicast	0.00	0.00	0.00	0.00
			Multicast	0.00	0.00	0.01	0.01
		Even VLAN	Voice	0.04	0.02	0.02	0.02
			Unicast	0.02	0.01	0.00	0.00
			Multicast	0.03	0.01	0.01	0.01
Fail both WAN links on N-PE1	Shut	Odd VLAN	Voice	3.48	3.46	3.48	3.48
			Unicast	3.48	3.48	3.48	3.48
			Multicast	3.49	3.47	3.48	3.48
		Even VLAN	Voice	0.00	0.00	0.00	0.00
			Unicast	0.00	0.00	0.00	0.00
			Multicast	0.00	0.00	0.00	0.00
	No shut	Odd VLAN	Voice	1.44	1.42	1.44	1.44
			Unicast	1.43	1.43	1.44	1.44
			Multicast	5.25	3.61	1.44	1.44
		Even VLAN	Voice	0.00	0.00	0.00	0.00
			Unicast	0.00	0.00	0.00	0.00
			Multicast	0.00	0.00	0.00	0.00
Fail both WAN links on N-PE2	Shut	Odd VLAN	Voice	0.00	0.00	0.02	0.02
			Unicast	0.00	0.00	0.00	0.00
			Multicast	0.01	0.00	0.01	0.01
		Even VLAN	Voice	2.26	2.22	2.26	2.26
			Unicast	2.25	2.24	2.25	2.24
			Multicast	4.05	2.42	2.25	2.25
	No shut	Odd VLAN	Voice	0.02	0.02	0.00	0.00
			Unicast	0.00	0.00	0.00	0.00
			Multicast	0.00	0.00	0.01	0.01
		Even VLAN	Voice	1.23	1.20	1.20	1.20
			Unicast	1.21	1.21	1.21	1.21
			Multicast	3.58	1.22	1.22	1.22
Clear entire routing table on N-PE1	Clear	Odd VLAN	Voice	0.00	0.00	0.00	0.00
			Unicast	0.00	0.00	0.00	0.00
			Multicast	0.04	0.02	0.02	0.01
		Even VLAN	Voice	0.00	0.00	0.00	0.00
			Unicast	0.00	0.00	0.00	0.00
			Multicast	0.04	0.02	0.02	0.01
Clear entire routing table on N-PE2	Clear	Odd VLAN	Voice	0.00	0.00	0.00	0.00
			Unicast	0.00	0.00	0.00	0.00
			Multicast	0.00	0.00	0.00	0.00
		Even VLAN	Voice	0.00	0.00	0.00	0.00
			Unicast	0.00	0.00	0.00	0.00
			Multicast	0.00	0.00	0.00	0.00

Table 9-8 *Convergence Numbers for Link and Node Failures for Multidomain H-VPLS with N-PE Redundancy Using EEM Semaphore: EEM Option 4a Solution*

Failure Type	Action	VLAN	Traffic Type	Traffic Direction			
				LON → SJ		SJ → LON	
				Max	Min	Max	Min
Clear dynamic MAC address table on N-PE1	Clear	Odd VLAN	Voice	0.00	0.00	0.00	0.00
			Unicast	0.00	0.00	0.00	0.00
			Multicast	0.04	0.02	0.02	0.01
		Even VLAN	Voice	0.00	0.00	0.00	0.00
			Unicast	0.00	0.00	0.00	0.00
			Multicast	0.40	0.02	0.02	0.01
Clear dynamic MAC address table on N-PE2	Clear	Odd VLAN	Voice	0.00	0.00	0.00	0.00
			Unicast	0.00	0.00	0.00	0.00
			Multicast	0.00	0.00	0.01	0.00
		Even VLAN	Voice	0.00	0.00	0.00	0.00
			Unicast	0.00	0.00	0.00	0.00
			Multicast	0.00	0.00	0.01	0.00

[1]Under certain conditions, especially when using a P-core, a node may delay new PW LDP label advertisement toward peers until a background timer, currently hard-coded to 10 seconds, expires. When this situation occurs, a PW may not be activated before 10 seconds. Cisco defect CSCso99838 documents this issue.

[2]In normal conditions, when N-PE routers advertise labels to new peers, convergence of unicast traffic takes approximately 2 seconds.

Server Cluster Tests

Event logs are captured from the Event Viewer of the Microsoft cluster server. The logs are in the reverse order, showing the last event first. It is best to view the time stamps when analyzing these logs.

Table 9-9 shows the event logs from the Event Viewer of the Microsoft cluster server.

Table 9-9 *Event Logs for H-VPLS with N-PE Redundancy Using EEM Semaphore: EEM Option 4a*

Test Case	Time (Seconds)	Event Logs with Time Stamps for consistency from Microsoft Server			
		12/19/2008	4:32:48 PM	CAMP3-SERVER3	Cluster service successfully joined the server cluster CLUSTER-MNS
		12/19/2008	4:32:41 PM	CAMP3-SERVER3	The node (re)established communication with cluster node 'CAMP3-SERVER2' on network 'private(1)'.
		12/19/2008	4:32:41 PM	CAMP3-SERVER3	The node (re)established communication with cluster node 'CAMP3-SERVER2' on network 'public'.
		12/19/2008	4:32:41 PM	CAMP3-SERVER3	The node (re)established communication with cluster node 'CAMP3-SERVER1' on network 'public'
		12/19/2008	4:32:41 PM	CAMP3-SERVER3	The node (re)established communication with cluster node 'CAMP3-SERVER1' on network 'private(1)'.
Establish L2 Connectivity between Microsoft Server Nodes	No Convergence	12/19/2008	4:32:41 PM	CAMP3-SERVER2	The interface for cluster node 'CAMP3-SERVER3' on network 'private(1)' is operational (up). The node can communicate with all other available cluster nodes on the network.
		12/19/2008	4:32:41 PM	CAMP3-SERVER2	The interface for cluster node 'CAMP3-SERVER3' on network 'public' is operational (up). The node can communicate with all other available cluster nodes on the network.
		12/19/2008	4:32:40 PM	CAMP3-SERVER1	The node (re)established communication with cluster node 'CAMP3-SERVER3' on network 'private(1)'.
		12/19/2008	4:32:40 PM	CAMP3-SERVER1	The node (re)established communication with cluster node 'CAMP3-SERVER3' on network 'public'.
		12/19/2008	4:32:40 PM	CAMP3-SERVER2	The node (re)established communication with cluster node 'CAMP3-SERVER3' on network 'public'.
		12/19/2008	4:32:40 PM	CAMP3-SERVER2	The node (re)established communication with cluster node 'CAMP3-SERVER3' on network 'private(1)'.

Table 9-9   *Event Logs for H-VPLS with N-PE Redundancy Using EEM Semaphore: EEM Option 4a*

Test Case	Time (Seconds)	Event Log with Time Stamp from Microsoft Server			
		11/26/2008	11:49:35 AM	CAMP3-SERVER2	The Cluster Service brought the Resource Group "ClusterGroup" online.
		11/26/2008	11:47:57 AM	CAMP3-SERVER2	The Cluster Service is attempting to bring online the Resource Group "ClusterGroup".
		11/26/2008	11:47:57 AM	CAMP3-SERVER2	Cluster network 'public' is operational (up). All available server cluster nodes attached to the network can communicate using it.
		11/26/2008	11:47:57 AM	CAMP3-SERVER2	The interface for cluster node 'CAMP3-SERVER2' on network 'public' is operational (up). The node can communicate with all other available cluster nodes on the network.
Shut Down Both N-PEs in a Data Center	124	11/26/2008	11:47:57 AM	CAMP3-SERVER2	The interface for cluster node 'CAMP3-SERVER1' on network 'public' is operational (up). The node can communicate with all other available cluster nodes on the network.
		11/26/2008	11:47:57 AM	CAMP3-SERVER2	Cluster node CAMP3-SERVER3 was removed from the active server cluster membership. Cluster service may have been stopped on the node, the node may have failed, or the node may have lost communication with the other active server cluster nodes.
		11/26/2008	11:47:34 AM	CAMP3-SERVER1	The node lost communication with cluster node 'CAMP3-SERVER3' on network 'private(1)'.
		11/26/2008	11:47:31 AM	CAMP3-SERVER1	The node lost communication with cluster node 'CAMP3-SERVER3' on network 'public'.

Table 9-9 *Event Logs for H-VPLS with N-PE Redundancy Using EEM Semaphore: EEM Option 4a*

Test Case	Time (Seconds)	Event Log with Time Stamp from Microsoft Server			
Power Off Access Switch	195	11/25/2008	6:53:35 PM	CAMP3-SERVER2	The Cluster Service brought the Resource Group "ClusterGroup" online.
		11/25/2008	6:51:05 PM	CAMP3-SERVER2	The Cluster Service is attempting to bring online the Resource Group "ClusterGroup".
		11/25/2008	6:51:05 PM	CAMP3-SERVER2	Cluster node CAMP3-SERVER3 was removed from the active server cluster membership. Cluster service may have been stopped on the node, the node may have failed, or the node may have lost communication with the other active server cluster nodes.
		11/25/2008	6:50:43 PM	CAMP3-SERVER2	The node lost communication with cluster node 'CAMP3-SERVER3' on network 'public'.
		11/25/2008	6:50:43 PM	CAMP3-SERVER2	The node lost communication with cluster node 'CAMP3-SERVER3' on network 'private(1)'.
		11/25/2008	6:50:20 PM	CAMP3-SERVER1	The node lost communication with cluster node 'CAMP3-SERVER3' on network 'public'.
		11/25/2008	6:50:20 PM	CAMP3-SERVER1	The node lost communication with cluster node 'CAMP3-SERVER3' on network 'private (1)'.
Shut Down Active Node	210	12/19/2008	4:30:31 PM	CAMP3-SERVER2	The Cluster Service brought the Resource Group "ClusterGroup" online.
		12/19/2008	4:28:53 PM	CAMP3-SERVER2	Cluster node CAMP3-SERVER3 was removed from the active server cluster membership. Cluster service may have been stopped on the node, the node may have failed, or the node may have lost communication with the other active server cluster nodes.
		12/19/2008	4:26:59 PM	CAMP3-SERVER1	The node lost communication with cluster node 'CAMP3-SERVER3' on network 'public'.
		12/19/2008	4:26:59 PM	CAMP3-SERVER1	The node lost communication with cluster node 'CAMP3-SERVER3' on network 'private(1)'.
		12/19/2008	4:26:59 PM	CAMP3-SERVER2	The node lost communication with cluster node 'CAMP3-SERVER3' on network 'public'.
		12/19/2008	4:26:59 PM	CAMP3-SERVER2	The node lost communication with cluster node 'CAMP3-SERVER3' on network 'private(1)'.

Table 9-9   *Event Logs for H-VPLS with N-PE Redundancy Using EEM Semaphore: EEM Option 4a*

Test Case	Time (Seconds)	Event Log with Time Stamp from Microsoft Server			
Private VLAN NPE Reload	7	12/3/2008	6:49:00 PM	CAMP3-SERVER2	Cluster network 'private(1)' is operational (up). All available server cluster nodes attached to the network can communicate using it.
		12/3/2008	6:49:00 PM	CAMP3-SERVER2	The interface for cluster node 'CAMP3-SERVER3' on network 'private(1)' is operational (up). The node can communicate with all other available cluster nodes on the network.
		12/3/2008	6:49:00 PM	CAMP3-SERVER2	The interface for cluster node 'CAMP3-SERVER1' on network 'private(1)' is operational (up). The node can communicate with all other available cluster nodes on the network.
		12/3/2008	6:49:00 PM	CAMP3-SERVER2	The interface for cluster node 'CAMP3-SERVER2' on network 'private(1)' is operational (up). The node can communicate with all other available cluster nodes on the network.
		12/3/2008	6:49:00 PM	CAMP3-SERVER2	The node (re)established communication with cluster node 'CAMP3-SERVER3' on network 'private(1)'.
		12/3/2008	6:48:58 PM	CAMP3-SERVER3	The node (re)established communication with cluster node 'CAMP3-SERVER1' on network 'private(1)'.
		12/3/2008	6:48:58 PM	CAMP3-SERVER3	The node (re)established communication with cluster node 'CAMP3-SERVER2' on network 'private(1)'.
		12/3/2008	6:48:54 PM	CAMP3-SERVER2	The node lost communication with cluster node 'CAMP3-SERVER3' on network 'private(1)'.
		12/3/2008	6:48:53 PM	CAMP3-SERVER3	The node lost communication with cluster node 'CAMP3-SERVER1' on network 'private(1)'.
		12/3/2008	6:48:53 PM	CAMP3-SERVER3	The node lost communication with cluster node 'CAMP3-SERVER2' on network 'private(1)'.

Table 9-9   *Event Logs for H-VPLS with N-PE Redundancy Using EEM Semaphore: EEM Option 4a*

Test Case	Time (Seconds)	Event Log with Time Stamp from Microsoft Server			
Unplug Active Server	125	12/3/2008	12:11:26 PM	CAMP3-SERVER2	The Cluster Service brought the Resource Group "ClusterGroup" online.
		12/3/2008	12:09:47 PM	CAMP3-SERVER2	The Cluster Service is attempting to bring online the Resource Group "ClusterGroup".
		12/3/2008	12:09:47 PM	CAMP3-SERVER2	Cluster node CAMP3-SERVER3 was removed from the active server cluster membership. Cluster service may have been stopped on the node, the node may have failed, or the node may have lost communication with the other active server cluster nodes.
		12/3/2008	12:09:26 PM	CAMP3-SERVER2	The interface for cluster node 'CAMP3-SERVER3' on network 'public' failed. If the condition persists, check the cable connecting the node to the network. Next, check for hardware or software errors in node's network adapter. Finally, check for failures in any network components to which the node is connected such as hubs, switches, or bridges.
		12/3/2008	12:09:25 PM	CAMP3-SERVER2	The node lost communication with cluster node 'CAMP3-SERVER3' on network 'private(1)'.
		12/3/2008	12:09:21 PM	CAMP3-SERVER2	The node lost communication with cluster node 'CAMP3-SERVER3' on network 'public'.

Multidomain H-VPLS with Dedicated U-PE: EEM Option 4b

The "multidomain H-VPLS with dedicated U-PE: EEM option 4b" solution is intended mainly for outsourcers or service providers that are willing to propose a DCI solution that is completely nonintrusive to data center devices. This solution does not require any scripting on the existing devices and supports VLAN overlapping.

Figure 9-22 illustrates the EEM option 4b solution.

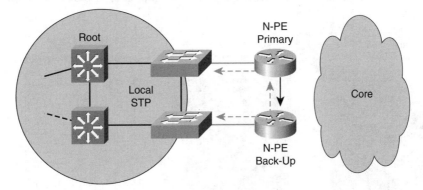

Figure 9-22 *Multidomain H-VPLS with dedicated U-PE: EEM option 4b.*

This solution is identical to EEM option 4a except that an intermediate U-PE device (Layer 2 switch) is inserted between the aggregation switch and the N-PE. This U-PE device performs the same function as the aggregation switches in the EEM option 4a solution. Because of its insertion, there is no need to modify any configuration on the existing aggregation switches within the data center.

This solution could be appropriate for the following situations:

- Service provider that offers data center interconnectivity but that does not own aggregation switches and so cannot install clear MAC address scripts on the distribution boxes.

- Aggregation switches in the data center do not support EEM to control data-plane links and redundant VPLS PWs.

This solution has not been validated by Cisco and therefore does not include deployment details.

Multidomain H-VPLS with Multichassis EtherChannel: EEM Option 5a

The Cisco Catalyst 6500 series Virtual Switching System (VSS) allows merging two physical Cisco Catalyst 6500 series switches together into one single entity.

Figure 9-23 illustrates the VSS concept, in which two 9-slot Cisco Catalyst 6509 chassis can be managed as one 18-slot chassis after enabling VSS.

VSS also introduces Multichassis EtherChannel (MEC), which allows EtherChannel to span across two physical switches. With MEC, all the dual-homed connections to and from the upstream and downstream devices can be configured as EtherChannel, as opposed to individual links. As a result, MEC allows Layer 2 multipathing without the reliance on the Layer 2 redundancy protocols such as STP.

Figure 9-24 illustrates VSS and MEC. Edge devices recognize VSS systems as only one switch.

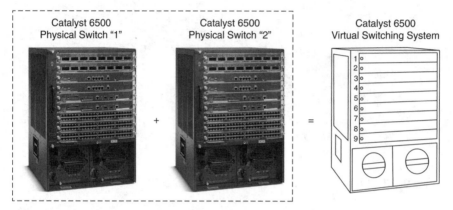

Figure 9-23   *VSS: Logical view.*

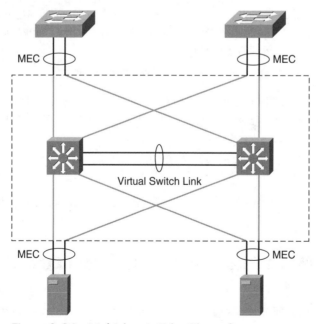

Figure 9-24   *Multichassis EtherChannel.*

As with regular Cisco EtherChannel interfaces, all ports within the MEC link share the same source index, regardless of the chassis in which they are physically present. This approach makes it possible to apply a single IP address for Layer 3 EtherChannel links or for STP to view, such an EtherChannel interface as one logical port.

Note   For information about VSS and MEC technologies, refer to www.http://tinyurl.com/5zph8e.

This solution leverages the benefits of VSS technology on Cisco Catalyst 6500 and vPC (virtual PortChannel available from NX-OS 4.1) on Cisco Nexus 7000 systems.

Figure 9-25 shows a VSS system at the edge of the VPLS.

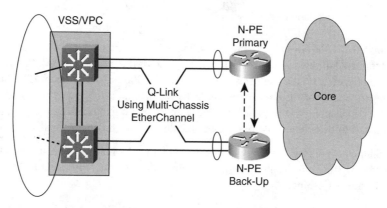

Figure 9-25   *VSS/vPC deployed in the aggregation layer.*

With the deployment of VSS and MEC, scalable H-VPLS solutions can be enhanced to provide link- and chassis-level redundancy and faster convergence during link and node failures.

In this architecture, an MEC system (either VSS or Nexus vPC) in the aggregation layer connects using one EtherChannel toward each N-PE. LACP or PAgP allows Cisco switches to manage Ethernet channeling and protects EtherChannel, while an EEM script ensures availability of N-PE nodes. An EEM script also ensures that only one EtherChannel is cross-connected toward the multipoint VPLS at any time, thus avoiding a loop in the topology.

Because only one MEC is active at a time, MAC address flushing can be easily achieved by flapping the unused MEC. In addition, EEM scripts can be added to track the MEC status. However, this approach adds to the configuration complexity and requires one semaphore per MEC rather than one per node.

Solution Positioning

EEM option 5a is an efficient solution to interconnect data centers using VPLS. Some of the key benefits of this solution are as follows:

- Very simple implementation when MEC tracking is not required.

- Only one EtherChannel (two forwarding links) per N-PE.

- Highly scalable (maximum 4096 VLAN per port, multiplied by number of edge ports).

- One semaphore/EEM script per N-PE when not tracking MEC.

- When tracking MEC, an additional semaphore/EEM script is required per MEC.

- The N-PE node does not participate in local STP.

- Supports overlapping VLANs.

Because the N-PE does not participate in local STP, multitenant and overlapping VLANs are supported in this solution, which makes it one of the most preferred designs. This solution depends on the use of the Cisco Catalyst 6500 or Cisco Nexus 7000 in the aggregation layer of the data center and is by far the most simple and highly scalable solution applicable to enterprise customers, ASPs, and outsourcers that require thousands of VLANs to be extended across geographically dispersed data centers.

To maintain simplicity, this design does not provide VLAN load balancing between the two MECs. This solution also does not require an E-semaphore link and EEM script for MAC address flushing.

This solution has not been validated by Cisco and therefore does not include deployment details.

Multidomain H-VPLS with MEC and VLAN Load Balancing: EEM Option 5b

As of this writing, EEM option 5b is the most deployed solution for VPLS node redundancy in greenfield data centers.

This solution combines the features of EEM option 3 (selective QinQ) with EEM option 5a (VSS and MEC) solutions to provide key features for a large DCI with high scalability and the capability to load balance VLANs across two MECs. This design provides complete independence between N-PE and the aggregation layer. Multiple tenants and overlapping VLANs are supported because N-PE nodes do not participate in local STP. In addition, selective QinQ ensures scalability of VLANs that can be extended across remote sites. These advantages make this solution attractive for deployment in multitenant data centers and for large enterprise customers and outsourcers. However, MAC address overlapping can be an issue in some implementations. See the section "QinQ MAC Overlapping" in Chapter 11 for design considerations.

In this architecture, even though N-PE routers do not participate in the local STP, VPLS topology changes must be communicated to the aggregation switches. This communication is achieved via MAC address flush EEM scripts installed in the aggregation switches that will be triggered from the N-PE routers.

Because of VPLS topology changes, there are several ways to flush MAC addresses. However, to maintain compatibility with various models of aggregation switches already deployed in the data centers, this solution triggers MAC address flushing though flapping a dedicated physical link, called the E-link or E-semaphore, between the N-PE routers and aggregation switches.

If Cisco Nexus 7000s are deployed in the aggregation layer, this E-link can be replaced by an E-semaphore, which can be triggered by tracking an IP route. In this option, control and data planes share the same physical resources.

Figure 9-26 illustrates the EEM option 5b solution.

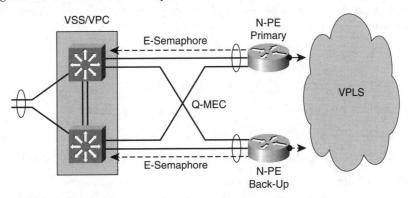

Figure 9-26 *H-VPLS with VSS/vPC and MEC: EEM option 5b.*

In this solution, QinQ VLAN (also known as the core VLAN) cross-connects using only one VFI toward all other remote data centers. The N-PE router performs QinQ encapsulation or adds a QinQ outer tag to the received dot1q traffic on the Q-link (the port that faces the edge on the N-PE to aggregation link) before forwarding the traffic via the VFI.

The Q-link interface on the N-PE side can either be a LAN port on a 67xx module or an interface on an ES module:

- **LAN port:** Selective QinQ is *not* supported, so only one QinQ tag can be added per port.

- **ES module:** Selective QinQ is supported, which allows the configuration of multiple *service instances* mapped to multiple QinQ VLANs. This configuration enables distribution of VLANs across multiple EVCs and load repartition of traffic flows on the core links.

In this solution, the Q-link is a MEC that connects both the aggregation switches to each N-PE router. This dual-connectivity approach gives a notion of primary and backup Q-link with load repartition.

In this architecture, tracking the Q-link is not critical because MEC at the edge provides connectivity to both the aggregation switches. Nevertheless, this design was validated with tracking Q-link failure, even though its failure is highly improbable.

EEM option 5a outlines a simple solution if VLAN load balancing between the two MECs is not desired. However, for implementing server clusters, VLAN load balancing is recommended. The solution is to implement E-semaphore to trigger MAC address flushing on the aggregation switches.

When using an ES20 module facing edge, selective QinQ is configured to load balance traffic from Q-link over multiple VFIs. Load repartition becomes easy via the use of selective QinQ. VLANs are groomed into two VFIs, where one VFI can be active for a certain set of VLANs and a second VFI is the backup for another set of VLANs. This approach requires two semaphores, one for each VFI.

In this solution, the core VLANs imposed by QinQ are as follows:

- **N-PE1:** 3001 for odd VLANs grooming into VFI 3001

  3004 for even VLANs acting as backup for N-PE2 core VLAN 3002 into VFI 3002

- **N-PE2:** 3002 for even VLANs grooming into VFI 3002

  3003 for odd VLANs acting as backup for N-PE1 core VLAN 3001 into VFI 3001

Even though the VPLS core ensures that these core VLANs are locally significant, Cisco recommends the use of unique core VLAN numbers on N-PE1 and N-PE2 within the data center.

On the N-PE routers, when an interface on a LAN module is used for connectivity to the aggregation switches, QinQ tagging can be achieved only on a per-port basis. Usage of LAN modules at the edge implies that all traffic on the Q-link is encapsulated into only one core VLAN. Therefore, VLAN load repartition can be performed only per port with one semaphore protection.

EEM scripts are used to guard against N-PE node failure, Q-link failure including edge aggregation failure, and VPLS node isolation from the core.

The following actions are taken when the primary node detects a core link failure or when the backup N-PE detects that the primary node is down:

- Semaphore and PW management, identical to all EEM-based solutions.
- MAC address flushing on the aggregation device is executed by EEM scripts on aggregation triggered by flapping E-semaphore.

Control Plane

In addition to QinQ, the independence of STP, VPLS, and MPLS core domains also provide scalability and availability of this solution. To accomplish this, there are three independent control planes:

- **Spanning tree:** N-PE devices do not participate in local STP.

  Spanning-tree BPDUs are not transmitted over VPLS.

  Local data center MAC address flushing is executed via an EEM script triggered by the E-link or E-semaphore.

- **VPLS:** P- and B-semaphores allow active/standby state between primary and backup N-PE nodes.

  For load balancing, two semaphore pairs are configured, one for active/standby and one for standby/active.

- **MPLS core:** LDP and IGP protocols are enabled in the core.

Data Plane

Incoming traffic on the Q-link is encapsulated into either of the two core VLANs. In this design, selective QinQ is configured, and odd VLANs and even VLANs are split into two different core VLANs. These core VLANs are attached to two core VFIs, and each VFI is connected to other data center VFIs with partially meshed PWs. However, the backup VFI connects only to all other data centers' primary nodes. Associated VFIs are load balanced on both N-PEs, and PW load balancing is achieved on the core links. In the case of equal-cost multipath into the core, PWs are load balanced based on destination N-PE/VCID, which is nothing but the destination VLAN.

Theory of Operation

This section analyzes EEM option 5b behavior in normal and failure states.

Normal Mode

Each N-PE router is configured with just two VFIs, one for all the odd VLANs and one for all the even VLANs. In normal mode, odd VLANs on N-PE1 are connected to an active VFI while the active VFI associated with even VLANs is on N-PE2.

In this solution, failure conditions include the following:

- Aggregation switch failure (covered via MEC, but it is still considered)

- Q-link failure

- Primary N-PE failure

- Backup N-PE failure

- Main core link (MPLS) failure

- All core links failure on primary N-PE (node isolation)

- All core links failure on backup N-PE

The following are the main recovery mechanisms that react to these failures:

- E-semaphore to trigger MAC flushing on aggregation switches

- EEM semaphores for N-PE node failure or node isolation

- LDP for core link failure without isolation

Primary N-PE Node Failure

Consider the following analysis of the condition when a primary node loses connectivity to the VPLS domain, either because it is down or because it gets isolated from data center or the MPLS core.

Figure 9-27 shows the link and PW state after primary node or edge link failure in EEM option 5b.

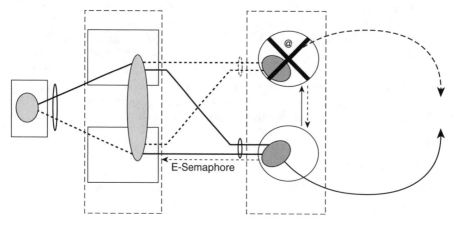

Figure 9-27   *Primary N-PE failure.*

When the primary N-PE fails or becomes isolated from the core, its P-semaphore is no longer advertised by the core IGP.

As soon as the backup N-PE node detects that the primary node is down, the PW-ID loopback interface is brought up, which enables the backup PWs that are connected to the primary N-PE nodes at other remote sites. In addition, to prevent an active/active state, the backup N-PE raises its own B-semaphore, preventing the primary N-PE from becoming active.

An EEM script on the backup N-PE transitions backup PWs to active state. The backup N-PE node flaps the E-link, which triggers an EEM script running on the aggregation switch, forcing it to flush local MAC addresses.

Primary N-P Node Recovers After the Failure

When the primary node initializes and becomes ready, it receives the B-semaphore route and therefore stays in standby mode. The primary N-PE raises the P-semaphore, which is announced by the core IGP. When the backup N-PE node learns the P-semaphore route, it starts a delay timer (recommended and configured to 100 sec). The traffic continues to forward through the backup PWs via the backup Q-link (MEC) until the delay timer expires. When the delay timer expires, the backup node disables the backup PW by shutting down the B-semaphore loopback interface. This action allows the primary node to become active and return to normal state.

Because VSS combines both the aggregation switches into one logical switch, MAC address flushing is executed on both the MECs via only one EEM script.

Figure 9-28 shows the configuration on the primary node requesting the aggregation switch to manage MAC address flushing when it changes the state to active. This request is made by flapping the E-link, in this case interface gig2/1.

```
event manager applet VPLS_ODD-VLAN_B_Semaphore-is-down

 event track 11 state down

 action 1.0 cli command "enable"

 action 2.0 cli command "conf t"

 action 4.0 cli command "int lo91"          ◄──  Start Xconnect

 action 4.1 cli command "no shutdown"

 action 5.0 cli command "int gig 2/1"

 action 5.1 cli command "shutdown"          ◄──  Request aggregation mac-flush

 action 5.2 cli command "no shutdown"

 action 9.0 syslog msg "Backup N-PE has become Standby, Primary is Active"
```

Figure 9-28 *E-semaphore trigger on N-PE.*

Figure 9-29 shows the EEM script on the aggregation switch. When the N-PE flaps the E-link, as shown in Figure 9-28, the EEM script running on the aggregation switch detects the change in interface state and flushes local MAC addresses.

Figure 9-30 shows the EEM script for MAC address flushing on the aggregation switch. Tracking an interface is supported from EEM Version 2.4 and later.

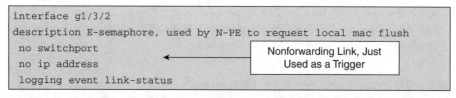

```
interface g1/3/2
description E-semaphore, used by N-PE to request local mac flush
 no switchport                        Nonforwarding Link, Just
 no ip address                           Used as a Trigger
 logging event link-status
```

```
event manager applet N-PE_is_requesting_mac-table-flush
 event syslog pattern ": Interface GigabitEthernet1/3/2, changed state
   to down"
 action 1.0 cli command "enable"
 action 5.0 cli command "clear mac-add dyn port-channel1"
 action 9.0 syslog msg "Local MAC Flush executed on VPLS N-PE request"
```

Figure 9-29 *EEM script on aggregation switch for MAC address flushing.*

```
track 30 interface g1/3/2 line-protocol

event manager applet N-PE_is_requesting_flush
 event track 30 state down
 action 1.0 cli command "enable"
 action 5.0 cli command "clear mac-add dyn port-channel1"
 action 9.0 syslog msg "Local MAC-flush executed on VPLS N-PE request"
```

Figure 9-30 *MAC address flushing script installed on aggregation switch.*

N-PE Routers: Hardware and Software

Table 9-10 compares the hardware and software that can be used for N-PE nodes. Cisco 7600 routers were used as N-PEs for all the MST- and EEM-based solutions that this book describes. In this solution, selective QinQ with two EVCs was configured using ES20 modules facing the aggregation. Also, the aggregation switches must support the EEM script, which can be triggered on a specific syslog message or on the link state.

Table 9-10 *Hardware and Software for N-PE Nodes*

Cisco 7600 Router	Cisco Catalyst 6500
Interfaces on SIP or ES modules are required for connectivity toward the VPLS core.	Interface on SIP module is required for connectivity toward the VPLS core.
ES module: Selective QinQ. 67xx module: Plain QinQ tagging, one QinQ tag per port.	ES module: Not supported. 67xx module: Plain QinQ tagging, one QinQ tag per port.
Interface on any 67xx LAN or ES module; does not carry any traffic.	Interface on 67xx LAN module; does not carry any traffic.
Cisco IOS 12.2(33)SRC1.	Cisco IOS 12.2(33)SXI.

Implementing EEM Option 5b

EEM option 5b requires that the two aggregation switches be converted to VSS or Nexus vPC and connected to both N-PEs via MEC.

> **Note** For step-by-step procedures about how to convert the standalone Catalyst 6500 switches to VSS, refer to the "Configuring Virtual Switching Systems" portion of the *Catalyst 6500 Release 12.2SXH and Later Software Configuration Guide*, available at www.http://tinyurl.com/dfdlhe.

The following list provides snippets of configuration from the N-PE and aggregation devices and output from various **show** commands for verification:

Step 1.   Configure the core IGP, MPLS, and targeted LDP as documented in the section "VPLS with N-PE Redundancy Using EEM Semaphore: EEM Option 2."

Step 2.   Configure the Q-link as MEC, including per-VLAN load repartition using selective QinQ on the N-PE side:

```
! On N-PE1:

sj-n-pe1# show run interface port-channel 31

!

interface Port-channel31

 description Q-link to sj-agg-1/2

 mtu 9216

 no ip address

 logging event link-status

 load-interval 30

 mls qos trust dscp

 service instance 3001 ethernet

  encapsulation dot1q 3,5,7,9,11,13,15,17,19,21,23,25,27,.....257,259

  bridge-domain 3001

 !

 service instance 3004 ethernet

  encapsulation dot1q
2,4,6,8,10,12,14,16,18,20,22,24,26,28,.....258,260

  bridge-domain 3004

 !

end

sj-n-pe1# show run int g4/0/4
```

```
!
interface GigabitEthernet4/0/4
 description MEC(Po31) to sj-agg-1 1/2/3
 dampening
 mtu 9216
 ip arp inspection limit none
 no ip address
 logging event link-status
 load-interval 30
 carrier-delay msec 0
 udld port
 mls qos trust dscp
 channel-group 31 mode active
end
sj-n-pe1# show run int g4/0/5
!
interface GigabitEthernet4/0/5
 description MEC(Po31) to sj-agg-2 2/2/12
 dampening
 mtu 9216
 ip arp inspection limit none
 no ip address
 logging event link-status
 load-interval 30
 carrier-delay msec 0
 udld port
 mls qos trust dscp
 channel-group 31 mode active
end
sj-n-pe1#
! On N-PE2:
sj-n-pe2# show run int port-channel 32
!
interface Port-channel32
 description Q-link to sj-agg-1/2
 mtu 9216
 no ip address
```

```
  logging event link-status
  load-interval 30
  mls qos trust dscp
  service instance 3002 ethernet
   encapsulation dot1q
2,4,6,8,10,12,14,16,18,20,22,24,26,28,.....258,260
   bridge-domain 3002
  !
  service instance 3003 ethernet
   encapsulation dot1q 3,5,7,9,11,13,15,17,19,21,23,25,27,.....257,259
   bridge-domain 3003
  !
end


sj-n-pe2# show run int g4/0/4
!
interface GigabitEthernet4/0/4
 description MEC(Po32) to sj-agg-1 2/2/3
 dampening
 mtu 9216
 ip arp inspection limit none
 no ip address
 logging event link-status
 load-interval 30
 carrier-delay msec 0
 udld port
 mls qos trust dscp
 channel-group 32 mode active
end


sj-n-pe2# show run int g4/0/5
!
interface GigabitEthernet4/0/5
 description MEC(Po32) to sj-agg-1 1/2/12
 dampening
 mtu 9216
 ip arp inspection limit none
```

```
    no ip address

    logging event link-status

    load-interval 30

    carrier-delay msec 0

    udld port

    mls qos trust dscp

    channel-group 32 mode active

   end


   sj-n-pe2#
```

Step 3.   Configure MEC on the VSS-facing N-PEs and the access switches:

```
! MEC on aggregation switches with N-PEs:
sj-agg-1# show run int port-channel 31
!
interface Port-channel31

 description Q-link to sj-n-pe1

 switchport

 switchport trunk encapsulation dot1q

 switchport trunk allowed vlan 1-61,201-260

 switchport mode trunk

 switchport nonegotiate

 mtu 9216

 logging event link-status

 logging event spanning-tree status

 load-interval 30

 spanning-tree portfast trunk

 spanning-tree link-type point-to-point


sj-agg-1# show run int g2/2/12
!
interface GigabitEthernet2/2/12

 description MEC(Po31) to sj-n-pe1

 switchport

 switchport trunk encapsulation dot1q

 switchport trunk allowed vlan 2-61,201-260

 switchport mode trunk
```

```
 switchport nonegotiate

 mtu 9216

 logging event link-status

 logging event spanning-tree status

 load-interval 30

 spanning-tree portfast trunk

 spanning-tree link-type point-to-point

 channel-group 31 mode active
end
```

sj-agg-1# **show run int g1/2/3**

```
!

interface GigabitEthernet1/2/3

 description MEC(Po31) to sj-n-pe1

 switchport

 switchport trunk encapsulation dot1q

 switchport trunk allowed vlan 2-61,201-260

 switchport mode trunk

 switchport nonegotiate

 mtu 9216

 logging event link-status

 logging event spanning-tree status

 load-interval 30

 spanning-tree portfast trunk

 spanning-tree link-type point-to-point

 channel-group 31 mode active
end
```

```
sj-agg-1#
! MEC on aggregation switches with SJ-Access1:
interface Port-channel1

 description Port-channel to sj-access1

 switchport

 switchport trunk encapsulation dot1q

 switchport trunk allowed vlan 1-61,100-200

 switchport mode trunk

 switchport nonegotiate
```

```
  mtu 9216

  logging event link-status

  logging event spanning-tree status

  load-interval 30

 !

interface GigabitEthernet1/2/24

  description port-channel 1 interface to sj-a1

  switchport

  switchport trunk encapsulation dot1q

  switchport trunk allowed vlan 1-61,100-200

  switchport mode trunk

  switchport nonegotiate

  mtu 9216

  logging event link-status

  logging event spanning-tree status

  load-interval 30

  channel-group 1 mode active

 !

interface GigabitEthernet2/2/23

  description port-channel 1 interface to sj-a1

  switchport

  switchport trunk encapsulation dot1q

  switchport trunk allowed vlan 1-61,100-200

  switchport mode trunk

  switchport nonegotiate

  mtu 9216

  logging event link-status

  logging event spanning-tree status

  load-interval 30

  channel-group 1 mode active
```

Step 4.   Configure MEC for connectivity toward access switches. This is not related to VPLS but is a recommended design for a data center:

```
! On Access1:
sj-access1# show cdp neighbor
Capability Codes: R - Router, T - Trans Bridge, B - Source Route Bridge
                  S - Switch, H - Host, I - IGMP, r - Repeater, P -
Phone
```

Device ID	Local Intrfce	Holdtme	Capability	Platform	Port ID
campus3-223sw1	Gig 5/2	137	S I	WS-C2950-	Fas 0/3
sj-agg-1	Gig 2/23	175	R S I	WS-C6509-	Gig 2/2/23
sj-agg-1	Gig 2/24	158	R S I	WS-C6509-	Gig 1/2/24

sj-access1# **show run int port-channel 1**

```
!
interface Port-channel1
 switchport
 switchport trunk encapsulation dot1q
 switchport mode trunk
 switchport nonegotiate
 mtu 9216
 logging event link-status
 logging event spanning-tree status
end
```

sj-access1# **show run int g2/23**

```
!
interface GigabitEthernet2/23
 description L2 trunk connection to sj-agg-2
 switchport
 switchport trunk encapsulation dot1q
 switchport mode trunk
 switchport nonegotiate
 mtu 9216
 logging event link-status
 logging event spanning-tree status
 channel-group 1 mode active
end
```

sj-access1# **show run int g2/24**

```
!
interface GigabitEthernet2/24
 description L2 trunk connection to sj-agg-1
```

```
      switchport
      switchport trunk encapsulation dot1q
      switchport mode trunk
      switchport nonegotiate
      mtu 9216
      logging event link-status
      logging event spanning-tree status
      channel-group 1 mode active
end
```

```
sj-access1# show etherchannel port-channel
                  Channel-group listing:
                  _ _ _ _ _ _ _ _ _ _ _.


Group: 1
_ _ _ _ _
                  Port-channels in the group:
                  _ _ _ _ _ _ _ _ _ _ _


Port-channel: Po1    (Primary Aggregator)


_ _ _ _ _ _


Age of the Port-channel    = 0d:00h:02m:41s
Logical slot/port   = 14/1          Number of ports = 2
HotStandBy port = null
Port state          = Port-channel Ag-Inuse
Protocol            =   LACP
Fast-switchover     = disabled


Ports in the Port-channel:
```

```
Index   Load   Port    EC state        No of bits

———+———+———+———————————+————-.

  0     55    Gi2/23  Active    4

  1     AA    Gi2/24  Active    4


Time since last port bundled:    0d:00h:02m:12s    Gi2/24
```

Step 5.   Create QinQ VLANs and create one SVI and VFI per QinQ VLAN.

On N-PE1	**On N-PE2**

```
lon-n-pe1#                                  lon-n-pe2#
...                                         ...
!                                           !
mpls ldp neighbor 10.76.70.12 targeted ldp  mpls ldp neighbor 10.76.70.11 targeted ldp
mpls ldp neighbor 10.76.70.21 targeted ldp  mpls ldp neighbor 10.76.70.21 targeted ldp
mpls ldp neighbor 10.76.70.22 targeted ldp  mpls ldp neighbor 10.76.70.22 targeted ldp
mpls ldp neighbor 10.76.70.31 targeted ldp  mpls ldp neighbor 10.76.70.31 targeted ldp
mpls ldp neighbor 10.76.70.32 targeted ldp  mpls ldp neighbor 10.76.70.32 targeted ldp
mpls ldp tcp pak-priority                   mpls ldp tcp pak-priority
mpls ldp session protection                 mpls ldp session protection
no mpls ldp advertise-labels                no mpls ldp advertise-labels
mpls ldp advertise-labels for 76            mpls ldp advertise-labels for 76
mpls label protocol ldp                     mpls label protocol ldp
xconnect logging pseudowire status          xconnect logging pseudowire status
!                                           !
access-list 76 permit 10.76.0.0 0.0.255.255 access-list 76 permit 10.76.0.0 0.0.255.255
!                                           !
lon-n-pe1#                                  lon-n-pe1#
 !                                           !
vlan 3001                                   vlan 3002
 name H-VPLS_Primary_core_VLAN               name H-VPLS_Primary_core_VLAN
!                                           !
vlan 3004                                   vlan 3003
 name H-VPLS_Backup_core_VLAN                name H-VPLS_Backup_core_VLAN
!                                           !
l2 vfi VFI-Even manual                      l2 vfi VFI-Even manual
 vpn id 3002                                 vpn id 3002
 neighbor 10.76.90.32 encapsulation mpls     neighbor 10.76.90.31 encapsulation mpls
 neighbor 10.76.90.22 encapsulation mpls     neighbor 10.76.90.32 encapsulation mpls
!                                            neighbor 10.76.90.21 encapsulation mpls
l2 vfi VFI-Odd manual                        neighbor 10.76.90.22 encapsulation mpls
 vpn id 3001                                !
 neighbor 10.76.91.31 encapsulation mpls    l2 vfi VFI-Odd manual
 neighbor 10.76.91.32 encapsulation mpls     vpn id 3001
 neighbor 10.76.91.21 encapsulation mpls     neighbor 10.76.91.31 encapsulation mpls
 neighbor 10.76.91.22 encapsulation mpls     neighbor 10.76.91.21 encapsulation mpls
!                                           !
```

On N-PE1	On N-PE2
| ```
interface Vlan3001
 description Primary Core QinQ VLAN - used
 to transport Odd edge VLAN
 mtu 9216
 no ip address
 xconnect vfi VFI-Odd
!
interface Vlan3004
 description Backup Core QinQ VLAN - used
 to transport Even edge VLAN
 mtu 9216
 no ip address
 xconnect vfi VFI-Even
!
``` | ```
interface Vlan3002
 description Primary Core QinQ VLAN - used to
transport Even edge VLAN
 mtu 9216
 no ip address
 xconnect vfi VFI-Even
!
interface Vlan3003
 description Backup Core QinQ VLAN - used to
transport Odd edge VLAN
 mtu 9216
 no ip address
 xconnect vfi VFI-Odd
!
``` |

```
lon-n-pe1# show mpls l2transport vc 3001


Local intf     Local circuit
Dest address   VC ID     Status
— — — — — —·   — — — — — — — — — — — —  —
— — — — — —·   — — — — —  — — — —

VFI VFI-Odd    VFI
10.76.91.31    3001      UP
VFI VFI-Odd    VFI
10.76.91.32    3001      DOWN
VFI VFI-Odd    VFI
10.76.91.21    3001      UP
VFI VFI-Odd    VFI
10.76.91.22    3001      DOWN
```

Step 6.   Verify the EtherChannel configuration to ensure that the EtherChannel is formed with all the configured member interfaces:

```
! On N-PE1:

sj-n-pe1# show etherchannel port-channel

                  Channel-group listing:

                  — — — — — — — — — —·


     Group: 31

     — — — —

                  Port-channels in the group:

                  — — — — — — — — — —
```

```
Port-channel: Po31     (Primary Aggregator)


    — — — — —


Age of the Port-channel   = 1d:00h:57m:09s
Logical slot/port    = 14/1            Number of ports = 2
HotStandBy port = null
Passive port list    = Gi4/0/4 Gi4/0/5
Port state           = Port-channel L3-Ag Ag-Inuse
Protocol             =   LACP
Fast-switchover      = disabled
Direct Load Swap     = disabled


Ports in the Port-channel:

Index   Load   Port     EC state        No of bits
— — —+— — —+— — —+— — — — — — — —+— — — — ·
   0     0F    Gi4/0/4    Active     4
   1     F0    Gi4/0/5    Active     4


Time since last port bundled:    0d:00h:40m:26s    Gi4/0/5
Time since last port Un-bundled: 0d:00h:50m:15s    Gi4/0/5
! On N-PE2:
sj-n-pe2# show etherchannel port-channel
             Channel-group listing:
             — — — — — — — — — — — ·


Group: 32
    — — — — —
             Port-channels in the group:
             — — — — — — — — — —


Port-channel: Po32     (Primary Aggregator)


    — — — — —
```

```
Age of the Port-channel    = 1d:00h:33m:57s

Logical slot/port    = 14/1          Number of ports = 2

HotStandBy port = null

Passive port list    = Gi4/0/4 Gi4/0/5

Port state            = Port-channel L3-Ag Ag-Inuse

Protocol            =    LACP

Fast-switchover    = disabled

Direct Load Swap    = disabled


Ports in the Port-channel:


Index   Load   Port    EC state        No of bits

———+———+———+———————————+————— ·

  1     55    Gi4/0/4    Active    4

  0     AA    Gi4/0/5    Active    4


Time since last port bundled:    0d:00h:31m:44s    Gi4/0/4
Time since last port Un-bundled: 0d:00h:41m:28s    Gi4/0/4
```

Step 7.   Configure an E-link on the N-PEs to allow the EEM script on aggregation switches to trigger MAC flushing. This link does not forward any data traffic and is provisioned only to trigger an EEM script running on aggregation switches for MAC address flushing when the interface state changes.

On N-PE1	On N-PE2
```interface GigabitEthernet2/1``` ```no ip address```	```interface GigabitEthernet2/1``` ```no ip address```

Step 8.   Configure object tracking using EEM. Use the **show running-config | begin event manager** command to display EEM applets that are configured:

```
! On N-PE1:
!
process-max-time 50
!
track timer ip route 1
!
track 10 ip route 10.76.80.12 255.255.255.255 reachability
```

```
  delay up 100
!
track 11 ip route 10.76.81.12 255.255.255.255 reachability
!
track 20 interface Port-channel31 line-protocol
!
track 25 list boolean or
 object 110
 object 112
 delay up 40
!
track 110 interface GigabitEthernet4/0/19 line-protocol
 delay down 5 up 60
!
track 112 interface GigabitEthernet4/0/0 line-protocol
!
event manager applet VPLS_EVEN-VLAN_P_semaphore-is-down
 event track 10 state down
 action 1.0 cli command "enable"
 action 2.0 cli command "conf t"
 action 3.0 cli command "int lo80"
 action 3.1 cli command "no shut"
 action 4.0 cli command "int lo90"
 action 4.1 cli command "no shut"
 action 9.0 syslog msg "Backup PW is active"
event manager applet VPLS_EVEN-VLAN_P_semaphore-is-up
 event track 10 state up
 action 1.0 cli command "enable"
 action 2.0 cli command "conf t"
 action 3.0 cli command "int lo90"
 action 3.1 cli command "shut"
 action 4.0 cli command "int lo80"
 action 4.1 cli command "shut"
 action 5.0 cli command "int gi2/1"
 action 5.1 cli command "shut"
 action 5.2 cli command "no shut"
```

```
   action 9.0 syslog msg "Backup PW is shutdown"
event manager applet VPLS_ODD-VLAN_B_semaphore-is-up
 event track 11 state up
 action 1.0 cli command "enable"
 action 2.0 cli command "conf t"
 action 4.0 cli command "int lo91"
 action 4.1 cli command "shut"
 action 9.0 syslog msg "Backup N-PE is Active, Force Primary in
   Standby"
event manager applet VPLS_ODD-VLAN_B_semaphore-is-down
 event track 11 state down
 action 1.0 cli command "enable"
 action 2.0 cli command "conf t"
 action 4.0 cli command "int lo91"
 action 4.1 cli command "no shut"
 action 9.0 syslog msg "Backup N-PE has become Standby, Primary runs
   Active"
event manager applet Track_MEC_link_failure
 event track 20 state down
 action 1.0 cli command "enable"
 action 2.0 cli command "conf t"
 action 3.0 cli command "int lo91"
 action 3.1 cli command "shut"
 action 4.0 cli command "int lo81"
 action 4.1 cli command "shut"
 action 9.0 syslog msg "Aggregation link is failing, Force Primary
   in Standby"
event manager applet Track_MEC_link_recovery
 event track 20 state up
 action 1.0 cli command "enable"
 action 2.0 cli command "conf t"
 action 4.0 cli command "int lo81"
 action 4.1 cli command "no shut"
 action 9.0 syslog msg "Aggregation link as recover, Primary requests
   to become active"
event manager applet WAN_links_down
 event track 25 state down
 action 1.0 cli command "enable"
```

```
 action 2.0 cli command "conf t"

 action 3.0 cli command "interface port-channel 31"

 action 3.1 cli command "shut"

 action 9.0 syslog msg "Both WAN Links are down. Shutting down Q Link"

event manager applet Oneofthe_WAN_Link_is_UP

 event track 25 state up

 action 1.0 cli command "enable"

 action 2.0 cli command "conf t"

 action 3.0 cli command "interface port-channel 31"

 action 3.1 cli command "no shut"

 action 9.0 syslog msg "One of the WAN link is up. Bring up Q link"

event manager applet Backup-node_ready

 event track 110 state up

 action 1.0 cli command "enable"

 action 2.0 cli command "conf t"

 action 3.0 cli command "track 10 ip route 10.76.80.12 255.255.255.255
   reachability"

 action 3.2 cli command "delay up 100"

 action 9.0 syslog msg "Backup node is operational"

event manager applet Backup-node_not_ready

 event track 110 state down

 action 1.0 cli command "enable"

 action 2.0 cli command "conf t"

 action 3.0 cli command "no track 10"

 action 4.0 cli command "int lo90"

 action 4.1 cli command "shut"

 action 5.0 cli command "int lo80"

 action 5.1 cli command "shut"

 action 9.0 syslog msg "Backup node not operational"

 !

event manager history size events 20

event manager history size traps 20

end
```

Step 9.   Configure the EEM script on the aggregation device to flush MAC addresses:

```
! On Agg-1:

interface GigabitEthernet1/3/2

 description "Dedicated link for E-Semaphore connected to N-PE1.
Logging of link status must be enabled for EEM script to function"
```

```
        no switchport

        no ip address

        logging event link-status

      !

     event manager applet VPLS_Edge_Semaphore_from_N-PE1

       event syslog pattern "%LINK-3-UPDOWN: Interface GigabitEthernet1/3/2,
         changed state to down"

       action 1.0 cli command "enable"

       action 5.0 cli command "clear mac-address-table dynamic interface
         port-channel 31"

       action 5.1 cli command "clear mac-address-table dynamic interface
         port-channel 32"

       action 9.0 syslog msg "Local MAC flushing executed for VPLS access
         links"

     ! On Agg-2:

     interface GigabitEthernet2/3/2

       description "Dedicated link for E-Semaphore connected to N-PE2.
     Logging of link status must be enabled for EEM script to function"

       no switchport

       no ip address

       logging event link-status

      !

     event manager applet VPLS_Edge_Semaphore_from_N-PE2

       event syslog pattern "%LINK-3-UPDOWN: Interface GigabitEthernet2/3/2,
         changed state to down"

       action 1.0 cli command "enable"

       action 5.0 cli command "clear mac-address-table dynamic interface
         port-channel 31"

       action 5.1 cli command "clear mac-address-table dynamic interface
         port-channel 32"

       action 9.0 syslog msg "Local MAC flushing executed for VPLS access
         links"

      !
```

Convergence Tests

The traffic profile outlined in Chapter 7 was used to determine end-to-end convergence for unidirectional voice, unicast, and multicast traffic. Links and nodes were failed to simulate network failures.

Table 9-11 shows results of various node and link failures. Convergence numbers (max and min) are in seconds.

Table 9-11 *Convergence Numbers for Link and Node Failures for Multidomain H-VPLS with VSS and VLAN Load Balancing: EEM Option 5b*

Failure Type	Action	VLAN	Traffic Type	Traffic Direction			
				LON → SJ		SJ → LON	
				Max	Min	Max	Min
Fail VSS active	Reload	Odd VLAN	Voice	0.00	0.00	0.02	0.00
			Unicast	0.00	0.00	0.00	0.00
			Multicast	0.01	0.00	1.36	0.01
		Even VLAN	Voice	0.02	0.00	0.02	0.00
			Unicast	0.00	0.00	0.00	0.00
			Multicast	0.01	0.00	1.36	0.00
	Restore	Odd VLAN	Voice	0.02	0.02	0.02	0.00
			Unicast	0.00	0.00	0.00	0.00
			Multicast	0.03	0.01	0.06	0.01
		Even VLAN	Voice	0.04	0.02	0.02	0.00
			Unicast	0.00	0.00	0.00	0.00
			Multicast	0.04	0.01	0.05	0.01
Fail VSS standby	Reload	Odd VLAN	Voice	0.02	0.02	0.41	0.41
			Unicast	0.01	0.01	0.41	0.41
			Multicast	0.02	0.01	0.43	0.01
		Even VLAN	Voice	0.02	0.02	0.40	0.40
			Unicast	0.01	0.01	0.41	0.41
			Multicast	0.02	0.01	0.43	0.01
	Restore	Odd VLAN	Voice	0.20	0.12	0.12	0.12
			Unicast	0.17	0.17	0.08	0.08
			Multicast	0.19	0.17	0.10	0.05
		Even VLAN	Voice	0.24	0.20	0.12	0.12
			Unicast	0.22	0.22	0.08	0.08
			Multicast	0.25	0.22	0.10	0.05
VSS forced switchover from Agg-2 to Agg-1	Switch over	Odd VLAN	Voice	0.04	0.02	0.30	0.30
			Unicast	0.02	0.01	0.30	0.30
			Multicast	0.03	0.01	0.30	0.00
		Even VLAN	Voice	0.08	0.06	0.30	0.30
			Unicast	0.07	0.07	0.30	0.30
			Multicast	0.08	0.06	0.30	0.30
VSS forced switchover from Agg-1 to Agg-2	Switch over	Odd VLAN	Voice	0.04	0.00	0.02	0.00
			Unicast	0.00	0.00	0.00	0.00
			Multicast	0.02	0.01	1.47	0.01
		Even VLAN	Voice	0.02	0.00	0.02	0.00
			Unicast	0.00	0.00	0.00	0.00
			Multicast	0.01	0.01	1.47	0.01
Fail N-PE1	Reload	Odd VLAN	Voice	1.28	1.24	1.28	1.24
			Unicast	1.26	1.26	1.26	1.26
			Multicast	1.28	1.25	1.27	1.25
		Even VLAN	Voice	0.02	0.02	0.02	0.00
			Unicast	0.00	0.00	0.00	0.00
			Multicast	0.03	0.01	0.01	0.00
	Restore	Odd VLAN	Voice	1.00	0.92	0.96	0.96
			Unicast	0.97	0.95	0.95	0.95
			Multicast	1.73	1.21	0.96	0.93
		Even VLAN	Voice	0.02	0.02	0.02	0.00
			Unicast	0.00	0.00	0.00	0.00
			Multicast	0.01	0.01	0.01	0.00

Table 9-11 *Convergence Numbers for Link and Node Failures for Multidomain H-VPLS with VSS and VLAN Load Balancing: EEM Option 5b*

Failure Type	Action	VLAN	Traffic Type	LON → SJ Max	LON → SJ Min	SJ → LON Max	SJ → LON Min
Fail N-PE2	Reload	Odd VLAN	Voice	0.02	0.02	0.02	0.00
			Unicast	0.00	0.00	0.00	0.00
			Multicast	0.01	0.01	0.01	0.00
		Even VLAN[1,2]	Voice	3.08	3.02	3.08	3.06
			Unicast	3.04	3.04	3.06	3.06
			Multicast	4.14	3.06	3.08	3.05
	Restore	Odd VLAN	Voice	0.04	0.02	0.02	0.00
			Unicast	0.01	0.01	0.00	0.00
			Multicast	0.02	0.01	0.01	0.00
		Even VLAN	Voice	0.98	0.94	0.98	0.93
			Unicast	0.95	0.95	0.95	0.94
			Multicast	1.94	1.92	0.95	0.94
Fail VSL control link	Shut	Odd VLAN	Voice	0.00	0.00	0.00	0.00
			Unicast	0.00	0.00	0.00	0.00
			Multicast	0.00	0.00	0.00	0.00
		Even VLAN	Voice	0.00	0.00	0.00	0.00
			Unicast	0.00	0.00	0.00	0.00
			Multicast	0.00	0.00	0.00	0.00
	No shut	Odd VLAN	Voice	0.00	0.00	0.00	0.00
			Unicast	0.00	0.00	0.00	0.00
			Multicast	0.00	0.00	0.00	0.00
		Even VLAN	Voice	0.00	0.00	0.00	0.00
			Unicast	0.00	0.00	0.00	0.00
			Multicast	0.00	0.00	0.00	0.00
Fail VSL noncontrol link	Shut	Odd VLAN	Voice	0.00	0.00	0.00	0.00
			Unicast	0.00	0.00	0.00	0.00
			Multicast	0.00	0.00	0.00	0.00
		Even VLAN	Voice	0.00	0.00	0.00	0.00
			Unicast	0.00	0.00	0.00	0.00
			Multicast	0.00	0.00	0.00	0.00
	No shut	Odd VLAN	Voice	0.00	0.00	0.00	0.00
			Unicast	0.00	0.00	0.00	0.00
			Multicast	0.00	0.00	0.00	0.00
		Even VLAN	Voice	0.00	0.00	0.00	0.00
			Unicast	0.00	0.00	0.00	0.00
			Multicast	0.00	0.00	0.00	0.00
Fail VSL by unplugging both physical links	Unplug	Odd VLAN	Voice	0.02	0.00	0.04	0.00
			Unicast	0.00	0.00	0.01	0.01
			Multicast	0.01	0.00	1.10	0.01
		Even VLAN	Voice	0.02	0.00	0.02	0.00
			Unicast	0.00	0.00	0.00	0.00
			Multicast	0.01	0.00	1.08	0.01
	Plug	Odd VLAN	Voice	0.02	0.02	0.02	0.00
			Unicast	0.00	0.00	0.00	0.00
			Multicast	0.01	0.01	0.01	0.01
		Even VLAN	Voice	0.02	0.02	0.02	0.00
			Unicast	0.00	0.00	0.00	0.00
			Multicast	0.01	0.01	0.01	0.01

Table 9-11 *Convergence Numbers for Link and Node Failures for Multidomain H-VPLS with VSS and VLAN Load Balancing: EEM Option 5b*

Failure Type	Action	VLAN	Traffic Type	Traffic Direction LON → SJ Max	Min	SJ → LON Max	Min
Fail MEC physical link between N-PE1 and Agg active	Shut	Odd VLAN	Voice	0.02	0.02	0.02	0.00
			Unicast	0.00	0.00	0.00	0.00
			Multicast	0.01	0.01	0.30	0.01
		Even VLAN	Voice	0.02	0.02	0.02	0.00
			Unicast	0.00	0.00	0.00	0.00
			Multicast	0.01	0.01	0.01	0.00
	No shut	Odd VLAN	Voice	0.02	0.00	0.02	0.00
			Unicast	0.00	0.00	0.00	0.00
			Multicast	0.02	0.00	0.01	0.00
		Even VLAN	Voice	0.02	0.00	0.02	0.00
			Unicast	0.00	0.00	0.00	0.00
			Multicast	0.01	0.00	0.01	0.00
Fail MEC physical link between N-PE1 and Agg standby	Shut	Odd VLAN	Voice	0.20	0.16	0.18	0.16
			Unicast	0.18	0.17	0.14	0.14
			Multicast	0.19	0.16	0.25	0.01
		Even VLAN	Voice	0.02	0.02	0.02	0.00
			Unicast	0.00	0.00	0.00	0.00
			Multicast	0.01	0.01	0.01	0.01
	No shut	Odd VLAN	Voice	0.12	0.08	0.14	0.12
			Unicast	0.11	0.11	0.13	0.12
			Multicast	0.11	0.10	0.13	0.01
		Even VLAN	Voice	0.02	0.02	0.02	0.00
			Unicast	0.00	0.00	0.00	0.00
			Multicast	0.01	0.01	0.01	0.01
Fail MEC PortChannel between N-PE1 and Agg	Shut	Odd VLAN[1,2]	Voice	3.04	2.98	2.82	2.80
			Unicast	3.02	3.01	2.81	2.81
			Multicast	3.03	2.79	2.82	2.80
		Even VLAN	Voice	0.02	0.02	0.02	0.00
			Unicast	0.00	0.00	0.00	0.00
			Multicast	0.01	0.01	0.01	0.01
	No shut	Odd VLAN	Voice	1.04	0.98	1.02	0.98
			Unicast	1.00	1.00	1.01	1.01
			Multicast	1.40	1.04	1.02	1.00
		Even VLAN	Voice	0.02	0.02	0.02	0.00
			Unicast	0.00	0.00	0.00	0.00
			Multicast	0.01	0.00	0.01	0.01
Fail MEC physical link between N-PE2 and Agg active	Shut	Odd VLAN	Voice	0.02	0.00	0.06	0.04
			Unicast	0.00	0.00	0.03	0.03
			Multicast	0.01	0.00	0.04	0.02
		Even VLAN	Voice	0.02	0.02	0.00	0.00
			Unicast	0.00	0.00	0.00	0.00
			Multicast	0.07	0.00	0.30	0.00
	No shut	Odd VLAN	Voice	0.02	0.00	0.02	0.00
			Unicast	0.00	0.00	0.00	0.00
			Multicast	0.01	0.00	0.01	0.00
		Even VLAN	Voice	0.02	0.00	0.00	0.00
			Unicast	0.00	0.00	0.00	0.00
			Multicast	0.01	0.00	0.01	0.00

Table 9-11 *Convergence Numbers for Link and Node Failures for Multidomain H-VPLS with VSS and VLAN Load Balancing: EEM Option 5b*

Failure Type	Action	VLAN	Traffic Type	LON → SJ Max	LON → SJ Min	SJ → LON Max	SJ → LON Min
Fail MEC physical link between SJ N-PE2 and Agg standby	Shut	Odd VLAN	Voice	0.02	0.02	0.02	0.00
			Unicast	0.00	0.00	0.00	0.00
			Multicast	0.01	0.00	0.01	0.00
		Even VLAN	Voice	0.02	0.02	0.34	0.32
			Unicast	0.01	0.01	0.33	0.32
			Multicast	0.02	0.01	0.37	0.01
	No shut	Odd VLAN	Voice	0.02	0.02	0.02	0.00
			Unicast	0.00	0.00	0.00	0.00
			Multicast	0.01	0.01	0.01	0.01
		Even VLAN	Voice	0.12	0.08	0.10	0.08
			Unicast	0.11	0.10	0.09	0.09
			Multicast	0.12	0.09	0.10	0.01
Fail MEC PortChannel between N-PE2 and Agg	Shut	Odd VLAN	Voice	0.04	0.02	0.02	0.00
			Unicast	0.00	0.00	0.00	0.00
			Multicast	0.04	0.01	0.01	0.01
		Even VLAN[1,2]	Voice	3.64	3.58	3.64	3.58
			Unicast	3.60	3.60	3.61	3.61
			Multicast	5.45	3.98	3.62	3.59
	No shut	Odd VLAN	Voice	0.02	0.02	0.02	0.00
			Unicast	0.01	0.00	0.00	0.00
			Multicast	0.02	0.00	0.01	0.01
		Even VLAN	Voice	1.18	1.14	1.20	1.18
			Unicast	1.16	1.16	1.18	1.18
			Multicast	1.46	1.33	1.19	1.17
Fail MEC physical link between Access1 and Agg active	Shut	Odd VLAN	Voice	0.00	0.00	0.02	0.00
			Unicast	0.00	0.00	0.00	0.00
			Multicast	0.01	0.00	0.01	0.00
		Even VLAN	Voice	0.02	0.02	0.02	0.00
			Unicast	0.00	0.00	0.00	0.00
			Multicast	0.01	0.00	0.01	0.00
	No shut	Odd VLAN	Voice	0.02	0.00	0.02	0.00
			Unicast	0.00	0.00	0.00	0.00
			Multicast	0.01	0.00	0.01	0.00
		Even VLAN	Voice	0.02	0.00	0.02	0.00
			Unicast	0.00	0.00	0.00	0.00
			Multicast	0.01	0.00	0.01	0.00
Fail MEC physical link between Access1 and Agg standby	Shut	Odd VLAN	Voice	0.20	0.14	0.02	0.00
			Unicast	0.17	0.17	0.00	0.00
			Multicast	0.17	0.12	0.01	0.00
		Even VLAN	Voice	0.20	0.14	0.02	0.00
			Unicast	0.17	0.17	0.00	0.00
			Multicast	0.17	0.12	0.01	0.00
	No shut	Odd VLAN	Voice	0.04	0.02	0.02	0.00
			Unicast	0.03	0.02	0.00	0.00
			Multicast	0.04	0.02	0.01	0.01
		Even VLAN	Voice	0.06	0.02	0.02	0.00
			Unicast	0.03	0.03	0.00	0.00
			Multicast	0.04	0.02	0.01	0.01

Table 9-11 *Convergence Numbers for Link and Node Failures for Multidomain H-VPLS with VSS and VLAN Load Balancing: EEM Option 5b*

Failure Type	Action	VLAN	Traffic Type	LON → SJ Max	LON → SJ Min	SJ → LON Max	SJ → LON Min
Fail MEC physical link between Access2 and Agg active	Shut	Odd VLAN	Voice	0.02	0.02	0.02	0.00
			Unicast	0.00	0.00	0.00	0.00
			Multicast	0.01	0.01	1.03	0.01
		Even VLAN	Voice	0.02	0.02	0.02	0.00
			Unicast	0.00	0.00	0.00	0.00
			Multicast	0.01	0.01	1.03	0.01
	No shut	Odd VLAN	Voice	0.02	0.02	0.02	0.00
			Unicast	0.00	0.00	0.00	0.00
			Multicast	0.01	0.01	0.02	0.01
		Even VLAN	Voice	0.02	0.02	0.02	0.00
			Unicast	0.00	0.00	0.00	0.00
			Multicast	0.01	0.01	0.01	0.01
Fail MEC physical link between Access2 and Agg standby	Shut	Odd VLAN	Voice	0.02	0.02	0.50	0.50
			Unicast	0.00	0.00	0.46	0.46
			Multicast	0.00	0.00	0.48	0.02
		Even VLAN	Voice	0.02	0.02	0.50	0.50
			Unicast	0.00	0.00	0.46	0.46
			Multicast	0.01	0.00	0.48	0.02
	No shut	Odd VLAN	Voice	0.02	0.02	0.04	0.04
			Unicast	0.00	0.00	0.05	0.04
			Multicast	0.00	0.00	0.05	0.01
		Even VLAN	Voice	0.02	0.02	0.04	0.04
			Unicast	0.00	0.00	0.05	0.04
			Multicast	0.01	0.00	0.05	0.01
Fail WAN link between N-PE1 and N-PE2	Shut	Odd VLAN	Voice	0.00	0.00	0.00	0.00
			Unicast	0.00	0.00	0.00	0.00
			Multicast	0.00	0.00	0.00	0.00
		Even VLAN	Voice	0.00	0.00	0.00	0.00
			Unicast	0.00	0.00	0.00	0.00
			Multicast	0.00	0.00	0.00	0.00
	No shut	Odd VLAN	Voice	0.00	0.00	0.00	0.00
			Unicast	0.00	0.00	0.00	0.00
			Multicast	0.00	0.00	0.00	0.00
		Even VLAN	Voice	0.00	0.00	0.00	0.00
			Unicast	0.00	0.00	0.00	0.00
			Multicast	0.00	0.00	0.00	0.00
Fail WAN link facing core on N-PE1	Shut	Odd VLAN	Voice	0.14	0.08	0.14	0.08
			Unicast	0.11	0.11	0.11	0.11
			Multicast	0.12	0.10	0.12	0.10
		Even VLAN	Voice	0.02	0.02	0.02	0.00
			Unicast	0.00	0.00	0.00	0.00
			Multicast	0.01	0.00	0.01	0.01
	No shut	Odd VLAN	Voice	0.02	0.00	0.02	0.00
			Unicast	0.00	0.00	0.00	0.00
			Multicast	0.01	0.00	0.01	0.01
		Even VLAN	Voice	0.02	0.00	0.02	0.00
			Unicast	0.00	0.00	0.00	0.00
			Multicast	0.01	0.00	0.01	0.00

Table 9-11 *Convergence Numbers for Link and Node Failures for Multidomain H-VPLS with VSS and VLAN Load Balancing: EEM Option 5b*

Failure Type	Action	VLAN	Traffic Type	Traffic Direction LON → SJ Max	Min	SJ → LON Max	Min
Fail WAN link facing core on N-PE2	Shut	Odd VLAN	Voice	0.00	0.12	0.00	0.00
			Unicast	0.00	0.00	0.00	0.00
			Multicast	0.00	0.00	0.00	0.00
		Even VLAN	Voice	0.12	0.10	0.12	0.12
			Unicast	0.12	0.11	0.12	0.11
			Multicast	0.13	0.11	0.12	0.11
	No shut	Odd VLAN	Voice	0.02	0.02	0.02	0.00
			Unicast	0.00	0.00	0.00	0.00
			Multicast	0.01	0.00	0.01	0.00
		Even VLAN	Voice	0.04	0.02	0.04	0.00
			Unicast	0.00	0.00	0.00	0.00
			Multicast	0.02	0.00	0.02	0.00
Fail both WAN links on N-PE1	Shut	Odd VLAN[1,2]	Voice	5.32	5.26	5.28	5.26
			Unicast	5.28	5.27	5.27	5.27
			Multicast	5.31	5.26	5.29	5.27
		Even VLAN	Voice	0.02	0.02	0.02	0.00
			Unicast	0.00	0.00	0.00	0.00
			Multicast	0.02	0.01	0.00	0.00
	No shut	Odd VLAN	Voice	0.68	0.62	0.68	0.64
			Unicast	0.65	0.65	0.66	0.66
			Multicast	1.66	0.80	0.68	0.65
		Even VLAN	Voice	0.02	0.02	0.02	0.00
			Unicast	0.00	0.00	0.00	0.00
			Multicast	0.01	0.01	0.01	0.01
Fail both WAN links on N-PE2	Shut	Odd VLAN	Voice	0.00	6.92	0.02	0.00
			Unicast	0.00	0.00	0.00	0.00
			Multicast	0.00	0.00	0.01	0.00
		Even VLAN[1,2]	Voice	6.94	6.85	6.94	6.92
			Unicast	6.92	6.92	6.93	6.92
			Multicast	7.67	6.89	6.93	6.90
	No shut	Odd VLAN	Voice	0.02	0.02	0.02	0.00
			Unicast	0.00	0.00	0.00	0.00
			Multicast	0.01	0.01	0.01	0.01
		Even VLAN	Voice	0.62	0.58	0.66	0.64
			Unicast	0.60	0.60	0.63	0.63
			Multicast	1.48	1.38	0.65	0.63
Clear dynamic MAC address table on Agg	Clear	Odd VLAN	Voice	0.00	0.00	0.00	0.00
			Unicast	0.00	0.00	0.00	0.00
			Multicast	0.00	0.00	0.00	0.00
		Even VLAN	Voice	0.00	0.00	0.00	0.00
			Unicast	0.00	0.00	0.00	0.00
			Multicast	0.00	0.00	0.00	0.00
Clear CEF adjacencies on N-PE1	Clear	Odd VLAN	Voice	0.00	0.00	0.00	0.00
			Unicast	0.00	0.00	0.00	0.00
			Multicast	0.00	0.00	0.00	0.00
		Even VLAN	Voice	0.00	0.00	0.00	0.00
			Unicast	0.00	0.00	0.00	0.00
			Multicast	0.00	0.00	0.00	0.00

Table 9-11 *Convergence Numbers for Link and Node Failures for Multidomain H-VPLS with VSS and VLAN Load Balancing: EEM Option 5b*

Failure Type	Action	VLAN	Traffic Type	Traffic Direction			
				LON → SJ		SJ → LON	
				Max	Min	Max	Min
Clear IP routing table on N-PE1	Clear	Odd VLAN	Voice	0.00	0.00	0.00	0.00
			Unicast	0.00	0.00	0.00	0.00
			Multicast	0.00	0.00	0.00	0.00
		Even VLAN	Voice	0.00	0.00	0.00	0.00
			Unicast	0.00	0.00	0.00	0.00
			Multicast	0.00	0.00	0.00	0.00
Clear dynamic MAC address table on N-PE1	Clear	Odd VLAN	Voice	0.00	0.00	0.00	0.00
			Unicast	0.00	0.00	0.00	0.00
			Multicast	0.00	0.00	0.00	0.00
		Even VLAN	Voice	0.00	0.00	0.00	0.00
			Unicast	0.00	0.00	0.00	0.00
			Multicast	0.00	0.00	0.00	0.00

[1]Under certain conditions, especially when using a P-core, a node may delay new PW LDP label advertisement toward peers until a background timer, currently hard coded to 10 seconds, expires. When this situation occurs, a PW may not be activated before 10 seconds. Cisco defect CSCso99838 documents this issue.

[2]Under normal conditions, when N-PE routers advertise labels to new peers, convergence of unicast traffic takes approximately 2 seconds when N-PE1 or N-PE2 is reloaded

Server Tests

Event logs are captured from the Event Viewer of the Microsoft cluster server. The logs are in the reverse order, showing the last event first. It is best to view the time stamps when analyzing these logs.

Table 9-12 shows the event logs from the Event Viewer of the Microsoft cluster server.

Table 9-12 *Event Logs for Multidomain H-VPLS with MEC and VLAN Load Balancing: EEM Option 5b*

Test Case	Time in Seconds	Event Logs with Time Stamps from Microsoft Server			
Establish L2 connectivity	No convergence	5/21/2008	11:24:17 AM	CAMP3-SERVER2	The time service is now synchronizing the system time with the time source camp3-server1.camp3.com (ntp.d|10.10.5.102:123->1.1.1.1:123).
		5/21/2008	11:24:17 AM	CAMP3-SERVER2	The time provider NtpClient is currently receiving valid time data from camp3-server1.camp3.com (ntp.d|10.10.5.102:123->1.1.1.1:123).

Table 9-12 *Event Logs for Multidomain H-VPLS with MEC and VLAN Load Balancing: EEM Option 5b*

Test Case	Time in Seconds	Event Logs with Time Stamps from Microsoft Server			
Power off both N-PEs	115	5/21/2008	11:36:35 AM	CAMP3-SERVER1	The cluster service brought the resource group "Cluster Group" online.
		5/21/2008	11:35:04 AM	CAMP3-SERVER1	The cluster service is attempting to bring online the resource group "Cluster Group."
		5/21/2008	11:35:04 AM	CAMP3-SERVER1	Cluster node CAMP3-SERVER2 was removed from the active server cluster membership. Cluster service may have been stopped on the node, the node may have failed, or the node may have lost communication with the other active server cluster nodes.
		5/21/2008	11:34:41 AM	CAMP3-SERVER1	The node lost communication with cluster node 'CAMP3-SERVER2' on network 'private 2(1).'
		5/21/2008	11:34:41 AM	CAMP3-SERVER1	The node lost communication with cluster node 'CAMP3-SERVER2' on network 'public.'
		5/21/2008	11:34:40 AM	CAMP3-SERVER1	The node lost communication with cluster node 'CAMP3-SERVER2' on network 'private(1).'
		5/21/2008	11:34:41 AM	CAMP3-SERVER3	The node lost communication with cluster node 'CAMP3-SERVER2' on network 'private 2(1).'
		5/21/2008	11:34:41 AM	CAMP3-SERVER3	The node lost communication with cluster node 'CAMP3-SERVER2' on network 'public.'
		5/21/2008	11:34:40 AM	CAMP3-SERVER3	The node lost communication with cluster node 'CAMP3-SERVER2' on network 'private(1).'
Power off access switch	208	5/20/2008	6:59:52 PM	CAMP3-SERVER1	The cluster service brought the resource group "Cluster Group" online.
		5/20/2008	6:59:05 PM	CAMP3-SERVER1	The cluster service is attempting to bring online the resource group "Cluster Group."
		5/20/2008	6:59:05 PM	CAMP3-SERVER1	Cluster node CAMP3-SERVER2 was removed from the active server cluster membership. Cluster service may have been stopped on the node, the node may have failed, or the node may have lost communication with the other active server cluster nodes.
		5/20/2008	6:58:42 PM	CAMP3-SERVER1	The node lost communication with cluster node 'CAMP3-SERVER2' on network 'private(1).'
		5/20/2008	6:58:43 PM	CAMP3-SERVER3	The node lost communication with cluster node 'CAMP3-SERVER2' on network 'private(1).'

Table 9-12 *Event Logs for Multidomain H-VPLS with MEC and VLAN Load Balancing:*
EEM Option 5b

Test Case	Time in Seconds	Event Logs with Time Stamps from Microsoft Server			
Power off active node	119	5/20/2008	6:49:20 PM	CAMP3-SERVER3	The cluster service brought the resource group "Cluster Group" online.
		5/20/2008	6:48:44 PM	CAMP3-SERVER2	Cluster service is attempting to failover the Cluster Resource Group 'Cluster Group' from node CAMP3-SERVER2 to node CAMP3-SERVER3.
		5/20/2008	6:48:51 PM	CAMP3-SERVER3	The time provider NtpClient is currently receiving valid time data from camp3-server1.camp3.com (ntp.d|172.25.196.28:123->1.1.1.1:123).
		5/20/2008	6:48:06 PM	CAMP3-SERVER3	The cluster service is attempting to bring online the resource group "Cluster Group."
		5/20/2008	6:47:21 PM	CAMP3-SERVER2	The cluster service brought the resource group "Cluster Group" offline.
Private VLAN N-PE reload	2	5/20/2008	6:38:21 PM	CAMP3-SERVER2	The node (re)established communication with cluster node 'CAMP3-SERVER3' on network 'private(1).'
		5/20/2008	6:38:20 PM	CAMP3-SERVER2	The node (re)established communication with cluster node 'CAMP3-SERVER1' on network 'private(1).'
		5/20/2008	6:38:19 PM	CAMP3-SERVER2	The node lost communication with cluster node 'CAMP3-SERVER3' on network 'private(1).'
		5/20/2008	6:38:19 PM	CAMP3-SERVER2	The node lost communication with cluster node 'CAMP3-SERVER1' on network 'private(1).'
Private VLAN N-PE reload	2	5/20/2008	6:38:21 PM	CAMP3-SERVER2	The node (re)established communication with cluster node 'CAMP3-SERVER3' on network 'private(1).'
		5/20/2008	6:38:20 PM	CAMP3-SERVER2	The node (re)established communication with cluster node 'CAMP3-SERVER1' on network 'private(1).'
		5/20/2008	6:38:19 PM	CAMP3-SERVER2	The node lost communication with cluster node 'CAMP3-SERVER3' on network 'private(1).'
		5/20/2008	6:38:19 PM	CAMP3-SERVER2	The node lost communication with cluster node 'CAMP3-SERVER1' on network 'private(1).'
Unplug active server	98	5/20/2008	7:11:07 PM	CAMP3-SERVER1	The cluster service brought the resource group "Cluster Group" online.
		5/20/2008	7:10:00 PM	CAMP3-SERVER1	The cluster service is attempting to bring online the resource group "Cluster Group."
		5/20/2008	7:10:00 PM	CAMP3-SERVER1	Cluster node CAMP3-SERVER2 was removed from the active server cluster membership. Cluster service may have been stopped on the node, the node may have failed, or the node may have lost communication with the other active server cluster nodes.
		5/20/2008	7:09:39 PM	CAMP3-SERVER1	The node lost communication with cluster node 'CAMP3-SERVER2' on network 'private(1).'
		5/20/2008	7:09:38 PM	CAMP3-SERVER3	The node lost communication with cluster node 'CAMP3-SERVER2' on network 'private(1).'
		5/20/2008	7:09:29 PM	CAMP3-SERVER2	The time service is now synchronizing the system time with the time source camp3-server1.camp3.com (ntp.d|10.10.5.102:123->1.1.1.1:123).
		5/20/2008	7:09:29 PM	CAMP3-SERVER2	The time provider NtpClient is currently receiving valid time data from camp3-server1.camp3.com (ntp.d|10.10.5.102:123->1.1.1.1:123).

Multidomain H-VPLS with MEC and VLAN Load Balancing: PWs on Active and Standby VPLS Nodes in Up/Up State: EEM Option 5c

All EEM-based solutions that this book describes are based on the up/down PW model. The PW on the primary N-PE is in up state, and the PW on the standby N-PE is in down state. There are several benefits to this approach. In the case of an unexpected split-brain condition between VPLS nodes, this approach ensures that there are no potential dual active paths between sites, and it avoids Layer 2 loops in the global topology. In addition, EEM semaphore scripts are independent of bridge domain and Ethernet virtual circuit (EVC) configuration. However, the disadvantage of this approach is the convergence speed, because the backup PW must transition to up state before it can transport traffic. This action sometimes takes a few seconds and could be avoided with an up/up PW approach.

The EEM option 5c solution presents an alternative that allows PWs on the backup N-PEs to also be in up state. This accelerates the activation of the backup path in the event of a failure in the primary path.

Figure 9-31 provides an overview of up/up PW concept.

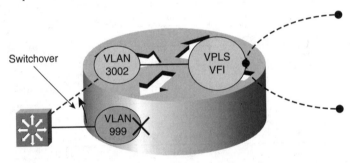

Figure 9-31 *Switchover between a stub and active VLAN for VPLS VFI connectivity.*

In this EEM option 5c solution, the PWs on the backup N-PE are also in up state. The concept is to forward edge traffic to a null QinQ VLAN until the backup path needs to be activated, thus avoiding Layer 2 loops in the global topology. In the event of a failure in the primary path, EEM maps the edge traffic to a QinQ VLAN that is connected to the VFI.

Although every EEM-based deployment model that this book describes can benefit from the up/up PW option, this solution describes its applicability only to the "multidomain H-VPLS with MEC and VLAN load balancing: EEM option 5b" solution.

This solution is similar to EEM option 5b in which the MEC system (either VSS or Nexus vPC) in the aggregation layer is connected using one EtherChannel toward each N-PE. The only difference is that the PWs on both the active and the standby N-PEs are in up/up state. The backup PW also is in up state, but does not forward any traffic. An

EEM script ensures that one service instance within an EtherChannel is cross-connected toward only one multipoint VFI at any time, thus avoiding loops in the topology.

As with all the EEM-based deployment models, the PW topology is based on the split-horizon concept. All primary N-PE routers are fully meshed with all primary and backup N-PE routers. The backup N-PE routers have only PWs toward the remote primary N-PEs; there are no PWs configured between the backup N-PE routers.

In PW up/down approach, the PWs are up on the primary N-PE and down on the back-up node. In an up/up approach, the PWs on the primary and backup N-PEs are always in up state, and the service instance is attached/detached from the bridge domain on the backup N-PE.

With the up/up option, a dummy edge VLAN (for example, 998) is configured solely to keep the VFI in up state and to prevent the autostate function from automatically shutting down the VFI.

In normal mode, which is under no failure condition, VLANs are associated with a null bridge domain on the QinQ link connecting the backup N-PE to the aggregation switch.

Figure 9-32 shows the association of edge VLAN, service instance, bridge domain, VFI, and PWs.

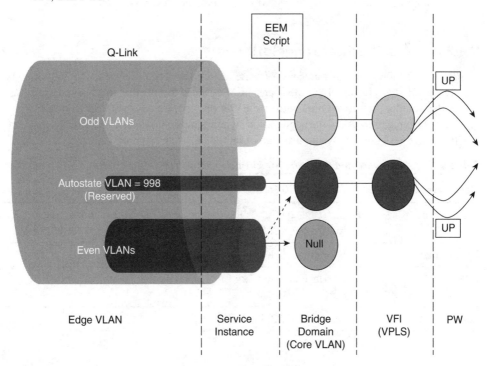

Figure 9-32 *Usage of EVC to create the up/up PW concept.*

Selective QinQ is configured on the N-PE side of the link connection to aggregation. This configuration allows the creation of several service instances to groom the edge VLAN. Each service instance is associated with a bridge domain that is cross-connected to a VFI, and this VFI has a PW to connect over the core toward the remote nodes.

When a failure occurs in the primary path, the EEM script on the backup N-PE router attaches a backup service instance (even VLAN bridge domain 3002) to the active bridge domain VLAN 3002, thus providing connectivity to the VPLS cloud.

When the primary N-PE recovers from failure, the backup N-PE transitions back to standby mode, and the service instance for customer VLANs is bridged again to the stub VLAN.

This approach allows the definition of a set of preprovisioned VFIs that are ready to be used and does not require modification of EEM scripts when a new edge domain needs to be added.

When compared to other EEM-based deployment models described earlier in this chapter, the key difference in this approach is the creation of an additional service instance and a bridge domain, 998. All the even VLANs on the primary N-PE are connected to this dummy bridge domain, 998, which is not cross-connected to any VFI. Therefore, in normal mode, the primary N-PE node does not transport even VLANs.

N-PE Routers: Hardware and Software

Table 9-13 shows the hardware and software required for N-PE nodes. Cisco 7600 routers were used as N-PEs for all the MST- and EEM-based solutions that this book describes. In this solution, selective QinQ with two EVCs was configured using ES20 modules facing the aggregation. Also, the aggregation switches must support an EEM script that can be trigged on a specific syslog message or on the link state.

Table 9-13 *Hardware and Software for N-PE Nodes*

Hardware/Software	Cisco 7600 Router
Facing core	Interfaces on SIP or ES modules are required for connectivity toward the VPLS core.
Facing edge	ES module: Selective QinQ is required in this solution.
E-link	Interface on any 67xx LAN or ES module; does not carry any traffic.
Software	Cisco IOS 12.2(33)SRC1.

Configuration Summary

The following configuration from N-PE1 and N-PE2 routers highlights the framework of the up/up PW solution.

On N-PE1	On N-PE2

```
vlan 2-61,201-260,998-999
!
vlan 3001
 name H-VPLS_Primary_core_VLAN
!
vlan 3004
 name H-VPLS_Backup_core_VLAN
!
l2 vfi VFI-Even manual
 vpn id 3002
 neighbor 10.76.90.22 encapsulation mpls
 neighbor 10.76.90.32 encapsulation mpls
!
l2 vfi VFI-Odd manual
 vpn id 3001
 neighbor 10.76.91.32 encapsulation mpls
 neighbor 10.76.91.31 encapsulation mpls
 neighbor 10.76.91.21 encapsulation mpls
 neighbor 10.76.91.22 encapsulation mpls
!
interface Vlan3001
 description Primary Core QinQ VLAN - used
to transport Odd edge VLAN
 mtu 9216
 no ip address
 xconnect vfi VFI-Odd
!
interface Vlan3004
 description Backup Core QinQ VLAN - used
to transport Even edge VLAN
 mtu 9216
 no ip address
 xconnect vfi VFI-Even

interface Port-channel31
 description used for QinQ ES20 card fac-
ing Aggregation (Multi-Etherchannel toward
 VSS)
 mtu 9216
```

```
vlan 2-61,201-260,998-999
!
vlan 3002
 name H-VPLS_Primary_core_VLAN
!
vlan 3003
 name H-VPLS_Backup_core_VLAN
!
l2 vfi VFI-Even manual
 vpn id 3002
 neighbor 10.76.90.21 encapsulation mpls
 neighbor 10.76.90.22 encapsulation mpls
 neighbor 10.76.90.31 encapsulation mpls
 neighbor 10.76.90.32 encapsulation mpls
!
l2 vfi VFI-Odd manual
 vpn id 3001
 neighbor 10.76.91.21 encapsulation mpls
 neighbor 10.76.91.31 encapsulation mpls
!
interface Vlan3002
 description Primary Core QinQ VLAN - used
to transport Even edge VLAN
 mtu 9216
 no ip address
 xconnect vfi VFI-Even
!
interface Vlan3003
 description Backup Core QinQ VLAN - used
to transport Odd edge VLAN
 mtu 9216
 no ip address
 xconnect vfi VFI-Odd

interface Port-channel32
 description used for QinQ ES20 card facing
Aggregation (Multi-Etherchannel toward VSS)
 mtu 9216
 ip arp inspection limit none
```

On N-PE1	On N-PE2

```
logging event bundle-status          logging event link-status
load-interval 30                     load-interval 30
mls qos trust dscp                   mls qos trust dscp
spanning-tree portfast trunk         spanning-tree portfast trunk
service instance 998 ethernet        service instance 998 ethernet
description Dummy to hold Vlan 3004 up   description Dummy to hold Vlan 3002 up
encapsulation dot1q 998              encapsulation dot1q 998
bridge-domain 3004                   bridge-domain 3002
!                                    !
service instance 999 ethernet        service instance 999 ethernet
description Dummy to hold Vlan 3001 up   description Dummy to hold Vlan 3003 up
encapsulation dot1q 999              encapsulation dot1q 999
bridge-domain 3001                   bridge-domain 3003
!                                    !
service instance 3001 ethernet       service instance 3002 ethernet
encapsulation dot1q                  encapsulation dot1q
1,3,5,7,9,11,13,15,17,19,21,23,25,27,29,31,   2,4,6,8,10,12,14,16,18,20,22,24,26,28,30,32,
  33,35,37,39,41,43,45,47,49,51,53,55,57,       34,36,38,40,42,44,46,48,50,52,54,56,58,
  59,61,201,203,205,207,209,211,213,215,        60,202,204,206,208,210,212,214,216,218,
  217,219,221,223,225,227,229,231,233,235,      220,222,224,226,228,230,232,234,236,238,
  237,239,241,243,245,247,249,251,253,255,      240,242,244,246,248,250,252,254,256,
  257,259                                       258,260
bridge-domain 3001                   bridge-domain 3002
!                                    !
service instance 3004 ethernet       service instance 3003 ethernet
encapsulation dot1q                  encapsulation dot1q
2,4,6,8,10,12,14,16,18,20,22,24,26,28,30,   1,3,5,7,9,11,13,15,17,19,21,23,25,27,29,
  32,34,36,38,40,42,44,46,48,50,52,54,56,       31,33,35,37,39,41,43,45,47,49,51,53,55,
  58,60,202,204,206,208,210,212,214,216,        57,59,6 1,201,203,205,207,209,211,213,
  218,220,222,224,226,228,230,232,234,236,      215,217,219,2 21,223,225,227,229,231,
  238,240,242,244,246,248,250,252,254,256,      233,235,237,239,241,243,245,247,
  258,260                                       249,251,253,255,257,259
bridge-domain 998                    bridge-domain 999
```

```
lon-n-pe1# sh cdp neigh
Capability Codes: R - Router, T - Trans
Bridge, B - Source Route Bridge
                S - Switch, H - Host, I
- IGMP, r - Repeater, P - Phone

Device ID        Local Intrfce    Holdtme
Capability  Platform  Port ID
campus3-223sw8   Gig 1/2          156
S I    WS-C2950T Fas 0/2
lon-n-pe2        Ten 4/0/0        127
R S I    CISCO7604 Ten 4/0/0
```

On N-PE1   **On N-PE2**

```
lon-agg-1          Ten 2/0/1          135
R S I      WS-C6509- Ten 2/7/12
lon-agg-1          Ten 3/1            179
R S I      WS-C6509- Ten 1/7/6
lon-agg-1          Ten 2/0/0          138
R S I      WS-C6509- Ten 1/7/11
CRS1-mpls-p1       Ten 4/0/1          147
R          CRS-1      TenGigE0/0/0/0
lon-core1          Ten 3/2            161
R S I      WS-C6506  Ten 1/2
lon-n-pe1#


lon-n-pe1#sh mpls l2transport vc


Local intf      Local circuit
Dest address    VC ID      Status
— — — — — —·   — — — — — — — — — — — —
— — — — — — —·  — — — — —  — — — — —
VFI VFI-Odd     VFI
10.76.70.21     3001       UP
VFI VFI-Odd     VFI
10.76.70.22     3001       UP
VFI VFI-Even    VFI
10.76.70.22     3002       UP
VFI VFI-Odd     VFI
10.76.70.31     3001       UP
VFI VFI-Odd     VFI
10.76.70.32     3001       UP
VFI VFI-Even    VFI
10.76.70.32     3002       UP
lon-n-pe1#
```

EEM scripts on the N-PE router alternatively position the even VLANs in nonforwarding bridge domain 998 and the forwarding bridge domain 3004:

```
! On N-PE1:
process-max-time 50
!
track timer ip route 1
!
track 10 ip route 10.76.80.12 255.255.255.255 reachability
 delay up 100
```

```
!
track 11 ip route 10.76.81.12 255.255.255.255 reachability
!
track 20 interface Port-channel31 line-protocol
!
track 25 list boolean or
 object 110
 object 112
 delay up 40
!
track 40 ip route 10.76.81.32 255.255.255.255 reachability
!
track 110 interface TenGigabitEthernet4/0/1 line-protocol
 delay down 5 up 60
!
track 112 interface TenGigabitEthernet4/0/0 line-protocol
!
event manager applet VPLS_EVEN-VLAN_P_semaphore-is-down
 event track 10 state down
 action 1.0 cli command "enable"
 action 2.0 cli command "conf t"
 action 3.0 cli command "interface port-channel 31"
 action 3.1 cli command "service instance 3004 ethernet"
 action 3.2 cli command "bridge-domain 3004"
 action 4.0 cli command "int lo80"
 action 4.1 cli command "no shut"
 action 9.0 syslog msg "Backup PW is active"
event manager applet VPLS_EVEN-VLAN_P_semaphore-is-up
 event track 10 state up
 action 1.0 cli command "enable"
 action 2.0 cli command "conf t"
 action 3.0 cli command "interface port-channel 31"
 action 3.1 cli command "service instance 3004 ethernet"
 action 3.2 cli command "bridge-domain 998"
 action 4.0 cli command "int lo80"
 action 4.1 cli command "shutdown"
 action 5.0 cli command "int Te3/1"
 action 5.1 cli command "shut"
 action 5.2 cli command "no shut"
 action 9.0 syslog msg "Backup PW is shutdown"
event manager applet VPLS_ODD-VLAN_B_semaphore-is-up
 event track 11 state up
 action 1.0 cli command "enable"
 action 2.0 cli command "conf t"
 action 4.0 cli command "interface port-channel 31"
```

```
 action 4.1 cli command "service instance 3001 ethernet"
 action 4.2 cli command "bridge-domain 999"
 action 9.0 syslog msg "Backup N-PE is Active, Force Primary in Standby"
event manager applet VPLS_ODD-VLAN_B_semaphore-is-down
 event track 11 state down
 action 1.0 cli command "enable"
 action 2.0 cli command "conf t"
 action 4.0 cli command "interface port-channel 31"
 action 4.1 cli command "service instance 3001 ethernet"
 action 4.2 cli command "bridge-domain 3001"
 action 9.0 syslog msg "Backup N-PE has become Standby, Primary runs Active"
event manager applet Track_Aggregation_link_failure
 event track 20 state down
 action 1.0 cli command "enable"
 action 2.0 cli command "conf t"
 action 3.0 cli command "int lo81"
 action 3.1 cli command "shutdown"
 action 4.0 cli command "interface port-channel 31"
 action 4.1 cli command "service instance 3001 ethernet"
 action 4.2 cli command "bridge-domain 999"
 action 9.0 syslog msg "Aggregation link is failing, Force Primary in Standby"
event manager applet Track_Aggregation_link_recovery
 event track 20 state up
 action 1.0 cli command "enable"
 action 2.0 cli command "conf t"
 action 4.0 cli command "int lo81"
 action 4.1 cli command "no shutdown"
 action 9.0 syslog msg "Aggregation link as recover, Primary requests to become
   active"
event manager applet Backup-node_ready
 event track 110 state up
 action 1.0 cli command "enable"
 action 2.0 cli command "conf t"
 action 3.0 cli command "track 10 ip route 10.76.80.12 255.255.255.255 reacha
   bility"
 action 3.1 cli command "delay up 100"
 action 9.0 syslog msg "Backup node is operational"
event manager applet Backup-node_not_ready
 event track 110 state down
 action 1.0 cli command "enable"
 action 4.0 cli command "configure t"
 action 5.0 cli command "no track 10"
 action 5.1 cli command "interface port-channel 31"
 action 5.2 cli command "service instance 3004 ethernet"
 action 5.3 cli command "bridge-domain 998"
 action 5.4 cli command "int lo80"
```

```
   action 5.5 cli command "shutdown"
   action 9.0 syslog msg "Backup node not operational"
event manager applet MPLS_Interfaces_Down
 event track 25 state down
 action 1.0 cli command "enable"
 action 2.0 cli command "config t"
 action 4.0 cli command "interface port-channel 31"
 action 4.1 cli command "shut"
 action 9.0 syslog msg "Both MPLS Interfaces are down. Shutting down ES20 link"
event manager applet MPLS_Either_Interface_up
 event track 25 state up
 action 1.0 cli command "enable"
 action 2.0 cli command "config t"
 action 3.0 cli command "interface port-channel 31"
 action 4.0 cli command "no shut"
 action 9.0 syslog msg "One MPLS Int is up. Unshutting ES20 link"
event manager applet SJ-Odd-VLAN_B-Semaphor-up
 event track 40 state up
 action 1.0 cli command "enable"
 action 2.0 cli command "clear mac-address-table dynamic"
event manager applet SJ-Odd-VLAN_B-Semaphor-down
 event track 40 state down
 action 1.0 cli command "enable"
 action 2.0 cli command "clear mac-address-table dynamic"
 !
```

Convergence Tests

The traffic profile outlined in Chapter 7 was used to determine end-to-end convergence for unidirectional voice, unicast, and multicast traffic. Links and nodes were failed to simulate network failures.

Table 9-14 shows results of various node and link failures. Convergence numbers (max and min) are in seconds.

Table 9-14 *Convergence Numbers for Link and Node Failures for VPLS with N-PE Redundancy Using EEM Semaphore with All PWs Up Solution: EEM Option 5c*

Failure Type	Action	VLAN	Traffic Type	Traffic Direction			
				LON → SJ		SJ → LON	
				Max	Min	Max	Min
Reload Agg-1	Reload	Odd VLAN	Voice	0.04	0.02	0.02	0.02
			Unicast	0.01	0.00	0.00	0.00
			Multicast	0.44	0.01	0.01	0.01
		Even VLAN	Voice	0.02	0.02	0.02	0.02
			Unicast	0.00	0.00	0.00	0.00
			Multicast	0.43	0.42	0.01	0.01
	Restore	Odd VLAN	Voice	0.26	0.24	0.00	0.00
			Unicast	0.24	0.24	0.00	0.00
			Multicast	0.25	0.00	0.64	0.00
		Even VLAN	Voice	0.24	0.24	0.00	0.00
			Unicast	0.24	0.24	0.00	0.00
			Multicast	0.25	0.00	0.14	0.00
Reload Agg-2	Reload	Odd VLAN	Voice	0.02	0.02	0.02	0.02
			Unicast	0.00	0.00	0.02	0.02
			Multicast	0.21	0.02	0.08	0.03
		Even VLAN	Voice	0.00	0.02	0.00	0.00
			Unicast	0.00	0.00	0.02	0.02
			Multicast	0.22	0.01	0.07	0.02
	Restore	Odd VLAN	Voice	0.06	0.02	0.02	0.02
			Unicast	0.03	0.03	0.02	0.02
			Multicast	0.22	0.02	0.07	0.02
		Even VLAN	Voice	0.04	0.02	0.00	0.00
			Unicast	0.01	0.01	0.02	0.02
			Multicast	0.22	0.01	0.06	0.01
Agg forced switchover	Reload	Odd VLAN	Voice	0.02	0.02	0.02	0.02
			Unicast	0.00	0.00	0.02	0.02
			Multicast	0.48	0.38	0.13	0.02
		Even VLAN	Voice	0.02	0.02	0.04	0.04
			Unicast	0.00	0.00	0.03	0.03
			Multicast	0.40	0.01	0.15	0.04
	Restore	Odd VLAN	Voice	0.12	0.02	0.02	0.02
			Unicast	0.09	0.09	0.00	0.00
			Multicast	0.10	0.00	0.00	0.00
		Even VLAN	Voice	0.14	0.08	0.02	0.02
			Unicast	0.09	0.09	0.00	0.00
			Multicast	0.54	0.00	0.00	0.00
Reload N-PE2	Reload	Odd VLAN	Voice	0.04	0.02	0.00	0.00
			Unicast	0.02	0.01	0.00	0.00
			Multicast	0.04	0.00	0.00	0.00
		Even VLAN	Voice	0.52	0.48	0.52	0.52
			Unicast	0.50	0.50	0.52	0.52
			Multicast	2.59	0.53	0.52	0.52
	Restore	Odd VLAN	Voice	0.14	0.02	0.02	0.02
			Unicast	0.08	0.05	0.00	0.00
			Multicast	0.12	0.02	0.00	0.00
		Even VLAN	Voice	0.42	0.38	0.42	0.42
			Unicast	0.40	0.39	0.40	0.40
			Multicast	2.17	0.46	0.39	0.39

Table 9-14 *Convergence Numbers for Link and Node Failures for VPLS with N-PE Redundancy Using EEM Semaphore with All PWs Up Solution: EEM Option 5c*

Failure Type	Action	VLAN	Traffic Type	Traffic Direction LON → SJ Max	Min	SJ → LON Max	Min
Fail VSL control link	Shut	Odd VLAN	Voice	0.04	0.02	0.02	0.02
			Unicast	0.01	0.01	0.00	0.00
			Multicast	0.03	0.00	0.00	0.00
		Even VLAN	Voice	0.00	0.02	0.02	0.02
			Unicast	0.00	0.00	0.00	0.00
			Multicast	0.00	0.00	0.00	0.00
	No shut	Odd VLAN	Voice	0.02	0.00	0.00	0.00
			Unicast	0.00	0.00	0.00	0.00
			Multicast	0.01	0.00	0.00	0.00
		Even VLAN	Voice	0.02	0.00	0.00	0.00
			Unicast	0.00	0.00	0.00	0.00
			Multicast	0.02	0.00	0.00	0.00
Fail VSL	Shut	Odd VLAN	Voice	0.04	0.02	0.02	0.02
			Unicast	0.01	0.01	0.00	0.00
			Multicast	0.03	0.00	0.00	0.00
		Even VLAN	Voice	0.00	0.02	0.02	0.02
			Unicast	0.00	0.00	0.00	0.00
			Multicast	0.00	0.00	0.00	0.00
	No shut	Odd VLAN	Voice	0.02	0.00	0.00	0.00
			Unicast	0.00	0.00	0.00	0.00
			Multicast	0.01	0.00	0.00	0.00
		Even VLAN	Voice	0.02	0.00	0.00	0.00
			Unicast	0.00	0.00	0.00	0.00
			Multicast	0.02	0.00	0.00	0.00
Fail link between N-PE1 and Agg-1	Shut	Odd VLAN	Voice	0.44	0.26	0.00	0.00
			Unicast	0.37	0.27	0.00	0.00
			Multicast	0.41	0.01	0.00	0.00
		Even VLAN	Voice	0.02	0.00	0.00	0.00
			Unicast	0.00	0.00	0.00	0.00
			Multicast	0.00	0.00	0.00	0.00
	No shut	Odd VLAN	Voice	0.24	0.06	0.00	0.00
			Unicast	0.17	0.07	0.00	0.00
			Multicast	0.26	0.01	0.01	0.01
		Even VLAN	Voice	0.02	0.00	0.00	0.00
			Unicast	0.00	0.00	0.00	0.00
			Multicast	0.00	0.00	0.01	0.01
Fail link between N-PE1 and Agg-2	Shut	Odd VLAN	Voice	0.02	0.02	0.10	0.10
			Unicast	0.01	0.00	0.09	0.09
			Multicast	0.37	0.00	0.09	0.09
		Even VLAN	Voice	0.02	0.02	0.02	0.02
			Unicast	0.00	0.00	0.00	0.00
			Multicast	0.01	0.00	0.02	0.00
	No shut	Odd VLAN	Voice	0.04	0.00	0.02	0.02
			Unicast	0.01	0.01	0.00	0.00
			Multicast	0.03	0.01	0.01	0.01
		Even VLAN	Voice	0.00	0.02	0.00	0.00
			Unicast	0.00	0.00	0.00	0.00
			Multicast	0.01	0.00	0.00	0.00

Table 9-14 *Convergence Numbers for Link and Node Failures for VPLS with N-PE Redundancy Using EEM Semaphore with All PWs Up Solution: EEM Option 5c*

| | | | | Traffic Direction | | | |
| | | | | LON → SJ | | SJ → LON | |
Failure Type	Action	VLAN	Traffic Type	Max	Min	Max	Min
Fail link between N-PE2 and Agg-1	Shut	Odd VLAN	Voice	0.04	0.02	0.02	0.02
			Unicast	0.01	0.01	0.00	0.00
			Multicast	0.02	0.00	0.01	0.01
		Even VLAN	Voice	0.44	0.26	0.02	0.02
			Unicast	0.38	0.28	0.00	0.00
			Multicast	0.38	0.00	0.01	0.01
	No shut	Odd VLAN	Voice	0.02	0.02	0.00	0.00
			Unicast	0.01	0.00	0.00	0.00
			Multicast	0.02	0.01	0.01	0.01
		Even VLAN	Voice	0.38	0.06	0.00	0.00
			Unicast	0.28	0.06	0.00	0.00
			Multicast	0.36	0.00	0.01	0.01
Fail link between N-PE2 and Agg-2	Shut	Odd VLAN	Voice	0.02	0.02	0.00	0.00
			Unicast	0.01	0.00	0.00	0.00
			Multicast	0.01	0.00	0.01	0.01
		Even VLAN	Voice	0.02	0.00	0.10	0.10
			Unicast	0.00	0.00	0.09	0.09
			Multicast	0.59	0.50	0.10	0.10
	No shut	Odd VLAN	Voice	0.02	0.02	0.00	0.00
			Unicast	0.00	0.00	0.00	0.00
			Multicast	0.02	0.01	0.01	0.01
		Even VLAN	Voice	0.02	0.00	0.00	0.00
			Unicast	0.00	0.00	0.00	0.00
			Multicast	0.02	0.01	0.01	0.01
Fail link between Access1 and Agg-1	Shut	Odd VLAN	Voice	0.04	0.02	0.02	0.02
			Unicast	0.01	0.00	0.00	0.00
			Multicast	0.02	0.00	0.01	0.01
		Even VLAN	Voice	0.02	0.02	0.02	0.02
			Unicast	0.01	0.00	0.00	0.00
			Multicast	0.02	0.00	0.01	0.01
	No shut	Odd VLAN	Voice	0.04	0.02	0.02	0.02
			Unicast	0.02	0.02	0.00	0.00
			Multicast	0.03	0.01	0.01	0.01
		Even VLAN	Voice	0.04	0.02	0.02	0.02
			Unicast	0.02	0.02	0.00	0.00
			Multicast	0.02	0.00	0.01	0.01
Fail link between Access1 and Agg-2	Shut	Odd VLAN	Voice	0.10	0.02	0.00	0.00
			Unicast	0.03	0.01	0.00	0.00
			Multicast	0.06	0.00	0.01	0.00
		Even VLAN	Voice	0.02	0.00	0.00	0.00
			Unicast	0.00	0.00	0.00	0.00
			Multicast	0.03	0.01	0.01	0.00
	No shut	Odd VLAN	Voice	0.04	0.02	0.02	0.02
			Unicast	0.01	0.01	0.00	0.00
			Multicast	0.02	0.00	0.01	0.01
		Even VLAN	Voice	0.02	0.02	0.02	0.02
			Unicast	0.01	0.01	0.00	0.00
			Multicast	0.01	0.00	0.01	0.01

Table 9-14   *Convergence Numbers for Link and Node Failures for VPLS with N-PE Redundancy Using EEM Semaphore with All PWs Up Solution: EEM Option 5c*

Failure Type	Action	VLAN	Traffic Type	Traffic Direction LON → SJ Max	Min	SJ → LON Max	Min
Fail link between Access2 and Agg-1	Shut	Odd VLAN	Voice	0.02	0.02	0.58	0.44
			Unicast	0.00	0.00	0.53	0.44
			Multicast	0.01	0.00	0.54	0.39
		Even VLAN	Voice	0.02	0.02	0.00	0.00
			Unicast	0.00	0.00	0.00	0.00
			Multicast	0.01	0.00	0.01	0.01
	No shut	Odd VLAN	Voice	0.00	0.02	0.28	0.06
			Unicast	0.00	0.00	0.18	0.02
			Multicast	0.01	0.00	0.29	0.03
		Even VLAN	Voice	0.02	0.02	0.02	0.02
			Unicast	0.00	0.00	0.00	0.00
			Multicast	0.01	0.00	0.00	0.00
Fail link between Access2 and Agg-2	Shut	Odd VLAN	Voice	0.16	0.02	0.02	0.02
			Unicast	0.06	0.04	0.00	0.00
			Multicast	0.10	0.01	0.03	0.01
		Even VLAN	Voice	0.02	0.02	0.42	0.42
			Unicast	0.00	0.00	0.41	0.41
			Multicast	0.02	0.00	0.42	0.35
	No shut	Odd VLAN	Voice	0.02	0.02	0.02	0.02
			Unicast	0.00	0.00	0.00	0.00
			Multicast	0.01	0.01	0.00	0.00
		Even VLAN	Voice	0.02	0.02	0.00	0.00
			Unicast	0.00	0.00	0.02	0.02
			Multicast	0.01	0.00	0.03	0.01
Fail WAN link facing core on N-PE1	Shut	Odd VLAN	Voice	0.24	0.20	0.06	0.06
			Unicast	0.21	0.21	0.06	0.05
			Multicast	0.23	0.20	0.06	0.06
		Even VLAN	Voice	0.02	0.02	0.00	0.00
			Unicast	0.00	0.00	0.00	0.00
			Multicast	0.00	0.00	0.00	0.00
	No shut	Odd VLAN	Voice	0.04	0.02	0.02	0.02
			Unicast	0.03	0.03	0.00	0.00
			Multicast	0.04	0.02	0.01	0.01
		Even VLAN	Voice	0.02	0.02	0.02	0.02
			Unicast	0.00	0.00	0.00	0.00
			Multicast	0.01	0.00	0.01	0.01
Fail both WAN links on N-PE2	Shut	Odd VLAN	Voice	0.06	0.02	0.02	0.02
			Unicast	0.01	0.01	0.00	0.00
			Multicast	0.04	0.00	0.00	0.00
		Even VLAN	Voice	0.71	0.67	0.54	0.54
			Unicast	0.69	0.69	0.53	0.53
			Multicast	2.50	1.09	0.54	0.52
	No shut	Odd VLAN	Voice	0.04	0.02	0.00	0.00
			Unicast	0.02	0.01	0.00	0.00
			Multicast	0.05	0.01	0.00	0.00
		Even VLAN	Voice	0.74	0.70	0.72	0.72
			Unicast	0.71	0.71	0.71	0.71
			Multicast	2.05	0.81	0.71	0.71

Table 9-14 *Convergence Numbers for Link and Node Failures for VPLS with N-PE Redundancy Using EEM Semaphore with All PWs Up Solution: EEM Option 5c*

| Failure Type | Action | VLAN | Traffic Type | Traffic Direction | | | |
| | | | | LON → SJ | | SJ → LON | |
				Max	Min	Max	Min
Clear dynamic MAC address table on aggregation switches	Clear	Odd VLAN	Voice	0.02	0.00	0.00	0.00
			Unicast	0.00	0.00	0.00	0.00
			Multicast	0.01	0.00	0.00	0.00
		Even VLAN	Voice	0.02	0.00	0.00	0.00
			Unicast	0.00	0.00	0.00	0.00
			Multicast	0.02	0.00	0.00	0.00
Clear IP routing table on both N-PEs	Clear	Odd VLAN	Voice	0.02	0.00	0.00	0.00
			Unicast	0.00	0.00	0.00	0.00
			Multicast	0.01	0.00	0.00	0.00
		Even VLAN	Voice	0.02	0.00	0.00	0.00
			Unicast	0.00	0.00	0.00	0.00
			Multicast	0.02	0.00	0.00	0.00
Clear dynamic MAC address table on both N-PEs	Clear	Odd VLAN	Voice	0.02	0.00	0.00	0.00
			Unicast	0.00	0.00	0.00	0.00
			Multicast	0.01	0.00	0.00	0.00
		Even VLAN	Voice	0.02	0.00	0.00	0.00
			Unicast	0.00	0.00	0.00	0.00
			Multicast	0.02	0.00	0.00	0.00

Summary

H-VPLS solutions that use the EEM semaphore protocol offer the most scalability among the solutions that this chapter presents. These solutions easily adapt to various data center formats and constraints through various options for connecting to the aggregation. The solutions that options 4a and 5b describe are widely deployed in organizations that have data centers with multiple bridging domains. However, the up/up PW approach in EEM option 5c makes it the solution that provides the fastest convergence times.

Chapter 10

GRE-Based Deployment Model

Typically, Ethernet over Multiprotocol Label Switching (EoMPLS) and Virtual Private LAN Service (VPLS) technologies have required an MPLS switching core for Layer 2 extension over long distances. When the core network is not dedicated for Layer 2 virtual private network (L2VPN) extension, migrating an existing IP core to MPLS can be complex. Also, MPLS and its related technologies require expertise for deployment and maintenance. To ease the adoption of Layer 2 extension, Cisco offers solutions to encapsulate EoMPLS or VPLS traffic over generic routing encapsulation (GRE) tunnels. These solutions allow transporting all Layer 2 traffic across data centers over the existing IP core. EoMPLS / VPLS over GRE is also known as Any Transport over MPLS over GRE (AToMoGRE) or Layer 2 VPN over GRE (L2VPNoGRE).

GRE-based deployment models focus on using L2VPN over an IP core network, which eliminates MPLS switching in the core. These deployment models provide Layer 2 extension over a WAN and take advantage of Layer 3 fast convergence and Embedded Event Manager (EEM) to interconnect geographically dispersed data centers.

The Cisco Catalyst 6500 series switch with a SIP-400 module running Cisco IOS Software Release 12.2(33)SXI or later supports multipoint bridging using VPLSoGRE over an IP network with STP isolation.

In VPLSoGRE, IP GRE tunnels are established between the core routers within each data center. MPLS Label Distribution Protocol (LDP) sessions are established through these GRE tunnels, which provide MPLS connectivity. MPLS connectivity over GRE tunnels is known as MPLSoGRE. VPLS virtual circuits are then established over MPLSoGRE tunnels, which provide multipoint connectivity over an IP network.

Figure 10-1 shows VPLS connectivity across an IP network.

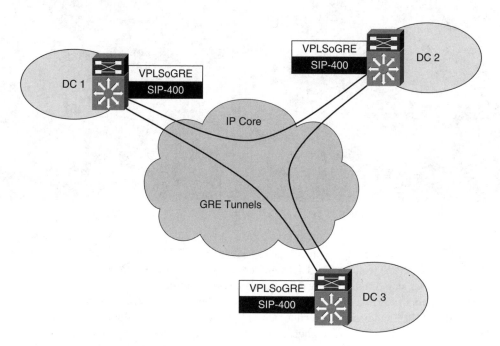

Figure 10-1   *VPLSoGRE Using Cisco Catalyst 6500*

This book focuses on interconnecting multiple data centers; therefore, only VPLSoGRE-based solutions are discussed in this chapter.

VPLSoGRE with Network-facing Provider Edge (N-PE) redundancy using EEM semaphore (EEM option 2) and Multidomain H-VPLS (EEM option 4a) were validated in Cisco labs. Chapter 9, "EEM-Based Deployment Models," provides detailed descriptions and the theory of operation of these solutions. However, all MST-based solutions documented in Chapter 8, "MST-Based Deployment Models," and EEM-based solutions documented in Chapter 9 can provide redundant access to the IP core via GRE.

This chapter provides the key configurations steps required to establish VPLS virtual circuits over MPLSoGRE tunnels. Implementing N-PE redundancy within the data center and EEM semaphore concepts are identical to EEM-based deployment models discussed in Chapter 9 and are not repeated in this chapter.

Key Configuration Steps for VPLSoGRE-Based Solutions

The following configuration from N-PE1 and N-PE2 routers highlights the framework of the VPLSoGRE solution based on the network topology outlined in Figure 7-2 in Chapter 7, "Data Center Multilayer Infrastructure Design."

Step 1. Create GRE tunnels between N-PEs and enable MPLS on these GRE tunnels. Ensure that the tunnel destination is reachable via a Gigabit Ethernet interface on the SIP-400 module. The following shows the configuration for N-PE1:

```
lon-n-pe1-cat6500#
!
interface Loopback1
 description tunnel source for VPLSoGRE
 ip address 99.1.1.11 255.255.255.255
!
interface Loopback2
 description tunnel source for VPLSoGRE
 ip address 99.1.1.13 255.255.255.255
!
interface Loopback3
 description tunnel source for VPLSoGRE
 ip address 99.1.1.15 255.255.255.255
!
interface Loopback4
 description tunnel source for VPLSoGRE
 ip address 99.1.1.17 255.255.255.255
!
interface Tunnel1121
 description to sin-n-pe1 Tunnel2111
 ip address 200.1.1.1 255.255.255.252
 ip ospf network point-to-point
 mpls ip
 tunnel source 99.1.1.15
 tunnel destination 99.1.1.21
!
interface Tunnel1122
 description to sin-n-pe2 tunn2211
 ip address 200.1.2.1 255.255.255.252
 ip ospf network point-to-point
 mpls ip
 tunnel source 99.1.1.17
 tunnel destination 99.1.1.22
!
interface Tunnel1131
```

```
   description to sj-n-pe1 Tunnel3111
   ip address 200.1.3.1 255.255.255.252
   ip ospf network point-to-point
   mpls ip
   tunnel source 99.1.1.11
   tunnel destination 99.1.1.31
  !
  interface Tunnel1132
   description to sj-n-pe2 Tunnel3211
   ip address 200.1.4.1 255.255.255.252
   ip ospf network point-to-point
   mpls ip
   tunnel source 99.1.1.13
   tunnel destination 99.1.1.32
```

Step 2. MPLS LDP neighbors should be reachable via GRE tunnels. Configure static routes to reach the LDP neighbors via the tunnels configured in Step 1. The following shows the configuration for N-PE1:

```
lon-n-pe1-cat6500#
!
! Tunnels for LDP peering with N-PEs in remote data centers
ip route 10.76.70.21 255.255.255.255 Tunnel1121
ip route 10.76.70.22 255.255.255.255 Tunnel1122
ip route 10.76.70.31 255.255.255.255 Tunnel1131
ip route 10.76.70.32 255.255.255.255 Tunnel1132
!
! Tunnels to enable backup PWs for even VLANs to N-PE2's in
remote data centers
ip route 10.76.90.22 255.255.255.255 Tunnel1122
ip route 10.76.90.32 255.255.255.255 Tunnel1132
!
! Tunnels to enable primary PWs for odd VLANs on N-PE1's in
remote data centers
ip route 10.76.91.21 255.255.255.255 Tunnel1121
ip route 10.76.91.31 255.255.255.255 Tunnel1131
!
! Tunnels to enable backup PWs for odd VLANs on N-PE2's in
remote data centers
ip route 10.76.91.22 255.255.255.255 Tunnel1122
ip route 10.76.91.32 255.255.255.255 Tunnel1132
```

Step 3. Verify that OSPF neighbors and LDP peers are established via these GRE tunnels:

```
lon-n-pe1-cat6500#show ip ospf neighbor
```

Neighbor ID	Pri	State		Dead Time	Address	Interface
99.1.1.38	0	FULL/	-	00:00:33	200.1.4.2	Tunnel1132
99.1.1.37	0	FULL/	-	00:00:33	200.1.3.2	Tunnel1131
99.1.1.28	0	FULL/	-	00:00:32	200.1.2.2	Tunnel1122

```
 99.1.1.27      0   FULL/  -   00:00:33  200.1.1.2    Tunnel1121
 116.5.200.77   0   FULL/  -   00:00:37  192.168.41.12 Gigabit
                                                      Ethernet3/0/0
 12.12.12.12    0   FULL/  -   00:00:39  192.168.13.2  Gigabit
                                                      Ethernet3/0/1
 13.13.13.13    0   FULL/  -   00:00:33  10.11.11.2    Gigabit
                                                      Ethernet2/8
```

```
lon-n-pe1-cat6500#show mpls ldp neighbor | begin 10.76.70.31

Peer LDP Ident: 10.76.70.31:0; Local LDP Ident 10.76.70.11:0
  TCP connection: 10.76.70.31.30021 - 10.76.70.11.646
  State: Oper; Msgs sent/rcvd: 287/257; Downstream
  Up time: 01:26:33
  LDP discovery sources:
    Targeted Hello 10.76.70.11 -> 10.76.70.31, active, passive
    Targeted Hello 10.76.70.11 -> 10.76.91.31, active
    Tunnel1131, Src IP addr: 200.1.3.2
    Targeted Hello 10.76.91.11 -> 10.76.70.31, passive
      Addresses bound to peer LDP Ident:
        31.31.31.31  99.1.1.31    99.1.1.33    99.1.1.35
        99.1.1.37    10.76.70.31  10.76.81.31  223.255.103.61
        10.13.11.1   192.168.61.3 192.168.33.3 200.1.11.2
        200.1.15.2   10.76.91.31  200.1.3.2    200.1.7.2
```

```
lon-n-pe1-cat6500#show ip route 10.76.70.31

Routing entry for 10.76.70.31/32
  Known via "static", distance 1, metric 0 (connected)
  Routing Descriptor Blocks:
  * directly connected, via Tunnel1131
      Route metric is 0, traffic share count is 1
```

```
lon-n-pe1-cat6500#show cdp neighbors
Capability Codes: R - Router, T - Trans Bridge, B - Source
Route Bridge
                    S - Switch, H - Host, I - IGMP, r -
Repeater, P - Phone


Device ID  Local Intrfce  Holdtme Capability Platform  Port ID
lon-agg-1  Gig 2/7          179     R S I     WS-C6509- Gig 2/3
lon-core1  Gig 2/8          159     R S I     WS-C6506  Gig 3/8
mpls-p1    Gig 3/0/0        140     R S I     WS-C6506  Gig 5/1
lon-n-pe2-
cat6500

           Gig 3/0/1        155     R S I     WS-C6506- Gig 3/0/1
lon-n-pe2-
cat6500

           Gig 2/2          146     R S I     WS-C6506- Gig 2/2
lon-n-pe2-
cat6500

           Gig 2/1          133     R S I     WS-C6506- Gig 2/1
lon-n-pe1-
cat6500#
```

Step 4.   Configure VPLS sessions:

- For one virtual forwarding instance (VFI) per VLAN to be transported across data centers, follow the steps outlined in the section "VPLSoGRE with N-PE Redundancy Using EEM Semaphore."

- For one VFI per group of VLANs to be transported across data centers, follow the steps outlined in the section "VPLSoGRE Multidomain with H-VPLS."

VPLSoGRE with N-PE Redundancy Using EEM Semaphore

Create one VFI per VLAN, which is cross-connected (xconnected) to the primary and backup nodes in other data centers. Taking VLAN 7 as an example, under normal mode, traffic from VLAN 7 is forwarded via N-PE1, which is the primary node for odd VLANs.

VFI for VLAN 7 on N-PE1 is xconnected to primary and backup N-PEs in other data centers. On N-PE2, which is the backup node for odd VLANs, VFI for VLAN 7 is xconnected to all primary nodes in other data centers. Example 10-1 shows these configurations for N-PE1 and N-PE2.

Example 10-1   *MPLS, VFI, and SVI Configuration and Verification*

```
! On N-PE1:
lon-n-pe1-cat6500#
...
!
mpls ldp neighbor 10.76.70.12 targeted ldp
mpls ldp neighbor 10.76.70.21 targeted ldp
mpls ldp neighbor 10.76.70.22 targeted ldp
mpls ldp neighbor 10.76.70.31 targeted ldp
mpls ldp neighbor 10.76.70.32 targeted ldp
mpls ldp tcp pak-priority
mpls ldp session protection
no mpls ldp advertise-labels
```

Example 10-1   *MPLS, VFI, and SVI Configuration and Verification*

```
mpls ldp advertise-labels for 76
mpls label protocol ldp
xconnect logging pseudowire status
!
access-list 76 permit 10.76.0.0 0.0.255.255

! VFI for VLAN 7
l2 vfi VFI-7 manual
 vpn id 7
 neighbor 10.76.91.21 encapsulation mpls
 neighbor 10.76.91.32 encapsulation mpls
 neighbor 10.76.91.31 encapsulation mpls
 neighbor 10.76.91.22 encapsulation mpls
!
interface Vlan7
 mtu 9216
 no ip address
 xconnect vfi VFI-7
end


lon-n-pe1-cat6500# show mpls l2transport vc 7


Local intf     Local circuit            Dest address      VC ID      Status
-------.       ----------------- -------.  -----  -----
VFI VFI-7      VFI                      10.76.91.21       7          UP
VFI VFI-7      VFI                      10.76.91.22       7          DOWN
VFI VFI-7      VFI                      10.76.91.31       7          UP
VFI VFI-7      VFI                      10.76.91.32       7          DOWN
lon-n-pe1-cat6500#

! On N-PE2:
lon-n-pe2# show mpls l2transport vc 7


Local intf     Local circuit            Dest address      VC ID      Status
------.        --------------- -------.  -----  -----
VFI VFI-7      VFI                      10.76.91.21       7          DOWN
VFI VFI-7      VFI                      10.76.91.31       7          DOWN
lon-n-pe2#
```

Convergence Tests

The traffic profile outlined in Chapter 7 was used to determine end-to-end convergence for unidirectional voice, unicast, and multicast traffic. Links and nodes were failed to simulate network failures.

Table 10-1 shows results of various node and link failures for the VPLSoGRE with N-PE redundancy using EEM semaphore solution. Convergence numbers (max and min) are in seconds.

Table 10-1   *Convergence Numbers for Link and Node Failures for the VPLSoGRE with N-PE Redundancy Using EEM Semaphore Solution*

| | | | | Traffic Direction | | | |
| | | | | LON → SJ | | SJ → LON | |
Failure Type	Action	VLAN	Traffic Type	Max	Min	Max	Min
Reload N-PE1	Reload	Odd VLAN	Voice	2.82	0.02	2.82	2.74
			Unicast	2.81	2.75	2.81	2.67
		Even VLAN	Voice	0.02	0.02	0.02	0.02
			Unicast	0.00	0.00	0.00	0.00
	Restore	Odd VLAN	Voice	1.54	1.14	1.24	1.14
			Unicast	1.50	1.48	1.22	1.08
		Even VLAN	Voice	0.00	0.02	0.02	0.02
			Unicast	0.00	0.00	0.00	0.00
Reload N-PE2	Reload	Odd VLAN	Voice	0.02	0.02	0.00	0.00
			Unicast	0.00	0.00	0.00	0.00
		Even VLAN	Voice	2.92	2.34	2.89	2.87
			Unicast	2.91	2.35	2.92	2.35
	Restore	Odd VLAN	Voice	0.04	0.02	0.00	0.00
			Unicast	0.01	0.01	0.00	0.00
		Even VLAN	Voice	3.42	3.36	6.20	6.20
			Unicast	3.39	3.38	6.21	6.21
Reload Agg-1	Reload	Odd VLAN	Voice	0.50	0.46	0.98	0.42
			Unicast	0.48	0.47	0.99	0.43
		Even VLAN	Voice	0.02	0.02	0.00	0.00
			Unicast	0.00	0.00	0.00	0.00
	Restore	Odd VLAN	Voice	0.24	0.20	2.64	0.22
			Unicast	0.21	0.21	2.61	0.20
		Even VLAN	Voice	0.00	0.00	0.02	0.02
			Unicast	0.00	0.00	0.00	0.00
Reload Agg-2	Reload	Odd VLAN	Voice	0.02	0.02	0.02	0.02
			Unicast	0.00	0.00	0.00	0.00
		Even VLAN	Voice	0.76	0.72	0.02	0.02
			Unicast	0.73	0.73	0.72	0.72
	Restore	Odd VLAN	Voice	0.00	0.00	0.00	0.00
			Unicast	0.00	0.00	0.00	0.00
		Even VLAN	Voice	0.18	0.12	0.12	0.10
			Unicast	0.16	0.12	0.12	0.09

Table 10-1 *Convergence Numbers for Link and Node Failures for the VPLSoGRE with N-PE Redundancy Using EEM Semaphore Solution (continued)*

Failure Type	Action	VLAN	Traffic Type	Traffic Direction			
				LON → SJ		SJ → LON	
				Max	Min	Max	Min
Fail L2 link between N-PE1 and Agg-1	Shut	Odd VLAN	Voice	0.10	0.06	0.08	0.02
			Unicast	0.08	0.07	0.08	0.02
		Even VLAN	Voice	0.00	0.02	0.00	0.00
			Unicast	0.00	0.00	0.00	0.00
	No shut	Odd VLAN	Voice	0.04	0.02	2.74	0.06
			Unicast	0.03	0.03	2.72	0.03
		Even VLAN	Voice	0.02	0.02	0.02	0.02
			Unicast	0.00	0.00	0.00	0.00
Fail L2 link between N-PE2 and Agg-2	Shut	Odd VLAN	Voice	0.02	0.02	0.02	0.02
			Unicast	0.00	0.00	0.00	0.00
		Even VLAN	Voice	0.16	0.14	0.18	0.10
			Unicast	0.15	0.15	0.15	0.07
	No shut	Odd VLAN	Voice	0.02	0.02	0.02	0.02
			Unicast	0.00	0.00	0.00	0.00
		Even VLAN	Voice	0.02	0.02	0.04	0.04
			Unicast	0.01	0.00	0.02	0.01
Fail L2 link between Agg-1 and Agg-2	Shut	Odd VLAN	Voice	0.00	0.02	0.02	0.02
			Unicast	0.00	0.00	0.00	0.00
		Even VLAN	Voice	0.02	0.02	0.02	0.02
			Unicast	0.00	0.00	0.00	0.00
	No shut	Odd VLAN	Voice	0.02	0.02	0.00	0.00
			Unicast	0.00	0.00	0.00	0.00
		Even VLAN	Voice	0.02	0.00	0.00	0.00
			Unicast	0.00	0.00	0.00	0.00
Fail L2 link between N-PE1 and N-PE2	Shut	Odd VLAN	Voice	0.02	0.02	0.00	0.00
			Unicast	0.00	0.00	0.00	0.00
		Even VLAN	Voice	0.00	0.00	0.00	0.00
			Unicast	0.00	0.00	0.00	0.00
	No shut	Odd VLAN	Voice	0.00	0.00	0.00	0.00
			Unicast	0.00	0.00	0.00	0.00
		Even VLAN	Voice	0.02	0.00	0.00	0.00
			Unicast	0.00	0.00	0.00	0.00
Fail WAN link facing core on N-PE1	Shut	Odd VLAN	Voice	1.12	1.10	0.02	0.02
			Unicast	1.10	1.10	0.00	0.00
		Even VLAN	Voice	0.02	0.02	0.02	0.02
			Unicast	0.00	0.00	0.00	0.00
	No shut	Odd VLAN	Voice	0.00	0.00	0.00	0.00
			Unicast	0.00	0.00	0.00	0.00
		Even VLAN	Voice	0.02	0.00	0.00	0.00
			Unicast	0.00	0.00	0.00	0.00

continues

Table 10-1   *Convergence Numbers for Link and Node Failures for the VPLSoGRE with N-PE Redundancy Using EEM Semaphore Solution (continued)*

Failure Type	Action	VLAN	Traffic Type	Traffic Direction			
				LON → SJ		SJ → LON	
				Max	Min	Max	Min
Fail WAN link facing core on N-PE2	Shut	Odd VLAN	Voice	0.02	0.02	0.00	0.00
			Unicast	0.00	0.00	0.00	0.00
		Even VLAN	Voice	0.66	0.62	0.24	0.24
			Unicast	0.63	0.63	0.23	0.23
	No shut	Odd VLAN	Voice	0.02	0.02	0.02	0.02
			Unicast	0.00	0.00	0.00	0.00
		Even VLAN	Voice	0.00	0.00	0.02	0.02
			Unicast	0.00	0.00	0.00	0.00
Fail both WAN links on N-PE1	Shut	Odd VLAN	Voice	1.24	0.02	1.56	1.48
			Unicast	1.22	1.22	1.53	1.41
		Even VLAN	Voice	0.02	0.02	0.02	0.02
			Unicast	0.00	0.00	0.00	0.00
	No shut	Odd VLAN	Voice	1.26	0.52	1.24	1.18
			Unicast	1.26	0.53	1.25	0.34
		Even VLAN	Voice	0.02	0.02	0.00	0.00
			Unicast	0.00	0.00	0.00	0.00
Fail both WAN links on N-PE2	Shut	Odd VLAN	Voice	0.00	0.00	0.00	0.00
			Unicast	0.00	0.00	0.00	0.00
		Even VLAN	Voice	2.08	1.82	1.88	1.84
			Unicast	2.07	1.81	1.88	1.77
	No shut	Odd VLAN	Voice	0.02	0.02	0.02	0.02
			Unicast	0.00	0.00	0.00	0.00
		Even VLAN	Voice	2.18	1.50	2.22	2.18
			Unicast	2.18	1.49	2.19	1.30
Clear entire routing table on both N-PEs	*Clear	Odd VLAN	Voice	0.02	0.02	0.00	0.00
			Unicast	0.00	0.00	0.00	0.00
		Even VLAN	Voice	5.16	4.96	4.96	4.96
			Unicast	5.14	4.98	4.96	4.92
Clear dynamic MAC address table on both N-PEs	Clear	Odd VLAN	Voice	0.02	0.02	0.00	0.00
			Unicast	0.00	0.00	0.00	0.00
		Even VLAN	Voice	0.02	0.00	0.00	0.00
			Unicast	0.00	0.00	0.00	0.00

*Installing static routes may take up to 6 seconds when the **clear ip route** * command is executed to clear all the routes. Cisco defect number CSCsk10711 documents this issue.

Cluster Server Tests

Table 10-2 shows event logs from the Event Viewer of a Microsoft cluster server. The logs are in the reverse order, showing the last event first. It is best to view the timestamps while analyzing these logs.

Table 10-2   *Event Logs for the VPLSoGRE with N-PE Redundancy Using EEM Semaphore Solution*

Test Case	Time in Seconds	Event Logs with Time Stamps from Microsoft Server			
		1/12/2009	12:44:21 PM	CAMP3-SERVER3	Cluster service successfully joined the server cluster CLUSTER-MNS.
		1/12/2009	12:44:13 PM	CAMP3-SERVER2	The interface for cluster node 'CAMP3-SERVER3' on network 'private(1)' is operational (up). The node can communicate with all other available cluster nodes on the network.
		1/12/2009	12:44:12 PM	CAMP3-SERVER2	The interface for cluster node 'CAMP3-SERVER3' on network 'public' is operational (up). The node can communicate with all other available cluster nodes on the network.
		1/12/2009	12:44:11 PM	CAMP3-SERVER3	The node (re)established communication with cluster node 'CAMP3-SERVER1' on network 'public.'
		1/12/2009	12:44:11 PM	CAMP3-SERVER3	The node (re)established communication with cluster node 'CAMP3-SERVER1' on network 'private(1).'
Establish L2 connectivity between Microsoft server nodes	No convergence	1/12/2009	12:44:11 PM	CAMP3-SERVER3	The node (re)established communication with cluster node 'CAMP3-SERVER2' on network 'public.'
		1/12/2009	12:44:11 PM	CAMP3-SERVER3	The node (re)established communication with cluster node 'CAMP3-SERVER2' on network 'private(1).'
		1/12/2009	12:44:10 PM	CAMP3-SERVER2	The node (re)established communication with cluster node 'CAMP3-SERVER3' on network 'private(1).'
		1/12/2009	12:44:10 PM	CAMP3-SERVER2	The node (re)established communication with cluster node 'CAMP3-SERVER3' on network 'public.'
		1/12/2009	12:44:10 PM	CAMP3-SERVER1	The node (re)established communication with cluster node 'CAMP3-SERVER3' on network 'public.'
		1/12/2009	12:44:10 PM	CAMP3-SERVER1	The node (re)established communication with cluster node 'CAMP3-SERVER3' on network 'private(1).'

continues

Table 10-2   *Event Logs for the VPLSoGRE with N-PE Redundancy Using EEM Semaphore Solution (continued)*

Test Case	Time in Seconds	Event Logs with Time Stamps from Microsoft Server			
Shut down both N-PEs in a data center	119	1/8/2009	5:34:00 PM	CAMP3-SERVER2	The cluster service brought the resource group "ClusterGroup" online.
		1/8/2009	5:32:25 PM	CAMP3-SERVER2	The cluster service is attempting to bring online the resource group "ClusterGroup."
		1/8/2009	5:32:25 PM	CAMP3-SERVER2	Cluster node CAMP3-SERVER3 was removed from the active server cluster membership. Cluster service may have been stopped on the node, the node may have failed, or the node may have lost communication with the other active server cluster nodes.
		1/8/2009	5:32:01 PM	CAMP3-SERVER1	The node lost communication with cluster node 'CAMP3-SERVER3' on network 'private(1).'
		1/8/2009	5:32:01 PM	CAMP3-SERVER1	The node lost communication with cluster node 'CAMP3-SERVER3' on network 'public.'
Power off access switch	160	1/8/2009	5:04:07 PM	CAMP3-SERVER2	The cluster service brought the resource group "ClusterGroup" online.
		1/8/2009	5:01:50 PM	CAMP3-SERVER2	The cluster service is attempting to bring online the resource group "ClusterGroup."
		1/8/2009	5:01:50 PM	CAMP3-SERVER2	Cluster node CAMP3-SERVER3 was removed from the active server cluster membership. Cluster service may have been stopped on the node, the node may have failed, or the node may have lost communication with the other active server cluster nodes.
		1/8/2009	5:01:28 PM	CAMP3-SERVER2	The node lost communication with cluster node 'CAMP3-SERVER3' on network 'public.'
		1/8/2009	5:01:29 PM	CAMP3-SERVER2	The node lost communication with cluster node 'CAMP3-SERVER3' on network 'private(1).'
		1/8/2009	5:01:27 PM	CAMP3-SERVER1	The node lost communication with cluster node 'CAMP3-SERVER3' on network 'public.'
		1/8/2009	5:01:28 PM	CAMP3-SERVER1	The node lost communication with cluster node 'CAMP3-SERVER3' on network 'private(1).'

Table 10-2   *Event Logs for the VPLSoGRE with N-PE Redundancy Using EEM
Semaphore Solution*

Test Case	Time in Seconds	Event Logs with Time Stamps from Microsoft Server			
Shut down both N-PEs in a data center	119	1/8/2009	5:34:00 PM	CAMP3-SERVER2	The cluster service brought the resource group "ClusterGroup" online.
		1/8/2009	5:32:25 PM	CAMP3-SERVER2	The cluster service is attempting to bring online the resource group "ClusterGroup."
		1/8/2009	5:32:25 PM	CAMP3-SERVER2	Cluster node CAMP3-SERVER3 was removed from the active server cluster membership. Cluster service may have been stopped on the node, the node may have failed, or the node may have lost communication with the other active server cluster nodes.
		1/8/2009	5:32:01 PM	CAMP3-SERVER1	The node lost communication with cluster node 'CAMP3-SERVER3' on network 'private(1).'
		1/8/2009	5:32:01 PM	CAMP3-SERVER1	The node lost communication with cluster node 'CAMP3-SERVER3' on network 'public.'
Power off access switch	160	1/8/2009	5:04:07 PM	CAMP3-SERVER2	The cluster service brought the resource group "ClusterGroup" online.
		1/8/2009	5:01:50 PM	CAMP3-SERVER2	The cluster service is attempting to bring online the resource group "ClusterGroup."
		1/8/2009	5:01:50 PM	CAMP3-SERVER2	Cluster node CAMP3-SERVER3 was removed from the active server cluster membership. Cluster service may have been stopped on the node, the node may have failed, or the node may have lost communication with the other active server cluster nodes.
		1/8/2009	5:01:28 PM	CAMP3-SERVER2	The node lost communication with cluster node 'CAMP3-SERVER3' on network 'public.'
		1/8/2009	5:01:29 PM	CAMP3-SERVER2	The node lost communication with cluster node 'CAMP3-SERVER3' on network 'private(1).'
		1/8/2009	5:01:27 PM	CAMP3-SERVER1	The node lost communication with cluster node 'CAMP3-SERVER3' on network 'public.'
		1/8/2009	5:01:28 PM	CAMP3-SERVER1	The node lost communication with cluster node 'CAMP3-SERVER3' on network 'private(1).'

continues

Table 10-2   *Event Logs for the VPLSoGRE with N-PE Redundancy Using EEM Semaphore Solution (continued)*

Test Case	Time in Seconds	Event Logs with Time Stamps from Microsoft Server			
Shut down active node	103	1/8/2009	6:25:40 PM	CAMP3-SERVER2	The cluster service brought the resource group "ClusterGroup" online.
		1/8/2009	6:24:36 PM	CAMP3-SERVER3	Cluster service is attempting to fail over the cluster resource group 'ClusterGroup' from node CAMP3-SERVER3 to node CAMP3-SERVER2.
		1/8/2009	6:24:17 PM	CAMP3-SERVER2	The cluster service is attempting to bring online the resource group "ClusterGroup".
		1/8/2009	6:23:56 PM	CAMP3-SERVER2	The node lost communication with cluster node 'CAMP3-SERVER3' on network 'public.'
		1/8/2009	6:23:57 PM	CAMP3-SERVER1	The node lost communication with cluster node 'CAMP3-SERVER3' on network 'public.'
Private VLAN NPE reload	4	1/8/2009	5:51:27 PM	CAMP3-SERVER3	The node (re)established communication with cluster node 'CAMP3-SERVER1' on network 'private(1).'
		1/8/2009	5:51:27 PM	CAMP3-SERVER1	The node (re)established communication with cluster node 'CAMP3-SERVER3' on network 'private(1).'
		1/8/2009	5:51:27 PM	CAMP3-SERVER2	The node (re)established communication with cluster node 'CAMP3-SERVER3' on network 'private(1).'
		1/8/2009	5:51:26 PM	CAMP3-SERVER3	The node (re)established communication with cluster node 'CAMP3-SERVER2' on network 'private(1).'
		1/8/2009	5:51:24 PM	CAMP3-SERVER3	The node lost communication with cluster node 'CAMP3-SERVER1' on network 'private(1).'
		1/8/2009	5:51:24 PM	CAMP3-SERVER3	The node lost communication with cluster node 'CAMP3-SERVER2' on network 'private(1).'
		1/8/2009	5:51:24 PM	CAMP3-SERVER1	The node lost communication with cluster node 'CAMP3-SERVER3' on network 'private(1).'
		1/8/2009	5:51:23 PM	CAMP3-SERVER2	The node lost communication with cluster node 'CAMP3-SERVER3' on network 'private(1).'

Table 10-2   *Event Logs for the VPLSoGRE with N-PE Redundancy Using EEM Semaphore Solution*

Test Case	Time in Seconds	Event Logs with Time Stamps from Microsoft Server			
Unplug active server	104	1/8/2009	6:25:40 PM	CAMP3-SERVER2	The cluster service brought the resource group "ClusterGroup" online.
		1/8/2009	6:24:36 PM	CAMP3-SERVER2	Cluster service is attempting to fail over the cluster resource group 'ClusterGroup' from node CAMP3-SERVER3 to node CAMP3-SERVER2.
		1/8/2009	6:24:17 PM	CAMP3-SERVER2	The cluster service is attempting to bring online the resource group "ClusterGroup."
		1/8/2009	6:24:05 PM	CAMP3-SERVER2	The interface for cluster node 'CAMP3-SERVER3' on network 'public' failed. If the condition persists, check the cable connecting the node to the network. Next, check for hardware or software errors in node's network adapter. Finally, check for failures in any network components to which the node is connected such as hubs, switches, or bridges.
		1/8/2009	6:23:56 PM	CAMP3-SERVER2	The node lost communication with cluster node 'CAMP3-SERVER3' on network 'public.'

VPLSoGRE: Multidomain with H-VPLS Solution

To configure one VFI per group of VLANs to be transported across data centers, follow these steps:

Step 1.   Create QinQ VLANs on both N-PEs. Configure QinQ using dot1q-tunnel on the Q-links between N-PEs and aggregation switches.

> **Note**   The Cisco Catalyst 6500 does not support selective QinQ. Two physical links were provisioned between N-PEs and aggregation switches to load balance traffic between odd and even VLANs.

On N-PE1

```
vlan 4001
name H-
VPLS_Primary_core_VLAN_for_odd_vlans
vlan 4004
name H-
VPLS_Backup_core_VLAN_for_even_vlans
!
interface GigabitEthernet2/5
 description QinQ link for Odd Vlans -
connected to LON-Agg-1
 switchport
 switchport access vlan 4001
 switchport trunk allowed vlan
1,3,5,7,9,11 ..
 switchport mode dot1q-tunnel
 mtu 9216
 spanning-tree bpdufilter enable
!
interface GigabitEthernet2/6
 description QonQ link for Even Vlans
-connected to LON-Agg-1
 switchport
 switchport access vlan 4004
 switchport trunk allowed vlan
2,4,6,8,10,12 ..
 switchport mode dot1q-tunnel
 mtu 9216
 spanning-tree bpdufilter enable
!
end
```

On N-PE2

```
vlan 4004
name H-
VPLS_Primary_core_VLAN_for_even_vlans
vlan 4001
name H-
VPLS_Backup_core_VLAN_for_odd_vlans
!
interface GigabitEthernet2/5
 description QinQ link for Even Vlans
connected to LON-Agg-2
 switchport
 switchport access vlan 4004
 switchport trunk allowed vlan 2,4,6,8,10
..
 switchport mode dot1q-tunnel
 mtu 9216
 spanning-tree bpdufilter enable
!
interface GigabitEthernet2/6
 description QinQ link for Odd Vlans
connected to LON-Agg-2.
 switchport
 switchport access vlan 4001
 switchport trunk allowed vlan
1,3,5,7,9,11 ..
 switchport mode dot1q-tunnel
 mtu 9216
 spanning-tree bpdufilter enable
!
end
```

On N-PE1

```
interface GigabitEthernet2/2
 description Odd-Vlans QinQ Link to lon-
n-pe1-cat6500 g2/5
 switchport
 switchport trunk encapsulation dot1q
 switchport trunk allowed vlan
1,3,5,7,9,11 ..
 switchport mode trunk
 mtu 9216
 spanning-tree portfast trunk
 spanning-tree bpdufilter enable
!
interface GigabitEthernet2/4
 description Even Vlans QinQ link to
lon-n-pe1-cat6500 g2/6
 switchport
 switchport trunk encapsulation dot1q
 switchport trunk allowed vlan
2,4,6,8,10,12 ..
 switchport mode trunk
 mtu 9216
 spanning-tree portfast trunk
 spanning-tree bpdufilter enable
end
```

On N-PE2

```
interface GigabitEthernet2/2
 description Even-Vlans QinQ Link to lon-
n-pe2-cat6500 gi2/5
 switchport
 switchport trunk encapsulation dot1q
 switchport trunk allowed vlan
2,4,6,8,10,12 ..
 switchport mode trunk
 mtu 9216
 spanning-tree portfast trunk
 spanning-tree bpdufilter enable
!
interface GigabitEthernet2/4
 description Odd-Vlans QiQ Link to lon-n-
pe2-cat6500 g2/6
 switchport
 switchport trunk encapsulation dot1q
 switchport trunk allowed vlan
1,3,5,7,9,11 ..
 switchport mode trunk
 mtu 9216
 spanning-tree portfast trunk
 spanning-tree bpdufilter enable
end
```

Step 2. Create one VFI per QinQ VLAN to be connected to other data centers and create one switched virtual interface (SVI) per QinQ VLAN as shown here for N-PE1 and N-PE2:

On N-PE1

```
lon-n-pe1-cat6500#
!
l2 vfi VFI-4001 manual
 vpn id 4001
 neighbor 10.76.91.31 encapsulation mpls
 neighbor 10.76.91.22 encapsulation mpls
 neighbor 10.76.91.21 encapsulation mpls
 neighbor 10.76.91.32 encapsulation mpls
!
l2 vfi VFI-4004 manual
 vpn id 4004
 neighbor 10.76.90.22 encapsulation mpls
 neighbor 10.76.90.32 encapsulation mpls


lon-n-pe1-cat6500#
...
!
mpls ldp neighbor 10.76.70.12 targeted
ldp
mpls ldp neighbor 10.76.70.21 targeted
ldp
mpls ldp neighbor 10.76.70.22 targeted
ldp
mpls ldp neighbor 10.76.70.31 targeted
ldp
mpls ldp neighbor 10.76.70.32 targeted
ldp
mpls ldp tcp pak-priority
mpls ldp session protection
no mpls ldp advertise-labels
mpls ldp advertise-labels for 76
mpls label protocol ldp
xconnect logging pseudowire status
!
access-list 76 permit 10.76.0.0
0.0.255.255
!
```

On N-PE2

```
lon-n-pe2-cat6500#
!
l2 vfi VFI-4001 manual
 vpn id 4001
 neighbor 10.76.91.31 encapsulation mpls
 neighbor 10.76.91.21 encapsulation mpls
!
l2 vfi VFI-4004 manual
 vpn id 4004
 neighbor 10.76.90.22 encapsulation mpls
 neighbor 10.76.90.21 encapsulation mpls
 neighbor 10.76.90.32 encapsulation mpls
 neighbor 10.76.90.31 encapsulation mpls


lon-n-pe2-cat6500#
...
!
mpls ldp neighbor 10.76.70.11 targeted
ldp
mpls ldp neighbor 10.76.70.21 targeted
ldp
mpls ldp neighbor 10.76.70.22 targeted
ldp
mpls ldp neighbor 10.76.70.31 targeted
ldp
mpls ldp neighbor 10.76.70.32 targeted
ldp
mpls ldp tcp pak-priority
mpls ldp session protection
no mpls ldp advertise-labels
mpls ldp advertise-labels for 76
mpls label protocol ldp
xconnect logging pseudowire status
!
access-list 76 permit 10.76.0.0
0.0.255.255
!
```

On N-PE1

```
lon-n-pe1-cat6500#


lon-n-pe1-cat6500#
!
interface Vlan4001
 description Primary Core QinQ VLAN -
used to transport Odd edge VLAN
 mtu 9216
 no ip address
 xconnect vfi VFI-4001
!
interface Vlan4004
 description Backup Core QinQ VLAN -
used to transport Even edge VLAN
 mtu 9216
 no ip address
 xconnect vfi VFI-4004
```

On N-PE2

```
lon-n-pe2-cat6500#


lon-n-pe2-cat6500#
!
interface Vlan4004
 description Primary Core QinQ VLAN -
used to transport Even edge VLAN
 mtu 9216
 no ip address
 xconnect vfi VFI-4004
!
interface Vlan4001
 description Backup Core QinQ VLAN - used
to transport odd edge VLAN
 mtu 9216
 no ip address
 xconnect vfi VFI-4001
```

```
lon-n-pe1-cat6500#show mpls l2 vc
```

Local intf	Local circuit	Dest address	VC ID	Status
VFI VFI-4004	VFI	10.76.90.22	4004	DOWN
VFI VFI-4004	VFI	10.76.90.32	4004	DOWN
VFI VFI-4001	VFI	10.76.91.21	4001	UP
VFI VFI-4001	VFI	10.76.91.22	4001	DOWN
VFI VFI-4001	VFI	10.76.91.31	4001	UP
VFI VFI-4001	VFI	10.76.91.32	4001	DOWN

```
lon-n-pe1-cat6500#
```

```
lon-n-pe2-cat6500#show mpls l2 vc
```

Local intf	Local circuit	Dest address	VC ID	Status
VFI VFI-4004	VFI	10.76.90.21	4004	DOWN
VFI VFI-4004	VFI	10.76.90.22	4004	UP
VFI VFI-4004	VFI	10.76.90.31	4004	DOWN
VFI VFI-4004	VFI	10.76.90.32	4004	UP
VFI VFI-4001	VFI	10.76.91.21	4001	DOWN
VFI VFI-4001	VFI	10.76.91.31	4001	DOWN

```
lon-n-pe2-cat6500#
```

Convergence and Cluster Server Tests

The traffic profile outlined in Chapter 7 was used to determine end-to-end convergence for unidirectional voice, unicast, and multicast traffic. Links and nodes were failed to simulate network failures.

Table 10-3 shows results of various node and link failures for the VPLSoGRE Multidomain with H-VPLS solution. Convergence numbers (max and min) are in seconds.

Table 10-3   *Convergence Numbers for Link and Node Failures for the VPLSoGRE Multidomain with H-VPLS Solution*

Failure Type	Action	VLAN	Traffic Type	Traffic Direction			
				LON → SJ		SJ → LON	
				Max	Min	Max	Min
Reload N-PE1	Reload	Odd VLAN	Voice	2.46	0.02	2.62	2.62
			Unicast	2.43	2.43	2.62	2.62
		Even VLAN	Voice	0.02	0.02	0.02	0.02
			Unicast	0.00	0.00	0.00	0.00
	Restore	Odd VLAN	Voice	0.90	0.88	0.88	0.88
			Unicast	0.89	0.89	0.87	0.87
		Even VLAN	Voice	0.00	0.00	0.00	0.00
			Unicast	0.00	0.00	0.00	0.00
Reload N-PE2	Reload	Odd VLAN	Voice	0.02	0.00	0.02	0.02
			Unicast	0.00	0.00	0.00	0.00
		Even VLAN	Voice	1.40	1.38	1.36	1.36
			Unicast	1.38	1.38	1.36	1.36
	Restore	Odd VLAN	Voice	0.02	0.02	0.02	0.02
			Unicast	0.00	0.00	0.00	0.00
		Even VLAN	Voice	0.58	0.56	0.55	0.55
			Unicast	0.57	0.57	0.55	0.55
Reload Agg-1	Reload[1]	Odd VLAN	Voice	5.56	5.54	3.58	3.58
			Unicast	5.55	5.55	3.58	3.58
		Even VLAN	Voice	0.02	0.02	0.00	0.00
			Unicast	0.06	0.00	0.05	0.01
	Restore	Odd VLAN	Voice	0.62	0.02	0.86	0.64
			Unicast	0.61	0.61	0.86	0.64
		Even VLAN	Voice	0.00	0.00	0.00	0.00
			Unicast	0.00	0.00	0.00	0.00
Reload Agg-2	Reload	Odd VLAN	Voice	0.02	0.02	0.00	0.00
			Unicast	0.00	0.00	0.00	0.00
		Even VLAN	Voice	2.14	2.12	2.12	2.12
			Unicast	2.13	2.13	2.13	2.13
	Restore	Odd VLAN	Voice	0.00	0.00	0.00	0.00
			Unicast	0.00	0.00	0.00	0.00
		Even VLAN	Voice	1.18	1.10	1.50	1.50
			Unicast	1.17	1.12	1.50	1.12

Table 10-3 *Convergence Numbers for Link and Node Failures for the VPLSoGRE Multidomain with H-VPLS Solution*

Failure Type	Action	VLAN	Traffic Type	Traffic Direction			
				LON → SJ		SJ → LON	
				Max	Min	Max	Min
Fail L2 link between N-PE1 and Agg-1	Shut	Odd VLAN	Voice	2.68	2.65	2.64	2.62
			Unicast	2.68	2.68	2.64	2.61
		Even VLAN	Voice	0.02	0.02	0.00	0.00
			Unicast	0.00	0.00	0.00	0.00
	No shut	Odd VLAN	Voice	1.44	1.44	1.44	1.44
			Unicast	1.44	1.44	1.42	1.42
		Even VLAN	Voice	0.02	0.02	0.02	0.02
			Unicast	0.00	0.00	0.00	0.00
Fail L2 link between N-PE2 and Agg-2	Shut	Odd VLAN	Voice	0.00	0.00	0.02	0.02
			Unicast	0.00	0.00	0.00	0.00
		Even VLAN	Voice	2.26	2.24	2.30	2.30
			Unicast	2.26	2.26	2.28	2.27
	No shut	Odd VLAN	Voice	0.02	0.02	0.02	0.02
			Unicast	0.00	0.00	0.00	0.00
		Even VLAN	Voice	1.10	1.08	1.10	1.10
			Unicast	1.09	1.09	1.07	1.07
Fail L2 link between Agg-1 and Agg-2	Shut	Odd VLAN	Voice	0.02	0.02	0.02	0.02
			Unicast	0.00	0.00	0.00	0.00
		Even VLAN	Voice	0.02	0.02	0.02	0.02
			Unicast	0.00	0.00	0.00	0.00
	No shut	Odd VLAN	Voice	0.02	0.02	0.00	0.00
			Unicast	0.00	0.00	0.00	0.00
		Even VLAN	Voice	0.02	0.00	0.00	0.00
			Unicast	0.00	0.00	0.00	0.00
Fail WAN link facing core on N-PE1	Shut	Odd VLAN	Voice	1.18	1.14	0.00	0.00
			Unicast	1.16	1.16	0.00	0.00
		Even VLAN	Voice	0.00	0.00	0.00	0.00
			Unicast	0.00	0.00	0.00	0.00
	No shut	Odd VLAN	Voice	0.00	0.00	0.00	0.00
			Unicast	0.00	0.00	0.00	0.00
		Even VLAN	Voice	0.02	0.00	0.00	0.00
			Unicast	0.00	0.00	0.00	0.00
Fail WAN link facing core on N-PE2	Shut	Odd VLAN	Voice	0.00	0.00	0.00	0.00
			Unicast	0.03	0.00	0.00	0.00
		Even VLAN	Voice	1.02	1.00	0.00	0.00
			Unicast	1.00	1.00	0.00	0.00
	No shut	Odd VLAN	Voice	0.00	0.00	0.02	0.02
			Unicast	0.00	0.00	0.00	0.00
		Even VLAN	Voice	0.02	0.02	0.02	0.02
			Unicast	0.00	0.00	0.00	0.00

continues

Table 10-3   *Convergence Numbers for Link and Node Failures for the VPLSoGRE Multidomain with H-VPLS Solution (continued)*

Failure Type	Action	VLAN	Traffic Type	Traffic Direction			
				LON → SJ		SJ → LON	
				Max	Min	Max	Min
Fail both WAN links on N-PE1	Shut	Odd VLAN	Voice	1.76	1.74	1.84	1.84
			Unicast	1.74	1.74	1.80	1.80
		Even VLAN	Voice	0.02	0.02	0.04	0.04
			Unicast	0.00	0.00	0.00	0.00
	No shut	Odd VLAN	Voice	0.50	0.48	0.52	0.52
			Unicast	0.48	0.47	0.48	0.47
		Even VLAN	Voice	0.02	0.02	0.04	0.04
			Unicast	0.00	0.00	0.00	0.00
Fail both WAN links on N-PE2	Shut	Odd VLAN	Voice	0.02	0.02	0.04	0.04
			Unicast	0.00	0.00	0.00	0.00
		Even VLAN	Voice	1.39	1.36	1.64	1.64
			Unicast	1.37	1.37	1.60	1.60
	No shut	Odd VLAN	Voice	0.02	0.02	0.02	0.02
			Unicast	0.00	0.00	0.00	0.00
		Even VLAN	Voice	0.40	0.36	0.42	0.42
			Unicast	0.38	0.38	0.41	0.41
Clear entire routing table on both N-PE1	Clear[2]	Odd VLAN	Voice	5.02	4.98	4.98	4.98
			Unicast	4.99	4.98	4.96	4.96
		Even VLAN	Voice	0.02	0.02	0.02	0.02
			Unicast	0.00	0.00	0.00	0.00
Clear dynamic MAC address table on both N-PEs	Clear	Odd VLAN	Voice	0.02	0.02	0.00	0.00
			Unicast	0.00	0.00	0.00	0.00
		Even VLAN	Voice	0.00	0.00	0.00	0.00
			Unicast	0.00	0.00	0.00	0.00

[1] Under certain conditions, especially when using a P-core, a node may delay new PW LDP labels advertisement toward remote peers until a background timer, currently hard-coded to 10 seconds, expires. Whenever this situation occurs, the PW may not be activated before 10 seconds. Cisco defect CSCso99838 documents this issue.

[2] Installing static routes may take up to 6 seconds when the **clear ip route** * command is executed to clear all the routes. Cisco defect number CSCsk10711 documents this issue.

Cluster Server Tests

Table 10-4 shows event logs from the Event Viewer of a Microsoft cluster server. The logs are in the reverse order showing the last event first. It is best to view the timestamps while analyzing these logs.

Table 10-4 *Event Logs for the VPLSoGRE Multidomain H-VPLS Solution*

Test Case	Time in Seconds	Event Logs with Time Stamps from Microsoft Server			
		1/15/2009	4:19:44 PM	CAMP3-SERVER2	Cluster service successfully joined the server cluster CLUSTER-MNS.
		1/15/2009	4:19:31 PM	CAMP3-SERVER2	The node (re)established communication with cluster node 'CAMP3-SERVER3' on network 'public.'
		1/15/2009	4:19:31 PM	CAMP3-SERVER2	The node (re)established communication with cluster node 'CAMP3-SERVER3' on network 'private(1)'.
		1/15/2009	4:19:31 PM	CAMP3-SERVER2	The node (re)established communication with cluster node 'CAMP3-SERVER1' on network 'public.'
		1/15/2009	4:19:31 PM	CAMP3-SERVER2	The node (re)established communication with cluster node 'CAMP3-SERVER1' on network 'private(1).'
Establish L2 connectivity between Microsoft Server nodes	No convergence	1/15/2009	4:19:26 PM	CAMP3-SERVER3	The interface for cluster node 'CAMP3-SERVER2' on network 'private(1)' is operational (up). The node can communicate with all other available cluster nodes on the network.
		1/15/2009	4:19:26 PM	CAMP3-SERVER3	The interface for cluster node 'CAMP3-SERVER2' on network 'public' is operational (up). The node can communicate with all other available cluster nodes on the network.
		1/15/2009	4:19:24 PM	CAMP3-SERVER3	The node (re)established communication with cluster node 'CAMP3-SERVER2' on network 'private(1).'
		1/15/2009	4:19:24 PM	CAMP3-SERVER3	The node (re)established communication with cluster node 'CAMP3-SERVER2' on network 'public.'
		1/15/2009	4:19:24 PM	CAMP3-SERVER1	The node (re)established communication with cluster node 'CAMP3-SERVER3' on network 'public.'
		1/15/2009	4:19:24 PM	CAMP3-SERVER1	The node (re)established communication with cluster node 'CAMP3-SERVER3' on network 'private(1).'

continues

Table 10-4   *Event Logs for the VPLSoGRE Multidomain H-VPLS Solution (continued)*

Test Case	Time in Seconds	Event Logs with Time Stamps from Microsoft Server		
Shut down both N-PEs in a data center	237	1/15/2009	5:23:17 PM	CAMP3-SERVER2	The cluster service brought the resource group "ClusterGroup" online.
		1/15/2009	5:20:50 PM	CAMP3-SERVER2	The cluster service is attempting to bring online the resource group "Cluster Group."
		1/15/2009	5:20:50 PM	CAMP3-SERVER2	Cluster node CAMP3-SERVER3 was removed from the active server cluster membership. Cluster service may have been stopped on the node, the node may have failed, or the node may have lost communication with the other active server cluster nodes.
		1/15/2009	5:20:28 PM	CAMP3-SERVER2	The node lost communication with cluster node 'CAMP3-SERVER3' on network 'private(1).'
		1/15/2009	5:20:26 PM	CAMP3-SERVER2	The node lost communication with cluster node 'CAMP3-SERVER3' on network 'public.'
		1/15/2009	5:20:22 PM	CAMP3-SERVER1	The node lost communication with cluster node 'CAMP3-SERVER3' on network 'public.'
		1/15/2009	5:20:20 PM	CAMP3-SERVER1	The node lost communication with cluster node 'CAMP3-SERVER3' on network 'private(1).'
Power off access switch	156	1/15/2009	5:43:30 PM	CAMP3-SERVER2	The cluster service brought the resource group "ClusterGroup" online.
		1/15/2009	5:41:22 PM	CAMP3-SERVER2	The cluster service is attempting to bring online the resource group "ClusterGroup."
		1/15/2009	5:41:22 PM	CAMP3-SERVER2	Cluster node CAMP3-SERVER3 was removed from the active server cluster membership. Cluster service may have been stopped on the node, the node may have failed, or the node may have lost communication with the other active server cluster nodes.
		1/15/2009	5:41:00 PM	CAMP3-SERVER2	The node lost communication with cluster node 'CAMP3-SERVER3' on network 'public.'
		1/15/2009	5:41:00 PM	CAMP3-SERVER2	The node lost communication with cluster node 'CAMP3-SERVER3' on network 'private(1)'.
		1/15/2009	5:40:54 PM	CAMP3-SERVER1	The node lost communication with cluster node 'CAMP3-SERVER3' on network 'public.'
		1/15/2009	5:40:54 PM	CAMP3-SERVER1	The node lost communication with cluster node 'CAMP3-SERVER3' on network 'private(1).'

Table 10-4 *Event Logs for the VPLSoGRE Multidomain H-VPLS Solution*

Test Case	Time in Seconds	Event Logs with Time Stamps from Microsoft Server			
		1/15/2009	5:07:52 PM	CAMP3-SERVER2	Cluster service successfully joined the server cluster CLUSTER-MNS.
		1/15/2009	5:07:46 PM	CAMP3-SERVER2	The interface for cluster node 'CAMP3-SERVER3' on network 'private(1)' is operational (up). The node can communicate with all other available cluster nodes on the network.
		1/15/2009	5:07:46 PM	CAMP3-SERVER2	The interface for cluster node 'CAMP3-SERVER3' on network 'public' is operational (up). The node can communicate with all other available cluster nodes on the network.
		1/15/2009	5:07:44 PM	CAMP3-SERVER2	The node (re)established communication with cluster node 'CAMP3-SERVER3' on network 'private(1).'
Shut down active node	14	1/15/2009	5:07:44 PM	CAMP3-SERVER2	The node (re)established communication with cluster node 'CAMP3-SERVER3' on network 'public.'
		1/15/2009	5:07:40 PM	CAMP3-SERVER3	The node (re)established communication with cluster node 'CAMP3-SERVER2' on network 'private(1).'
		1/15/2009	5:07:40 PM	CAMP3-SERVER3	The node (re)established communication with cluster node 'CAMP3-SERVER2' on network 'public'.
		1/15/2009	5:07:39 PM	CAMP3-SERVER3	The node (re)established communication with cluster node 'CAMP3-SERVER1' on network 'private(1).'
		1/15/2009	5:07:39 PM	CAMP3-SERVER3	The node (re)established communication with cluster node 'CAMP3-SERVER1' on network 'public.'
		1/15/2009	5:07:38 PM	CAMP3-SERVER1	The node (re)established communication with cluster node 'CAMP3-SERVER3' on network 'private(1)'.
		1/15/2009	5:07:38 PM	CAMP3-SERVER1	The node (re)established communication with cluster node 'CAMP3-SERVER3' on network 'public.'

continues

Table 10-4   *Event Logs for the VPLSoGRE Multidomain H-VPLS Solution (continued)*

Test Case	Time in Seconds	Event Logs with Time Stamps from Microsoft Server			
Private VLAN N-PE reload	2	1/15/2009	1:09:46 PM	CAMP3-SERVER3	The node (re)established communication with cluster node 'CAMP3-SERVER2' on network 'private(1).'
		1/15/2009	1:09:45 PM	CAMP3-SERVER1	The node (re)established communication with cluster node 'CAMP3-SERVER3' on network 'private(1).'
		1/15/2009	1:09:45 PM	CAMP3-SERVER2	The node (re)established communication with cluster node 'CAMP3-SERVER3' on network 'private(1).'
		1/15/2009	1:09:45 PM	CAMP3-SERVER3	The node (re)established communication with cluster node 'CAMP3-SERVER1' on network 'private(1).'
		1/15/2009	1:09:45 PM	CAMP3-SERVER3	The node lost communication with cluster node 'CAMP3-SERVER1' on network 'private(1).'
		1/15/2009	1:09:45 PM	CAMP3-SERVER1	The node lost communication with cluster node 'CAMP3-SERVER3' on network 'private(1).'
		1/15/2009	1:09:44 PM	CAMP3-SERVER2	The node lost communication with cluster node 'CAMP3-SERVER3' on network 'private(1).'
Unplug active server	114	1/15/2009	4:33:19 PM	CAMP3-SERVER2	The cluster service brought the resource group "ClusterGroup" online.
		1/15/2009	4:31:53 PM	CAMP3-SERVER2	The cluster service is attempting to bring online the resource group "ClusterGroup."
		1/15/2009	4:31:53 PM	CAMP3-SERVER2	Cluster node CAMP3-SERVER3 was removed from the active server cluster membership. Cluster service may have been stopped on the node, the node may have failed, or the node may have lost communication with the other active server cluster nodes.
		1/15/2009	4:31:30 PM	CAMP3-SERVER2	The node lost communication with cluster node 'CAMP3-SERVER3' on network 'public.'
		1/15/2009	4:31:25 PM	CAMP3-SERVER1	The node lost communication with cluster node 'CAMP3-SERVER3' on network 'public.'
		1/15/2009	4:33:19 PM	CAMP3-SERVER2	The cluster service brought the resource group "ClusterGroup" online.

Summary

This chapter described the VPLSoGRE technology for interconnecting data centers when the core network is IP-based. For related information, see Chapter 11, "Additional Data Center Interconnect Design Considerations."

Additional Data Center Interconnect Design Considerations

This chapter addresses several key technologies and issues that you should consider when interconnecting data centers, including the following:

- Multicast

- Alignment of spanning tree, HSRP, and active service modules

- Routing design

- QinQ MAC overlapping

- Storm control

- QoS considerations

- Stateful switchover

- OSPF cost

- Anycast RP and router IDs

Multicast Deployment in a Layer 2 Environment

An Ethernet switch learns MAC addresses from the source MAC address field of the Ethernet frame it receives. This is because a source MAC address of any packet will always be an address of a device and will never be a multicast or a broadcast MAC address. However, a switch, by default, floods multicast traffic within the broadcast domain. Flooding can consume significant bandwidth if many multicast servers are sending streams to the segment. Internet Group Management Protocol (IGMP) snooping provides a solution to this issue, as described in detail in the sections that follow.

Multicast at Layer 2

Configuring static MAC addresses for each group and each client would solve the immediate problem of flooding, but such a solution is neither scalable nor dynamic. The most efficient solution is to forestall the problem by using IGMP snooping. In IGMP snooping, the switch intercepts IGMP messages from the host to the router and uses these messages to update its MAC address table.

IP multicast uses the host signaling protocol IGMP to indicate the presence of multicast receivers interested in multicast group traffic. IGMP snooping is a multicast constraining mechanism that runs on a Layer 2 (L2) LAN switch but requires the switch to examine some Layer 3 information (IGMP join/leave messages) in the IGMP packets sent between the host and the router. When the switch hears a host issue an *IGMP host report* message, it adds the port number of the host to the associated multicast table entry. When the switch hears the host issue the *IGMP leave group* message, the switch removes the host entry from the table. Using information gained from IGMP snooping, the LAN switch avoids flooding the subnet with multicast traffic.

Any IP Version 4 (IPv4) traffic with a destination IP address in the range of 224.0.0.0 to 239.255.255.255 is a multicast stream. All IPv4 multicast packets map to a predefined IEEE MAC address that has the format 01.00.5e.xx.xx.xx.

Note   IGMP snooping works only if the multicast MAC address maps to this IEEE-compliant MAC range. By design, some reserved multicast ranges are excluded from being snooped. If a nonconforming multicast packet is sourced on a switched network, the packet is flooded throughout that VLAN, which means that it is treated like broadcast traffic.

IGMP snooping is enabled on Catalyst switches by default, but it is not supported on any Catalyst platform that lacks a multicast router. The presence of at least one multicast router port (which, from a switch perspective, is simply a port that connects to a multicast router) is essential for IGMP snooping to work across switches. Unless the switches somehow learn of or know about a multicast router port, the IGMP snooping mechanism breaks down.

Under some circumstances, multicast traffic may not pass across Catalyst switches, even in the same VLAN. For deployment of multicast in a campus network and for problems and solutions related to IGMP snooping in a switched environment, refer to the Cisco document "*Multicast Does Not Work in the Same VLAN in Catalyst Switches*" (Document ID: 68131), available at www. http://tinyurl.com/dqs4k.

Tuning the IGMP Query Interval

Example 11-1 shows a sample configuration of how to tune the IGMP query interval. This configuration requires that Protocol Independent Multicast (PIM) be enabled on the switched virtual interface (SVI).

Example 11-1   *Tuning the Multicast IGMP Query Interval*

```
lon-agg-1# config t
Enter configuration commands, one per line.  End with CNTL/Z.
lon-agg-pe1(config)# int vlan 13
lon-agg-pe1(config-if)# ip pim sparse-mode
lon-agg-pe1(config-if)# ip igmp snooping querier
lon-agg-pe1(config-if)# ip igmp query-interval 3
lon-agg-pe1(config-if)# ip igmp query-max-response-time 1
lon-agg-pe1(config-if)#

lon-agg-pe1# show ip igmp int vlan 13
Vlan13 is up, line protocol is up
  Internet address is 10.10.13.11/24
  IGMP is enabled on interface
  Current IGMP host version is 2
  Current IGMP router version is 2
  IGMP query interval is 3 seconds
  IGMP querier timeout is 6 seconds
  IGMP max query response time is 1 seconds
  Last member query count is 2
  Last member query response interval is 1000 ms
  Inbound IGMP access group is not set
  IGMP activity: 11 joins, 11 leaves
  Multicast routing is enabled on interface
  Multicast TTL threshold is 0
  Multicast designated router (DR) is 10.10.13.12
  IGMP querying router is 10.10.13.11 (this system)
  No multicast groups joined by this system
  IGMP snooping is globally enabled
  IGMP snooping CGMP-AutoDetect is globally enabled
  IGMP snooping is enabled on this interface
  IGMP snooping fast-leave (for v2) is disabled and querier is disabled
  IGMP snooping explicit-tracking is enabled
  IGMP snooping last member query response interval is 1000 ms
IGMP snooping report-suppression is enabled
```

Note   You cannot configure **ip igmp query-interval** without configuring **ip pim** on the SVI. Cisco defect CSCsq77111 addresses this issue.

Spanning Tree, HSRP, and Service Module Design

When using active/standby service module pairs, it becomes important to align traffic flows so that the active/primary service modules are the preferred path to a particular server application. Aligning the spanning-tree root, the Hot Standby Router Protocol (HSRP) default gateway, and active service modules on the same aggregation switch is desirable because this alignment creates a design that is more deterministic and easier to troubleshoot.

An aligned design becomes particularly important in failure scenarios such as the inter-switch trunk failure. When all active service modules are aligned in the same switch, flows between service modules stay on the local switching bus without traversing the trunk between aggregation switches. Otherwise, traffic flows can hop back and forth between aggregation switches, creating undesirable conditions that are unpredictable and difficult to troubleshoot.

This alignment of service is particularly true for a multisite data center. Cisco recommends that you maintain alignment within the same site toward one aggregation switch with local backup of the service.

With the extension of a VLAN across multiples sites, you must also extend the associated IP subnet. Cisco recommends that HSRP redundancy be local in each site, with a different HSRP group for each location. An IP subnet is then backed up locally with the site HSRP group.

Cisco does not recommend extending other network services, such as firewalls or load balancers, in active/active state across multiple locations.

The solutions that this book describes assume local backup for network services and target VLAN extensions for application services such as clusters and VMotion.

For detailed information about implementing the Spanning Tree Protocol (STP), HRSP, and services modules in data center aggregation switches and with different failure scenarios, refer to the document available at www. http://tinyurl.com/27rscs.

Routing Design

One of the common concerns for extended L2 LAN segments is the presence of identical subnets in data centers whose subnets are usually summarized according to routing best practices. Although the practice of having the same subnet in two data centers is not a standard routing best practice, it must be supported when deploying high-availability (HA) clusters and virtual machines.

For detailed information about advertising cluster subnet and Route Health Injection (RHI) , refer to the Cisco documents "*Data Center High Availability Clusters Design Guide*" and "*Cisco Data Center Infrastructure 2.5 Design Guide*" available at www. http://tinyurl.com/ct4cw8 and www. http://tinyurl.com/27rscs, respectively.

> **Note**   Spanning tree, HSRP, and services module design, along with routing design within a data center, are beyond the scope of this design guide. They are documented here simply to highlight their importance. URLs are provided for easy reference.

QinQ MAC Overlapping

As discussed in Chapter 2, "Appraising Virtual Private LAN Service," Hierarchical-Virtual Private LAN Service (H-VPLS) uses a VLAN encapsulation option referred to as *802.1Q in 802.1Q* (or just *QinQ*) to achieve scalability and VLAN independence. QinQ inserts a core VLAN tag into the edge frame and uses this tag to bridge the frame, which is then passed to the VPLS process.

If the requirement is to transport several hundred VLANs over the VPLS cloud, the optimum approach is to enable QinQ and use only one virtual forwarding instance (VFI) for this QinQ VLAN.

Figure 11-1 illustrates QinQ frame encapsulation.

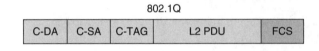

Figure 11-1   *QinQ frame encapsulation.*

Per the 802.1Q standard, edge frame information consists of the customer destination address (C-DA), customer source address (C-SA), customer VLAN tag (C-TAG) and a payload (PDU). With QinQ enabled, the switch also receives a service provider VLAN tag (S-TAG).

QinQ provides significant scalability and ease of configuration in a H-VPLS deployment. However, with QinQ, every VLAN shares the same core bridging domain. VLAN is encapsulated, but MAC addresses are not. Therefore, QinQ does not support MAC address overlapping.

Figure 11-2 shows a scenario under which MAC overlapping can occur.

MAC addresses are significant within a LAN segment. It is not a problem if devices in separate LAN segments or VLANs have the same MAC address. Figure 11-2 illustrates this example:

- Multiple devices in the same site have the same MAC address (A).

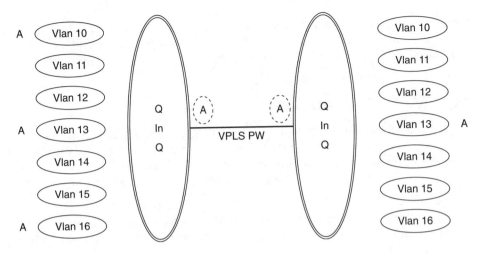

Figure 11-2 *QinQ and MAC address overlapping.*

- These devices are in VLANs 10 and 16.

- These devices connect to a site with VLAN 13 that also has a device with MAC address A.

In this example, a conflict arises: QinQ shares the same core bridge domain for all VLANs, and so in the core, MAC address A appears on the left and right at the same time.

In most cases, a device's MAC address is hard-coded, so the same MAC address cannot be present in multiple sites at the same time. This situation is clearly the case for server applications such as clusters or VMotion. However, certain devices such as firewalls, HSRP, and load balancers use virtual MAC addresses, which are not necessarily unique. So while H-VPLS provides a scalable solution for L2 extension, QinQ cannot be easily used for extending network services across multiple sites.

Consider the following cases that share the QinQ bridge domain:

- **HSRP:** By default, HSRP uses the same virtual MAC address per group, so it is not possible to extend a group across QinQ. You must configure different HSRP groups for each data center to provide router redundancy for the same IP subnet. Alternatively, if this approach is not practicable, you can change the group number of each VLAN, with a maximum of 255 groups.

- **VMware machines:** When VMware machines are configured, by default they use the same MAC address in all VLAN interfaces. However, because this MAC address is the physical address of the server that hosts the virtual machine (VM), it changes when you move a VM to another server. Multisite MAC address overlapping cannot occur with VMotion; however, a MAC move is possible.

- **Firewall Service Module (FWSM) and Adaptive Security Appliance (ASA):** When in an active/active state, firewalls use the same MAC address for each member of the cluster. In addition, firewalls frequently use STP signaling packets to synchronize state. Therefore, because of the MAC address overlapping issue, it is not recommended that you extend firewalls in active/active state across multiple sites. If firewall services are configured for active/standby mode or if MAC addresses are kept local, MAC address overlapping is not a problem.

- **SVIs:** Another issue is pinging the aggregation switch from a remote site when the same MAC address is configured in all SVIs of the switch. In the QinQ bridge domain, permanent MAC moves occur between local VLANs. Because of these MAC moves, the switch may not find the destination MAC address in its content-addressable memory (CAM) table when a ping packet arrives. Pinging is not a problem when MAC addresses remain local to a single data center.

In most cases, a VPLS node connects to the aggregation switches in the data center by using only one link or port channel. In this scenario, there is no benefit to the node learning local MAC addresses, because it accesses all local devices through the same interface. In these cases, it is recommended that you disable MAC address learning on the link between the VPLS node and aggregation switch. Here is a sample configuration command:

no mac-address-table learning interface GigabitEthernet4/0/4

In the near future, the issue of MAC address overlapping in the QinQ bridge domain will be eliminated by the implementation of 802.1ah standard. This standard proposes to encapsulate both the VLAN and the MAC address field. Figure 11-3 illustrates MACinMAC encapsulation.

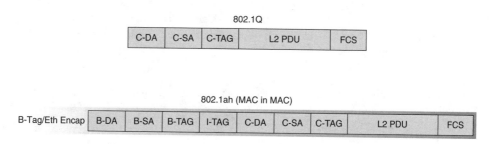

Figure 11-3 *MACinMAC encapsulation.*

In the 802.1ah standard, the customer (C-) frame is encapsulated with a backbone (B-) header that includes a backbone VLAN tag (B-TAG) and backbone destination and source addresses (B-DA, B-SA) that point toward the backbone node that performs encapsulation. With this approach, the backbone no longer sees any edge VLAN or edge MAC addresses. An additional field, the service instance tag (I-TAG), encapsulates customer addresses and includes the service instance identifier (I-SID), which identifies the individual customer instance.

With the implementation of 802.1ah, QinQ encapsulation will allow scalability without the MAC overlapping issue. An ES+ line card on a Cisco 7600 router configured as a VPLS node will support the 802.1ah protocol. Although QinQ provides significant scalability, it currently has limitations in extending network services. Therefore, data center interconnect (DCI) solutions are targeted only for server and application extensions such as clustering and VMs. With the implementation of the 802.1ah standard, which will resolve problems arising from MAC address overlapping, the extension of network services may be possible.

Storm Control

VPLS with Network-facing Provider Edge (N-PE) redundancy solves two of the four main issues with L2 extension:

- Link quality with L3 protection

- STP isolation (L2 control-plane isolation) using several node redundancy approaches

In addition, VPLS over GRE solves a third issue: L2 extension over the IP core. The fourth issue, data-plane storm control, is not resolved.

L2 bridging or switching relies on a broadcast and flooding mechanism to discover devices over a loop-free topology built by STP. Without STP enabled or if there is an error in the configuration of STP, redundant links in an L2 network create loops. In this situation, L2 frames that do not have a Time-To-Live (TTL) field in the data-link portion of the Ethernet frame loop forever, which creates a data-plane storm.

For HA, a data center must implement STP best practices. These best practices include STP enhancement features such as RootGuard, bridge protocol data unit (BPDU) filtering, and PortFast BPDU guard. In addition, LoopGuard provides additional protection against Layer 2 forwarding loops.

Note   For more information, refer to the white paper *"Best Practices for Catalyst 6500/6000 Series and Catalyst 4500/4000 Series Switches Running Cisco IOS Software,"* available at www. http://tinyurl.com/6634p.

Implementation of VPLS allows STP isolation, which decreases STP domain size, reducing the burden on the control plane. VPLS is a virtual bridge that allows broadcast and flooding of packets, however, and does not reduce the propagation of data-plane storms.

In situations where multiple data centers are interconnected to provide L2 extensions across these data centers, STP failures in one data center can cause data-plane storms in other data centers. Consider the following traffic types when you implement methods to address data-plane storms:

- L2 control plane

- L2 broadcast

- L2 multicast

- L2 known unicast

- L2 unknown unicast (UU)

The lack of TTL field implementation in the L2 header of the Ethernet frame allows traffic storms to continue until you manually disconnect redundant links. In these situations, some frames hit the CPU, and some just overflow the links. DCI solutions mitigate the effect of a data storm for each of the traffic types.

VPLS significantly reduces control-plane constraints; however, you must still manage the data plane carefully. As discussed in the sections that follow, even though STP isolation is achieved through implementing VPLS to interconnect data centers, these data centers remain prone to storms that can affect device CPUs and congest links. When designing a solution, consider the trade-off between HA and flexibility.

> **Note**   For storm control details and caveats, refer to the Cisco document *"Configuring Traffic-Storm Control,"* available at www. http://tinyurl.com/cdtsfk.

L2 Control-Plane Packet Storm Toward N-PE

In the Multiple Spanning Tree (MST)-based deployment models, options 1a and 1b, discussed in Chapter 8, "MST-Based Deployment Models," and the Embedded event Manager (EEM)-based deployment models, options 2 and 3 discussed in Chapter 9, "EEM-Based Deployment Models," N-PE participates in local STP. Therefore, the N-PE receives BPDUs, which are the STP control packets and Address Resolution Protocol (ARP) broadcast packets. If a data storm occurs, the node CPU can become overloaded, which can disrupt control-plane traffic.

Figure 11-4 illustrates the effect of a data storm when N-PE participates in STP.

Several actions must be taken to protect VPLS nodes:

- Implement standard loop protection mechanisms, such as RootGuard, BPDU filtering, BPDU guard, or LoopGuard.

- Implement control-plane policing (CoPP) to protect the CPU against infinite BPDU, ARP, and other control-plane packet floods.

- To alleviate ARP impact, do not specify an IP address for cross-connected bridge domains.

When N-PE does not participate in local STP, as in EEM deployment models 4 and 5 discussed in Chapter 9, or with the multichassis Link Aggregation Control Protocol (mLACP)/Inter-Chassis Communication Protocol (ICCP), the node is isolated from local STP and is not subject to CPU disturbances due to control-plane packets.

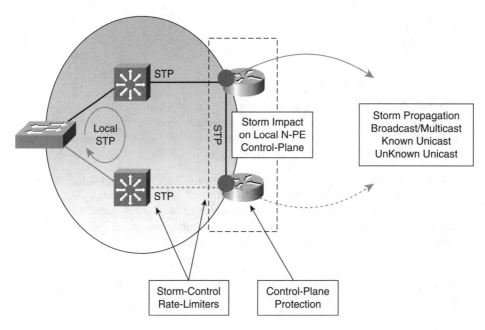

Figure 11-4   *Data storm and N-PE participating in local STP.*

L2 Broadcast and Multicast Packet Storm

L2 broadcast and multicast storms are detrimental to CPUs and negatively affect all switches within that broadcast domain, which includes switches in local and remote data centers. To rate-limit intersite broadcast traffic, use the **storm-control broadcast level** *threshold* command. Similarly, use the **storm-control multicast level** *threshold* command to rate-limit multicast traffic. The *threshold* parameter specifies the limit (percentage) placed on broadcast or multicast traffic. A threshold value of 100 percent means that no limit is placed on broadcast traffic. Valid entries are from 1 to 100.

> **Note**   In this book, the storm-control level for broadcast and multicast was set to 5. However, Cisco does not recommend 5 or any specific value. Some required protocols such as Address Resolution Protocol (ARP) and Dynamic Host Configuration Protocol (DHCP) use broadcasts. Organizations should look at their own applications and specific traffic patterns to determine the optimal value.

Figure 11-5 illustrates where to place storm control rate limiters.

Install storm control rate limiters on both sides of the link between data center aggregation and the N-PE:

■   Rate-limiting on the N-PE side stops the storm before it gets out to the VPLS network. Broadcast/multicast storm control is supported on a LAN-type port and a non-EtherChannel ES20 line card (Cisco IOS Software Release 12.2(33)SRD). As of today, storm control is not supported on EtherChannel with an ES20 card.

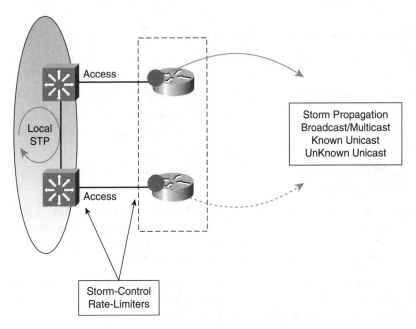

Figure 11-5 *N-PEs and storm control.*

- Rate-limiting on the aggregation side stops the storm from getting into the data center from the VPLS network. This type of rate-limiting is supported on any port/EtherChannel/Virtual Switching System (VSS) and Nexus 7000 for broadcast or multicast (and for unicast).

L2 Known Unicast Packet Storm

An L2 known unicast frame is a packet that has a destination MAC address that is populated in the N-PE CAM table. In an uncontrolled known unicast data storm, standard unicast frames do not reach the CPU, but large amounts of useless data congest the links.

With VLAN extension using VPLS, two scenarios exist:

- **N-PE participates in the local STP:** The MAC address table is likely flushed due to STP instability. Because of this flushing, all local MAC addresses become unknown. In this situation, what was a known MAC address storm converts to an unknown MAC address storm.

- **N-PE does not participate in the local STP:** Local STP instability does not cause flushing of the N-PE MAC address. In this situation, N-PE does not transmit storms that point to a local MAC address but does transmit storms that point to a remote MAC address.

There is no easy way to rate-limit an uncontrolled known unicast data storm because neither VPLS nor plain switching can differentiate between a looping frame and a good frame.

L2 Unknown Unicast Packet Storm

An unknown unicast (UU) frame is a frame that has a destination MAC address that is not known in the MAC address table of an L2 device (a bridge or a switch). The learning bridge uses the flood mechanism to populate MAC addresses in the CAM table.

In a loop condition, UU flooding creates a data storm because frames lack TTL. Just as with any unicast storm, UU frames never reach the CPU, so an uncontrolled storm leads to congested links.

It is difficult to distinguish UU frames from known frames, but if you want to control this large amount of garbage traffic, you can implement some optional processes.

One approach is to use the hardware-based Unknown Unicast Flood Rate Limiter (UFRL) that the Cisco Catalyst 6500 with Supervisor 10G supports. UFRL is a global rate limiter and cannot be configured on an interface or VLAN basis. Organizations should consider their traffic patterns to determine the optimal value.

Another approach, which is complex but efficient, is to rely on a unique characteristic of storm frames, which is flooding. This approach requires one dedicated port (either with a modified cable to have the port always up or with a wrap cable) that is used as a witness port to monitor traffic. Because this witness port has no MAC address, no good intersite traffic reaches it, but it is found by all unknown, broadcast, and multicast traffic, which makes it a good way to probe dangerous traffic.

If you set up a monitoring script, you can specify a number of actions to take whenever this traffic reaches a threshold. You can, for example, block all UU traffic from being sent to other sites. To do so, the script installs a dynamic unknown unicast blocking (UUB) command on the link connecting to the data center, which protects other sites from the UU storm. Another approach is to isolate the site under storm conditions and stop all traffic.

Figure 11-6 illustrates the use of a witness port to achieve storm control.

Use EEM to dynamically install the UUB command on transmitting ports to stop flooding when a storm is detected. You have three choices:

- Stop flooding only at the interconnection point. (Do not affect local data center behavior.)

- Stop flooding only for extended VLANs. (Do not affect running local VLANs.)

- Totally stop the storm, not just rate-limit it.

Example 11-2 shows a sample configuration to implement such an approach.

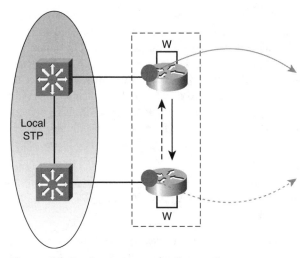

Figure 11-6   *Storm control using a witness port.*

Example 11-2   *Preventing UU Flooding*

```
event manager applet rate_above
 event snmp oid ifOutUcastPkts.2
  get-type exact entry-op ge entry-val 1000 entry-type
  increment poll-interval 10
    action 2.0 counter name flood_set op set value 2

event manager applet flood_control
event counter name flood_set
 entry-op eq entry-val 2 exit-op eq exit-val 1
   action 1.0 cli command "enable"
   action 2.0 cli command "conf t"
   action 3.0 cli command "int gig 1/2"
   action 3.1 cli command "switchport block unicast"
   action 3.2 cli command "exit"

event manager applet activate
  event none
  action 1.0 counter name flood_set op set value 1
```

QoS Considerations

Multiple types of traffic pass between data centers, including client traffic, server exchange traffic, server-to-server L3 traffic, server-to-server L2 traffic, and control-plane packets.

One approach to quality of service (QoS) is simply to overprovision links to avoid congestion. Many networks implement this simple approach. However, DCI is a special case because it transports L2 bridged packets, for which bandwidth use is not easy to control, especially when transient or permanent loops occur. A safe approach to QoS for DCI is to isolate L2 traffic from regular L3 traffic. The differentiated services (DiffServ) model, with its separated allocation scheme for queues, is perfectly suited for this requirement. This model allows dedicating one class of service (CoS) for L2 traffic, with a minimum bandwidth assigned to this class. If L2 traffic overflows the buffers, the CoS assigned to any other traffic is not subjected to disruption. Implementing this model is quite easy: You just force the Multiprotocol Label Switching (MPLS) EXP bits on the port-facing aggregation either at the port or at the Ethernet virtual circuit (EVC) level. This approach enables MPLS to transport all L2 frames via this dedicated CoS, which isolates L2 traffic from other types of traffic.

In addition, Cisco recommends that you enable policing to rate-limit ingress bridged traffic for a single VLAN or a group of VLANs. The policer can be applied at the port level, the SVI level, or the EVC level.

Another approach to QoS for DCI is to classify and mark real-time and important bridged traffic from other L2 flows to differentiate and prioritize this traffic. This classification and marking of the interested traffic can be achieved by relying on the 802.1Q CoS bits preset by the aggregation switches. Trusting these 802.1Q CoS bits maps the MPLS EXP bit to the CoS value. This approach is appealing. However, an MPLS core cannot offer more than eight CoS values, and it reserves two of those values for signaling. The allocation of the remaining six CoS bits must be carefully considered.

The CoS allocation scheme varies from network to network. The example supplied here applies in many instances.

There are two primary considerations regarding the number of required classes of services:

■   Defining traffic classification in term of marking

■   Defining how many queues per link serve these classes

An IP differentiated services code point (DSCP) marking field can identify up to 64 classes of traffic, whereas technologies such as switching (L2 or MPLS) support only 8 class markings. Generally, hardware physical constraints limit the number of queues on a physical interface to fewer than 64. Even if 64 or more queues were supported, allocating bandwidth to them would be extremely complex. Therefore, the typical recommendation is to use four to six queues on an interface, especially for high-speed links, such as 1-Gbps and 10-Gbps links. For example, five queues could be configured as follows:

■   **Expedite Forwarding (EF5):** Strict priority queue for low-bandwidth traffic, primarily voice, that is sensitive to packet jitter

■   **Assured Forwarding (AF4):** Real-time queue for high-bandwidth traffic, such as video, that is sensitive to packet jitter

■   **Assured Forwarding (AF3):** Critical business traffic (for example, TCP and Network File System [NFS]), with congestion-avoidance mechanisms

■ **Assured Forwarding (AF1):** L2 DCI traffic

■ **Best Effort (BE or AF0):** Best-effort traffic with congestion-avoidance mechanisms

It is often recommended, but not mandatory, that you create a specific class (AF6) for signaling traffic used by routing protocols to protect the stability of a network in the case of link congestion. However, it also is common to map this traffic to a critical traffic queue.

In the preceding example, AF1 is dedicated to L2 traffic, which eliminates any influence from L2 flooding toward other classes.

The following example illustrates the configuration of DiffServ on a core MPLS link. In this example, real-time (RT) traffic and important traffic is isolated from the class default. Absolute priority up to 20 Mbps is assigned to RT traffic, and a minimum of 30 percent of the link capability is allocated to important traffic. In addition, because core link capacity is not offered at full link speed by service providers, N-PE is shaping egress traffic to a service level agreement (SLA). In this example, the SLA is 500 Mbps:

Step 1. Define a class map for RT and important traffic:

```
class-map match-all exp-RT

match mpls experimental topmost 5

class-map match-all exp-Important

match mpls experimental topmost 4
```

Step 2. Create a policy map to prioritize, rate-limit, and allocate bandwidth:

```
policy-map child-queueing

class exp-RT

priority

police cir 20000000 conform transmit exceed drop

class exp-Important

bandwidth percent 30

class class-default

bandwidth remaining percent 70
```

Step 3. Create a policy map for all the other traffic types that does not meet the RT and important traffic profile. Shape traffic to 500 Mbps:

```
policy-map shaper-core

class class-default

shape average 500000000

service-policy child-queueing
```

Step 4. Apply the policy outbound to the core link:

```
interface GigabitEthernet3/0/1

 ip address 10.10.20.4 255.255.255.0

 mpls ip

 service-policy output shaper-core
```

Stateful Switchover Considerations

When an N-PE router reloads, power to the LAN modules is enabled before WAN modules are powered on. Because of this sequencing, LAN interfaces are enabled before route reachability to the core can be tracked via EEM. When the LAN interfaces become active, the spanning tree converges and places the interface between N-PEs and aggregation switches in forwarding mode. Therefore, traffic is black-holed because the WAN interfaces might still be in down state or the path to the core network might not be available.

The EEM reboot applet ensures that LAN interfaces are in shut state until the IP route configured in the **track** command is reachable after the router initializes. Stateful switchover (SSO) synchronizes the states of line cards and protocols, so it is not recommended for deployment on N-PEs.

IGP (OSPF) Cost

In situations where the inter-N-PE link speed is lower than the core link speed between the N-PE and the P-router, the preferred path for routes between the N-PEs is via the core. In such situations, reduce IGP cost on inter-N-PE interfaces to establish an IGP neighbor relationship via the inter N-PE link. The following example shows an Open Shortest Path First (OSPF) cost value of 1 assigned to the interface:

```
interface GigabitEthernet4/0/2
 description L3 connection between sj-n-pe1 and sj-n-pe2
ip ospf cost 1
```

When deploying traffic-engineering tunnels, take care when calculating the cost of the entire tunnel and the link cost across all paths. In situations where the cost is misconfigured, the backup pseudowire from the backup N-PE to the primary N-PE at the remote end might not follow the directly connected physical link, but instead go over the primary link, which is a suboptimal configuration.

Router ID Selection

MPLS selects the highest loopback interface as the router ID. If Anycast RP (Rendezvous Point) is configured, routers configured as MPLS neighbors do not form neighbor relationships (because of duplicate router IDs). The Cisco recommendation is that you configure **mpls ldp router-id loopback** *x* **force** to use a specific loopback interface for the router ID. The following example shows a configuration that forces the use of loopback 70 for the MPLS LDP router ID:

```
lon-n-pe1# config t
Enter configuration commands, one per line.  End with CNTL/Z.
lon-n-pe1(config)# mpls ldp router-id Loopback70 force
lon-n-pe1(config)#
```

Summary

This chapter described several technologies that should be considered when designing and deploying DCI. These technologies may apply when you implement the solutions that this book describes.

## Chapter 12

VPLS PE Redundancy Using Inter-Chassis Communication Protocol

Virtual Private LAN Service (VPLS) requires node redundancy to implement robust multipoint connectivity. A definitive solution for a VPLS node redundancy standard is under work at the Internet Engineering Task Force (IETF) and will be subject to code implementation. Although the approach outlined in this chapter is still under draft, it should be considered the main solution when it becomes ready for application.

In its initial phase, VPLS redundancy for Provider Edge (PE) routers relies on the following elements that this chapter describes in more detail:

■ Attachment circuit (AC) redundancy using multichassis Link Aggregation Control Protocol (mLACP)

■ Synchronization of nodes using Inter-Chassis Communication Protocol (ICCP)

■ Pseudowire (PW) redundancy using standby states

■ MAC address flushing provided through mLACP/PW state changes

Although subsequent phases will define additional ways of providing AC side elements with the objective of extending the list of supported topologies, this initial phase provides an efficient approach for data center interconnect (DCI).

Because ICCP is the determining factor, this model is referenced as the *ICCP model* throughout this chapter.

Figure 12-1 illustrates the overall application of the ICCP model.

In this figure, you can see that the broadcast domain at each site is built upon a local spanning tree and is determined by a Spanning Tree Protocol (STP) that is totally isolated from other sites. VPLS interconnects these broadcast domains in a no-loop condition that an mLACP-controlled EtherChannel offers and that allows a unique connection to the multipoint VPLS network. Synchronization of PE nodes is ensured through ICCP.

Figure 12-1 demonstrates the naming convention used in this chapter. The switch that performs bridging access toward the VPLS is called CE (for Customer Edge); in DCI, it is the aggregation switch. The node that performs the VPLS encapsulation is called PE (for Provider Edge); in DCI, it is called N-PE. (N-PE stands for Network-side PE and is commonly used for a node performing VPLS functionality.) The pseudowires linking VPLS instances (VFI, virtual forwarding instance) are called PWs.

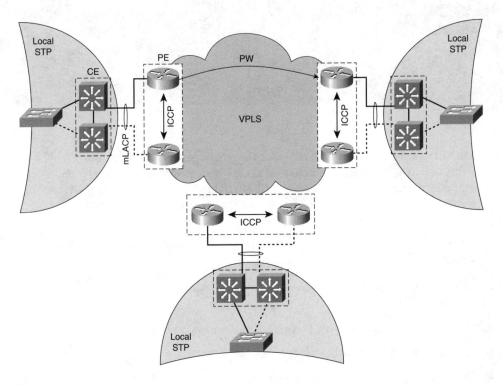

Figure 12-1 *ICCP model for N-PE redundancy in a VPLS network.*

The following sections discuss ICCP in more detail, with a focus on the four keys elements that enable VPLS node redundancy.

Introducing ICCP

The ICCP model targets the carrier Ethernet aggregation domain, a much larger problem than DCI. This chapter restricts its focus to DCI applications.

The protocol runs within a set of two (or more) PEs that form a redundancy group (RG) for the purpose of synchronizing data among the systems. It accommodates both a multi-chassis AC and PW redundancy mechanisms.

ICCP will support several topologies, some of which include an access network at the edge and the option not to collocate PEs on the same site. This overview focuses on an edge box dual system connected to two collocated PEs connected via EtherChannel.

In addition to ICCP concepts, Figure 12-1 shows a typical example on this collocation design.

ICCP provides a reliable communication channel to client applications (for example, mLACP or PW redundancy). This channel allows remote-state synchronization for AC and PW redundancy management.

ICCP takes advantage of the Label Distribution Protocol (LDP) extension, which offers reliable, in-order, stateful message delivery and capability negotiation between PEs and secure authentication mechanisms. It runs over the core or over the Multiprotocol Label Switching (MPLS) link, redundantly interconnecting both PEs.

ICCP relies also on a common mechanism to actively monitor the health of PEs in an RG, with the goal of achieving subsecond (approximately 50 to 150 ms) detection of loss of a remote node to give the client applications (redundancy mechanisms) enough reaction time to achieve subsecond service restoration time. In addition, ICCP provides an event-driven state update for immediate notification of client application state changes.

ICCP notifies its client applications when a remote PE that is a member of the RG fails. ICCP does not define its own keepalive mechanism, but rather reuses existing fault-detection mechanisms. The following mechanisms may be used by ICCP to detect PE node failure:

- **Bidirectional Forwarding Detection (BFD):** Run a BFD session between the PEs that are members of a given RG, and use that data to detect PE node failure. This method of fault detection assumes that resiliency mechanisms are in place to protect connectivity to the remote PE nodes, so loss of periodic BFD messages from a given PE node can mean only that the node itself has failed.

- **IP reachability monitoring:** It is possible for a PE to monitor IP layer connectivity to other members of a RG that are participating in Interior Gateway Protocol/Border Gateway Protocol (IGP/BGP) routing. When connectivity to a PE is lost, the local PE interprets the event to mean loss of the remote PE node. This method of fault detection assumes that resiliency mechanisms are in place to protect the route to the remote PE nodes, and hence loss of IP reachability to a given node can mean only that the node itself has failed.

Now that nodes are synchronized via ICCP to form a redundant cluster, the section that follows covers how they are interacting with the edge and core.

Interaction with AC Redundancy Mechanisms

The AC for an RG consists of two links groomed in a bundle with "max_link" parameter =1 on the CE side, which means that only one link is active while the other is in standby mode. The selection of the active link should be performed on both sides as follows:

- By the CE, based on priority. (LACP fast switchover helps accelerate switching from a failing link toward the backup one.)

- By the PE, based on link information exchanged via ICCP.

Figure 12-2 illustrates the interaction between the AC mechanism, mLACP, and node synchronization via ICCP.

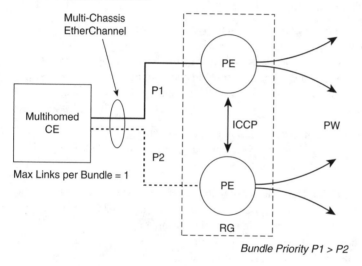

Figure 12-2   *ICCP Interaction with AC redundancy.*

This dual-side redundancy control ensures that the failover mechanism is always controlled by the PE side, which protects against CE misconfiguration and prevents susceptibility to the split-brain problem.

On the data center side, the multihomed CE is either a Catalyst 6500 Virtual Switching System (VSS) or a Nexus 7000 using virtual PortChannel (vPC) to form a Multichassis EtherChannel (MEC). On the PE side, the VPLS boxes are two Cisco 7600 units forming RGs with mLACP technology. As VPLS redundancy evolves, more types of AC topologies will be supported.

Interaction with PW Redundancy Mechanisms

RFC 4447 defines the PW edge-to-edge emulation (PWE3) control protocol exchanged through LDP, which uses the following status codes to indicate the operational state for an AC and a PW to a remote node:

- **0x00000000:** Pseudowire forwarding (clear all failures)

- **0x00000001:** Pseudowire not forwarding

- **0x00000002:** Local attachment circuit (ingress) receive fault

- **0x00000004:** Local attachment circuit (egress) transmit fault

- **0x00000008:** Local PSN-facing PW (ingress) receive fault

- **0x00000010:** Local PSN-facing PW (egress) transmit fault

  A new draft RFC proposes to extend the control word with two new codes:

- **0x00000020:** Status code for PW preferential forwarding status:

  When the bit is set, it indicates "PW forwarding standby."

  When the bit is cleared, it indicates "PW forwarding active."

- **0x00000040:** Status code for PW request switchover status:

  When the bit is set, it represents "Request switchover to this PW."

  When the bit is cleared, it represents no specific action.

Until this proposal, the status of a PW was either up or down; a new intermediate status is introduced that allows a PW to be in standby mode, which means that the PW is waiting for final activation to begin forwarding frames.

The PW state depends on the AC state. If an AC (or one of multiple ACs) is active, the PWs are active. If an AC (or all the ACs) is in standby, the associated PWs are in standby mode. A PW is end-to-end connected when both sides are active. From that point, it can forward frames. Status-change requests are performed through LDP. In the case of a large number of PWs (which is not foreseen for DCI), hot-standby PW functionality allows status-change scalability.

Figure 12-3 illustrates ICCP interaction with PW redundancy.

In Figure 12-3, the PE on the bottom left has activated its AC within the bundle connecting to the left CE, while the top-right PE has done the same. The only forwarding PW here is the one running diagonally up.

This solution presents dual protection against a loop induced by an unexpected split-brain problem, one at the PW level and one at the AC level.

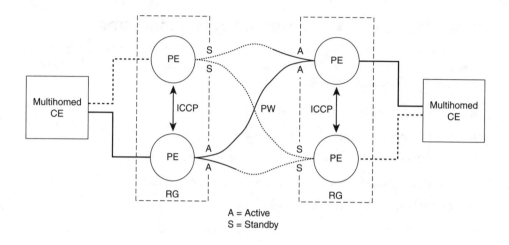

Figure 12-3   *ICCP interaction with PW redundancy.*

Configuring VPLS PE Redundancy Using ICCP

At this stage in writing, it is a bit early to foresee the exact configuration scheme for VPLS PE redundancy using ICCP, but Example 12-1 provides an initial direction.

Example 12-1   *Sample Configuration*

```
redundancy
 interchassis group rg id
  member ip peer ip address
  monitor peer [bfd ¦ route-watch]
! for fast PE failure detection
  mlacp node-id node id
  backbone interface backbone if
! for network isolation tracking

l2 vfi vfi name manual
  vpn id vpn id
  status coupled
! active/standby PW
  neighbor neighbor ip address
  neighbor neighbor ip address
  ...

interface Port-channel1
 no ip address
 lacp fast-switchover
 lacp max-bundle 2
```

```
! 2 on PE side, 1 on CE side
 mlacp interchassis group rg id
 service instance 1 ethernet
  encapsulation dot1q 100
! non QinQ or MACinMAC case
  bridge-domain 200

interface Vlan200
 no ip address
 xconnect vfi vfi name
```

Summary

In conclusion, in term of positioning versus other solutions discussed in this book, although the Embedded Event Manager (EEM) semaphore protocol offers an effective and proven solution, the solution often is complex. When available, ICCP may provide an equally effective solution, but one that is easier to implement. You might want to consider the ICCP solution when it becomes available and reliable.

## Chapter 13

Evolution of Data Center Interconnect

This chapter provides a speculative overview of the emerging technologies and architectures that could revolutionize the future of data center interconnect (DCI) without compromising the stability of large bridging domains.

A Larger Problem to Solve

The need to extend a VLAN across multiple sites is a key reason why DCI is a primary focus of the application and server side of the IT community.

The key question is this: Will this requirement last for long or will server-to-server applications evolve and integrate IP routing for their control-plane traffic? It is difficult to predict the future, especially in the world of virtualization, which is in its inception. Nevertheless, it is worthwhile to compare the two approaches: Layer (L2) bridging and IP routing.

No one will challenge the fact that IP is the best compromise between ease of use and deployment and availability. It has long been proven that IP scales easily and resists strong perturbation. One driver for its scalability is its use of subnets, which allows entities to structure networks geographically and then give them a strong and static organization. The price for geographical configuration is lack of mobility. Despite significant work on IP mobility (either around Mobile IP tunnels or proxy Address Resolution Protocol [proxy ARP]), an efficient solution has yet to be invented.

On the other hand, L2 bridging is natively mobile because it has no concept of edge node organization. L2 bridging determines localization dynamically through broadcast and flooding; however, the price for this dynamic localization is fragility and scalability.

So, on one hand, L2 bridging is flexible, but it requires broadcasting throughout the entire domain, so it lacks scalability and robustness. On the other hand, at Layer 3 (L3), IP networks scale by confining the broadcast domain to a limited subnet area, so they lack mobility and transparency.

Server and application vendors do not care about networking constraints; what they require is ease of use, ease of deployment, and transparency. In addition, virtualization initiatives are pushing strongly toward mobility. Therefore, you can expect that the requirement of L2 bridging within and between data centers will last a long time. Still, scaling requirements mean that there is no chance that client/server solutions will follow the same path. IP routing will remain the only solution in the WAN space. Therefore, IP will have to evolve to consider virtualization. A key piece of this evolution is Virtual Routing and Forwarding (VRF), which allows the existence of IP virtual private networks (VPN). Another networking domain that is going toward L2 bridging is the service provider WAN aggregation layer, which now is called *Carrier Ethernet*. During the past few years, a wide variety of networking software has been developed to handle this huge market, and DCI benefits from it.

After years of battle between networking experts who debate whether L2 is evil or essential, it is now increasingly accepted that some VLANs must be extended across multiple data center sites. So, the question is no longer "Should we do it?" but instead "How do we do it best?"

Networking Technology: Research Directions

The networking community is working hard on several paths to resolve VLAN extension across multiple sites. Depending on the background, the research direction might focus on hardening L2 bridging, increasing IP flexibility, or a combination of both via either a tunneling approach or a fusion of concepts. The following sections consider three main approaches that relate to future developments:

- Improving legacy L2 bridging with Spanning Tree Protocol

- Creating a new concept with an L2 bridging data plane and routed control plane

- Offering an L2 service over L3 transport with an overlay approach

Improving Legacy L2 Bridging

Significant development will continue to take place to improve the reliability of standard L2 bridging with Spanning Tree Protocol (STP). This development will include the following approaches:

- STP scaling with innovations such as Reverse Layer 2 Gateway Protocol (R-L2GP), which allows the building of STP domains that are interconnected via gateways.

- Automatic STP failure detection and correction; guard and bridging assurance are typical features in this domain.

- Increasing use of Multichassis EtherChannel (MEC) in multiple implementations such as Virtual Switching System (VSS) and virtual PortChannel (vPC). The idea is to use a channeling protocol such as Link Aggregation Control Protocol (LACP) to perform local repairs, thus providing link and node redundancy with STP remaining transparent to these local repairs.

Despite these improvements in L2 bridging, which may be adequate for the needs of most medium-sized data centers, STP is losing favor when extending its control beyond the access layer. The reason behind this sentiment is debatable, but the fact remains: A new approach is required to increase the high availability and efficiency of bridging domains.

New Concepts in L2 Bridging

The effort of the networking community seems to be split in two main directions:

- One group is working on intra-DC scalability and availability.

- One group is focusing on data center interconnect (DCI).

The networking community is working to make Ethernet scalable, lossless, and efficient. To do so, it is creating a new concept for Ethernet L2 bridging and approaching this concept from multiple directions: data-plane flow control and priority storage-area network (SAN) traffic integration; data-plane encapsulation for scalability; data-plane loop avoidance using the hop-count field; and routed control-plane that allows loop-free multipath transmission of unicast, unicast flooding, multicast, and broadcast traffic.

Several initiatives are ongoing with Cisco Data Center Ethernet (DCE), Converged Enhanced Ethernet, IEEE 802.1 DCB WG (Data Center Bridging working group), the IETF Transparent Interconnection of Lots of Links (TRILL) proposal, and many other proposals. These initiatives include IEEE Shortest Path Bridging 802.1aq, Congestion Notification 802.1Qau, and Enhanced Transmission Selection 802.1Qaz. It is still unclear which initiative will be the final one; most probably a merged approach will succeed.

This book does not address the issue of convergence on a single network infrastructure for various types of traffic such as LAN and SAN, because this approach is more of an intra-DC issue. However, it is worthwhile to pause for a more in-depth analysis of the potential replacements for STP.

The DCE and TRILL initiatives revolve primarily around the concept of the routing bridge (Rbridge). A good reference for understanding the control-plane approach is the TRILL working group at IETF.org.

These new approaches rely on the following concepts:

- The ingress (customer) bridge frame should be encapsulated in a backbone MAC frame to avoid core switches to the bridge on the user MAC address. This approach is the *MACinMAC* concept; however, diverse approaches to this concept might propose quite different encapsulation formats.

- An edge Rbridge acts as a classic learning bridge, and learns every MAC address in the domain, but core Rbridges never see any edge MAC addresses.

- The backbone MAC frame should include a hop count field that decrements on each hop and that drops the frame when the count reaches zero. With such a field, which is inherited from IP, no storm can occur if a control-plane creates permanent or transient loops.

- The Intermediate System-to-Intermediate System (IS-IS) protocol should be used rather than STP to create paths between core nodes for the following reasons:

    - IS-IS creates loop-free unicast paths between edge nodes, the multicast replication tree, and the broadcast tree.

    - Switching benefits from IS-IS Equal Cost Multi-Path (ECMP) technology that allows the network to efficiently balance traffic over multiple paths.

In short, the concept of Rbridging allows the network to benefit from the IP control-plane and the data-plane hop-count stormbreaker concept without having to encapsulate L2 frames in IP. The IP control plane replaces STP, but the data plane still bridges.

With the TRILL/DCE approach, the switch uses the data plane to learn of the site and the Rbridge where remote MAC addresses belong. An initial unknown frame is flooded via a safe tree, and the table is populated with the reply packet.

Another emerging idea is to avoid even the concept of learning bridges. A MAC routing approach will likely emerge soon. The concept is to populate the MAC address table of the ingress device via IS-IS by using the control plane rather than the data plane.

L2 Service over L3 Transport: MPLS or IP? Battle or Coexistence?

With this evolution in L2 bridging, the choice to encapsulate frames via MACinMAC implies that core nodes must be L2 switches. In several cases, the interconnection of data centers might need to rely on an L3 protocol, which means relying on either IP or Multiprotocol Label Switching (MPLS).

MPLS already offers such a transport: Virtual Private LAN Service (VPLS; the main subject of this book). MPLS offers the maximum toolset; it solves the L2 extension with the VPLS option and offers L3 virtualization with its extended VRF concept. In the service provider domain, MPLS is enriched with powerful features such as the capability to engineer traffic and reserve resources with local repair via Fast Reroute (FRR). In addition, MPLS is clearly the solution chosen by service providers to solve L2 aggregation of their WANs. These MPLS-based solutions use Ethernet over MPLS (EoMPLS) or MPLS Transport Profile (MPLS-TP). Although MPLS is promising, it is just emerging in the multicast world.

Many ongoing developments allow the same or an equivalent L2 transport approach over an IP network. However, a simple IP-based solution is required, because even though MPLS is well accepted by service providers, very large enterprises, and public organizations, it is not accepted by most other enterprises. For these organizations, two solutions will probably arise:

- Encapsulating MPLS over IP with configuration simplification (see Chapter 10, "GRE-Based Deployment Models")

- Natively encapsulating L2 frames over IP in an over-the-top approach, in which the IP tunnel transports L2 unicast traffic over IP unicast, but uses native IP multicast to transport L2 multicast and broadcast

It might be relevant to understand that one of the main IP routing protocols is IS-IS, which is the driver for MAC routing. You can expect to see the two features merge to offer a powerful MAC routing over IP solution. With this union, reconvergence events, broadcasts, and unknown unicast flooding can be totally localized and kept from propagating to multiple data centers.

Summary

The networking community is slowly moving away from STP for data centers. The emerging model is based on the IS-IS shortest-path concept. To implement this new model, however, Ethernet frame headers must be modified to incorporate hop-count loop breakers. Proposed multiple concurrent or complementary encapsulation formats can transport a bridging frame over the core; this concept scales from a simple MACinMAC encapsulation up to an IP or an MPLS encapsulation. In the world of intra-DC scalability, no one is thinking about IP or MPLS, so approaches like TRILL and DCE will probably succeed.

For DCI, the MPLS approach is by far the most ready and is gaining momentum despite its complexity. In simple situations, however, TRILL and DCE could be adopted. Most of the enterprise community expects IP to fulfill expectations. If it does, it will probably become the main approach.

Glossary

802.1q IEEE 802.1q is an industry-standard VLAN trunking protocol that enables a single link to carry the traffic of multiple VLANs.

AC An attachment circuit is the customer connection to a service provider network. An AC may be a physical port or a virtual port and may be any transport technology (for example, Frame Relay DLCI, ATM PVC, or Ethernet VLAN). In the context of a VPLS, an AC typically is an Ethernet port.

Agg Aggregation is an Ethernet switch that aggregates several access switch connections for onward connection to the N-PE.

BFD Bidirectional Forwarding Detection provides a rapid and consistent method of link, device, or protocol failure detection. BFD can be used with BGP, IS-IS, EIGRP, OSPF, and MPLS-TE protocols.

B-semaphore The primary VPLS node tracks a dedicated IP address on the backup N-PE. This IP address is called a backup semaphore.

Core Intersite network, which includes VPLS (N-PE) and MPLS (P) devices.

CVD Cisco Validated Design. The CVD program consists of systems and solutions that are designed, tested, and documented to facilitate and improve customer deployments.

DR Designated router. OSPF elects a DR and a backup designated router (BDR) for each segment in a broadcast or multiaccess network such as Ethernet. The DR sends a Network LSA (Type 2 LSA) with information that pertains to that segment.

Edge Layer 2 devices, including aggregation and access switches, within a data center network.

EEM Embedded Event Manager is a powerful and flexible subsystem in Cisco IOS that provides real-time network event detection and automation. Organizations can adapt the behavior of their network devices to align with their business needs.

EoMPLS   Ethernet over MPLS is a point-to-point Layer 2 VPN technology that transports Ethernet frames across an MPLS core network.

EVC   Ethernet virtual circuit is an association of two or more user-to-networks (UNI) and is an end-to-end representation of a single instance of a Layer 2 service being offered by a provider to a customer.

HA   High availability is the technology that enables networkwide resiliency to increase IP network availability. It ensures continuous access to applications, data, and content if a network or device failure occurs.

H-VPLS   Hierarchical Virtual Private LAN Service is a Layer 2 VPN service over Ethernet networks. H-VPLS introduces the hierarchy by partitioning VPLS, which improves the scalability of VPLS.

ICCP   Inter-Chassis Communication Protocol is used between N-PEs in a redundancy group to enable dual-homed interconnect to a customer edge device. This protocol provides VPLS node redundancy by monitoring and communicating the status of each N-PE in the redundancy group.

IGP   Interior Gateway Protocol, such as IS-IS, OSPF, EIGRP, and RIP.

IGMP   Internet Group Management Protocol is a multicast protocol in the Internet protocols family. It is used by IP hosts to report their host group memberships to any immediately neighboring multicast routers.

GigE   Gigabit Ethernet is a version of Ethernet that offers bandwidth of 1 gigabit per second (Gbps).

LAN   Local-area network. A high-speed, low-error data network that covers a relatively small geographic area. LANs connect workstations, peripheral devices, terminals, and other devices in a single building or other geographically limited area.

LDP   Label Distribution Protocol. A signaling protocol in the MPLS architecture. It is used between label switch routers (LSR).

LER   Label edge router. A router that operates at the edge of an MPLS network. The LER initially adds or ultimately removes a label from a packet.

LSP   Label switch path. A specific path that MPLS traffic passes through.

MAN   Metropolitan-area network. A network that covers an area larger than a local-area network, such as a city or a school district.

MEC   Multichassis EtherChannel. A Layer 2 multipathing technology that allows a connected node to terminate an EtherChannel across two physical Cisco Catalyst 6500 series switches that make up a Virtual Switching System.

Mono-tenant   A data center with only one Layer 2 domain.

MPLS   Multiprotocol Label Switching. A label-based packet-forwarding technology.

MST   Multiple Spanning Tree Protocol. Enables multiple VLANs to be mapped to the same spanning-tree instance. In this way, it reduces the number of spanning-tree instances that are required to support a large number of VLANs.

Multi-tenant   Refers to a data center that hosts multiple independent Layer 2 domains (for example, an outsourcer's data center).

NIC   Network interface card. A card installed in a computer to provide network communication capabilities to and from that computer.

N-PE   Network-facing Provider Edge router. Acts as a gateway between the MPLS core and edge domain.

OSPF   Open Shortest Path First Protocol. An Interior Gateway Protocol that is used for routing between routers that belong to a single autonomous system.

P router   Provider router. An LSR that functions as a transit router in an MPLS core network.

PE router   Provider Edge router. A router that is part of a service provider's network and is connected to a customer edge (CE) router.

P-semaphore   The backup VPLS node tracks a dedicated IP address on the primary N-PE. This IP address is called a primary semaphore.

PIM   Protocol Independent Multicast. Refers to a family of multicast routing protocols, each optimized for a different environment. The primary PIM protocols are PIM Sparse Mode and PIM Dense Mode.

POS   Packet over Synchronous Optical network is a technology that maps IP datagrams into the SONET frame payload by using PPP.

PW   Pseudowire. A virtual connection that connects two virtual switch instances in a VPLS. It is bidirectional and consists of a pair of unidirectional MPLS virtual circuits (VCs). A PW also can be used to connect a point-to-point circuit, also referred to as an emulated circuit.

QinQ   The IEEE 802.1Q-in-Q VLAN tag provides a VLAN tunneling mechanism by encapsulating a frame tagged with an 802.1q header with another 802.1q header.

Redundancy   The duplication of devices, services, or connections so that, if a failure occurs the redundant devices, services, or connections can perform the work of those that failed.

SAN   Storage-area network. A specialized network that interconnects servers and storage devices. By combining LAN networking models with the core building blocks of server performance and mass storage capacity, a SAN eliminates the bandwidth bottlenecks and scalability limitations imposed by previous SCSI bus-based architectures.

SONET   Synchronous Optical Network. Enables transmission of synchronous data over a fiber-optic network.

Split brain   Split brain occurs when all the links of private network fail, but the cluster nodes continue to run. In this situation, each node in the cluster assumes that the other nodes are dead and attempts to start services that other nodes are still running.

TenGigE   Ten Gigabit Ethernet is an emerging Ethernet technology that offers bandwidth of 10 gigabits per second.

TLS   Transparent LAN Service. A transport service that service providers offer as a way to link remote Ethernet networks.

Tunnel label   An outer label used to switch packets across a provider network.

VC   Virtual circuit. A logical connection between two network devices.

VC label   A virtual circuit label is an inner label used to bind the L2 interface to which packets must be forwarded.

VFI   Virtual forwarding instance. A collection of data structures used by the software- or hardware-based data plane to forward packets to one or more VCs.

VLAN   Virtual LAN. Comprises a group of devices that are located on various physical LAN segments but are configured so that they can communicate as if they were attached to the same wire.

VLAN overlapping   In a multi-tenant data center, outsourcers host several customers on the same site. Therefore, the VPLS nodes are shared between independent domains. VLAN overlapping occurs when multiple customers connected to the same N-PE use the same VLAN number.

vPC   Virtual PortChannel. A port channel between a single device and two upstream switches. Currently, it is supported in Nexus switches only.

VPLS   Virtual Private LAN Service. A method for providing Ethernet-based multipoint communication over IP/MPLS networks. VPLS allows geographically dispersed sites to share an Ethernet broadcast domain by connecting the sites through pseudowires.

VPN   Virtual private network. Allows IP traffic to travel securely over public TCP/IP networks and the Internet by encapsulating and encrypting all IP packets.

VRF   VPN Routing and Forwarding. A technology that allows multiple instances of a routing table to coexist in the same router.

VSI   Virtual switch instance. Describes an Ethernet bridge function that equates to a multipoint L2 VPN within an N-PE. A VSI terminates PW virtual interfaces, in comparison to an Ethernet bridge, which terminates physical Ethernet interfaces.

VSS   Virtual Switching System. System virtualization technology that allows the pooling of two Cisco Catalyst 6500 switches into a single virtual switch.

WAN   Wide-area network. A network that provides connectivity for multiple physical locations that typically are separated by large distances. For example, a WAN could span a city, or country, or across countries.

Index

Symbols

D

F

K-L

P

T

FREE Online Edition

Your purchase of **Interconnecting Data Centers Using VPLS** includes access to a free online edition for 45 days through the Safari Books Online subscription service. Nearly every Cisco Press book is available online through Safari Books Online, along with more than 5,000 other technical books and videos from publishers such as Addison-Wesley Professional, Exam Cram, IBM Press, O'Reilly, Prentice Hall, Que, and Sams.

SAFARI BOOKS ONLINE allows you to search for a specific answer, cut and paste code, download chapters, and stay current with emerging technologies.

Activate your FREE Online Edition at www.informit.com/safarifree

> **STEP 1:** Enter the coupon code: BJETREH.

> **STEP 2:** New Safari users, complete the brief registration form.
> Safari subscribers, just log in.

If you have difficulty registering on Safari or accessing the online edition, please e-mail customer-service@safaribooksonline.com